D0648427

WITHDRAWN

BY THE SAME AUTHOR

Charles M. Russell:
  The Life and Legend of America's Cowboy Artist

813
B945zt

TARZAN FOREVER

THE LIFE OF

Edgar Rice Burroughs,

CREATOR OF TARZAN

JOHN TALIAFERRO

SCRIBNER

SCRIBNER
1230 Avenue of the Americas
New York, NY 10020

Copyright © 1999 by John Taliaferro

All rights reserved, including the right of reproduction
in whole or in part in any form.

All Edgar Rice Burroughs family photographs, correspondence,
memorabilia, and other archival material are copyright © Edgar
Rice Burroughs, Inc.

SCRIBNER and design are trademarks of Simon & Schuster Inc.

Designed by Brooke Zimmer
Set in Stempel Garamond
Manufactured in the United States of America

1 3 5 7 9 10 8 6 4 2

Library of Congress Cataloging-in-Publication Data

Taliaferro, John
Tarzan forever: the life of Edgar Rice Burroughs, creator of
Tarzan/John Taliaferro
p. cm.
Includes bibliographical references.
1. Burroughs, Edgar Rice, 1875—1950. 2. Novelists, American—20th
century—Biography. 3. Adventure stories—Authorship. 4. Tarzan
(Fictitious character) I. Title.
PS3503.U687Z88 1999
813'.52—dc21   98–54707
[b]   CIP

ISBN 0-684-83359-X

To George McWhorter

06-18-1999   Gift   JUL 17 2000

ALLEGHENY COLLEGE LIBRARY

CONTENTS

Our civilization is still in a middle stage—scarcely beast, in that it is no longer wholly guided by instinct; scarcely human, in that it is not yet wholly guided by reason. On the tiger no responsibility rests. We see him aligned by nature with the forces of life—he is born into their keeping and without thought he is protected. We see man far removed out of the lairs of the jungles, his innate instincts dulled by too near an approach to free will, his free will scarcely sufficiently developed to replace his instincts and afford him perfect guidance. He is becoming too wise to hearken always to instincts and desires; he is still too weak to always prevail against them.

—Theodore Dreiser, *Sister Carrie* (1900)

1

THE SUM OF THE PARTS

"If you write one story, it may be bad; if you write a hundred, you have the odds in your favor," Edgar Rice Burroughs lectured young authors. In his case, though, it took far fewer to hit the mark. *Tarzan of the Apes,* written when he was thirty-six years old, was only the third story Burroughs submitted for publication. It ran in full in the October 1912 issue of *The All-Story,* taking up virtually the entire magazine. The reception exceeded the wildest dreams of author and editors alike and triggered a phenomenon unprecedented in publishing history. Dazzled readers proclaimed *Tarzan* one of the best adventure tales ever and pleaded for more. And so Burroughs obliged: twenty-three more Tarzan novels over the next thirty years, plus another fifty non-Tarzans, including eleven set on Mars, six at the center of the Earth, and five on Venus. A formal accounting of Burroughs's total sales has never been made, but the most conservative estimate is thirty million books sold during his lifetime; a more generous tally is sixty million. Considering that Burroughs's titles have been published in more than thirty languages and given the broad circulation of his stories in magazines and comics, there can be little question that he was the most widely read American author of the first half of the twentieth century.

"I had this story from one who had no business to tell it to me, or any other," he begins his chronicle of an orphaned child raised by apes. More truthfully, his tale was guided by a number of distinguishable sources, including the legend of Romulus and Remus, wild children of early Rome; Mowgli, the boy raised by wolves in Kipling's *The Jungle Book;* and travelogues of colonial Africa from the end of the nineteenth century. Burroughs had never heard of Rousseau's noble savage or Nietzsche's *Übermensch,* and though he owned a copy of Darwin's *The Descent of Man,* he never got much beyond sketching a monkey on the title page. Nevertheless, he had acquired a layman's grasp of one of the burning issues of the post-Victorian era—and for that matter, every period since. "I was mainly interested in playing with the idea of a contest between heredity and environment," he wrote in *Writer's Digest* twenty years after the first publication of *Tarzan of the Apes.* "For this purpose I selected an infant child of a race strongly marked by hereditary characteristics of the finer and nobler sort, and at an age at which he could not have been influenced by association with creatures of his own kind I threw him into an environment as diametrically opposite that to which he had been born as I might well conceive."

Baby Tarzan, as nearly everyone knows, grows up to become lord of the apes. He is a crafty woodsman and a silent stalker. His eyes, ears, and nose miss nothing. He "fills his belly by the chase" and prefers his meat raw. He backs down to neither man nor beast and does not recognize fear. "I know the word," he says in *Tarzan and the Leopard Men,* "but what has it to do with death?" Every Tarzan tale is full of stupendous action: mortal combat with apes and lions and breathtaking aerial traverses of the "middle terraces" of the African forest. In its sheer passion, Tarzan's yell, the victory bellow of the bull ape, is the supreme *cri de coeur,* and his romance with Jane is as primal and star-crossed as those of Romeo and Juliet or Beauty and the Beast.

But what many people forget—particularly those more familiar with Metro-Goldwyn-Mayer's and Johnny Weissmuller's film version of the Tarzan story—is that Tarzan, besides being king of the jungle, is also the son and rightful heir of England's Lord and Lady Greystoke, and in the final pages of *Tarzan of the Apes,* he must come to terms with his gentility. Loincloth, knife, and bow remain his preferred wardrobe, but he adjusts to tailored suits and cafe society with remarkable ease. In later episodes, he flies a plane, quotes Latin, and oversees English and African estates. Blood—in his case, blue blood—always tells, an axiom that Burroughs stresses in nearly all of his stories.

In his sublime synthesis of nature and nurture, Tarzan is as timely as he is timeless. By the turn of the nineteenth century, America's idol of earthy virtue, the frontiersman, had been crowded out by the decadent city slicker and by a new class of immigrants, mostly Mediterranean and Eastern European, who, in contrast to the fin de siècle bourgeoisie, were deemed too uncouth, too thick-wristed to enrich the American commonweal. Enter Tarzan, the embodiment of Teddy Roosevelt's "strenuous life," a latter-day Leatherstocking whose exuberant physicality and solid pedigree provided a welcome antidote to the mongrel modern age.

And in short order, he became a *super*hero, the first pop icon to attain global saturation. As such, he was the forefather of Superman and more recent real-life marvels such as Michael Jordan. Before Tarzan, nobody understood just how big, how ubiquitous, how marketable a star could be.

But while there can hardly be a person on the planet who has not heard of Tarzan, very few are familiar with Edgar Rice Burroughs. Most who recognize the stuffy triple name assume that, like Lord Greystoke, he must be British, when in fact he was a native of Chicago and the founder of—what else?—Tarzana, California. Despite his enormous appeal, his work is not taught in schools or welcomed in the American canon; as a result, only diehard Burroughs buffs—most of whom cherish their collections of Burroughs books and memorabilia like splinters from the true cross—have any feel for the clever and complex creator of the century's most popular hero.

One reason for Burroughs's undeserved ostracism is the stigma attached to pulp fiction. According to the laws of the cultural jungle, writers like Hemingway or Fitzgerald are literary lions; Burroughs and other paid-by-the-word authors of science fiction, westerns, whodunits, and romantic confessionals are monkeys with typewriters—hacks. Burroughs pretended not to mind his lowbrow status. "I don't think my work is 'literature,' I'm not fooling myself about that," he told the *Los Angeles Times*. Writers of his ilk, he volunteered with a shrug, belong "in the same class with the aerial artist, the tap dancer, and the clown." Even so, he tried again and again to break out of the pulp ghetto and place his stories

ALLEGHENY COLLEGE LIBRARY

in "slicks"—*The Saturday Evening Post, Cosmopolitan, Collier's*—where the money and prestige were better.

Because of his low regard for his profession and because he had backed into it at such a late age, Burroughs was always uncomfortable with his accomplishments. "If I had striven for long years of privation and effort to fit myself to become a writer, I might be warranted in patting myself on the back," he confessed to his brother George in 1929, "but God knows I did not work and still do not understand how I happened to succeed." Nevertheless, his imagination was evident from the start. He drew delightful caricatures and wrote clever verse as a young boy, creativity that was curbed by his short attention span and his unshakeable sense that he did not meet the standards of his father, Maj. George Tyler Burroughs, a well-to-do Civil War veteran. His academic record was erratic, demotions and dismissals negating any bursts of achievement. He won an appointment to West Point only to fail the entrance exam, and he never lasted long at jobs, even the ones at which he did well, such as supervising the stenography department at Sears, Roebuck. By the time he started writing in earnest, he did so more out of resignation than avocation. "I was sort of ashamed of it as an occupation for a big, strong, healthy man," he confessed.

To thrive in the pulp market, where a good rate was a penny a word, a natural flair for storytelling was essential. "Plots are in the air. All you have to do is reach out and take them," Burroughs said of his knack for spinning yarns with such apparent ease. But without his array of other talents, he might easily have failed. His energy was titanic, like that of his fictional heroes. In a morning, he could conjure and conquer entire worlds, pecking thousands of words or filling a half-dozen dictaphone cylinders, even with his children crawling at his feet and creditors buzzing around his ears. More remarkable still was his head for business. In 1923, he became one of the very first writers to incorporate, and over the years, Edgar Rice Burroughs, Inc., grew into a complex organism. Most of his stories were first serialized in inexpensive magazines—known as pulps, for the low-grade paper on which they were printed. After that, they were published in book form. Then the "first edition" books became "popular" editions, or cheap hardcovers, the forerunners of paperbacks. This progression was not unusual: most of Jack London's yarns of the Far North, Zane Grey's westerns, and H. Rider Haggard's African adventures also appeared in magazines before they became best-selling books. But in one very important respect, Burroughs was in a league all his own. In 1931, he grew weary of having to share his income with middlemen—"parasites," he called them—and began publishing his own books under the ERB, Inc., imprint. Still not content with the return on his creative capital, he struck deals to turn Tarzan into a radio show, a daily newspaper strip, a Sunday comic page, and, most lucrative of all, motion pictures. Though marketing experts and syndication agents warned that Tarzan on the radio would compete with Tarzan in the comics or that serial motion pictures would steal audiences from feature motion pictures, Burroughs was convinced that the total would exceed the sum of the parts. As he saw it, there was no such thing as overkill, and well before Walt Disney ever hawked his first mouse ears or Ninja Turtle "action figures" became film stars, Burroughs was already a grand master of a concept that would one day be known as multimedia. He licensed Tarzan statuettes, Tarzan bread, Tarzan ice cream, bubble gum, bathing suits, and puzzles, and he founded a national network of Tarzan "clans" to convert American youth to the Tarzan way.

Yet for all his ingenuity and diligence, too often his successes were offset by disappointment and liability. With only a couple of exceptions, he never did graduate from the pulps. He failed at two marriages and was obliged to subdivide his beloved Tarzana ranch, paving the way, literally and ironically, for a suburb of drive-ins, drive-throughs, and mini-malls. Despite his extraordinary popularity, he never made a killing on any one deal. Royalty checks came frequently, but they never amounted to more than a few thousand dollars. Even in years when his income exceeded one hundred thousand dollars—most years it was far less—his appetites and expenses always seemed to leave him cash poor. He had a weakness for Thoroughbreds and fast cars, and after he met his second wife, Florence, he made the mistake of trying to keep pace with the spendthrift elite of Hollywood and Palm Springs. Nor did it help his pocketbook and peace of mind to be perennially repelling lawsuits, mostly disagreements over permissions and royalties, or making legal thrusts of his own. And through it all, he had mouths to feed. Florence and her two children were but his latest dependents; his own children, Joan, Hully, and Jack, were on the ERB, Inc., payroll for much of their adult lives, as were his alcoholic first wife, Emma, his daughter's deadbeat husband, Jim Pierce, and his trusted man Friday, Ralph Rothmund.

Because of this relentless overhead, he could never afford to stop writing. The beast had to be fed constantly. Some years he wrote three or four hundred thousand words, four or five books' worth. Tarzan, naturally, was his mainstay; he averaged one a year. Yet it would be a mistake to dismiss the other fifty titles as chaff. His painstakingly researched a pair of novels about the Apache warrior Shoz-Dijiji are noteworthy for their progressive characterization of Native Americans. *The Girl from Hollywood,* his autobiographical novel about a California ranch family ruined by booze, dope, and movieland promiscuity, is an equally fascinating cultural document. He may not have been the first writer to fantasize about Mars, but in light of recent astrophysical evidence suggesting that life might once have existed there, and NASA's pledge to one day land on its surface, Burroughs, who grew up in an era before airplanes or automobiles, deserves a salute for fanning the dream.

It is true that some of his stories are duds. They suffer from continuity problems, and the gimmicks are threadbare. But considering how quickly he crafted his plots, most of them are amazingly tight and considered. He imbues each of his worlds, ape or alien, with what H. G. Wells called "practical incredibleness." Burroughs visualized them so completely, in fact, that he worked up maps of their kingdoms, sketches of their costumes, and alphabets and glossaries of their languages, including a comprehensive "Ape-English/English-Ape" dictionary. He took particular care in the taxonomy of monsters and beasts: for instance, the cyclopean Plant Men of Mars have hair follicles "the bigness of a large angle-worm" and the nose of "a fresh bullet hole that had not yet begun to bleed." ("Of the few stories that I have had rejected," he told a fan, "grewsomeness [*sic*] was the principal cause.")

In a typical Burroughs tale, the hero is a stranger in a strange land—Tarzan in the jungle, John Carter on Mars, David Innes in the Inner World, Carson Napier on Venus. He is a warrior by both breeding and training. Repeatedly he is chased, outnumbered by savage hordes, and thrown into a "Stygian" cell of "Cimmerian" darkness. "Where there is life there is hope," exclaims John Carter when the going gets roughest, an optimism shared by all Burroughs protagonists. By application of brawn, brains, and valor, he eventually prevails over his adversaries and either makes his way home or else finds a new and better home.

Always, too, the leading man is called on to rescue a damsel in distress with whom he inevitably falls in love. Boy meets girl was hardly a new motif by the time Burroughs got around to employing it, though, remarkably, he was the first to introduce it to science fiction. (The sub-genre would come to be labeled "scientific romance.") In most instances, the object of the hero's affections is well-born, beautiful, and though indubitably chaste, often provocatively clad—or in some instances, virtually unclad. Dejah Thoris, the Princess of Mars, parades through eleven novels seminude.

"Entertainment is fiction's purpose," Burroughs insisted time and time again, and he pleaded innocent to "disseminating any great truths or spreading any sort of propaganda" in his stories. Glib demurrals aside, however, he frequently held forth, usually allegorically but sometimes quite overtly, on a wide range of political and social issues. His vicious attacks on Germany during World War I in *Tarzan the Untamed* and *The Land That Time Forgot* eventually cost him his lucrative German audience. Infected by the postwar Red Scare, he railed against socialism at home and abroad in *The Moon Maid* and a number of other stories.

All of his plots, especially the Tarzans, boil down to survival of the fittest, a theme both romantic and political. Burroughs, like so many of his contemporaries, believed in a hierarchy of race and class. In the Tarzan stories, blacks are generally superstitious and Arabs rapacious. On Mars, the races descend from a Tree of Life and, like fruit, are color-coded red, green, yellow, and black. Burroughs was obsessed with his own genealogy and was extremely proud of his nearly pure Anglo-Saxon lineage. He came from "good" stock, a critical ingredient for good standing, he asserted. Over time, his fervid appreciation of genetic predetermination led him to the radical fringe of Darwinism: eugenics. At one point, he even wrote a column for the *Los Angeles Examiner* calling for the extermination of all "moral imbeciles" and their relatives, a doctrine that would soon be trumpeted by Adolf Hitler. In an unpublished essay, "I See a New Race," Burroughs offered his own Final Solution to the world's problems.

But he was also canny enough to play both sides of the street. Even as he was stressing Tarzan's and John Carter's superior bloodlines, he honored the Algeresque notion of the common man pulling himself up by the bootstraps. In 1911, when he submitted his first story, *A Princess of Mars*, to the Munsey family of magazines, he chose the pen name Normal Bean to signify that he saw himself as just a regular fellow, a man of the people. On one hand, he assumed a certain aristocratic detachment from his work; on the other, he attributed his success to the fact that he shared "a common weakness with 120,000,000 other Americans." Not surprisingly, Mark Twain's *The Prince and the Pauper* was one of his favorite books, and he borrowed Twain's trick of role reversal in many of his own stories. Another mentor was Jack London, whose proletarian heroes survive more through grit than through grace. No matter how well-born (or low) one might be, Burroughs realized, no one was perfect, least of all himself. "Are the heart and soul of man any better because of civilization," he asked, "or is the apparent betterment [of civilization] merely . . . veneer?"

Indeed, there were periods when Burroughs's blithe hauteur failed him entirely, when self-effacement edged toward self-loathing. One of the worst occurred in 1940 and 1941, after he and Florence moved to Hawaii.

He had first brought her to Oahu on their honeymoon in 1935, after a delicate divorce from his first wife and a bizarre courtship; Florence, a former silent-movie actress, had been married to one of his business partners and trusted friends. When they returned in April 1940, they were accompanied by Florence's two children, Caryl Lee and Lee. Burroughs was turning sixty-five; his wife was half his age. Back in Los Angeles, they had been living far beyond his means, and he had exhausted himself trying to keep up with her. Once in Hawaii, though, his strength returned and his spirits improved. As the celebrated master of Tarzan, he was welcomed by a loose fraternity of navy and army men with an unlimited quantity of booze on their hands. "All my plans for retiring into a hole and pulling the hole in after me have been shot to hell," he joked after one particularly enthusiastic run of revelry. "You just can't say no to the people over here." Florence, too, was a welcome addition to the mostly male gatherings, though to hear her tell it, her role soon devolved into chauffeuring her tipsy, sunburned husband home from luaus and wee-hour card games. If anything, she was having trouble keeping up with *him*.

But while Hawaii provided a welcome change of scenery, it offered no escape. Between bridge, cocktails, and sunbathing, Burroughs still had to keep the pages coming. By the end of 1940, he had finished Mars, Inner World, and Tarzan manuscripts and was commencing a new Venus story. Over a period of ten days before Christmas, he wrote more than forty thousand words. That month, he, Florence, and the children had moved into the Niumalu Hotel in Honolulu, their third address since arriving in Hawaii. They had their own bungalow and most of their neighbors were long-term residents. Still, it was by no means a proper home. The rooms were cramped, buggy, and damp, and the family took their meals communally in the hotel's dining room. By mid-March, Florence had had enough. On the fourteenth, she and the children sailed for California. Four months later, she would sue for divorce, citing mental cruelty.

Her chief complaint was that Burroughs had made her feel old, or, contrarily, that because she was thirty years younger, he had made a show of acting more youthful, but had succeeded only in behaving childishly. She, however, was not entirely exempt from blame herself. Money was always an issue with her: the Ed Burroughs she had first been attracted to was a natty, venerable, and, she assumed, prosperous gentleman. According to Burroughs's allies, she was crestfallen when he informed her that they had to hold their expenses, including rent, to two hundred and fifty dollars a month, which was all the salary he was drawing from ERB, Inc., in 1941. With money, he was doubtless a father figure, potent and protective. On a budget, he was just another bald, slightly overweight old man.

Alone for the first time in forty years, Burroughs became a virtual shut-in, hiding behind the drawn blackout curtains of his Niumalu bungalow and talking to no one for days. An old bladder problem flared up, and he was hospitalized. He suspected he was dying.

Somehow he managed to keep plugging away at *The Wizard of Venus*, though his introductory paragraph reads like a note in a bottle. "I believe it was [explorer and natural historian] Roy Chapman Andrews who said that adventures were the result of incompetence and inefficiency," the story's hero, Carson Napier, declaims. "If that be so, I must be the prize incompetent of two worlds; for I am always encountering the most amazing adventures. It seems to me that I always plan intelligently, sometimes over meticulously; and then up jumps the Devil and everything goes haywire. However, in all fairness, I must admit that it is usually my fault. . . . I am rash. I take chances. I know that that is stupid. The thing that reflects most discredit upon my intelligence is the fact that oftentimes I know the thing I am about to do is stupid, and yet I go ahead and do it. I gamble with Death; my life is the stake." Burroughs was writing about the blunder that had first steered Carson Napier's spaceship in the direction of Venus, but he was also reflecting on his own decision to move to Hawaii, where his life was now very much in jeopardy.

He might easily have perished in Honolulu if two events had not intervened. One was the arrival of his son Hully on an undisguised mission of mercy. The second was an event that changed millions of lives besides his own, though he was among the few who witnessed it first-hand.

Unlike his fictional alter-egos, Burroughs had never been to war. He had been a cowboy and gold miner in Idaho and served in the United States Cavalry in Arizona. He had sailed through the Panama Canal, but never set foot in Africa, a continent he virtually owned in the popular imagination. He wrote about action, but his published words spoke louder than his own experience. "All the interesting things in my life never happened," he once confessed to an editor. "I am always late for the thrill. I always get to the fire after it is out."

Until Sunday, December 7, 1941. That morning, Burroughs and Hully woke early to play tennis but were distracted by the sound of what they believed to be antiaircraft practice. They soon learned the truth: the Japanese were bombing Pearl Harbor.

That night, Burroughs and Hully patrolled the waterfront as volunteers in a civilian guard, and over the next four years, Burroughs made three trips to Pacific war zones and enjoyed the distinction of being the oldest American correspondent to cover World War II. His dispatches were not widely read, and he was far from a hero. Still, the tours of duty made up for a lot: his disillusionment as a cavalryman, his rejection by the Rough Riders in 1898, his relegation to the reserves during World War I, and the general sense of qualified achievement that had nagged him for most of his career.

He had never explicitly yearned for his life to imitate his art; just the same, it finally did. If writing *Tarzan of the Apes* had been the first big turning point in his life, World War II was the second and, in a way, it was the climax, as well. After the war, Burroughs returned to California, where he was at long last reunited with his children and grandchildren. He died not far from Tarzana in 1950, a relatively contented man.

Fifty years later, the time has come to reappreciate this imaginative, vigorous figure who played such a crucial role in shaping the century now so near its close. The life of Edgar Rice Burroughs is a chronicle of personal highs and lows, successes and insecurities that faithfully mirror the aspirations and tensions of the society around him. To be sure, pop culture—books, magazines, movies, radio, comics—would have burgeoned without Burroughs; but as one of its most innovative and prolific contributors, he truly had a Tarzan-size impact.

2

A Jungle of Sorts

If George Tyler Burroughs ever contemplated owning a house of his own, he discarded the notion on October 8, 1871. That night, he and his wife, Mary, stood on the roof of their leased townhouse at 650 Washington Boulevard and watched Chicago burn. Major Burroughs was no stranger to horror; he had witnessed wholesale death during his years in the Union army during the Civil War, and he and Mary together had observed the bombardment of Richmond in April 1865. But nothing equalled the sight of the firestorm that destroyed seventeen thousand buildings—roughly one third of Chicago—and left one hundred thousand citizens homeless.

The Burroughses' West Side neighborhood was spared and the family was safe, yet the fire singed them nonetheless. As Chicago rose from the ashes and families less well-to-do built or bought new houses, the Burroughses were an anomaly: for the next forty years, until his death, Major Burroughs never owned the roof over his family's heads. "I was born in [a] rented house," his son reminisced to *Perfect Home* magazine in 1942, hastening to add, "It was home to me in the real sense of the word, because my father and mother made it a home."

George Burroughs and Mary Evaline Zieger had planned to get married in the fall of 1861, but the onset of war and George's enlistment in the New York militia intervened. He survived Bull Run—his closest call a bullet "through his blouse"—and was later commissioned as a lieutenant and quartermaster in the New York infantry. He and Mary were finally married in her hometown of Iowa City, Iowa, and she spent the rest of the war following her husband from front to front; later she recorded the more pleasant details of their peregrinations in a book, *Memoirs of a War Bride.* Discharged a brevet major, George Burroughs applied his quartermaster's acumen to running a furniture business in Portland, Maine, then brought Mary and their two sons to Chicago in 1868.

Chicago was not exactly a jungle; it would take another forty years for Upton Sinclair to coin that nickname with his muckraking novel of life and death in the stockyards. The city that emerged from the great fire strove for refinement, funding canals, streetcar lines, a clean-water system, concert halls, museums, and the country's first skyscrapers, department stores, and suburbs. But like the winds that blew across Lake Michigan, there was always something raw and unruly about Chicago. For all its cosmopolitan pretensions, the city's leading attraction remained the stockyards and packing plants, where day in and day out the immigrant employees of Armour and Swift slaughtered cattle and hogs by the thousand. "It was all so very businesslike that one watched it fascinated," Upton Sinclair reported. Yet at the same time, "One could not stand and watch very long without . . . hear[ing] the hog-squeal of the universe."

No other American city has inspired more eloquent metaphors of barbarism. "It is inhabited by savages," Rudyard Kipling would conclude after a brief stopover. The Chicago Board of Trade was known universally as "the Pit," where novelist Frank Norris regarded the buying and selling of wheat and other commodities as "a chaotic spasm of a world-force, a primeval energy . . . raging and wrathful." Even mundane scenes seemed deserving of bestial comparison. Long before Carl Sandburg's fog had visited Chicago "on little cat feet," Hamlin Garland had noticed the city's streetcars "nosing along like vicious boars, with snouts close to the ground."

In the years immediately following the Civil War, the West Side of

Chicago was the home of the city's beau monde. The hub of the neighborhood was Union Park, with its sculpted lagoons and Gothic gazebos, and the main thoroughfare was Washington Boulevard, with its tree-shaded sidewalks and marble-fronted townhouses. Washington Boulevard, for instance, was where Mary Todd Lincoln chose to live after the assassination of her husband in 1865.

It was also where one of Lincoln's loyal soldiers chose to raise a family. Edgar Rice Burroughs was born at 650 Washington Boulevard on September 1, 1875, George and Mary Burroughs's fifth son. The eldest, George Jr., had been born in Portland nine years earlier; Harry, also born in Maine, was seven years Ed's senior; next came Frank, born in Chicago in 1872, seven months after the fire. The fourth, Arthur, lived only twelve days after his birth in 1874.

Growing up, Burroughs never particularly cared for the name Edgar—"the sillyassest name ever hitched to a male"—but he was extremely proud of his middle name and its attendant genealogy. Through his grandmother Mary Rice, he was related to Edmund Rice, one of the early Massachusetts pilgrims. Clara Barton, Samuel F. B. Morse, and Calvin Coolidge were said to be Rice descendants, also. But the roots of distinction ran even deeper than that. "I can trace my ancestry back to Deacon Edmund Rice," Burroughs has the hero of *Escape on Venus* attest, "and from him to Cole Codoveg, who was King of Briton in the third century." In an era when it was customary for authors to sign their full names to poems, plays, stories, and novels, Edgar Rice Burroughs did so as much out of genetic pride as literary pomp.

The Burroughs side of the family, likewise of British stock, immigrated to Massachusetts at about the same time as the Rices. A number of Burroughs ancestors, perhaps including Burroughs's great-great-grandfather, fought in the Revolution, and they passed on their rock-ribbed patriotism to future generations. One of the few glimpses of Burroughs's grandfather, Abner Tyler Burroughs (husband of Mary Rice), comes from a worn 1896 Chicago newspaper that Burroughs kept in his files. A native of Massachusetts, Mr. Burroughs had sold his farm and come to live with his daughter Caroline in Chicago. Interviewed on election day as he marched home from the polls, he boasted that at age ninety, he was the oldest voter in the city. Furthermore, he announced spunkily, "Since there has been a Republican Party, I have never voted any other ticket, and before that party was born, as an old-time Whig, I voted for straight Republican principles."

Edgar Rice Burroughs's blood was not entirely Yankee, however, or even purely Anglo-Saxon. His mother's father, Josiah Zieger, was Pennsylvania Dutch, a genealogical detail he tended to play down in his recitation of family history. Shaping truth into romance, he preferred to stress those relatives of Mary Evaline Zieger Burroughs who had settled in Virginia in the eighteenth century, including John Coleman, after whom Burroughs named his second son. In his mind's eye, he was the direct descendant of the fighting cavaliers of the Old Dominion, and in several of his novels he attributes the gallantry and valor of his heroes expressly to their Virginia lineage.

Burroughs's romantic streak did not come from his father, who was, above all, a pragmatist. Upon arriving in Chicago from Portland, George Tyler Burroughs had joined with several partners in the distillery business. Because of the availability of grain and the manifest thirst of the populace, liquor distilling was for a while the city's second-largest industry after meatpacking. No one recalls the variety or quality of the wet goods produced by the series of distilleries with which Major Burroughs was associated, though one, the Phoenix Distillery, was known around the city as "a very profitable establishment" even in later years when many other distillers were going under.

By all accounts, the Burroughses were quite well off, though they were not in the same league with the city's plutocrats—the Pullmans (railway cars), McCormicks (reapers), or Fields (department store)—and the Burroughses' Washington Boulevard address was modest compared with many of the neighboring houses. Toward the end of the century, as more and more of Chicago's gentility moved north to Lake Shore Drive or the suburb of Lake Forest, Major Burroughs insisted on staying put on the West Side, which was rapidly turning working-class and polyglot. "Once upon a time," Burroughs observes in the mystery story "Beware!" (set in New York but clearly inspired by Chicago), every "hideous, frowning" townhouse had been occupied by "a family of fashion and wealth, and even now some of the old timers remained in a few of them." In *The Mucker*, his novel about a West Side thug, he summons a childhood memory of "frowsy streets filled with frowsy women and frowsy children."

By contrast, the Burroughs home was a haven of late-Victorian decorum. Mary Burroughs, trim and petite, ran the house with the help of a cook and two Irish maids; she is remembered for her warmth and humor, and as the only person who could rein in the Major. George Burroughs was six feet tall—his wife could walk under his outstretched arm without mussing her hair—and because of a boyhood accident, he surveyed the world with only one good eye. He insisted the family keep to a tight schedule; mealtimes were sounded on a Chinese gong at precisely 7:30 A.M., noon, and 6:00 P.M. When he was ready for bed, he simply extinguished the gaslights in the house, and everyone else was expected to turn in accordingly.

There was no doubting his conservatism, either at home or throughout Chicago. He was an official witness to the execution of the convicted Haymarket bombers in 1887 and was once excused from jury duty for his prejudice against Roman Catholicism. "I do not believe in fanaticism anywhere," he testified. The greatest gift he and Mary gave to their children, Burroughs wrote in the foreword to his mother's *Memoirs*, was "the red blood of the Puritan and the Pioneer, bequeathed . . . uncontaminated." A Burroughs was expected to stand tall. Sons were supposed to live up to their heritage.

Ed, or Eddie, as he was often called, was a happy if somewhat rambunctious child. He was blue-eyed and sturdy, and being the youngest of the four boys, he was granted the most liberties. His grandfather Burroughs and his favorite aunt and uncle, Caroline and Charles McEntee, lived nearby, and the families visited back and forth frequently. Burroughs tagged along with his brothers to nearby Union Park, where the family at times pastured a milk cow. A favorite diversion was to throw peanuts to Old Bob, a trained bear exhibited there. One of the few sad notes in those early years was the death of Charles Stuart Burroughs, a younger brother. He was born two weeks before Burroughs's sixth birthday, and died five months later. The image of the lifeless infant in his mother's arms was one of Burroughs's earliest and most potent memories. In *Tarzan of the Apes,* written thirty years later, the ape Kala's baby falls from a tree, and "when she gathered the wee, mangled form to her bosom life had left it." Bereft and childless, Kala adopts the infant Tarzan as a surrogate.

Burroughs described his early education as "an advanced course in private kindergarten, where I majored in weaving mats from strips of colored paper." He then attended the Brown School, only a few blocks' walk from his house, until the sixth grade. Two other Brown graduates were Florenz Ziegfeld, the showman, and Emma Hulbert, whom Burroughs would marry in 1900. A diphtheria epidemic prompted his parents to withdraw him from Brown, which was public, and enroll him in private school; the most convenient was Mrs. K. S. Cooley's School for Girls, where he and several other boys finished out the year in good health but great embarrassment.

Burroughs next attended the Harvard School at Twenty-first Street and Indiana Avenue, but he never managed to find his footing. "I was never a student—I just went to school there," he later told the school alumni bulletin. "Bennie Marshall [who became a successful Chicago architect] and I used to sneak down to the breakwater and smoke cubeb cigarettes and feel real devilish." Mediocre report cards notwithstanding, he showed evidence of a fertile mind. He had drawn humorous sketches and written poetry since early childhood. A couplet written at age five declares, "I'm Dr. Burroughs come to town,/To see my patint [*sic*] Maria Brown." At age ten, he included silly drawings and verse with his frequent letters to his brothers George and Harry, who were attending the Sheffield Scientific School at Yale:

> *Once there was a man who thought himself quite grand*
> *There was a dagger in his belt and pistol in each hand*
> *But when he saw a poor blind mole*
> *He climbed far up a very tall pole. . . .*

In some respects, he received a better education from his family than from his teachers. He would later credit his success as a writer to the fact that he "never heard other than excellent English in my home." He joked that his lifelong hatred for Dickens came from listening to Major Burroughs read *Dombey and Son* aloud. He was much more receptive to classical literature, of which he received a heavy dosage. His brother George wrote from Yale in 1887, praising him for reading *Tales of Ancient Greece*, a collection of myths retold for children, and urging him to study more about Greece in the family's copy of *A Brief History of Ancient, Mediaeval, and Modern Peoples,* which begins with the ethnocentric declaration that "the only historic race is the Caucasian, the others having done little worth recording." Burroughs's favorite classical tale, though, was the account of Horatio at the Bridge, as translated by Thomas Macaulay in *Lays of Ancient Rome*. Echoes of Macaulay's stirring account of the Roman warrior Horatio battling bravely against a phalanx of enemies would be heard in Burroughs's fiction:

I, with two more to help me,
Will hold the foe in play.
In yon strait path a thousand
May well be stopped by three.
Now who will stand on either hand,
And keep the bridge with me?

Burroughs earned no laurels at Harvard School, and he did not graduate. A letter from the principal indicates that he left midway through
the 1890–91 school year "on account of ill-health." While he may well
have had bouts of illness, as all children do, any excessive concern for his
health, including the diphtheria scare, can just as easily be explained by
parental anxiety following the loss of two other siblings. Family photos
from the period reveal a strapping, bright-eyed lad, and Burroughs's own
autobiography suggests his parents' protectiveness was precautionary
rather than remedial. "Shortly after I exploded from Harvard School
there was an epidemic of what was then known as La Grippe in Chicago
and my parents shipped me out to a cattle ranch in Idaho," he notes in a
never-completed autobiography, begun in 1929. "Unquestionably my
destiny is closely interwoven with pestilences, which may or may not
account for my having become a writer."

He was not the first of the Burroughs boys to move to Idaho for his
health. In August 1885, the Phoenix Distillery had burned, and though
the business survived, its market share and revenues were diminished. In
response, Major Burroughs invested in the American Battery Company,
which made storage batteries used mainly for train signals. George Jr.
and Harry both had joined the firm after graduating from Yale together
in 1889. (George had been held back by illness.) Soon it was Harry's turn
to get sick; his doctor feared that fumes from battery chemicals had damaged his lungs, and he prescribed a cure of exercise and fresh air. Accordingly, the two eldest Burroughs brothers moved to southeastern Idaho in
1890 and became partners in a cattle ranch, along with a Yale classmate,
Lew Sweetser, son of one of the region's first stockmen. Fifteen-year-old
Ed Burroughs joined them at their ranch, the Bar Y—"Y" for Yale—in
the spring of 1891. It was his first trip away from home.

The Bar Y was located on the Raft River, near its confluence with the
Snake, and bestrode the ruts of the old Oregon Trail. By 1890, the Con-
estoga wagons were history; so, too, was the era of unfenced range, when

herds were uncountable and profits grand. Still, the parcel of land that the three Yale men had bought from Sweetser's father seemed plenty wild to a teenager from Chicago. "[T]hem was the days!" Burroughs wrote in his autobiography. His job was to grub sage with a horse-drawn plow and occasionally carry mail and supplies from American Falls to Yale, the name Sweetser and the Burroughs brothers had given to the post office they had established near the Bar Y.

He had ridden often in Chicago, but Idaho was the beginning of a deeper appreciation of horses and horsemanship. "[W]hen I got my leg over a horse I owned the world," he exclaimed, and he eventually imbued nearly all of his fictional heroes with a similar passion. John Carter conquers Mars on the back of an eight-legged thoat, a steed of Burroughs's invention; in *The Moon Men,* Julian 9th rides Red Lightning, "a bay with the temper of a Hellhound"; and even Tarzan rides horseback once he and Jane settle on their estate in East Africa. Naturally the Burroughs westerns—*The Bandit of Hell's Bend, Apache Devil, The War Chief,* and *The Deputy Sheriff of Comanche County*—are rich with equestrian escapades.

In Idaho, Burroughs received a crash course in riding rough stock. His instructor's name was Whiskey Jack, a black bronc that had "killed one man and maimed several others," he mentioned with characteristic embroidery. "[B]eing still short on brains, I asked the boss if I could use him." It took five men to get a saddle and bridle on Whiskey Jack, and they blindfolded the horse while Burroughs mounted. "When they yanked the blind off, he took two jumps, slipped and fell down on me. . . . He didn't break anything in me, but I certainly hurt. . . . After they caught him and brought him back, I tried it again and when he got through bucking I owned him."

Another of his favorite Idaho yarns was that of Texas Pete, "a very likable murderer," with whom Burroughs worked at the Bar Y. Pete told him that he and a man named Paxton had been hired to kill each other during a range war. Pete won the duel, and so lived to tell his violent tale, which, regardless of its veracity, made a lasting impression on Burroughs. Many years later, he shaped the shootout into a bunkhouse ballad, verses of which he sprinkled throughout *The Bandit of Hell's Bend.* "I am the original bad un, I am/I eats 'em alive an' I don't give a damn," he has Texas Pete recite. " 'Fer how fast they come er how many they be/Of all the bad hombres the wust one is me.' "

If the real Texas Pete truly had gunned down Paxton, he was never arrested for it, and he left the Bar Y on his own accord. Soon Burroughs was gone as well. His parents called him back to Chicago at the end of the summer of 1891 and in September put him on a train bound for Andover, Massachusetts. "From murderers, horse thieves and bad men I was transported to Phillips Academy," he wrote. "I presume there must have been another epidemic somewhere."

For Burroughs, who only weeks earlier had been riding the range in spurs, chaps, and broad-brimmed hat, Andover, as the academy was more widely known, came as quite a shock. The school's four hundred boys were prepared for college—predominantly the Ivy League—through a demanding curriculum of scientific, English, or classical coursework. Burroughs enrolled in the English course as a sixteen-year-old sophomore, or "junior middler."

Once again, he dropped out before the school year was over. Grades, not health, were the stumbling block this time, though he claimed that his poor performance was not entirely his own fault. "In early youth, before I had studied English grammar," he explained in a letter to Andover thirty-six years later, "I was taken out of public school and placed in a private school, the head master of which believed in . . . start[ing] at the bottom, with Greek and Latin leading up to English and I left the school before I had progressed as far as English, and left without knowing much about Greek or Latin, either. . . . When I came to Andover it was already presumed that I had studied English grammar, so they started me in on Greek and Latin again."

He may not have fit in academically at Andover, but he made his mark in other ways. He contributed a number of illustrations and a poem to *The Mirror*, the school literary magazine, and was so popular with his classmates that, upon returning from Christmas break, he was elected class president. It mattered little, however; less than a month after his election, he was back in Chicago. Almost immediately his father enrolled him in a new school—this one having even less tolerance for eccentricity.

Michigan Military Academy was in Orchard Lake, Michigan, twenty-five miles northwest of Detroit. It stressed military drill and discipline and, according to Burroughs, enjoyed "a sub rosa reputation as a polite reform school." As usual, he was slow to fall into formation. He hated the traditional hazing and amassed so many hours of punishment that he could never have walked them all off "if I remained there the rest of my life." Barely two months into his stay, he used a railway passbook that his father had given him and fled to Chicago, arriving home at about the same time as a telegram from the school: "Your son deserted Thursday. Letter will follow." The most noteworthy detail of the telegram—and it was indeed a stroke of fortune—was the signature: "Chas King, Commandant."

Capt. Charles King had been at the academy not much longer than Burroughs, and he stayed less than a year, but the effect that he had on Burroughs's life was nonetheless deep and permanent. A teenager during the Civil War, King had volunteered as an army orderly, then attended West Point. As a lieutenant in the Fifth Cavalry under General Thomas Crook, he was severely wounded in a skirmish with Apaches at Sunset Pass, Arizona Territory, in 1874. He was with Crook again in the summer of 1876, fighting Crazy Horse's Sioux on the Rosebud River of Wyoming and narrowly missing Custer's engagement on the Little Bighorn. He was on hand for Buffalo Bill's legendary "duel" with the Cheyenne chief Yellow Hand, and he helped chase Chief Joseph's Nez Percés across Montana. In the spring of 1892, he was still in uniform and serving as interim commandant at Orchard Lake, though he was also absorbed by his other love, writing.

Between 1880 and his death in 1933, King churned out some two hundred and fifty stories and more than sixty books, earning the nickname "America's Kipling"—not so much for his belletristic polish as for his original, if somewhat purple, depictions of soldiers at home and at war. King's first romance, *The Colonel's Daughter,* was published in 1883, though his career as an author did not really take off until 1890, with the release of a popular edition of his memoir, *Campaigning with Crook.* That same year, he published *Sunset Pass,* the first of many books he would produce with the aid of the Dictaphone, a method so new that it was mentioned in numerous newspaper and magazine profiles of him. Nowadays King is an obscure figure, read and collected mostly by buffs of the Indian Wars. Yet his popularity at the turn of the century was enormous. His stories are perhaps less ripsnorting than those of protopulp adventure writers such as G. A. Henty and Capt. Mayne Reid, but whatever they lack in breakneck drama, they make up for in authenticity. To Burroughs's generation, Captain King was a living legend.

The day after his desertion, Burroughs was back at Orchard Lake, walking punishment. "Cadet Burroughs' offenses have been most serious, but not irretrievably so," King wrote to Major Burroughs, explaining his reason for giving the boy a second chance. "He has been reckless; not vicious."

King's mercy worked. From then on, Burroughs's conduct at the academy was, if not impeccable, then at least not entirely reprehensible. As a former cavalryman, Commandant King took a particular interest in riding instruction, and Burroughs, with his Idaho experience, was a star pupil. "You rode well in 1892," King recalled. To have won the approval of one of the country's greatest warriors, an officer who had led numerous saber charges against desperate Indians, did wonders for Burroughs's confidence and resolve. The following fall when he returned to Michigan, King was no longer there, but Burroughs never lost touch with his straight-backed, kind-hearted mentor. Twenty-one years later, he wrote to King for advice when he was negotiating his first book deal for *Tarzan of the Apes,* and their correspondence continued well past the appearance of *The War Chief,* Burroughs's own novel of Indian fighting, published in 1927.

In the fall of 1892, he made the football team and did well enough in the classroom to warrant a letter of cautious praise from the new superintendent: "Cadet Burroughs has made excellent progress in his studies . . . and is satisfactory in discipline." The following winter, he persuaded his parents to buy him a horse, "too fiery and too good a horse for a lot of boys to ride," but perfect for a youth of his ability, he argued. Not long afterward, he and several of the best riders in the school's cavalry troop were invited to perform at the annual horse show at the Detroit Riding Club, where they thrilled the crowd with their skill and exuberance. "The cadets ride like the vaqueros . . . , like the fleet South American gauchos, the most skillful and daring riders in the world," observed one paper. As a finale, Burroughs and his cohorts drew their revolvers and "dashed madly around the ring, firing in all directions." Burroughs took second prize in the drill competition, winning a riding crop for himself and a red ribbon for his new horse, Captain.

More excitement awaited him when school let out in June. It was the summer of the World's Columbian Exposition, and ten million people, from dirt farmers to dignitaries, made the pilgrimage to Chicago. The fair's organizers had conceived the exposition as a celebration of the remarkable progress the United States had made since Columbus's arrival four hundred years earlier. Toward this end, they built a neoclassical "White City" along the shores of Lake Michigan, which they packed with a vast array of marvelous displays of American know-how. One of the biggest sensations was the Ferris wheel, the world's first, 260 feet tall, each car holding sixty people and affording a grand view of the fairgrounds, the lake, and the broad expanse of Chicago. Outshining all other innovations was electricity, the wonder of the age. Quite fittingly, it was electricity that provided eighteen-year-old Ed Burroughs with a front-row seat of the fair's myriad goings-on. Throughout the summer, he was assigned the pleasant task of driving around the fair in a "nine-seater horseless surrey" powered by one of his father's storage batteries. At least one published account touted the vehicle as Chicago's first automobile; quite possibly Burroughs's love of cars and his penchant for conjuring fantastic methods of propulsion had a simultaneous genesis.

Yet as remarkable as America's technological triumphs would have appeared to Burroughs and his fellow fairgoers, in the end they were mere symbols of an even greater national accomplishment—a gain that was best appreciated in evolutionary terms. At the Columbian Exposition, America brashly announced its arrival at the summit of the human pyramid: no culture was more advanced than that of the United States, a tout delivered most plainly in the Anthropological Building, where displays of ethnic costumes and handicrafts from around the world served as quaint counterpoint to the brilliant American inventions of the surrounding White City. Science spoke even louder than trinkets in the Anthropological hall, and thousands of tourists, curious to see where they ranked on the scale of human progress, lined up to have their heads measured—"anthropometry," it was called—by a team of anthropologists led by Franz Boas, who would soon thrust himself into the middle of the debate over eugenics and racial determinism, a topic that Burroughs himself would be drawn to.

If the Anthropological Building was about numerical and artifactual documentation of human evolution, the Midway Plaisance, the fair's most popular thoroughfare, offered a more anecdotal glimpse of the family of man. The mile-long Midway was a riot of racial and ethnic exhibitionism, a cosmic bazaar the likes of which the world had never witnessed. Lined up cheek by jowl were Africans, Indians, Bedouins, Laplanders, and South Sea Islanders, living in their respective huts, tents, and temples, wrapped in their respective robes, capes, kilts, and loincloths. "It was the reconvening of Babel," pronounced the *Chicago Tribune.* At the entrance to each "village," barkers hawked exotic wares or coaxed visitors through tent flaps, where, for a small fee, they might observe aboriginal maidens performing authentic dances such as the now legendary "hoochie coochie."

On the Midway, all manner of prurience and condescension fell under the rubric of "education." "What an opportunity was here afforded to the scientific mind to descend the spiral of evolution," the *Tribune* reflected, "tracing humanity [from] its highest phases down almost to its animalistic origin." In a genuine Irish cottage, a humble Irish matron busied herself with crochet, a living diorama of colonialism. Or one could gawk at Javanese "flying their queer kites and shooting darts from their bamboo blow pipes." Especially popular was the delegation of Dahomans from West Africa. "Sixty-nine of them are here in all their barbaric ugliness, blacker than buried midnight and as degraded as the animals which prowl the jungles of their dark land," reported *Frank Leslie's Popular Magazine.* "There is no doubt that the Dahomans are most closely allied with the cruel and superstitious practices of savagery than any other country represented," chorused *The Chautauquan.*

Burroughs never recorded his own impressions of the fair or mentioned which exhibits he had seen. Surely, though, he did not miss the Midway. Nor would he willingly have passed up Buffalo Bill Cody's "Wild West Show" (encamped right next to the fairgrounds) with its riding, shooting, and, in finale, a reenactment of Custer's last stand. Then, too, he would have been drawn to Carl Hagenbeck's Arena of Wild Animals, featuring "a giant lion riding around the ring on horseback." Given Burroughs's subsequent romance with lions and lion-training, one wonders if his enthusiasm was not first whetted in Chicago during the summer of 1893. These, anyway, were many of the sensational pieces that he would toy with and assemble in his fiction.

BACK AT Michigan Military Academy in the fall, he threw himself into work and play with unprecedented zeal. He captained the football team, a sinewy five-foot-ten, 165-pound quarterback. He made excellent grades for the first time in his life, and the academy's end-of-term letter to his parents called him "one of our best boys." Surprisingly, the letter made no mention of his December afternoon as a duelist, though it was one of the most remarkable incidents of his entire military career.

He and a fellow cadet named Campbell pretended to argue one afternoon in front of the barracks. Burroughs struck Campbell with his glove, and that evening Campbell delivered a note requesting that Burroughs give him "the satisfaction my insult demands." They decided on Springfield rifles at fifty paces, the duel to take place on the ice of the nearby lake at dusk the following day. According to Burroughs, the entire student body swallowed the hoax. Some cadets wanted to prevent the inevitable bloodshed by tattling to the commandant; others took sides and sat up guarding their respective comrades from preemptive attack. The next afternoon, Burroughs and his second jumped out of the barracks window and headed for the lake. "Just ahead of us were the men with the rifles," he recalled, "and as . . . I turned to look back, I saw a string of cadets a mile long following in our wake. . . . We waited for ten minutes before we saw [Campbell's] crowd coming and then the fellows began to shake hands with me and bid me 'good-bye.' They were so excited that some of them cried."

Right about then, Campbell's second arrived and reported that Campbell had been caught by the commandant. The duel was off. Called on the carpet himself, Burroughs had to produce two blank rifle shells and an ink-stained handkerchief from his shirt before he could convince his superiors that he and Campbell had never intended to shoot each other. The ruse was well worth the reprimand they received from the commandant and the buffeting that followed back at the barracks. Burroughs related the story with pride in a letter to his parents, and indeed, as plots go, it was every bit as clever as the capers he invented for *The Outlaw of Torn* or *The Mad King,* two Burroughs novels of court-and-castle subterfuge.

The remainder of his stay at Orchard Lake was not without incident or accolades. The football team held a heftier, older squad from the University of Michigan to a tie. He contributed humorous drawings to *The Adjutant,* the academy paper, and helped found a literary magazine, *The Military Mirror,* its name presumably inspired by the journal he had worked on at Andover. He performed well enough in the classroom and by the spring of his junior year had climbed in rank to second lieutenant, though, as he confessed in his autobiography, "I cannot understand why it was that I was so often promoted. I was not particularly neat in my personal appearance, except at ceremonies; I was not particularly amenable to discipline, and in the matter of observing regulations I was a rotten soldier. . . . [W]hat a young ass I must have been."

One breach of regulations is noteworthy, not so much because it caused Burroughs to be reduced in rank temporarily, but because of what it reveals about his relationship to authority and his parents at the time. One day in April 1894, while serving as officer of the day, he stood by while a fellow student struck another student, a boy whom Burroughs already disliked as a bully. He not only failed to report the incident, but also stuck up for the student who had done the hitting. The "gross neglect of duty" nearly got him expelled; in the end, he was reduced in rank to private and confined to his room. In an eleven-page letter of explanation to his father, he questioned the "manliness" of the superintendent for punishing him and confessed he didn't give "two whoops in hades" for school. Then, turning contrite, he added that "if I could only feel that you and Mother hadn't lost confidence in me *again* on acct of this, it wouldn't be so hard."

His father's letter to the superintendent reveals that Major Burroughs was not exactly the curmudgeon that others have made him out to be: "I need not tell you that [the notice of my son's punishment] brought to me humiliation and pain. What more can I say? My son knows what I expect of him. His sense of duty to his school and his parents should guide all his actions. . . . If he will not obey he must take the consequences and his parents must suffer with him." Then, before signing off, the Major tendered a father's appeal for leniency: "I hope it does not mean confinement in his room for such a long time when we are likely to have hot weather."

Burroughs bounced back and by the end of his senior year, had been promoted to second-ranking captain; only one other student at the academy outranked him. "I loved everything military," he announced, and as graduation neared, he set his sights on West Point. Winning an appointment as a Chicagoan or Michigander was apparently too difficult, so he appealed to his brothers George and Harry, who were now well-connected stockmen in Idaho. George campaigned hard, and on May 6, 1895, he was able to wire that Idaho Congressman Edgar Wilson had awarded Burroughs the appointment. Four days later, he received an official notification from the Office of the Secretary of War that he had been selected *conditionally*. First he had to pass an entrance exam on June 13. "Your friends have done all for you now that is in their power," George Burroughs wrote. "I feel sure you will pass, Ed, but remember the exam is a rigid one, don't spare yourself in the short time left you to prepare."

He left Orchard Lake a week before graduation, presumably so he could be in West Point on time. Whether or not he crammed for the exam is not known. Either way, the trip was in vain. Of the 118 who sat for the exam, only fourteen passed; Burroughs was not among them, and there was nothing to be done. Instead of a summer preparing for enrollment at the United States Military Academy, he was obliged to return to Chicago and take a job as bill collector for an ice company owned by the family of one of his classmates, Robert Lay. In the fall, he found himself back at Michigan Military Academy, where he took a thirty-five-dollar-a-month job teaching cavalry, Gatling gun, and geology as one of several assistant commandants.

In a sense, he was merely a twenty-year-old postgraduate, editing *The Adjutant* and captaining the football team. More accurately, though, he had become the mirror image of his former unruly self. "I am afraid that I was a rather strict disciplinarian," he reflected. "I was supposed to ferret out infractions of regulations and [superintendent] Colonel Rogers could scarcely have selected a better man, as I had broken every regulation myself while I was a cadet." The students expressed their hatred for him by throwing lightbulbs and ink bottles at him from the barracks windows at night. Amid such animosity, Burroughs found the job lonely and less than fulfilling, and he came to the realization that "my position as Assistant Commandant gave me really less freedom than I had as a cadet, principally since I was forced to behave myself." By the end of the school year, he had decided to join the regular army, hoping that once he was in the ranks, he could win a commission as an officer.

ON MAY 13, 1896, Burroughs traveled to Detroit and enlisted. He gave his age as twenty-one, the minimum age at which one could join up without parental permission, though in truth he was three and a half months shy of his twenty-first birthday. The army had its doubts and checked with his father, who gave his blessing anyway. Two days later, Burroughs was assigned to the Seventh Cavalry at Fort Grant, Arizona Territory. The "Bloody Seventh" was a name that he and most every other American knew well. The Seventh had fought and fallen at the Little Bighorn in 1876, spilled more blood at Wounded Knee in 1890, and in the action perhaps freshest in Burroughs's consciousness, had quelled the famous Pullman strike on the streets of Chicago in the summer of 1894. Of Fort

Grant, he knew next to nothing, except that the recruiting sergeant in Detroit had assured him it was "absolutely the worst assignment in the United States Army."

He took a train as far as Willcox, in southeastern Arizona Territory, noting in his autobiography that he was able to afford only a seat in a day coach and that he was so hungry that "at one of the stops I swiped the lunch of a Mexican who had gotten off to stretch his legs." He made the twenty-six-mile trip to Fort Grant by stagecoach, accompanied by a young prostitute employed at the nearby brothel that catered to the troops.

The fort was situated in the foothills of the rugged Pinaleño Mountains, superimposed, as he recalled, "upon a chaos of enormous boulders." It had been built in 1872, at the height of the army's war against the Apaches. With the surrender of Geronimo in 1886 and the containment of the Apaches on the nearby San Carlos reservation, the mission of Fort Grant had become less urgent. Its two hundred soldiers were there to ensure that the Indians stayed put and to pursue the rare few who did not. Always remote, and increasingly superfluous, Grant was by the time of Burroughs's arrival a down-at-the-heels collection of adobe and rough-timbered structures surrounding a parade ground. He was assigned to Company B and, because of overcrowding, quartered in a Sibley tent. His bunkies were mostly foreign-born, and he was surprised to find that they made good soldiers. He was likewise impressed by the black troops at Fort Grant. "I worked under colored sergeants," he attested much later, "and without exception they were better to work under than our white sergeants."

He was not the wide-eyed youngster who had detrained in Idaho five years earlier, and the hardships and strictures of military life did not catch him off guard. He intended to take the army on its own terms, to excel, to become an officer. What he did not count on was that he would become sick. One of the few purported amenities at Fort Grant was its abundant supply of water, collected from mountain springs. In most years the water was clear and potable; 1896 was an exception. "They told me that it hadn't rained at Fort Grant for seventeen years," he recalled, "but shortly after I came it commenced. . . . The drinking water became impossible . . . and I presently achieved dysentery. I did not want to go to the hospital, but I finally became so weak that I had to and there I was in [the] charge of an ape named Costello, a hospital steward, the one man in the world whom I have ever sworn to kill. He was a beast, as unfit to care for sick men as were the drunken doctors assigned to the post."

His illness dragged on through the hot Arizona summer, though he was pronounced fit for duty within a week, a decision he blamed on Colonel Edwin "Bull" Sumner, the fort's commander. "He was what was then known as a pick-and-shovel man," Burroughs explained, "and he kept us busy building boulevards . . . where no one needed a boulevard." Sumner's very appearance made the back-breaking work all the more irksome. Burroughs insisted Sumner was so fat that he "conducted regimental maneuvers from an army ambulance," and it required "nothing short of a derrick to hoist him onto a horse." To his mind, Sumner was "the ultimate zero in cavalry officers."

By midsummer, he was fed up with Fort Grant. In a letter home on August 25, he mentioned the possibility of buying himself a transfer to Fort Sheridan, Illinois, but doubted that Sumner would allow it. "I made my bed and I will lie in it," he said dejectedly.

It was not that simple. During his hospitalization, one of the doctors had determined that Burroughs had a complication, which he described as "tobacco heart"—most likely an irregular heartbeat. Because of his condition, he could not receive an officer's commission; nor would Sumner transfer him; and Washington could not decide whether or not to discharge him. Able to chuckle at his conundrum thirty-five years later, Burroughs recalled pressing his doctor for an honest prognosis. "He was quite reassuring. He told me that I might live for six months, but on the other hand I might drop dead at any moment."

None of these vagaries kept him from active cavalry service, though. Two weeks after his discharge from the hospital, but by no means cured of his dysentery, he and twenty-two other enlisted men of Troop B rode from Fort Grant in pursuit of renegade Apaches.

The fear that Apaches might break out from the reservation and attack the ranchers who had usurped their historic domain was not entirely unwarranted. The previous winter and spring, several whites had been murdered, and Apaches had been blamed. Fort Grant routinely sent out patrols; the chance of actually catching renegades was remote, but the very presence of cavalry in the region was considered a worthwhile deterrent and usually received as a comfort by anxious settlers.

Heading the list of most-wanted Indians was an enigmatic figure whom the Americans had given the nickname the Apache Kid. He had once been a scout for the army, though no one had seen him for years; nor was it certain that he was even still alive. Nevertheless, the Apache Kid was still a prime suspect, along with the equally elusive Massai, who had surrendered with Geronimo ten years earlier but then had jumped from the train carrying the prisoners east. The most recent raid had been near a Mormon settlement, now the town of Solomon, north of Fort Grant across the Pinaleño Mountains, so it was in that direction Troop B headed on August 29.

In two novels that Burroughs set in Arizona, *Apache Devil* and *The War Chief,* he offers little description of the topography, except to say that it is mountainous, "sun-scorched," and "rugged." Clearly the stark majesty of the southwestern landscape was the last thing on his mind as his troop set out in search of Indians in a territory "into which could have been dumped the former German Empire and all of Greece." As they climbed the mountains, the pain in his abdomen became so severe that he could dismount only by falling off his horse. Somehow he was able to keep up with the troop, and eventually they reached Solomon. The Mormons, it turned out, were not keen to have the army in their midst, and as there had been no sightings of suspicious Indians in recent weeks, Troop B rode on to the Gila River, near the town of Duncan, and camped in a grove of cottonwoods. In the five weeks the troopers were away from Fort Grant, they scoured the hills but did not set eyes on a single hostile Apache. "It is just as well for us that there were no rene-gades about," Burroughs chuckled, "for those patrols [of two men each] would have been nothing more than animated targets that no self-respecting renegade could have ignored. As I look at it now, we were just bait."

The only Indians he ever got close to were the army's Apache scouts. On the Gila, he was wary of them at first. The scouts had their own camp a short distance from that of the cavalrymen, and at night, when owls were hooting, the men suspected that the scouts were signaling the rene-gades. This was not the case, and eventually Burroughs found himself drawn to his Indian comrades. "Their figures and carriages were magnif-icent and the utter contempt in which they held the white soldier was illuminating, to say the least." He befriended one scout in particular, "probably because I bought whiskey for him."

Corporal Josh, as he was called, had been a renegade, holding out in Mexico with the Apache Kid after Geronimo's surrender. One day, Josh "got homesick and wanted to come in," Burroughs remembered. "There was a standing order for the Kid, dead or alive, and Josh took advantage of this fact to win the favor and forgiveness of Uncle Sam. Being for some reason unable or unwilling to kill the Kid, he did the next best thing and killed one of the Kid's relatives, cut off his victim's head, put it in a gunny sack, tied it to the horn of his saddle and rode up from the Sierra Madres in Mexico to Fort Grant, where he dumped the head out on the floor of headquarters and asked for forgiveness and probably for a reward, so they let him enlist in the Apache scouts and made him a corporal."

Whether the story was true or not, a part of Burroughs wanted to believe it. He had read about primitive cultures in books, seen aborigines at the World's Fair. Now here before him, somewhat whiskey-sodden perhaps, was atavism incarnate. "[E]ver in the seed of the savage," he wrote in *The War Chief,* "is the germ of savagery that no veneer of civilization, no stultifying inhibitions seem able ever entirely to eradicate."

He made no such effort to understand his commanding officer, and he was not alone in his disdain. The army had received so many complaints about Colonel Sumner that it sent an inspector to investigate the possibility of a court-martial. Discipline in the meantime had eroded to the point where "an enlisted man dragged an officer from his mount at drill and beat him up" and men were boasting that "they would kill any officer they found out after dark." In the course of the army inspector's inquiry, members of Troop B were asked to sign a statement that they had never been mistreated by Colonel Sumner. Burroughs's signature is absent from the affidavit, and he never forgave his commanding officer for refusing to consider a discharge or transfer.

His situation could have been worse, however. Due to his lingering dysentery, as well as his ability with horses, he was given the "coffee-cooler" job of running the headquarters' stable. He shoveled manure, pitched hay, hauled grain, and groomed fourteen horses; compared with pick-and-shovel work, the assignment was considered salubrious. He had his own quarters separate from the vermin-infested adobe barracks where the rest of his troop was now housed. Living "the easy life of the plutocrat," he finally regained his health. In the field he had been obliged to live on jackrabbit and potatoes; as stableman, he enjoyed Thanksgiving and Christmas feasts of pork, mutton, venison, oysters, and plenty of beer.

"It was during these days," he wrote, "that several of us organized the 'The May Have Seen Better Days Club,'" the title itself suggesting a snobbish disdain for the social circumstances at Fort Grant. He was still a private, but he carried himself as an officer. "We were mostly from different troops and all were supposed to have known something better in life than building boulevards on sowbelly and spuds. . . . There was one chap whose father was a wealthy merchant from Boston; another was a Canadian; and a third was a chap by the name of Napier who had been an officer in the English army." They met in Burroughs's quarters near the stables once a month, usually right after payday, where they drank wine and imagined themselves proper clubmen in a city far away from Arizona.

By the beginning of 1897, better days were all he could think about, and his homesick letters finally moved his father to intercede on his behalf. Major Burroughs, who had once hosted a reception in Chicago for Fort Grant's namesake, Ulysses S. Grant, no longer had any contacts within the War Department, but he had friends who did. On March 11, two different scions of the Chicago business community wrote letters to Secretary of War Alger, requesting Burroughs be discharged for a variety of good reasons, not the least of which was that they would "esteem it a personal favor."

Four days later, orders were given to draw up the papers. Burroughs wound up serving only ten months of a three-year enlistment. His discharge listed his character as "excellent." Recommendations: "intelligent soldier." Expeditions: "None." Campaigns: "None." Wounds Received in Service: "None." Battles, Engagements, Affairs, or Skirmishes: "None." Remarks: "Service honest and faithful." Twenty-one years later, he summed up his army experience another way: "Chased the Apache Kid and his renegades about Arizona—never caught up with them. Made a bum soldier—except that I could ride well, the best thing I ever did. After my discharge from the army, I did various things."

The first of which was a cowpunching job for his brothers. Frank and George Burroughs were still in the cattle business in Idaho, along with their original partner, Lew Sweetser. As coincidence would have it (or perhaps as friends had orchestrated), Burroughs's discharge came through just in time for him to meet Harry in the Mexican border town of Nogales, very near Fort Grant, where Harry was to take delivery of a herd of Mexican cattle. Burroughs's responsibility was to help load them, then ride with the stock to Kansas City. It made army life seem like a lark. The cattle were in poor condition when they started, and "at every other stop, [we] dragged seven or eight dead animals out of each car," including those from a herd of Texas longhorns that had been added to the train. To keep the beasts from trampling one another, he had to enter the cars through a hatch in the roof and fight his way through the jam of hooves and horns and rouse the animals that had lost their footing. The trick was to twist the tail and heave until the animal took a notion to pick itself up.

After delivering the herd to Kansas City, he continued on to Chicago. Having scrapped his military career, he was at a loss for what to do next. Of all the Burroughs brothers, he was the one who had sought his father's approval most directly. Now he had no choice but to take a position at the American Battery Company. "I started at the bench and learned the business from the ground up," he stated. There is little to suggest that he was spoiled, though as an able-bodied twenty-one-year-old who lived off his parents, he may well have been seen that way. When he worked, he worked hard, and Major Burroughs would not have tolerated dilettantism. Still, no one believed that he was cut out for the battery business, and not long after starting his new job, he enrolled in a drawing class at the Chicago Art Institute. He had done some clever cartooning at Fort Grant and had occasionally mentioned wanting to pursue a career as a newspaper illustrator or political cartoonist. But his talent and talk still lacked the catalyst of ambition.

His one steady fixation seems to have been Emma Centennia Hulbert, a neighborhood girl he had known since Brown School days who owed her middle name to her birthday, January 1, 1876. Emma had matured into a bright and buxom young woman and had never entirely outgrown her front-stoop infatuation with Eddie Burroughs. They had traded letters while Burroughs was in the army, and now that he was back, they were not shy about seeing each other. Her father, Alvin Hulbert, was manager of several hotels, including the Tremont House on Michigan Avenue, one of the city's landmarks. Not surprisingly, he and Mrs. Hulbert were lukewarm toward Burroughs, whose background was solid but whose future was uncertain. Even so, they did not forbid the courtship, perhaps because Emma had assured them that she was not taking his eccentric suit seriously.

✳   ✳   ✳

WITH THE sinking of the battleship *Maine* in Havana harbor on February 15, 1898, and the prospect of war with Spain, Burroughs was suddenly keen to be back in uniform. He wrote to an old Michigan Military acquaintance seeking guidance on how to get into a fighting unit. The friend said he couldn't be of much help; once again, it looked as if Burroughs would miss the fire. Impulsively, he quit the American Battery Company and boarded a train for Idaho, where his brothers put him to work on the spring roundup. In May, a month before the invasion of Cuba, he made another stab at an army position, this time with the United States Volunteer Cavalry Regiment, better known as the Rough Riders. Part cavalryman, part cowboy, Burroughs was just the sort of man the Rough Riders were looking for to punish the oppressors of Cuban freedom. But regrettably, his only memento from the Spanish-American War was a letter from Lt. Col. Theodore Roosevelt: "I wish I could take you in, but I am afraid that the chances of our being over-enlisted forbid my bringing a man from such a distance." When the letter arrived, Burroughs was already driving cattle and camping in the hills of Idaho.

After the roundup was over, he moved to Pocatello, Idaho, and bought a stationery store and newsstand on Center Street. Pocatello, population 1,000, was fifty miles northeast of the Bar Y Ranch and the biggest town in the region. He sold cigars, sheet music, flags, magazines, books, and photographic supplies; he developed film, rented cameras, and for a while delivered newspapers on horseback. One of his advertisements in the local paper announced the arrival of "Capt. Chas. King's latest, 'A Wounded Name.'" "I had a book shop in Pocatello, Idaho," he wrote in a trade journal in 1921, "when cheap editions cost me fourteen cents and Munsey's Magazine sold for ten cents and cost me nine and weighed over a pound and the postage was a cent a pound and I am still trying to figure where my profits occurred. . . ." It was to the Munsey offices that he would choose to send his first story in 1911.

Despite his nascent knack for entrepreneurship, his store was "not a howling financial success," and by the winter he was obliged to return it to the previous proprietor. In the early spring of 1899, he once again joined his brothers' roundup. That same spring he made yet another attempt at a commission in the army. After the conclusion of the Spanish-American War the previous summer and the signing of the Treaty of Paris in December, Washington had considered retooling its force of volunteers as a standing army so as not to be caught unprepared again. Under such a plan, they would need officers. First Burroughs appealed to Congressman Wilson of Idaho, who had given him his appointment to West Point four years earlier. This time Wilson replied that Idaho had already used up its quota of appointments in the army; two days later, the Secretary of War's office advised Burroughs that all plans to organize the volunteers were on hold for the time being. There was no point in waiting, so when the roundup was over, he returned once more to Chicago, where a job was always waiting for him at the American Battery Company. Too, it was time to try again with Emma.

As it happened, three of the four Burroughs brothers were making comparable romantic advances of their own. Harry, the eldest, was the only one with a wife; he had married Ella Oldham, the daughter of close family friends, in 1891, and they were raising two children in Idaho. Then in the course of a single month, there was a virtual stampede to the altar: George married Edna McCoy in Idaho on January 10, 1900; Coleman married Grace Moss in Chicago on January 24; and Burroughs married Emma on January 31. None of them ever commented on why they had all made up their minds at the same time, but Emma, for one, must have seen some security in numbers. Burroughs had been making his pitch since his return from Idaho and, he claimed facetiously, "She got so tired of being proposed to that she just had to marry me to get a little rest."

The city directory for 1900 gives his and Emma's address as 194 Park Avenue, Emma's parents' house, but he hinted that they may have moved back and forth between the Hulberts and the Burroughses. Even after the battery company increased his salary from fifteen dollars a week to twenty, they still found it economical to eat meals at one house or the other.

For the next three years, Burroughs did his best to be a good husband and steady worker. All three of his brothers were in Idaho, even Coleman, his closest, who had never been tempted to go West before. Sweetser and the Burroughses were easing out of the livestock business and concentrating on dredging for gold in the Snake River. Burroughs was interested, but he held back.

Yet at least one document hints that he was not entirely consumed by the battery business during those quiet years between 1900 and 1903. It is a small, handmade book, bound with a shoelace, entitled *Snake*

River Cotton-Tail Tales. Inside the front cover is written, "Author's Autograph Edition . . . Limited to One Copy, of Which This Is No. 1." The recipients were seven-year-old Studley and five-year-old Evelyn Burroughs, Harry's children, who wintered with their mother in Chicago, but spent warmer months in Idaho. With no children of his own yet, Burroughs was wholeheartedly attached to his niece and nephew. He sent them several other one-of-a-kind books of nonsense verse, but *Cotton-Tail Tales* was the truest labor of love, and a small harbinger of things to come. Each of ten facing pages has a poem on the right, a witty, better-than-workmanlike illustration on the left. One depicts two rabbits in the garden:

> *Is that what they call a cabbage, ma,*
> *I've been eating for an hour?*
> *No, you silly little child*
> *It's what they cauliflower.*

Another shows the same two rabbits in the barnyard:

> *That great big ugly egg-plant, ma,*
> *Just bit me on the leg.*
> *That is a hen you foolish child.*
> *Well I saw her lay an egg.*

If Burroughs was no Edward Lear, he nonetheless had a demonstrable talent for telling delightful stories, a talent he would eventually hone into something much more elaborate.

3

THE EFFICIENCY
EXPERT

I t was only a matter of time before Burroughs lost interest in his father's business, and it was a measure of his dedication to Emma that he waited so long to quit. Finally, in the spring of 1903, he could sit still no more and announced to her that they were moving to Idaho.

Because dogs were normally forbidden on trains, Burroughs bribed the railway expressmen with liquor to allow their collie Rajah aboard, and he and Emma spent most of the trip in the express car, keeping the dog company and sharing the cheer. They rode the final stretch of the trip in an open Concord stagecoach. Burroughs photographed Emma seated among the baggage, looking like a frontier Queen Elizabeth in her grand girth and high collar. From the amount of personal belongings they carried, it must be assumed that they meant the move to be permanent.

Their destination was the Stanley Basin on the Salmon River, a tributary of the Snake. The Burroughs brothers had bought a new claim and had use for another man. Harry and George Burroughs were engineers by training, and during their years in the cattle business, they had studied the mineral potential of the Snake River. With Lew Sweetser, they had formed the Sweetser–Burroughs Mining Company in 1893 and, fueled by family capital, it had become one of the first outfits to attempt large-scale gold dredging on the broad and mostly navigable Snake. They built their own steam dredge, the *Argus,* and a tug to push it up and down the river. They also built a large houseboat—a barge with a two-story house onboard—which on some occasions was occupied by as many as five families, depending on the season and the work at hand. George Burroughs was the ramrod and spent the most time on the river. Harry, with two children, kept a house in Pocatello but worked closely with George. Coleman, who had opened a general store at Minidoka, a nearby railroad stop, pitched in as well. Even Major and Mrs. Burroughs had come out from Chicago on at least one occasion to check on the gold operation.

The business went well for several years. The dredge, manned around the clock in three shifts, sucked up sand from the river bottom, and the gold, of a flourlike consistency, was separated in successive stages of shaking and washing and settling. Eventually, Sweetser and the Burroughses added a second dredge, the *Yale,* and a second houseboat for employees. The work was demanding from the standpoint of both labor and logistics. Dredges and the tug had to be fueled and repaired; someone had to scout for the next likely anchorage; the houseboats then had to follow the dredges; crews had to be ferried back and forth; supplies had to be brought to the crews; and, to make money, the dredges were never allowed to stop. The industry of the *Argus* and the *Yale* was measured in ounces and pounds of gold, but also in the islands of tailings they left behind in the river.

Another challenge that had little to do with prospecting, but was just as crucial to the success of the business, was compatibility. In summer months, there were long stretches when Harry, Ella, George, Edna, Coleman, and Grace were all living on the bigger houseboat; they had christened it *El Nido*—the nest—though its eighteen rooms belied any inference of coziness. Harry's children, Evelyn and Studley, remember lots of gay times. A photo shows the families, in Sunday suits and dresses, gathered together in the barge's main room; there are curtains on the windows, cloths on the table, a Yale banner festooning the wall.

But for all the equanimity that these memories and mementos suggest, life on the Snake was not always idyllic. George Jr. was an unapologetic taskmaster, and the wives, though supportive of their husbands, were not so generous toward one another. The bickering was mostly over housework and who was or was not pulling her weight, and in the early going especially, the ill will was palpable and deleterious. By the time Burroughs and Emma arrived in Idaho a certain détente was in effect, but the notion that the Burroughses would continue as a big, happy family whose members could all work and live side by side had been seriously bruised.

In his 1929 autobiography, Burroughs makes no mention of any discord or hardship during this Idaho interlude, perhaps because he and Emma lived a good distance away from the Snake operation and were only occasional visitors to *El Nido* and Minidoka. He described the Stanley Basin as "the most beautiful spot in the United States," surrounded by snowcapped mountains and alive with deer, mountain sheep, and grizzly bears. Emma, whose childhood landscape ran more to plushly furnished hotels and whose only exposure to wilderness had been summer vacations at a well-kept lake house in Coldwater, Michigan, seems to have been a surprisingly good sport. At first she and Burroughs lived in a tent, assuredly a first for her, until they could build a cabin. Before they had a chance to settle in, though, the mining claim in the Stanley Basin proved a disappointment, and Burroughs and Emma were obliged to move on. Rather than join George and Coleman at Minidoka, they headed for Parma, Idaho, much farther downstream on the Snake, where Harry had moved one of the dredges.

Burroughs took no more than a superficial interest in dredging, and it was just as well, for in early 1904 the Sweetser–Burroughs mining interests failed for the same reasons most mining operations fail: high overhead, low production, and bad luck. It meant the end of fifteen years of toil by the brothers in Idaho.

While Harry and George were struggling to keep their business afloat, Burroughs's main concern seems to have been a correspondence course in drawing. How he supported Emma and himself is unclear; most likely he simply borrowed from his big brothers. Many years later, Lew Sweetser (who had gone on to prosper in other ventures and who became lieutenant governor of Idaho) wrote a brief description of Burroughs in the days before anyone ever guessed he would be famous. He portrayed him as an accomplished horseman but had no memory of him as a gold dredger. Mostly, Sweetser had been impressed by Burroughs's preoccupation with cartooning. "[H]e was ever drawing well-proportioned, six-shootered cowboys, and saddled, bucking broncs freeing themselves of sprawling riders. And sketches of the placer dredging boats on Snake river, and up in Stanley basin."

Certainly nobody figured Burroughs for a writer, not in 1903–04. His wife and family could only shake their heads and, if they were in an indulgent mood, smile, for now more than ever, Burroughs seemed to have embraced shiftlessness. His niece and nephew loved his funny stories and cartoons, but as far as his brothers and their wives were concerned, he was essentially a grown-up kid, unreliable when it came to prolonged or heavy labor. Most likely they barely listened when he announced that he was at work on something more substantial than the hasty nonsense poems or pen-and-ink caricatures he tossed off for the children. And in 1911, after he had written *A Princess of Mars,* the adults still had no recollection of *Minidoka 937th Earl of One Mile—Series M; An Historical Fairy Tale,* which he had written for young Studley and Evelyn Burroughs back in Idaho.

Minidoka is the embryo of the author eight years before his birth. He typed the first few pages on the backs of Yale Dredging Company forms; other bits are handwritten; all told, it is eighty-two pages of ungainly, unpolished fantasy. Some of the most bothersome nonsense may be excused as family jokes no longer decipherable, but much of the manuscript is clearly just puerile wordplay. The tale begins in "the Bradydom of Smith and the Connerdom of Bil which lay directly south of Basalt in the land of Bray Pzvrtjhk." The hero, Minidoka, has obviously borrowed his name from the Snake River hamlet, and his earldom, One Mile, is likely a location on the river, as well. The geography of the area is interpreted imaginatively: gold found in the river in recent times is the discard from the construction of the ancient palace of Pzvrtjhk; the basaltic rock formation "near Yale," a local landmark, was caused by the Spring of Fire, unleashed by Minidoka in an effort to rid the region of cockroaches and jackrabbits.

The plot, such as it is, follows that of a conventional fairy tale. As initiation into the Knights of the Spring of Fire, Minidoka must battle a Paleozoic monster called the Hookie-Dookie and a second beast, the Rhinogazarium, which lives in the Castle in the Air at the edge of the Earth. In victory, the earl is able to rescue the damsel Bodine, whom the Hookie-Dookie had turned into a coyote, and Rhi, the prince who had been metamorphosed into the form of the Rhinogazarium. The ingredients of so many of Burroughs's future stories are all present in cruder form: the clever names, the odyssey to other worlds, hand-to-hand combat with gargantuan monsters, sudden twists of fortune, and pseudoscientific asides. Burroughs borrows freely from Homer and Lewis Carroll, and his play on peerage in *Minidoka* suggests not just a familiarity with genealogy, but also with the genre of throne-room romance that was all the rage at the turn of the century. In 1894, Anthony Hope, a bored British barrister, had dashed off a tale about an Englishman who poses as the Prince of Ruritania, a fictional Central European kingdom, in order to save the crown and the life of the real prince, a distant relative. *The Prisoner of Zenda,* as the novel was titled, became an international best-seller (and would eventually be adapted to stage and screen). Inspired by Hope, in 1901 George Barr McCutcheon, an Indiana newspaperman, published *Graustark,* the first in a series of novels about a can-do American thrown into distinctly *Zenda*-esque circumstances, though McCutcheon gave his Ruritania the name Graustark. Like Hope, McCutcheon sold millions of books, and among their admirers was Edgar Rice Burroughs, who kept their titles in his library long after his own success had surpassed theirs.

The second half of *Minidoka* owes more to Jules Verne and to Jonathan Swift's *Gulliver's Travels.* The earl, accompanied by Bodine and Rhi, journeys to the center of the earth. Everything is backward at the core, beginning with its name, Nevaeh (heaven). As in Swift's land of the Houyhnhnms, humans are the beasts and the animals rule. Minidoka's tour guide is a monkey named Anthropop—a play on Darwin and perhaps an antecedent of the anthropoid apes of *Tarzan.* The reversal of roles is intended to shed satiric light on man's mistreatment of animals, a point made most blatantly on Minidoka's trip to the zoo (which bears a striking resemblance to the Chicago World's Fair grounds). Winged fish wearing halos "fish" in a lagoon for little boys, who are "hooked through the cheek and drawn ashore wriggling and squirming" and then thrown into a bag full of other little boys. The saga of Minidoka concludes with a fourteen-day fight between the earl and Rhi, who has threatened the honor of Bodine. Minidoka finally slays Rhi and turns him into a green-eyed monster, which he names Jealousy.

Instead of publishing *Minidoka* for his young nephew and niece, as he had done with *Cotton-Tail,* Burroughs filed it away with all of his other mementos of school, army, and the West, where it went undiscovered until after his death. It survives as proof that his decision in 1911 to write *A Princess of Mars,* his first legitimate novel, was not simply the impulse of a desperate salesman. He let eight years go by before endeavoring anything as elaborate as *Minidoka;* yet if he had never written it, regardless of its incompleteness and imperfections, he might never have come back to writing at all.

IN ONE curious respect, Burroughs's time in Parma, Idaho, was exactly like his cameo at Andover: he stayed just long enough to win an election. This time the office was that of alderman. "I do not know how I came to be nominated unless I nominated myself," he wrote in his autobiography. "I was running against a popular [incumbent] named Hanratty. . . . My campaigning method was simple. I button-holed every voter that I met, told them that I was running for office and that I did not want to be embarrassed by not getting a single vote." Enough sympathy votes won him the seat, though he held the job for less than a month. If nothing else, the experience provided a welcome lift to his self-esteem. He would become more guarded as he got older, but his hunger for attention never diminished; he liked being liked, even if it took a referendum to find out if he was.

Popularity was not one of the perks of his next job. After the gold dredges had shut down, Harry Burroughs, through a friend, found his brother a position as a depot policeman for the Oregon Short Line Railroad in Salt Lake City. Burroughs, Emma, and the dog Rajah left Idaho at the end of April. His principal duty was to roust drunks and hoboes, and though he must have derived some small pleasure from wearing a uniform, he hated the work. "Those yeggs were seldom as hard-boiled as they are painted," he explained, "and only on one or two occasions did I even have to flash my gun. The drunks were worse. If you have never tried to eject a drunk from a day-coach you have no idea how many arms and legs a man can have. One night I got a hurry-up call to search the yards for a murderer and being more conscientious than intelligent, I went through nearly a hundred dark coaches and box cars. The murderer may have been relieved that I did not find him, but he was no more relieved than I."

Years later, Burroughs would hold forth as an expert on police matters and often cited his experiences in Salt Lake as a credential. One of his chronic gripes was that policemen deserved higher pay. "The pride of these brave men keeps them from asking for assistance," he told the *New York Evening Journal* in 1929, recalling the months when he and Emma had nearly starved on a policeman's wages in Salt Lake. One can only imagine what Emma thought of their straits, but again the absence of recorded complaint suggests stoicism on her part. Burroughs noted that he did the washing and ironing, "[n]ot wishing to see Mrs. Burroughs do work of this sort." Money was so tight that he half-soled his own shoes.

He joked that he had taken the railroad job with the intention of working his way up to a "private car," meaning a position of executive opulence. But he could not even get promoted to fireman (of the engine). He and Emma yearned to be back in Chicago; all they lacked was coach fare home. "Then a brilliant idea overtook us," Burroughs related. "We had our household furniture with us, and we held an auction which was a howling success. People paid real money for the junk and we went back to Chicago first class."

By this time, October 1904, Burroughs's parents had moved from Washington Boulevard to a smaller rental house on Jackson Boulevard, six blocks away, so he and Emma moved in with Emma's family at 194 Park Avenue. George Jr., having closed out his interests in Idaho, rejoined American Battery. Harry and Coleman were either already back in Chicago at the time or would soon arrive—the chronology is not sharp. Harry had suffered an eye injury in Idaho and was nearly blind for a year; he eventually recovered well enough to take a job with a local telephone company. Coleman's store in Minidoka had burned, and he brought his family back to Chicago and took a job with a printer. The best Ed Burroughs could do was a job as timekeeper at a construction site, again arranged by his old Michigan Military roommate and riding chum, Bob Lay.

The next six years were possibly the worst of his life, spent in a cloud of self-doubt that he could never entirely shake. Two decades later, when he drew up an outline for his autobiography, he summarized the period between 1905 and 1911 with the simple, dreary statement: "I am a Flop." There was something plainly pathetic in his restiveness. He was a man of intelligence and integrity whose pattern of vapid jobs seems almost premeditated. In some cases, he took them merely to put food on the table;

in others, he held out the belief that he might actually get rich; but never did he take a job because it was what he really wanted to be doing or because it might prove to be his life's work. "I sold electric light bulbs to janitors, candy to drug stores and Stoddard's Lectures from door to door," he recalled humbly.

Peddling printed lectures fit his aptitude in a way, but surprisingly it was one of the jobs he was most ashamed of. "I wandered around a large city shoving my foot inside front doors before weary housewives could slam the doors in my face and if I succeeded in getting in . . . I commenced to recite, parrot-like, a long and hideous lie. . . . The initial and most colossal falsehood . . . still haunts my memories. It was: 'Mr. Stoddard has asked me to call on you, Mrs. Brown.' Even now I blush as I type it."

If nothing else, Burroughs's muddy résumé made good fodder for later stories. A 1921 story, "The Efficiency Expert," for example, is the adventure of a cocky young man who talks his way into a job for which he has no obvious qualifications. The hero of the story, Jimmy Torrance, disinherits himself from his father, a prosperous mill owner, because he wants to make his own way in the world. "Failure . . . unutterable failure," Jimmy mutters after an initial series of rejections. Finally, after working a few desultory jobs that pay the rent but scarcely "feed the inner man," he answers an ad for an "efficiency expert" in a Chicago plant. He reads a twenty-five-cent booklet on "How to Get More Out of Your Factory," dons a ready-made suit, and bluffs his way into the job. In true Horatio Alger fashion, he bears down, exposes embezzlers in the firm, and wins the president's daughter.

The real-life inspiration for "The Efficiency Expert" was considerably less romantic. "I had about decided that I was a total failure," his autobiography reports, "when I saw an advertisement in the *Chicago Tribune* which indicated that somebody wanted an expert accountant. Not knowing anything about what was expected of an expert accountant, I applied for the job and got it. . . . The break I got in this instance lay in the fact that my employer knew even less about the duties of an expert accountant than I did. I opened up an entire new set of books for him and because he couldn't understand them he thought that they must be good, so he gave me a permanent job as his office manager."

Burroughs might not have liked the job or have respected his boss, but he must have been at least competent. He had gained a passing familiarity with bookkeeping when he worked at American Battery several years earlier. (His title there had been treasurer.) And for all his apparent indifference toward his career, he did not want for organizational skills. He had a nervous, perhaps congenital, compulsion for order, made even more dogmatic by his military training. His chronic rebellion against authority hardly evidenced an anarchic streak; rather, it reflected an intense desire to control his world. And while imagination and story-telling flair were the qualities that would launch him as an author, his diligence and perspicacity in business would ensure his long-term success. Surely he would not have been promoted to office manager if he had not earned it.

Nor could he have bluffed his way into his next job: head of the stenographic department at Sears, Roebuck. All the evidence indicates that Burroughs excelled at Sears, and though he would later express a far greater nostalgia for his Wild West days, his experience overseeing one hundred and fifty office workers was surely just as seminal.

In 1907, the year he took the job, Sears was one of the fastest-growing companies in the country. Its thousand-page catalogue, mailed to more than three million customers, sold everything from hatpins to houses. In rural households, it was cherished nearly as dearly as the family Bible. Burroughs's department, made up mostly of women, turned out an average of four thousand letters a day. He was quickly singled out by higher-ups for his "professional manner" and his initiative in stream-lining operations, increasing productivity, and reducing costs.

The job could be hectic and frustrating at times, but he was able to find humor in the day-to-day drudgery. "I had my problems there," he acknowledges in his autobiography, "including the young lady who couldn't do as much work in the winter time as she could in the summer because the days were shorter." He drew a delightful series of caricatures which kidded the date-crazy stenographers with hair ribbons bigger than their brains; the gangly office boys consumed by "de Cubs" baseball team; and the mid-level drones who knew just what to say to the customer who had ordered a piano but received a toupee instead. "He seems to be conversant with every detail of the department," a superior complimented, though the man probably never saw the cartoons that bespoke Burroughs's true feelings toward the job at hand.

His future with Sears looked exceedingly bright, making his decision to quit seem like madness. The timing could not have been worse. It was one thing to expose Emma to hardship, quite another to subject his first-born child. Almost nine months exactly after Sears had named him head of the stenography department, Emma had given birth to a baby girl, Joan (pronounced Jo Ann). But instead of settling down, in August 1908, when Joan was four months old, Burroughs threw caution to the wind once again. "Having a good job and every prospect for advancement I decided to go into business for myself, with harrowing results," he recalled with only mild chagrin.

All that survives of the venture that drew him away from the security of Sears, Roebuck is a business card, "Burroughs & Dentzer, Advertising Contractors." Apparently it was an overnight failure that left him in dire circumstances. "I had no capital when I started," he noted, "and less when I got through."

He didn't seem to be doing much better on the home front, either, or so he tried to suggest in a humorous essay written shortly after Joan's birth. Except for the occasional light verse, "What Every Young Couple Should Know" was his first presentable piece of creative writing since *Minidoka* in 1903. It is a three-thousand-word manual of bad advice and humorous observation that reveals as much about Burroughs's maturation as a writer as it does about his ineptitude as a new father. "Babies born in captivity sometimes live to a great age," he begins. He recommends that infants not be permitted to walk at too early an age: "No case has come to my attention where a child has been permitted to during the first week." As for diet, "Raw ham should not be given to a baby until after the third month." He needles doctors, nurses, and relatives, and reserves his sagest counsel for fathers: "Papa should read as many biographies as possible. He will then learn that most great men are able to do with from ten to fifteen minutes sleep each day." In choosing a name for the baby, a father should keep silent. "If he did happen to suggest a pretty name the chances are that mamma would be annoyed to learn when it was too late that her baby was named after papa's stenographer."

Broke after his venture as an advertising contractor, Burroughs was unprepared for the expenses of parenthood: "A wise father expecting his first baby will purchase two hospitals and a drug store for cash. He will find this much cheaper than paying for them on the installment plan later." At the time, Burroughs, Emma, and an apparently colicky Joan were living in an apartment owned by, and across the street from, Emma's parents. He was so hard up that his father's Christmas present to him was a letter disclosing that the Major had paid off a three hundred dollar debt that Burroughs had owed one of his brothers since 1903. "I hope you will soon be in shape to pay any other indebtedness you have," Major Burroughs wrote in his holiday note. Burroughs expressed his filial gratitude publicly ten years later in "The Efficiency Expert." Jimmy Torrance makes a silent pledge to his father: "If he won't disinherit me, I am going to disinherit myself. I am going to make him proud of me. He's the best dad a fellow ever had, and I am going to show him that I appreciate him."

Burroughs's next job was nothing to brag about, though. Again he tried sales; the company bore the dignified name Physicians Co-Operative Association; its principal product was Alcola, billed as a cure for alcoholism. He and Emma both enjoyed drinking, so it is hard to imagine him putting his heart and soul into his sales pitch. Not that it would have mattered; Alcola was apparently worse than a placebo. The product died quickly, taking the recipe with it.

While working at Physicians Co-Operative, Burroughs and the company's owner, Dr. Stace, cooked up another sales scheme that they felt had much greater potential. In some ways, though, it was an even shakier and more shameful proposition than Alcola. Under the letterhead of the Stace–Burroughs Company, they sold a correspondence course in "scientific salesmanship" based, according to Burroughs, on his vast knowledge of "everything a salesman should not do." The program was probably not too much different from other self-improvement courses of the day, with one notable exception. "Along in the third or fourth lesson the joker appeared," he explained. "Purely as a matter of practice, [correspondents] had to sell goods in order to go on with the course. The fact that [Stace–Burroughs was] able to make a large profit on the goods . . . is merely incidental and we sure gave them a choice of things to pick from, our catalogs containing almost anything from aluminum pots to pianos." Like all the other get-rich ventures he had tried thus far, Stace–Burroughs soon "sank without a trace."

By this point, Burroughs had little to joke about. His thirty dollars a week from Stace–Burroughs had not covered expenses, especially after the birth of a second child, Hulbert, on August 12, 1909. To scrimp, he limited his lunch to three cents' worth of ginger snaps. At Christmas, he sent a card to brother Coleman with the message, "Please accept this little token/It would be more were I not broken."

Once more the chronology is hazy. When Stace–Burroughs failed is not exactly clear; it may have lasted through 1910. Certainly a period of unemployment followed. "I approached as near financial nadir as one may reach," Burroughs admitted starkly. He had no choice but to pawn his watch and Emma's jewelry. "Evidently there was not a job to be had in Chicago," he laments in his autobiography. "I got writer's cramp answering blind ads and wore out my shoes chasing after others. Then, somehow, I got hold of a few dollars and took an agency for the sale of a lead pencil sharpener." For an office, he borrowed space from old friend Bert Hall, a corset wholesaler.

In light of his future achievement, and in contrast to the heroes he would soon invent, nothing could have been more prosaic. Or perverse. Or, for that matter, more perfect. Edgar Rice Burroughs, thirty-five, husband, father of two children, and soon-to-be father of one of the greatest characters in popular literature, had become a check-suited drummer of twentieth-century gee-whizzery.

In his new job, he did not actually try to sell the pencil sharpeners himself. He was a jobber, a franchisee of some sort. His role was to hire sales agents, whom he sent into what he hoped was a dull but acquisitive world. Much to his disappointment, and the reading public's good fortune, his salesmen proved ineffectual. With scant business to transact, he filled the empty time reading cheap magazines, a habit he had acquired during his Alcola and Stace–Burroughs days, when he used to advertise his products in their pages. "[A]fter our advertisements were checked I sometimes took them home to read," he told the *Chicago Examiner* several years later. "There were several all-fiction publications among them—some that I had never before seen. I remember thinking that if other people got money for writing such stuff I might, too, for I was sure I could write stories just as rotten as theirs."

"Under the Moon of Mars," or *A Princess of Mars,* as it was eventually titled, is the tale of a soldier who falls into a trance in Arizona and wakes up on Mars. Over the years, more than a few readers have speculated that Burroughs's characters and the plot of *Princess* had come to him while in a trance of his own.

He never denied that he was a bit odd—he even encouraged his eccentric image as beneficial to his authorial mystique. And there is no doubt that his mind was unsettled at the time he wrote *Princess.* "I had worked steadily for six years without a vacation," he said of the period, "and for fully half of my working hours of that time I had suffered tortures from headaches." He attributed his condition to a blow to the head, received either in Idaho or during his stint as a railroad policeman. Along with the headaches came intense nightmares, "when I would see figures standing beside my bed, usually shrouded," he later revealed in a letter to the Boston Society of Psychic Research. Eventually the headaches subsided, but the nightmares never did. His children and both his wives gave up counting, but never got used to, the occasions when he woke them with his nocturnal thrashing and fulminations. Tent- and shipmates during World War II said they were regularly treated to the same alarming outbursts.

Yet the real impetus for *A Princess of Mars* had less to do with the supernatural ("in which I do not believe," he told the Boston psychics) than with the pressures of everyday life. To be sure, he needed more income. "I had a wife and two babies, a combination which does not work well without money," he told *The American Author* some years later. But even that explanation falls short. At the time he wrote *A Princess of Mars,* he had no earthly idea of the going rate for magazine stories; nor did he inquire—out of meekness perhaps, or more likely, because he was motivated by an impulse more basic than cash and more personal than he cared to admit in public. Stifled by a dull job, surrounded by a brood of demanding children, and under the scrutiny of a wife, parents, and in-laws whom he clearly wasn't impressing, he did what he had done so many times before: plotted escape. This, at least, clarifies why he was naturally so good at what he did and why his writing struck a chord with a wide audience of readers also looking for escape. "[S]urreptitiously," he said, "very surreptitiously, I started *A Princess of Mars.*"

HE BEGAN writing sometime in July of 1911. Meanwhile, slow sales had forced him to give up pencil sharpeners and go to work for his brother Coleman, who owned a firm that made stationery—"scratch pads," Burroughs belittled. He kept writing, though, and by mid-August had scribbled 43,000 words on the backs of old letterheads. On August 14, he paused, uncertain whether to keep going, but brave enough to submit what he had to one of the pulps. "Under separate cover," he wrote to *Argosy,* one of the Munsey magazines, "I am sending you by mail the first part of a manuscript of a story entitled: Dejah Thoris, Martian Princess. . . . The story contains sufficient action, love, mystery and 'horror' to render it entertaining to a large majority of readers. If it is acceptable to you, will you kindly advise me what you will pay me for it, and what total volume of manuscript you desire?" He signed the letter as he had bylined the manuscript: Normal Bean.

For once, he had not falsely advertised his merchandise. The story did indeed contain sufficient action, love, mystery, and horror, and it was light years ahead of *Minidoka,* his only other extended narrative to date. More than simply showing promise, it was a captivating piece of writing.

The story's hero and narrator, Captain John Carter, is a Civil War veteran and Indian fighter. Like Burroughs's own forebears and the hero of the well-known Owen Wister novel, Carter is a Virginian. (*The Virginian* was one of the few novels Burroughs claimed to have read more than once.) Carter is a superb horseman, marksman, swordsman, and the prototype for nearly all of Burroughs's heroes, including Tarzan: "He was a splendid specimen of manhood, standing a good two inches over six feet, broad of shoulder and narrow of hip, with the carriage of the trained fighting man. His features were regular and clear cut, his hair black and closely cropped, while his eyes were a steel gray, reflecting a strong and loyal character, filled with fire and initiative. His manners were perfect, and his courtliness was that of a typical southern gentleman of the highest type."

Carter tells his story in the first person, through the device of a manuscript left to a nephew after his apparent death. At the outset, he is prospecting in the mountains of Arizona. Pursued by Apaches, he hides in a cave, where he is overcome by an unexplainable lassitude. In an extreme effort to break out of his paralytic spell, he somehow triggers an out-of-body experience: "[T]here before me lay my own body as it had been lying all these hours. . . . I looked first at my lifeless clay there upon the floor of the cave and then down at myself in utter bewilderment; for there I lay clothed, and yet here I stood but naked as at the minute of my birth."

The task of transporting John Carter to Mars was even less problematic. By the turn of the century, the American public was already quite familiar with Ouija boards, seances, astral projection, and myriad strains of Theosophy. Even those who took a skeptical view of the paranormal could appreciate its usefulness as a literary device. Looking skyward,

Carter states, "My attention was quickly riveted by a large red star close to the distant horizon. As I gazed upon it I felt a spell of overpowering fascination—it was Mars, the god of war, and for me, the fighting man, it had always held the power of irresistible enchantment. As I gazed at it on that far-gone night it seemed to call across the unthinkable void. . . . My longing was beyond the power of opposition; I closed my eyes, stretched out my arms toward the god of my vocation and felt myself drawn with the suddenness of thought through the trackless immensity of space."

When John Carter opens his eyes, he knows instinctively that he is on Mars, though he is surprised to discover that Martian gravity is much less than Earth's. Already a figure of prowess in his own land, he is now a superman able to leap buildings in a single bound (twenty-three years before a caped Superman sprang from the pen of Cleveland writer Jerry Siegel).

The planet that Carter explores is not altogether alien, however. The atmosphere is breathable, and the landscape bears a strong resemblance to that of the American West. Tharks, the first Martians Carter encounters, are fifteen feet tall, with six limbs, green skin, red eyes, and tusks, but nonetheless bear a strong resemblance to American Indians. They carry spears and rifles and ride like the wind—though their mounts, called thoats, have eight legs and are controlled by telepathy. Later Carter befriends the Martian equivalent of a dog: the enormous, endearing "watch-thing," Woola.

Above all, Mars, or Barsoom, as it is known to its inhabitants, has a distinctly antiquarian familiarity. It is a feudal world ruled by chieftains, and John Carter for all intents and purposes becomes an interplanetary knight errant. Cannons may fire radioactive projectiles and airships are levitated and propelled by an "eighth ray," but when warriors clash, they still storm over each other's bulwarks and fight hand to hand in the manner of Horatio. Chariots are the preferred land vehicle, and at one point Carter must fight for his life as a gladiator in a ruined amphitheater. When it is time for bed, he wraps himself in furs and silks, like a medieval sultan.

This hybrid of the fantastic and old-fashioned makes Mars exotic, yet inherently plausible. Burroughs makes clear that he *knows* this planet—its geography, history, language, and mores—and he shares his comprehension with his heroes: they are strangers who are able to *adapt* to a strange land. John Carter masters the Barsoomian tongue and makes the thoats and the otherworldly gizmos work to his advantage. And it goes without saying that he makes the proper friends, thwarts the appropriate enemies, and wins the heart of the princess, Dejah Thoris.

Dejah Thoris is a red Martian, distinct from the gargoylish greens of Thark. Her Barsoomian homeland is called Helium, and her people are descendants of the planet's most cultivated race, who, once upon a time, were as white-skinned as John Carter. As the Martian seas gradually shrank, the civilization of these ancients withered as well, and they were obliged to mix with the darker races. The Heliumites, ascendant once again, now have reddish copper skins, but in nearly all other ways they are human, and quite appealingly so, as Carter attests unequivocally upon seeing Dejah Thoris for the first time: "Her face was oval and beautiful in the extreme, her every feature was finely chiseled and exquisite, her eyes large and lustrous."

When John Carter first encounters Dejah Thoris, she is a prisoner of the Tharks, arch-enemies of Helium and, under the current regime, a barbaric lot who live and multiply dispassionately, not unlike the manner in which "the owner of a Kentucky racing stud directs the scientific breeding of his stock for the improvement of the whole." Parents, for instance, are not permitted to hatch their own eggs—which is how all Barsoomians propagate—or to raise their own children.

With help from a sympathetic Thark slave, Carter and Dejah Thoris manage to escape and flee toward Helium, where her grandfather is the jeddak (king). Their journey is an unrelenting sequence of close calls, including one in which Carter snatches Dejah Thoris from the brink of a forced marriage to the jeddak of a rival city. "Things should not be too dull for your hero," Burroughs later explained to *The Writer's Monthly*, "and the better the fighting the more appreciated is the winning." True to form, the battles in *Princess* sometimes stretch for pages, like a Norse saga or a Douglas Fairbanks twelve-reeler. Burroughs actually approached Douglas Fairbanks in 1924 with a proposal that the dashing star play John Carter in the movies. Fairbanks declined, but he would have been a perfect fit, for he and Carter were two of the greatest swashbucklers of their day. The odds are always stacked against them, and when death seems inevitable, they vow to sell their lives as dearly as possible, their "long, straight, needle-like swords flashing in the sunlight."

For all its frantic action, however, *A Princess of Mars* would not have been a very memorable tale without a love story at its core. Before

Princess, the dominant trend in science fiction, in the pulps as well as the more elegant works of Jules Verne and H. G. Wells, was pure adventure—meaning *male* adventure, no women allowed. Men were too busy conquering new worlds and authors too preoccupied with taking society's foibles to millenarian extremes; they had no time for boy-meets-girl. But with the creation of Dejah Thoris, Burroughs proved that if fantasy was escape, then romantic fantasy, or "scientific romance," as the subgenre would soon be called, was the ultimate escape.

Though Burroughs prided himself on the "cleanliness" of his romances, he was not above adding spice when he thought it would improve the recipe. Throughout the entire narrative of *Princess*, for instance, Dejah Thoris is nearly as naked as an odalisque: "She was destitute of clothes," John Carter exclaims. "[I]ndeed, save for highly wrought ornaments she was entirely naked, nor could any apparel have enhanced the beauty of her perfect and symmetrical figure." Burroughs assumed correctly that a Martian context would keep such a revelation on a wholesome plane, but in 1911 the notion of women parading through a story unclad was nonetheless titillating; it borrowed as much from the *Police Gazette* as Greek iconography. Even today it is part of the great appeal of *A Princess of Mars*, most of whose admirers are still male.

Prolific nudity is not an invitation to carnal intimacy, however. Consensual sexual intercourse is conspicuously absent from *Princess* and the fiction of its ilk. In fact, the only instances in which sex is even suggested is in the context of rape; sooner or later in nearly every Burroughs story, the heroine must confront a "fate worse than death" at the hands of some ignoble lout. In the case of Dejah Thoris, who finds herself paired off unwillingly with the despicable Tal Hajus, jeddak of Thark, there is only one possible alternative to the unthinkable. "Far better that we save friendly bullets for ourselves at the last moment," Carter explains, "as did those brave frontier women . . . who took their own lives rather than fall into the hands of the Indian braves." Death and deflowering are always forestalled in the nick of time, thanks usually to the heroics of one good male or another—but not before the good reader has had an opportunity to savor a whiff of salaciousness without incurring a blemish on his sense of propriety.

As *Princess* dashes to its conclusion, John Carter unites the reds and the greens, rescues Dejah Thoris from the clutches of "abysmal atavism," and takes her for his wife. "Was there ever such a man!" Dejah Thoris exclaims. ". . . Alone, a stranger, hunted, threatened, persecuted, you have done in a few short months what in all the past ages of Barsoom no man has ever done." Their own snow white egg nestles in an incubator on the roof of the palace.

Instead of dropping the curtain on this happy scene, Burroughs offers a less snug ending. The Martian atmosphere plant has failed and the people are slowly suffocating. John Carter cracks the code (using "the nine thought waves") just before sinking into unconsciousness. When he wakes up, he is back on Earth, and the stage is set for a sequel. He sits at his desk, staring up at Mars: "I can see, across the awful abyss of space, a beautiful black-haired woman standing in the garden of a palace, and at her side is a little boy who puts his arm around her as she points into the sky. . . . I believe that they are waiting there for me, and something tells me that I shall soon know."

BURROUGHS never elaborated on why he chose Mars as the setting for *Princess,* but by 1911, the "red planet" was hardly an obscure subject. The first person to notice the signature markings on Mars's surface was Italian astronomer Giovanni Schiaparelli in 1879. To describe the matrix of straight lines he saw through the telescope, Schiaparelli chose the word *canali,* which translates as either "channels" or "canals." The latter definition was adopted by the English-speaking world, and soon semantics had command of logic. If immense man-made canals were possible on Earth—the Suez Canal had been completed ten years earlier—then the canals of Mars surely must be artificial, as well. In 1892, French astronomer Camille Flammarion made the pronouncement that "the present inhabitation of Mars by a race superior to ours is very possible."

The next noteworthy life-on-Mars theorist was an eccentric Boston Brahmin by the name of Percival Lowell. After distinguishing himself in mathematics and the classics at Harvard, Lowell had knocked around Europe and Asia for two decades, studying ancient cultures and philosophies. One of his lifelong passions was astronomy, and in 1894 Lowell decided to build an observatory in Flagstaff, Arizona, in order to study the latest object of his intellectual curiosity, the planet Mars. Because of the ellipticity of the Martian orbit, its proximity to Earth can range from thirty-five million miles to sixty-three million miles; every twenty-six months it draws near, and every fifteen years or so it draws especially near. Lowell's year, 1894, was a good time to look at Mars (as was Schiaparelli's).

The following year, Lowell published *Mars*, in which he seconded Schiaparelli's interpretation of the "canals." Lowell's second book, *Mars and Its Canals* (1906), was unwavering and more widely read, and his final treatise, *Mars as an Abode for Life* (1908), published three years before Burroughs wrote *A Princess of Mars,* was his most explosive. In it, he asserts that Mars was once covered by oceans, like Earth's. In the "struggle for existence" prompted by the drying up of the oceans, canals were "laid down by rule and compass" to draw water from the polar ice caps. Lowell presents actual maps of the canals, 437 in all, as "witness that life, and life of no mean order, at present inhabits the planet." In passing, he points out that a canal system of this magnitude would be easier to build on Mars than on his own planet because Martian gravity is 30 percent of Earth's. ("An elephant on Mars could jump like a gazelle.") And he ends with a note of sadness and caution: Mars is a very old, complex civilization, but it is dying. "The drying up of the planet is certain to proceed until its surface can support no life at all. Slowly but surely time will snuff it out. When the last ember is thus extinguished, the planet will roll a dead world through space, its evolutionary career forever ended." This after noting that our own oceans are receding as well.

Scientists continued to marginalize Lowell's reasoning, but the general public had already been softened up by a succession of fantastic novels on the subject. In 1894, the year Mars had come so close to Earth, Gustavus W. Pope had published *Journey to Mars,* a novel that bears a certain resemblance to *A Princess of Mars,* with its red princess, rainbow of races, swordplay, and an earthling hero whose prowess is enhanced by Martian gravity. A more famous Martian novel was H. G. Wells's *The War of the Worlds* (1898), in which giant Martians invade England. (Orson Welles turned H. G. Wells's book into a chilling radio program in the 1930s, and not until 1997, with the discovery in Antarctica of microscopic fossils in a Martian meteor, would the discussion of life on Mars again be so animated.)

Burroughs never acknowledged having read Pope or Wells, but he was clearly familiar with Lowell, most likely from the newspapers, which fed heavily on the Martian debate. Ancient civilization, empty sea beds, and diminished gravity are important elements of *A Princess of*

Mars and the other Martian stories that followed. At one point, Dejah Thoris takes a diamond from her hair and scratches what is obviously a Lowellian map of Barsoom on the marble floor: "It was crisscrossed in every direction with long straight lines, sometimes running parallel and sometimes converging toward some great circle." In recent years, science fiction enthusiasts have attempted to add more names to the list of influences on *Princess,* though the likelihood that Burroughs knew about them seems remote. All, anyway, owe at least an indirect debt to Percival Lowell.

ON AUGUST 24, ten days after submitting the first forty-three thousand words of *A Princess of Mars,* Burroughs received a letter from Thomas Newell Metcalf, managing editor of *The All-Story,* a sister to *Argosy* in the Munsey family. Frank Munsey, a Maine farmer's son who had become a New York publishing tycoon, had revolutionized the American magazine business in the 1890s by lowering the price of his general-interest flagship, *Munsey's Magazine,* from twenty-five cents to ten. Rival "slicks," *McClure's* and *Cosmopolitan,* so called because they were printed on smooth stock, did the same, and together they opened up an enormous, underappreciated middle-class market. With their fully illustrated mix of unstuffy journalism and able fiction accompanied by ads for nationally known products, ranging from automobiles to detergent, the slicks shouldered aside old-guard journals such as *Century, Harper's,* and *Scribner's,* and stole readers and advertisers from the daily newspapers and their Sunday supplements.

Munsey and his slick rivals also saw an opportunity to revitalize the all-fiction field, commandeering the audience of adolescent boys and working men who once had pledged allegiance to the dime novels. The dimes, best remembered for their Buffalo Bill westerns, Nick Carter detective stories, and the pluck-and-luck parables of Horatio Alger, had been crippled in 1897 by a regulation that raised the postal rate on irregularly circulated "periodicals." By 1910, a number of all-fiction monthlies had supplanted the dimes (most of which had actually cost a nickel). Some bore mild titles such as *Popular* or *Short Stories;* others, such as *Top Notch* and *Adventure,* waved bolder banners. Munsey's *Argosy* and *All-Story* were typical of the genre. Nicknamed for the cheap, rough paper on which they were printed, the early pulps carried very little illustration other than on the front cover. Type ran in two columns, pressing nearly to the margins of the seven-by-ten-inch format. A single issue might carry two or three novel-length stories in various stages of serialization, one story finishing up as another was beginning, plus shorter stories, advice columns, and an abundance of reader letters. The audience would always be largely male, but a surprising number of women were drawn to the murder mysteries, westerns, war stories, and science fiction adventures that were the pulp mainstay. (The time was coming when they would have their own pulps, the romance and true-confession magazines.) Advertising included major brand names as well as dubious tonics and fly-by-night correspondence courses similar to the one Burroughs had tried to sell while at Stace–Burroughs. Writing for the pulps was a shaky proposition at best. Had Burroughs inquired in advance, he might have been shocked to learn that some contributors earned as little as a tenth of a cent a word. Few pulp writers could work fast enough to make a living; fewer still ever graduated from the genre; O. Henry, Jack London, and Raymond Chandler are among the fortunate who made it out and up.

Argosy was Burroughs's first choice for *A Princess of Mars* because it was older and considered slightly higher-brow than the rest, but at either *Argosy* or *All-Story,* his timing could not have been better. Frank Munsey, pressed by rising printing costs, was planning to up the price of his pulps from ten cents to fifteen; to justify the hike, he intended to add more pages—and thus needed more stories.

"There are many things about the story I like," replied *All-Story*'s Metcalf, a twenty-eight-year-old Chicago native, "but on the other hand, there are points about which I am not so keen." He thought the beginning too slow and other parts inconsistent; too, he could not make a final judgment without reading the conclusion. If Burroughs would write another thirty thousand words "as ingenious as is the greater part of what I read," Metcalf wrote, "I should be very glad to consider it."

Burroughs completed the story in a month, following most of Metcalf's advice, including the suggestion that Carter fall unconscious at the end and wake up back in his Arizona cave. Burroughs was in such a tizzy to get the manuscript off that he miscalculated the postage and rushed a follow-up letter of apology to Metcalf in New York. He had to wait another five weeks for a decision. Finally, on November 4, Metcalf reported that "'The Martian Princess' story is in perfectly good form now and I should very much like to buy it." He offered four hundred dollars.

Burroughs was ecstatic. "I shall never make a million dollars," he predicted in his autobiography, "but if I do it cannot possibly give me the thrill that that four hundred dollar check gave me." Even so, he was cool in his reply to Metcalf. Though a novice fiction writer, he was a veteran business correspondent. In his August letter pitching the first installment of *Princess,* he had the presence of mind to request book rights; now he wanted to discuss money. "Your offer of $400.00 ... is acceptable to me," he wrote Metcalf, but in the next breath he politely petitioned for more. "Does the price at which I have sold you this first manuscript establish the rate for future stories? . . . I like the work. . . [but] it would not be worth my while to devote all my time to it at this rate." At the end, however, he let down his guard: "You may recall that I mentioned . . . that my prime object in writing the story was the urgent need I had for what it might bring, and I assure you that I will greatly appreciate anything you can do to expedite the forwarding of a check."

The check arrived two weeks later. Four hundred dollars, averaged out over the four months Burroughs had worked on the story, was not enough to liberate him from his brother's stationery company, but it was a step in the right direction. He had been so unsure of himself while writing *Princess* that he had kept the manuscript a secret from everyone except Emma. Now, with the money in hand and a promise from Metcalf that his story would be serialized from February to April (1912), he finally allowed himself to consider the possibility that one day he might make a living as a writer. The best news of all was that Metcalf had invited him to submit another story.

Metcalf had loved all the sword fighting and chivalry in *Princess,* and urged Burroughs to try "a serial of the regular romantic type, something like, say 'Ivanhoe,' or at least of the period when everybody wore armor and dashed about rescuing fair ladies." Burroughs needed no further prompting. A mere three weeks after receiving Metcalf's suggestion, he sent off *The Outlaw of Torn,* a book-length tale of thirteenth-century England. The hero is the fictitious second son of Henry III, who, like several other of Burroughs's subsequent protagonists, is ripped from his parents at an early age and brought up unaware of his true (and noble) origin. He becomes Norman of Torn, a Robin Hood-ish highwayman whose "clear eye and perfect figure" catch the eye of the fair Bertrade, daughter of a baron. Burroughs offers a short ration of history—he knew nothing about medieval England except what he extracted from a hasty reading of *Ivanhoe* and one or two other library books—but serves up a hearty feast of dungeons, secret passages, and archaisms such as "methought," "mayhap," and "it waxeth late." The duel between Norman and the devious DeVac, the man who had kidnapped him as a child and pretended to be his father, is epic. By the end, Norman saves England, reunites with his true parents, and nestles in the arms of Bertrade, who has loved him all along, not because of his outlaw's mask or royal crest, but because of the man beneath.

Burroughs believed he had written a masterpiece, but Metcalf was not so sanguine. "I am very doubtful about the story," he wrote on December 19. He liked the plot but wished for something more than one pulse-pounding scene after another. "You really didn't get the effect of the picturesqueness of Torne [*sic*]," he advised. "Opportunities for color and pageantry you have entirely missed." Metcalf tried to boost Burroughs's morale with a pledge that he would not have been so explicit in his criticisms if he did not believe in Burroughs's potential. Above all, he urged Burroughs not to be in such a rush.

Burroughs rebutted the allegation of haste with the explanation that he had worked "all day and late into the night. An experienced writer would doubtless cover much more ground in the same time." Other than that, he had no gripe with Metcalf's brief, and he cheerfully agreed to rewrite the story. Two months later he was done, though after reading several more books on the period, including Maurice Hewlitt's *Forest Lovers,* Howard Pyle's *Men of Iron,* and Mark Twain's *A Connecticut Yankee in King Arthur's Court,* he was convinced that "nobody knows anything about the manners, customs or speech of 13th Century England."

Metcalf did not like the second draft any better than the first, and suggested paying Burroughs a hundred dollars for the plot and turning it over to another writer with better descriptive skills. Burroughs said no, his pride obviously wounded. "I really think your readers would have liked that story," he told Metcalf. "I am not prone to be prejudiced in favor of my own stuff, in fact it all sounds like rot to me, but I tried the Mss on some young people, extremely superior, hypercritical young people, and some of them sat up all night reading it." He did not indicate who the readers had been, but if nothing else, his remark was evidence that he now had enough confidence in his writing to show it off. And this would not be the last time that Burroughs declared that he had a better feel for public taste than did his editors.

It must have been very hard to say no to Metcalf's money, even a hundred dollars. By that time, Champaign–Yardley was not doing well enough to pay both Burroughs and his brother a living wage. "We now had a recurrence of great poverty," Burroughs wrote in his autobiography, and he could only hope that he would have better luck with his next story.

As harsh as Metcalf had been in his criticism of *The Outlaw of Torn*, he still encouraged Burroughs to submit more romances. In particular, he was interested in a sequel to *A Princess of Mars*, this time urging him to explore "the Valley Dorr, the River Iss and the Sea of Korus, or those other semi-religious semi-mystical regions which you mentioned, but I believed never used. . . . Carter might get into some terrific rows, apropos of religion, with some of the Martian priests."

Burroughs wrote back on March 6, reporting that he already had in mind a follow-up to *Princess* but that he had not had a chance to get started on it. Instead, he said, "I have been working at odd moments on another of the 'improbable' variety of tale, and if I ever finish it I shall see what I can do in the way of a John Carter sequel." In two brief paragraphs, he sketched his new plot: "The story I am now on is of the scion of a noble English house—of the present time—who was born in tropical Africa where his parents died when he was about a year old. The infant was found and adopted by a huge she-ape, and was brought up among a band of fierce anthropoids.

"The mental development of this ape-man in spite of every handicap, of how he learned to read English without knowledge of the spoken language, of the way in which his inherent reasoning faculties lifted him high above his savage jungle friends and enemies, of his meeting with a white girl, how he came at last to civilization and to his own[,] makes most fascinating writing and I think will prove interesting reading, as I am especially adapted to the building of the 'damphool' species of narrative."

Metcalf's response a week later was undoubtedly the most important letter of his life: "I think your idea for a new serial is a cracker-jack and I shall be very anxious to have a look at it. You certainly have the most remarkable imagination of anybody whom I have run up against for some time, and I have come to the conclusion that I had very likely better not butt in on any of your schemes, but let you go ahead as you and your imagination see fit."

If Metcalf had thrown open his window and listened carefully, he might have heard the triumphant cry of the bull ape a thousand miles to his west.

4

WHITE APE

The first installment of *A Princess of Mars* was published in *The All-Story* and serialized monthly from February to July 1912. The magazine botched Burroughs's pen name, printing it as Norman Bean, instead of Normal. The error "ruined its subtle humor," Burroughs felt, and he never used the pseudonym again. Thereafter he submitted his manuscripts using his full name, Edgar Rice Burroughs.

By May, he was working for his brother's stationery company only three days a week and had taken a second job as manager of the business service department of *System*, a local business magazine. Subscribers would write in, asking for business advice, and Burroughs was charged with solving their problems, regardless of his own thin qualifications. "I knew little or nothing about business, had failed in every enterprise I had ever attempted and could not have given valuable advice to a peanut vendor," he would later write.

He hated the job and his boss, "an egotistical ass with the business morality of a peep show proprietor." He reported to Metcalf that he was making a decent salary, but wished fiction writing paid enough so he could quit. Metcalf could not promise anything close to a living wage, especially after Burroughs's lackluster showing with *The Outlaw of Torn,* but due to "certain changes in the future policy of *The All-Story,*" he was eager to read the "improbable" tale that Burroughs had been scribbling weekends and evenings since before Christmas. Burroughs's notes indicate that he finished the 504-page manuscript on May 14; but before he could mail it, he had to have a typist convert his sprawling penmanship to a more presentable form. Finally on June 11, he sent the typescript, which he had titled *Tarzan of the Apes,* to New York. "May I have an early decision?" he beseeched.

Metcalf took two weeks to respond: "I suppose by this time you have got a small souvenir from us to remind you of our attitude toward 'Tarzan of the Apes.'" In a separate envelope, Munsey's had sent a check for seven hundred dollars. Beyond that, Metcalf offered no overt praise. Instead he complained about the single-spacing of the typescript and the "appallingly thin paper" on which it was typed. Not until the September issue of *All-Story* did he acknowledge that *Tarzan* was something beyond the run of the mill. "If you will stop and realize how many thousands and thousands of stories an editor has to read, day in, day out," Metcalf wrote in his preview of *Tarzan,* slated to appear the following month, "you will be impressed when we tell you that we read this yarn at one sitting and had the time of our young lives. It is the most exciting story we have seen in a blue moon, and about as original as they make 'em." He and his staff liked *Tarzan* so much they planned to run the entire story in the October issue.

On the opening page of *Tarzan,* Burroughs offers the caveat typical of so many of the adventure stories he had read as a youth: "I do not say this story is true . . . but the fact that in the telling of it to you I have taken fictitious names for the principal characters quite sufficiently evidences the sincerity of my own belief that it *may* be true. . . . If you do not find it credible you will at least be as one with me in acknowledging that it is unique, remarkable, and interesting."

The tale begins in 1888, with John and Alice Clayton, Lord and Lady Greystoke, en route from England to West Africa, where Clayton has been sent by the British Colonial Office to investigate rumors that native British subjects are being enslaved by another European power (presumably Leopold II's Belgian Congo) to collect rubber and ivory. Clayton, like John Carter (another "JC"), is a "strong, virile man—mentally, morally, and physically." After a mutiny aboard ship, Lord and Lady Greystoke are set ashore on a remote, uninhabited coast. Clayton gives a pep talk to his petrified wife: "Hundreds of thousands of years ago our ancestors of the dim and distant past faced the same problems which we must face, possibly in these same primeval forests. . . . What they did may we not do? And even better for are we not armed with ages of superior knowledge, and have we not the means of protection, defense, and sustenance which science has given us . . . ?"

At first, their plight does not seem so bad. They have plenty of supplies, weapons, and of course, each other. Lady Alice pledges to her husband that she will do her best to be "a brave primeval woman, a fit mate for the primeval man." She bravely shoots a bull ape that has attacked them in their cabin, but the brush with brutal calamity sends her into a state of nervous dementia. That same night, she gives birth to a son, and a year later she dies. Lord Clayton writes in his diary, "My little son is crying for nourishment—O Alice, Alice, what shall I do?"

By way of answer, the focus shifts from man to apes. The reader is introduced to Kerchak, the king of the anthropoids, and Kala, a young female. Burroughs's knowledge of apes at the time was understandably vague; scientists had not yet begun to do fieldwork on primate taxonomy or behavior. And so he exercised his creative license and assigned Kerchak and Kala to a species "closely allied to the gorilla, yet more intelligent." No such animals exist in real life; there are only four species of anthropoid, or great, apes—gorillas, chimpanzees, orangutans, and gibbons—and Burroughs's apes are none of these.

Whatever gaps existed in Burroughs's knowledge of apes he patched over with scraps of fact and pseudoscience gathered from a lifetime of random reading and travel. One of the strongest influences was anthropometry, the measurement of man, a discipline that had caught his attention at the Chicago World's Fair in 1893. In *Tarzan of the Apes,* Kerchak's forehead is "extremely low and receding" and his eyes bloodshot, while Kala is a "splendid, clean-limbed animal, with a round, high forehead." In other words, Kala is more highly evolved, more like a human, than Kerchak is—a distinction that would soon figure in the fate of the baby Clayton.

As the story continues, the reader learns that Kala's first and only child has recently died in a fall, and she still clings to the corpse, absorbed in grief as her "tribe" of apes approaches the Clayton cabin.

Through the open door, they observe Lord Greystoke slumped over his diary, asleep. Kerchak enters silently and, without a thought, kills Clayton. Kala, meanwhile, snatches Clayton's infant son from its cradle, drops her own dead offspring in its place, and retreats to the treetops. "High up among the branches . . . she hugged the shrieking infant to her bosom, and soon the instinct that was dominant in this fierce animal . . . reached out to the tiny man-child's half-formed understanding, and he became quiet. Then hunger closed the gap between them, and the son of an English lord and an English lady nursed at the breast of Kala, the great ape."

Kala names her child Tarzan, ape-speak for "white skin." By the time Tarzan is ten, he is stronger and far more agile than any full-grown human athlete, able to swing through the trees effortlessly. Eventually a strange, unfathomable yearning, combined with sheer animal curiosity, leads him back to the cabin of his birth, which by luck has been locked and preserved since his abrupt departure.

It is here that Burroughs makes his next great leap—one that later would be eliminated in the Hollywood simplification of the Tarzan character. Searching the cabin, young Tarzan is drawn to the books, "which seemed to exert a strange and powerful influence over him." In his father's collection is a child's primer, some picture books, and a dictionary: "All of these he examined . . . though the strange little bugs which covered the pages where there were no pictures excited his wonder and deepest thought. . . . Squatting up on his haunches on the table top in the cabin his father had built—his smooth, brown, naked little body bent over the book which rested in his strong slender hands, and his great shock of long, black hair falling about his well-shaped head and bright, intelligent eyes—Tarzan of the apes, little primitive man, presented . . . an allegorical figure of the primordial groping through the black night of ignorance toward the light of learning."

Painstakingly, young Tarzan teaches himself to read and write, thanks to "a healthy mind endowed by inheritance." His wits, he discovers, are as nimble as his body, and soon a literate Tarzan is hunting with noose, bow and arrow, and the knife he has retrieved from the cabin. He kills most often for food, but, "being a man," he also kills for pleasure on occasion.

The lure of the apes is still dominant, however, and Tarzan finds himself participating instinctively and enthusiastically in the Dum-Dum, a ritual in which the apes gather in a circular clearing and beat on earthen drums to celebrate important tribal events. This primitive rite, Burroughs states, is "the antecedent of all the forms and ceremonies of modern church and state." (The annual gathering of the Burroughs Bibliophiles, the most dominant of the Burroughs fan clubs, is called the Dum-Dum, as well.)

In the countless interviews Burroughs gave in subsequent years, he never denied the gross implausibility of the Dum-Dum, the successful self-tutoring, or even the underlying premise of an infant surviving, and thriving, in a community of anomalous apes. "I do not believe that any human infant . . . could survive a fortnight in such an African environment," he volunteered, "and if he did he would develop into a cunning, cowardly beast, as he would have to spend most of his waking hours fleeing for his life. He would be underdeveloped from lack of proper and sufficient nourishment, from exposure to the inclemencies of the weather, and from lack of sufficient restful sleep." But suspension of disbelief came with the literary territory, and in most readers' minds, Burroughs's liberties were no more extreme than those of Poe, Verne, Haggard, Wells, Twain, or the myriad pulp writers he had scrutinized before entering the field himself.

Still, he did not escape the nitpickers entirely. One detail that readers pounced on was Sabor the tiger, nemesis of the apes. One day Sabor (not really an individual name, but ape-speak for tiger, the species) surprises Tarzan afoot on the jungle floor. It is too late to take to the trees. Tarzan manages to shoot two arrows into the charging Sabor, and as the tiger knocks him to the ground, he kills it with his knife. "With swelling breast, he placed a foot upon the body of his powerful enemy, and throwing back his fine young head, roared out the awful challenge of the victorious bull ape."

This scene, as anyone with the vaguest acquaintance with Tarzan must recognize, is one of the great moments in Tarzan's ascendancy. Nevertheless, when *Tarzan of the Apes* first appeared in the pages of *All-Story,* several readers fired off snippy letters informing the editors and Burroughs that tigers do not, and never have, prowled the African continent. In the book version of *Tarzan,* Sabor becomes a lioness, and thenceforth Burroughs determined to learn all he could about lions, apes, elephants, and all the other animals indigenous to Tarzan's environment.

The first human that Tarzan encounters, the black native hunter

Kulonga, is no more hospitable than Sabor. Kulonga stalks Tarzan's adoptive mother Kala, then kills her with a poisoned arrow through the heart. "Tarzan's grief and anger were unbounded. He roared out his hideous challenge time and again. . . . To lose the only creature in all the world who had ever manifested love and affection for him was the greatest tragedy he had ever known." In retribution, Tarzan follows Kulonga to the outskirts of his village, hangs him by the neck, then drives his knife into the black hunter's heart. "Tarzan of the Apes was no sentimentalist," Burroughs explains. "He knew nothing of the brotherhood of man," and the "jabbering," superstitious cannibals of Kulonga's tribe have not provided the best possible introduction.

Though Tarzan feels no bond to humans thus far, he finds himself ever so gradually growing apart from his ape relations. After a duel to the death with Kerchak, he assumes kingship of his tribe, then discovers that he has no affinity for the job of arbitrating domestic squabbles and other petty simian matters. For the first time, he dons a breechcloth, taken from a slain native. "Now indeed he was dressed as a man should be. None there was who could now doubt his high origin." He also begins wearing his mother's locket around his neck and starts shaving with his knife.

Here, midway in the story, Burroughs pauses to size up his hero: "The young Greystoke was indeed a strange and warlike figure, his mass of black hair falling to his shoulders behind and cut with his hunting knife to a rude bang upon his forehead. . . . His straight and perfect figure, muscled as the best of the ancient Roman gladiators . . . and yet with the soft and sinuous curves of a Greek god, told at a glance the wondrous combination of enormous strength with suppleness and speed." Now, if he could only find a mate.

Jane Porter is a spirited girl of nineteen (raised in Baltimore, not London, the birthplace of her film counterpart) when she arrives on the very beach where Tarzan's parents first landed. Like Lord and Lady Greystoke, she, too, has been set ashore by mutineers. At her side are her father, Professor Archimedes Porter; her father's secretary, Samuel T. Philander; her black maid, Esmerelda; and William Cecil Clayton, her suitor and, by sheer coincidence, Tarzan's cousin. Thusly configured, the cast is not unlike that of a conventional melodrama. Professor Porter and Philander are clumsy and absentminded, their refined intellects as ill-suited for the African jungle as their silk hats and swallow-tail coats.

Esmerelda is a rotund mammy, on stage for comic relief and, regrettably, to carry the message that "domestic" blacks are scarcely more sophisticated than the African natives whom Tarzan has taken such great pleasure in tormenting. Clayton is a good sort, true and chivalrous, but like Duncan Heyward, the worthy officer in James Fenimore Cooper's *The Last of the Mohicans* who must compete with the woodsy Hawk-eye for the love of heroine Cora, he is a man of urbane limitations. He also happens to carry the germ of inevitable discord: on the assumption that Lord and Lady Greystoke are dead—soon confirmed by the discovery of their skeletons, along with that of the infant ape, which is mistaken for the child described in Clayton's diary—William Clayton believes himself to be the rightful heir to the house of Greystoke.

The castaways settle into Tarzan's old cabin, hoping for rescue. Tarzan spies on them, and one by one, plucks them from the jaws of sure death. He pays particular attention to Jane's safety: "In his savage, untutored breast new emotions were stirring. . . . He knew that she was created to be protected, and that he was created to protect her." So far, though, he is too shy to introduce himself, and Jane and the others assume that their "forest god" is a different person from the Tarzan of the Apes who has left a handwritten note in the cabin.

Tarzan is not the only male with an eye on fair Jane. Clayton does his best to look after her, and Terkoz, a cruel and vicious outcast from Tarzan's old tribe of apes, has his own unspeakable design. At an opportune moment, Terkoz drops from a tree, throws Jane roughly across his broad, hairy shoulder, and carries her deep into the jungle. Tarzan catches up in time to keep Terkoz from having his way, and Jane finds herself observing the fierce, bloody battle between "primordial ape" and "primeval man" with a mixture of horror and fascination. As Tarzan's great muscles "knotted beneath the tension of his efforts . . . the veil of centuries of civilization and culture was swept from the blurred vision of the Baltimore girl." Finally, after Tarzan's knife "drank deep a dozen times of Terkoz' heart's blood, and the great carcass rolled lifeless on the ground, it was a primeval woman who sprang forward with outstretched arms toward the primeval man who had fought for her and won her." As for Tarzan, "He did what no red-blooded man needs lessons in doing. He took his woman in his arms and smothered her upturned, panting lips with kisses."

Clutching her tightly, Tarzan carries Jane deeper into the "savage fastness of the untamed forest," first on the ground and then, apelike, by swinging through the branches of the "middle terrace." In the chapter that follows, entitled "Heredity," he and Jane, unchaperoned, feel tentatively for common ground. Because Tarzan can only read and write but cannot speak English, their first communication is nonverbal. Nevertheless, Jane discovers that she has "never felt more secure in her whole life" than she does in the presence of this "perfect creature." He tenderly builds her a grass-lined bower and fetches a cornucopia of ripe fruit. She gently inspects the locket around his neck, which she discovers contains miniature photos of Lord and Lady Greystoke. She notes the similarity between Lord Greystoke and Tarzan, but does not make the deductive leap; nor does Tarzan yet grasp that the residents of the cabin where he found the locket were his biological mother and father. Jane kisses the locket before returning it, and Tarzan, "like some courtier of old," presses his lips where hers have been. "It was a stately and gallant little compliment performed with the grace and dignity of utter unconsciousness of self. It was the hall-mark of his aristocratic birth, the natural outcropping of many generations of fine breeding, an hereditary instinct of graciousness."

Throughout the day, Jane has admired "the graceful majesty of his carriage, the perfect symmetry of his magnificent figure." But as night approaches, she grows nervous. She need not worry, however, for Tarzan rises to the occasion. "He had not in one swift transition become a polished gentleman from a savage ape-man, but at last the instincts of the former predominated, and over all was the desire to please the woman he loved, and to appear well in her eyes." He hands her his knife and curls up outside her door. They do not kiss again until just before he returns her to her people. "I love you—I love you," she whispers.

The pace of the plot quickens from this point forward. While Tarzan and Jane are away, a French cruiser discovers the castaways and deploys a crew of armed men into the interior in search of Jane. One of its officers, Lieutenant D'Arnot, is captured by the natives. Tarzan rescues D'Arnot just as he is about to become the cannibals' supper. While D'Arnot recovers from his wounds, he and Tarzan exchange written notes, and D'Arnot teaches Tarzan to speak French. By the time they arrive back at the coast, Jane, Professor Porter, Philander, Esmerelda, and Cecil Clayton have departed on the cruiser, having left D'Arnot for dead. Before departing, Jane had discovered an early note from Tarzan in which he had pledged his love. ("I am Tarzan of the Apes. I want you. I am yours. You are mine. We will live here together always in my house. . . . I will hunt for you. I am the greatest of the jungle hunters.") She still does not connect the Tarzan of the letter with the "wood man" she had spent the night with, and so in the written reply she leaves behind, she says she has already pledged her love to another.

Going through the contents of the cabin, D'Arnot comes across Lord Greystoke's diary, written in French (Burroughs's contrivance to keep Tarzan from reading it), and a set of infant fingerprints; he speculates that Tarzan is the son of John and Alice Clayton, though Tarzan still believes his mother is Kala. Soon they leave the cabin behind—along with a treasure of gold originally discovered by Professor Porter—and make their way north to a mission outpost. In a matter of weeks, Tarzan is garbed in a white suit, and under D'Arnot's guidance, eating with knife and fork, sipping absinthe on the veranda, and answering to "Monsieur Tarzan." D'Arnot eventually takes Tarzan to Paris, though Tarzan is anxious to go to America and find Jane. Before Tarzan leaves, D'Arnot takes his fingerprints.

By now, Burroughs is clearly racing to wrap up the story within the word count prescribed by his editor. Jane is being pressed by not just Cecil Clayton, but also by a second suitor, Robert Canler, a man to whom her father owes a great deal of money. She retreats to the family farm in Wisconsin, Canler and Clayton in amorous pursuit. Caught in a forest fire, she kneels and prays for the strength to meet her fate bravely. Out of nowhere, Tarzan appears and once again carries her to safety.

In one respect, though, he is too late, for Jane tells him that she has already promised to marry Canler in order to relieve her father's debt. When Tarzan asks her if she would marry him if she hadn't already committed to Canler, she cannot answer. "I see now that you could not be happy with—an ape," he says somewhat bitterly.

The full cast assembles for the final act. Tarzan dispatches Canler first by physical threat and then by announcing to Professor Porter that the gold buried on the beach in Africa is more than sufficient to erase the looming debt. In a private moment, Jane then tells Clayton that she will marry him instead, having convinced herself that her fling with the jungle creature had been merely a "passing hallucination." When Tarzan gets his turn to propose, Jane can only bury her face in her arms. "What had she done? Because she had been afraid she might succumb to the pleas of the giant, she had burned her bridges behind her—in her groundless apprehension that she might make a terrible mistake, she had made a worse one." She stands by her commitment to Clayton.

Tarzan's shock at having been spurned is punctually interrupted by the arrival of a telegram from D'Arnot: "Fingerprints prove you Greystoke. Congratulations." Tarzan reads the wire to himself, then tucks it away. Just then, Clayton enters, overflowing with British cordiality. "If it's any of my business, how the devil did you ever get into that bally jungle?" asks the man who has claimed Tarzan's title and now his woman.

"I was born there," Tarzan responds. "My mother was an Ape, and of course she couldn't tell me much about it. I never knew who my father was."

And so ends the first book of Tarzan. Burroughs sensed that it was a good story, but had no idea just *how* good it was until Thomas Newell Metcalf began forwarding the letters that had flooded *All-Story* within days of the October 1912 number hitting the newsstands. "[S]well," "dandy," "splendid," "wonderful," "magnificent" were the superlatives of choice. "[T]o say that it is the best story I ever read would be putting it mildly," gushed one admirer. "Jules Verne has nothing on him," chimed another. Beside the Sabor slip, there was only one other thing that bothered readers: the ending. "Do not leave Tarzan suffering," was the consensus.

If anything, the gripes about the conclusion pleased Burroughs. "I am inclined to think that that is the feature of the story that really clinched their interest," he wrote to Metcalf. Metcalf concurred, and in the December *All-Story*, he teased the readers who were "barking for a sequel" by suggesting that another Tarzan was far from a sure thing. "Mr. Burroughs wrote us a letter the other day," Metcalf mentioned in his December Table Talk column, "and he ended by saying: 'About a score of readers have threatened my life unless I promise to write a sequel to "Tarzan"—shall I?'" The editor responded cattily, "We wonder." In fact, Burroughs had already sent Metcalf an outline for a follow-up, tentatively titled "Monsieur Tarzan."

WHERE HAD the idea for Tarzan come from? Burroughs never did come up with a pat explanation, perhaps because there was none. "I've been asked that hundreds of times and ought to have a good answer thought up by now, but haven't," he told the *Los Angeles Times* in 1929. "I suppose it was just because my daily life was full of business system, and I wanted to get as far from that as possible. My mind, in relaxation, preferred to roam in scenes and situations I'd never known. I find I can write better about places I've never seen than those I have."

He may never have seen Africa in person, but like many of his generation, he had an armchair familiarity with those who had. By 1912, the era of grueling, fever-ravaged African exploration was all but over, replaced by Europe's even more feverish scramble for colonial foothold. Still, few westerners were likely to forget the sensational years of African discovery and conquest: Sir Richard Burton's and John Speke's desperate search for the source of the Nile in 1858; journalist Henry Stanley's vainglorious expedition in relief of the African missionary David Livingstone in 1871; the annihilation of eight hundred British troops by Zulus in 1879, a debacle that eerily echoed the last stand of Custer's Seventh Cavalry on the Little Bighorn three years earlier; and the martyrdom of General Charles "Chinese" Gordon during the Arab siege of Khartoum in 1885. In the wake of its own imperialist victory in the Spanish-American War in 1898, America paid especially close attention to the Boer War, 1899–1902, a chapter in African history that generated more press than all the aforementioned dramas combined.

Not only Africa, but the entire globe was shrinking—an inevitability that only seemed to stimulate the public's appetite for terra incognita, real or imaginary. Fiction writers were more than willing to oblige. In *King Solomon's Mines* (1885), *She* (1887), and a dozen more hugely popular novels, H. Rider Haggard unveiled parts of the "dark continent" that no real-life safari had ever dreamed of. In W. H. Hudson's *Green Mansions* (1904), another best-seller and a book that has striking parallels to *Tarzan of the Apes,* a wandering white man falls in love with a feral nymph in the Amazon forest. And in Sir Arthur Conan Doyle's *The Lost World,* published the same year as the *All-Story* "Tarzan," a newspaper editor taunts a colleague with the declaration that "[t]he big blank spaces in the map are all being filled in, and there's no room for romance anywhere." Rising to the bait, the jaded journalist proceeds to discover a remote massif (also in South America) teeming with prehistoric life.

It was hardly a stretch, then, for Burroughs to set *Tarzan of the Apes* in a faraway jungle, but the genesis of Tarzan himself is a good deal harder to trace. If anything, Burroughs took a sort of perverse pleasure in perpetuating the mystery, and over the years, the task of tracking the ape-man's antecedents grew into a byzantine parlor game played by Burroughs devotees and detractors alike.

By far the most diligent digger into the roots of Tarzan during Burroughs's lifetime was Rudolph Altrocchi, a professor at the University of California, who spent two and a half years searching. A respected folklorist and closet Tarzan fan, Altrocchi first wrote to Burroughs in March 1937, averring ever so diplomatically that "the original idea for even the most original of artistic creations may at times have come to the artist from the outside. . . ."

Perhaps because he had never before received an inquiry as gently worded as Altrocchi's, Burroughs gave more than his usual enigmatic response: "I have tried to search my memory for some clue to the suggestions that gave me the idea, and as close as I can come to it I believe that it may have originated in my interest in Mythology and the story of Romulus and Remus. I also recall having read many years ago the story of the sailor who was shipwrecked on the Coast of Africa and who was adopted by and consorted with great apes to such an extent that when he was rescued a she-ape followed him into the surf and threw a baby after him.

"Then of course I read Kipling; so that it probably was a combination of all of these that suggested the Tarzan idea to me."

Romulus and Remus were, according to legend, the founders of ancient Rome who, as infants, had been suckled by a female wolf. Mowgli, the memorable hero of Rudyard Kipling's *The Jungle Book*, likewise benefitted from a lupine upbringing. Burroughs had enjoyed both yarns as a boy, and his letter to Altrocchi was by no means the first time he had cited them as inspirations for Tarzan. Kipling himself was quite aware of the connection, though he chose to repay Burroughs's tribute only backhandedly. Among the "zoos" of writers who had borrowed from *The Jungle Book*, Kipling allowed in *Something of Myself*, "the genius of the genii was the one who wrote a series called *Tarzan of the Apes*."

Altrocchi, too, had already made the Kipling and Romulus–Remus connection, but he was surprised, then stumped, by Burroughs's vague story of the shipwrecked man who consorts with the apes. Eventually he was convinced that it derived from French oral tradition, though he could find it published in only one text, an obscure seventeenth-century French novel, never translated into English or widely circulated in the United States. Altrocchi asked Burroughs several times where he had read the story, but Burroughs remained clueless.

Altrocchi stalked his thematic quarry into the fog of ancient history, locating fairy tales in which abandoned children are raised by wolves, bears, mares, cows, foxes, lions, pigs, deer, goats, gazelles, and even a woodpecker. He pursued the Romulus and Remus legend to Greece and then eastward (Cyrus of Persia was suckled by a dog) until he finally reached India, "the ultimate motherland of so much fantastic lore." Still determined, Altrocchi also turned up an assortment of medieval and more modern kin to Tarzan. Even Shakespeare, in *The Winter's Tale*, touches the universal totem:

> *Come on, poor babe,*
> *Some powerful spirit instruct the kites and the ravens*
> *To be thy nurses! Wolves and bears, they say,*
> *Casting their savageness aside, have done*
> *Like offices of pity.*

And *The Tempest* concerns a well-born European who is castaway on a wild island.

Ultimately Altrocchi coined a name for his newly circumscribed genre—"Aryan Exposure"—which he defined as instances in which humans "were nurtured by an animal foster mother, showed extraordinary resourcefulness in their jungly habitat and not only survived but also developed intelligently." If there ever was a motif that belonged in the public domain, he concluded, Aryan Exposure was it, and Burroughs offered no argument. "The fundamental idea is much older than Mowgli," he wrote Altrocchi, "so that after all there is nothing either new or remarkable about it."

Unfortunately, when Altrocchi got around to presenting his research at a meeting of the Philological Society of the Pacific Coast in Los Angeles, November 24, 1939, Burroughs was out of town. The two men never met.

Despite Altrocchi's prodigious research, he left a number of paths untrod in his quest for the origin of Tarzan. A humanist by profession and inclination, he did not explore the annals of science, which are in fact quite rich. In 1758, respected Swedish taxonomist Carl Linnaeus published *Systema naturae,* in which he distinguished *Homo ferus*—"feral man"—as a subset of *Homo sapiens.* His text iterated nine clear instances of feral man between 1544 and 1731. Between Linnaeus's day and Burroughs's, scientists and historians identified at least two dozen more wild men, including Wild Peter of Hanover, the Greek Sheep-boy, the Hessian Wolf-boy, the Bear-girl of Hungary, and, most famous of all, the Wild Boy of Aveyron (on whom François Truffaut based his 1969 film, *L'Enfant Sauvage—The Wild Child*). In the nineteenth century, British travelers in India—whence the wildman legend originated, according to Altrocchi—claimed to have spotted a number of different wild children, including children purported to have grown up with wolves, and their published hearsay and eyewitness accounts may well have lodged in the memory of Rudyard Kipling as well.

Typically, wild children of historical anecdote were precisely that: children who have been found living in rough and isolated circumstances. At the time of discovery, they are characteristically naked, hungry, unhousebroken, unable to speak, and extremely fearful of other humans. Efforts to "civilize" them, including teaching language, meet with limited success. Today it seems obvious that these children were handicapped, abused, traumatized, and abandoned, but in a darker era, when social and psychological safety nets were nonexistent, a wild child was perceived to be a creature unto itself.

The Wild Boy of Aveyron, France, was discovered by hunters in 1800; he was guessed to be about twelve and apparently had been on his own for five or six years. His story may have gone uncelebrated had he not happened to have lived during the age of Rousseau. As one of the leading freethinkers of the Enlightenment, Jean-Jacques Rousseau posited that man, though surely created by God, was born without the obvious fingerprint of God on his brow; rather, he is a blank slate, in a "state of nature," inherently good and balanced even in the absence of religious upbringing. How could this be proven? Enter the Wild Boy, who, once the dirt was scrubbed off, proved to be as white as any other Frenchman.

For the next five years, Victor, as he was named, was the ward of Parisian physician Jean-Marc-Gaspard Itard, a Rousseauvian of the first water, who patiently and gently undertook to "socialize" him. Victor developed emotionally, learned a modicum of manners, and most exciting to Itard, came to grasp the concept of "justice," considered the foundation of social order. Victor never learned to speak, however, and was never self-sufficient. As a humanitarian gesture, his education and care were worthwhile; as a controlled experiment in human nature, he raised more questions than he answered. Victor had been a wild child, but he was far from a noble savage.

Burroughs may not have heard of feral man when he wrote *Tarzan of the Apes;* he certainly never indicated that he had. But by 1915, when he sat down to write his fourth in the series, *The Son of Tarzan,* he was clearly up to speed on the clinical specifics. Tarzan's son Jack runs away from England and takes to the African jungle in much the same way Tarzan had done as a young man, and with the same wholesome result. A hunter who crosses his path is surprised to see Jack so fit and well-adjusted. "He appears to be an intelligent European," the hunter remarks, "and not much more than a lad. There is nothing of the imbecile or degenerate in his features or expression, as is usually true in similar cases, where some lunatic escapes into the woods and by living in filth and nakedness wins the title of wild man among the peasants of the neighborhood." (If art could imitate life, then turnabout was fair play. In 1933, the year after the release of MGM's first Tarzan film starring Johnny Weissmuller, a young boy, guessed to be five years old, was found living in the forest of El Salvador. He could not speak, but could swim, run, and climb very well. From all indications, he had survived solely on fruit and fish. Inevitably, he was given the name Tarzancíto, or "Little Tarzan.")

ANOTHER avenue of inquiry that Professor Altrocchi should have pursued but didn't was the recent popular press. Like H. Rider Haggard's tales of African exploration, stories of apes and ape-men were a well-established genre by the time Burroughs wrote *Tarzan of the Apes.* In 1861, British author R. M. Ballantyne, a mass-market peer of G. A. Henty, had published *The Gorilla Hunters,* in which he describes, among other things, the "certain air of tenderness" displayed by a mother gorilla, "[f]ierce and hairy though she was." In *The King of Apeland* by Harry Prentice (1888, republished as *Captured by Apes* in 1892), a young American animal trainer is marooned on an island in the East Indies and besieged by a highly organized and belligerent force of apes. And two years before the publication of *Tarzan of the Apes*, a four-part serial, "The Monkey Man," by pulp master William Tillinghast Eldridge, appeared in *All-Story*, a magazine Burroughs obviously knew well. After a mutiny and then a shipwreck, a man and a woman find themselves marooned on a remote Pacific island. Soon they discover that they are not alone; a hairy, wild-eyed "monkey-man" has been spying on them. The beast kidnaps the woman, her man comes to the rescue, and after a ferocious struggle, the monkey-man is killed. When the couple are finally rescued, they learn that the monkey-man was actually a sailor who had been set ashore long ago as punishment for unnamed misdeeds. Over the years, he had reverted to a wild state. (Eldridge in turn may have drawn his inspiration from Jules Verne's *Mysterious Island,* in which castaways encounter a creature whom they first believe is an ape, but in fact is a shipwrecked man who has "fallen to the lowest degree of brutishness.")

That Burroughs read any of these tales is impossible to prove, though in at least one instance the paper trail is quite compelling. The protagonist of Jack London's 1906 novel, *Before Adam,* is a modern youth who, through dreams triggered by deep atavistic impulses, is able to relive the experiences of a prehistoric forefather, an apelike creature dubbed Big-Tooth. Big-Tooth and his fellow prehumans swing through the trees, elude saber-toothed *tigers,* and communicate using a primitive vocabulary very similar to the one Tarzan learns from the anthropoids. Interestingly, Big-Tooth develops a bitter rivalry with a neighbor named Red-Eye, who like Tarzan's bloodshot Kerchak, is described as an "abysmal brute": "He was more primitive than any of us. . . . He tended to destroy the horde by his unsocial acts. He was really a reversion to an earlier type." More interesting still, Big-Tooth's horde practices a rhythmic log-beating ritual called the "hee-hee," which resembles Burroughs's Dum-Dum in both name and body language. "In ways the hee-hee council was an adumbration of the councils of primitive man," London observes, "and of the great national assemblies and international conventions of latter-day man." Burroughs says almost the same thing about the Dum-Dum.

In peeling the great onion that is *Tarzan,* there are so many sources beneath the sources. London freely admitted that he had based *Before Adam* on Stanley Waterloo's 1897 novel, *The Story of Ab,* though Waterloo's book provides nothing resembling a Dum-Dum or hee-hee. For this detail, London may well have tapped the journals of David Livingstone, which note that apes liked to "beat hollow trees as drums with hands, and then scream as music to it." Perhaps Burroughs read Livingstone, too. And if he explored any further in the Chicago library for other books on Africa, he might easily have come across Paul B. Du Chaillu's thrilling travelogue, *Explorations and Adventures in Equatorial Africa* (1862), which includes its own rendition of the victory cry of the bull ape: "It begins with a sharp *bark*, like an angry dog, then glides into a deep bass *roll*, which literally closely resembles the roll of distant thunder along the sky. . . . So deep is it that it seems to proceed less from the mouth and throat than from the deep chest and vast paunch."

Du Chaillu was the first white man to kill and closely examine gorillas, and his accounts of his hunts were so sensational that he eventually retold them in the form of a children's book, *Stories of the Gorilla Country* (1869). Esteemed ethnologist-explorer Sir Richard Burton was sufficiently taken with Du Chaillu's escapades that in 1862 he launched his own expedition to West Africa, which he later described in *Two Trips to Gorilla Land* (1876). Burton reported that Du Chaillu's portrayal of the gorilla as a "hellish dream creature, a being of that hideous order, half man, half beast" was wildly exaggerated; instead he saw the gorilla as another "poor devil ape." This more sympathetic view of gorillas is corroborated in another popular book of African adventure, J. W. Buel's *Heroes of the Dark Continent* (1890), published the same year as Henry Stanley's *In Darkest Africa*. In an observation that could be the source for both Ballantyne's "tender" gorilla and Burroughs's Kala, Buel notes that when an infant gorilla dies, "the mothers carry them about, closely pressed to them, till they fall from putrefaction." The page facing this passage presents a disturbing illustration of a female gorilla with her apparently deceased baby pressed to her breast.

It should also be noted that Buel and Du Chaillu, as well as Stanley, make frequent, if careless, references to African "tigers," and several other descriptions in their books strengthen the possibility that Burroughs thumbed through them before embarking on *Tarzan of the Apes*. Later in his career, he would amass an impressive library of Africana, though unfortunately it is now impossible to ascertain which titles he had owned or read by 1912.

*   *   *

THE MOST unsung inspiration for Tarzan had very little to do with literature or even Africa. By the turn of the century, America had codified its nostalgia for virgin wilderness and robust rural life in a variety of ways. The arcadian ideal—effectively a collective loss of Eden—had helped to spawn national parks and organizations such as the Boy Scouts and Camp Fire Girls. City-dwelling parents sent their children to newly established summer camps to learn woodcraft and pursued their own "outings," or at least enjoyed reading about them, in *Recreation, Field and Stream,* and other outdoor journals. The "strenuous life" became as voguish as straw hats.

So too did the Physical Culture movement, though its roots, while clearly intertwined with those of the new generation of "nature lovers," were even more urban. Physical Culture gathered its first followers in the years after the Civil War, when Americans began developing a passion for sports such as rowing, baseball, and football. Around the same time, the new discipline of physical "education" urged men and women to loosen their Victorian clothing and improve their health by swinging Indian clubs and lifting dumbbells. In the 1890s, America went mad for bicycles, and the revival of the Olympic Games in 1896 (and the first Olympics in the United States in 1904) signaled a formal reappreciation of sportsmanship and physicality. Institutions such as the YMCA linked exercise with wholesomeness, even piety.

The high priest of the Physical Culture movement was Bernarr Macfadden, a hard-luck Missouri farmboy turned strongman and promoter. He developed his own breakfast cereal (to compete with the products of Kellogg and Post), developed a chain of health food restaurants, and opened a series of spas, called healthatoriums. In 1899, Macfadden began publishing *Physical Culture,* a monthly magazine to promote clean living, good diet, and regular exercise. "Weakness is a sin," was one of his mottos, and he regularly published pictures of well-developed men and women to prove the counterpoint. (In 1905, Macfadden was arrested in New York for displaying a poster of a musclebound man wearing nothing besides a very Tarzanesque leopard skin loincloth.) By 1909, Macfadden had moved his business to Chicago, and in 1911, a year before Burroughs began writing *Tarzan of the Apes,* he published his two-thousand-page *Encyclopedia of Physical Culture,* in effect the bible of the movement.

Burroughs was obviously quite familiar with Macfadden and in his own way was a committed physical culturist. He fretted over his weight throughout his adult life and was a frequent dieter. He did not experiment with the exercise machines of the day, but he was fervent about the importance of daily exercise. Even into his seventies, he kept up the seventeen "setting-up" exercises outlined in his dog-eared copy of *Infantry Drill Regulations.* (Exercise 3: "Slowly describe a small circle, with each arm upward and backward. . . .") And while he never considered himself an exceptional physical specimen, he and the rest of the American public nonetheless had a well-formed opinion of what the ideal man (and woman) should look like. Bernarr Macfadden had made sure of that.

Yet Burroughs's Tarzan—"muscled as the best of the ancient Roman gladiators . . . and yet with the soft and sinuous curves of a Greek god"—was as much a reaction to Physical Culture as he was an exemplar of it. The real beauty of his physique is that he came by it naturally. There is nothing bulky about him, which could not be said for many of Macfadden's dumbbell-toting disciples (including, eventually, Charles Atlas). Tarzan, along with every other Burroughs protagonist, is limber and, above all, "clean-limbed," which *Webster's* defines as "well-proportioned," but in a Burroughs context also means not brutishly hairy. A clean-limbed man (or ape, such as Kala) is a product of good bloodlines and advanced breeding—to Burroughs's mind, one of the highest compliments that could be paid to anyone.

And therein lay yet another inspiration for Tarzan: Burroughs's lifelong fascination with evolution, an interest he shared with millions of his contemporaries. With the publication of Darwin's *On the Origin of Species* in 1859 and the gradual dissemination of his evolutionary theory, professional archeologists and amateur bonepickers had begun searching high and low for the "missing link" between modern man and his ape antecedent. The discovery of Neanderthal man (three years before Darwin's treatise) was followed by Cro-Magnon man, Heidelberg man, and then a Javanese skull belonging to *Pithecanthropus erectus,* who was either an apelike man or a mannish ape. In the fall of 1912, at almost the precise time that *All-Story* was running *Tarzan of the Apes,* the infamous Piltdown man—said to have the skull of a man and the jaw of an ape—was generating headlines in Great Britain and abroad. (Anglo-Saxons everywhere seemed actually *proud* of the fact that the first human, though an obvious brute, was one of *theirs,* an admission that was qualified, but not negated, when Piltdown man later proved to be a hoax.)

As the physical evidence accumulated, the links in the evolutionary chain suddenly seemed finite, almost countable. Now that modern man was able, in effect, to look his forefathers in the face, the gap didn't seem all that vast. Robert Louis Stevenson imagined that within every Jekyll was a potential Hyde. Jack London, an author whom Burroughs admired enormously, argued in a shelf of evocative novels that the "call of the wild" was still echoing in the inner ear of all domesticated animals, including humans. Similarly, Tarzan possesses "the best characteristics of the human family from which he was descended and the best of those which mark the wild beasts." That Tarzan is able to survive and flourish in the jungle reveals that even after millennia of evolution, civilization is still but a "taint," as insubstantial as Tarzan's loincloth and just as easily removed. But, Burroughs is quick to stress, it is also true that no matter how infinitesimal the taint of civilization may be, it can never be entirely eradicated by "uncouth and savage training."

HAVING STRUCK such a resonant note, Burroughs was not sure what to write next. Rather than start from scratch on a new story, he did several rewrites of *The Outlaw of Torn*, vowing to stick to it until his editor gave in. But Metcalf was unwavering, and in early December, Burroughs was obliged to cut his losses. Never again would he spend so much time reworking a story. In the future, when a submission was rejected, he would try another outlet or shelve it. Overhauling was not his style nor a good use of his time.

Stymied in his attempt to make *Outlaw* pay, he looked for a way to squeeze more money out of *Tarzan of the Apes*. For all the praise the story had received, *All-Story*'s audience was not enormous—perhaps two hundred thousand—and the October issue had in due course disappeared from newsstands. The logical next step was books. Ever the efficiency expert, Burroughs put together packets of the *All-Story Tarzan*, accompanied by a sampling of the laudatory letters written by *All-Story* readers, and mailed them to a likely list of publishing houses. To his disappointment, none thought it would make a worthy book. And so for the time being, he had to be satisfied with the knowledge that Munsey's had sold the newspaper serial rights to the *New York Evening World*, with the first installment to begin on January 6, 1913. Then, too, Metcalf had also accepted a second Mars story, which would begin running in January, also.

In *The Gods of Mars*, the sequel to *Princess*, John Carter again transports himself astrally to Barsoom, where he meets his red son Carthoris, who at the end of *Princess* was still just an egg, but now is a full-grown warrior in his own right. The bad news is that his wife, Carthoris's mother Dejah Thoris, has been kidnapped. In response to Metcalf's suggestion to stir up a "terrific row" over Martian religion, the campaign to rescue Dejah Thoris turns into a titanic holy war, bigger and more violent than any that Earth has ever known. (World War I was still two years away.) Carter marches at the head of a million-man army, "the fighting blood of [his] Virginia sires" coursing hot through his veins, his "seething blade" weaving "a web of death."

The leader of the religion against which Carter crusades is a flesh-eating priestess, a toothless, hawk-nosed crone with the classically derived name of Issus. The allegory is not explicit, but given the anti-Catholic leanings of Burroughs's father and the prevalence of anti-Catholic organizations at the time, the true target of his filibuster is not difficult to surmise. Martian religion, as preached by Issus and her network of cunning priests, is based on a "superstitious belief in lies that have been foisted upon us for ages by those directly above us, to whose personal profit and aggrandizement it was to have us continue to believe as they wished us to believe." For untold generations, Martians have journeyed faithfully down the Mysterious River Iss, believing they were bound for heaven. Instead, the passage is a trick to lure them to a fate worse than hell. By story's end, Carter exposes Issus as a false prophet, but just misses catching up to Dejah Thoris before she is locked up in the Golden Temple, the doors of which are unopenable for a year—leaving time and opportunity for another sequel.

In *Gods,* Burroughs also resumes his ruminations on race and evolution. Once upon a time, he explains, all Martians dangled, quite literally, from the Tree of Life. From this primordial fruit evolved white, green, yellow, and black men—from which, in turn, evolved the hybrid red men. Like most people of his day, Burroughs believed that there was a pecking order of "higher" and "lower" races. In a Swiftian twist on conventional wisdom, he arranges the Martian palette so that whites, closely related to apes, are at the bottom, and the blacks, the elite, purebred "First Born," are at the top. Yet to conclude from this hierarchy that he held a progressive view of race on his own planet would be to miss the playfulness of his Martian color code. Back on Earth, in the United States, where grew his own family tree, he clearly did not see the Negro race on top, a sentiment he would reiterate in nearly every Tarzan story.

*   *   *

IN DECEMBER 1912, after completing *The Gods of Mars,* he set to work on "Monsieur Tarzan," the plot of which he had outlined to Metcalf several months earlier. He threw everything he had into it: Tarzan (whose card reads "M. Jean C. Tarzan") works as an undercover agent for the French; tangles with the dastardly Russian spies, Rokoff and Paulvitch; lives among Saharan Arabs ("swarthy dark-eyed sons of the desert"); becomes chief of the black Waziri tribe ("savage friends"); and penetrates the lost city of Opar. The Oparians are the distant descendants of the doomed civilization of Atlantis; their men are bred to be like apes, while their women are bred for classic human beauty. Fairest of all is La, the high priestess, who is clearly derivative of Ayesha, the femme fatale of H. Rider Haggard's *She.* Tarzan eventually escapes from Opar with a fortune in gold and after many more intrigues finally gets around to rescuing Jane, who, along with fiancé Clayton and her father, has been marooned quite by chance on the very same shore where Tarzan was born and she and he first met. All ends well when Clayton, in sacrificing his life for Jane, produces a paper proving Tarzan's Greystoke birthright. At last Jane and Tarzan are married by an ordained Professor Porter in the cabin built by Tarzan's parents. "I know of no other place in which I should rather be married to my forest god," Jane exclaims, "than beneath the shade of his primeval forest."

By Christmas, Burroughs had every right to sit back with a feeling of accomplishment. Over the previous twelve months, at night and on weekends in his cramped West Side apartment, amid the mewling of two infant children, somehow he had managed to complete three novel-length stories, more than two hundred thousand words, and his only misstep had been *The Outlaw of Torn,* which hadn't been his idea to begin with. True, book publishers had been unreceptive, and he still could not afford to quit his job at *System* magazine, but on the other hand, one of the biggest newspapers in the country was about to serialize *Tarzan.* All in all, it had been quite a year.

But rather than partake of at least a small dram of self-satisfaction, as anyone else in similar circumstances would have done, he instead chose to turn the screws of self-doubt. "Nothwithstanding all the kind things you have said," he wrote to Metcalf in December, "I see my work just as I saw it before anyone said that he liked it. I see principally the many crudities." He had every confidence in his storytelling ability, he explained. Rather, it was his writing style—the "dress" of a story—he felt was lacking.

This was what it all came down to: a year into his career as an author and years before the nabobs of culture would pay enough attention to snub him, he had sized up his literary mortality perfectly, bitterly. He was a *storyteller*, and a good one—that much he knew. But deep down he feared that he would never be a *writer*.

Through Christmas and New Year's, even as he was finishing his next Tarzan, he couldn't leave the thought alone. On January 9, 1913, he wrote Metcalf to say that he was thinking of engaging a tutor to help him with his "rotten" English. He repeated the excuse of having been shuffled from school to school, where he received a rich dose of Greek and Latin, but "never was taught my mother tongue." Metcalf tried to put him at ease. "I don't see anything particular the matter with your grammar," he replied good-naturedly, offering no broader criticism of Burroughs's style than to note that some of the language in *The Outlaw of Torn* had been a tad contrived. But that was all in the past, Metcalf assured, and very much beside the point. For the second month in a row, the Table Talk section of *All-Story* was full of letters gushing over *Tarzan*. When could they read the next installment?

If Burroughs's anxiety was allayed, it did not remain so for long. On January 23, Metcalf's next letter had a decidedly cooler tone: he didn't like the new Tarzan story. He wasn't sure what to do about it, but then in his next letter, five days later, he rejected it outright. Groping for a diplomatic explanation, he said it lacked "balance."

Burroughs was crushed. If Tarzan had no future, nothing did. "There is so much uncertainty about the writing game," he wrote back despondently. Rather than lash out at Metcalf, as usual he directed his rancor at himself: "I probably lack balance myself—a well balanced mind would not turn out my kind of stuff. As long as I can't market it as it comes out it is altogether too much of a gamble, so I think I'll chuck it." Even his attempt at a gracious closing was pathetic: "Let me thank you once again for your many courtesies during the period of my incursion into literachoor."

For all Burroughs knew, his career had ended almost as abruptly as it had begun.

5

FAST AND FURIOUS

"**F**or the Love of Mike! Don't Get Discouraged!" Metcalf telegrammed immediately after reading Burroughs's facetious obituary.

But even before Metcalf sent his wire of encouragement, Burroughs had taken steps to save himself. Unbeknownst to Metcalf, he had mailed a second copy of "Monsieur Tarzan," now titled "The Ape-Man" (and eventually *The Return of Tarzan*), to Metcalf's principal rival, A. L. Sessions, editor of *New Story Magazine.* The tone of the accompanying letter reflected none of the self-pity Burroughs had expressed to Metcalf. Instead, he boasted of the success of *Tarzan of the Apes* in *All-Story* and hinted (or fibbed) that he had already received nibbles from a book publisher and motion picture company. Naturally he did not mention that "Ape-Man" had been turned down by Munsey; he was merely interested in enlarging his market, he explained, and besides, he had heard that *New Story*'s rates were higher.

New Story was owned by Street & Smith Publications, whose stable also included *The Popular Magazine* and *The People's Magazine.* The tug-of-war within the fiction market was fierce in those days, and Sessions, who must have envied the success that *All-Story* had enjoyed with *Tarzan of the Apes,* did not hesitate when the sequel dropped on his desk so unexpectedly. On February 8, he offered Burroughs one thousand dollars—roughly a penny a word, a much higher rate than that earned by the first Mars and Tarzan stories—which Burroughs promptly accepted. It was a great coup for writer and editor alike, just as Metcalf's rejection had been a huge tactical error. *New Story* had Tarzan and his enthusiastic audience, and *All-Story* had only egg on its face. For his part, Burroughs now had two very competitive publishers to play off each other. Shaky as he might still be as a writer, as a salesman and negotiator he was quite steady, as both magazines would soon discover.

Out of necessity, Burroughs had not quit writing in this period of uncertainty. He and Emma were still living week to week on his dismal paycheck from *System.* Somehow he managed to sit in an office by day, answering subscriber queries, and was still able to bear down on his fiction at night and on weekends. With the impending birth of a third child (John Coleman, on February 28), he and Emma were that much more beleaguered. Even if they had time for a social life or a few days off, they could not have afforded it. During January, immediately after completing "The Ape-Man," Burroughs had written "The Inner World" (*At the Earth's Core*), an account of the adventures of David Innes, who bores through the Earth's crust in an "iron mole." Innes and the machine's inventor, Abner Perry, discover a Stone Age world called Pellucidar, which is ruled by hideous reptiles (Mahars) whose gorillalike minions (Sagoths) have enslaved a race of "well-formed" but unsophisticated humans (gilaks), including the appropriately named Dian the Beautiful. Other Pellucidarians include the Mezops, an Indian-like tribe who have made peace with the Mahars.

Burroughs does not shirk in his rendering of this, his third imaginary world. Because Pellucidar is the inside of a sphere, the horizon is curved; the sun—the Earth's glowing core, actually—is stationary and neither rises nor sets; in Pellucidar there are no equivalents of years, days, or hours. Evolution is not entirely in arrears at the Earth's core, though it is decidedly topsy-turvy. For instance, male Mahars are extinct because the females have figured out a way to fertilize their own eggs. Endowed with the ability to exchange thoughts by the "fourth dimension," Mahars have no need for ears or spoken language. Yet they still must survive in a world of cave bears, saber-toothed tigers, and mastodons.

David Innes, like John Carter, is a charismatic demagogue who unites the humans and Mezops, defeats the Mahars, and leads "the races of men out of the darkness of ignorance into the light of advancement and civilization"—a cause that happens to be diametrically opposed to the one espoused by Tarzan, who strives to preserve primitive paradise by keeping civilization at bay. At story's end, Innes climbs aboard the iron mole and heads back to the Earth's surface to fetch the know-how and materials to make gunpowder. He thinks he is taking his sweetheart Dian with him, but at the last instant, a prankster sticks a grotesque Mahar in her place. Regardless of what happens after he reaches the surface, his love for Dian will now draw him back to Pellucidar—in a sequel, of course.

Burroughs kept the length of "Inner World" down to thirty thousand words at the request of John Phillips, editor of *American Magazine,* who had admired *A Princess of Mars* and *Tarzan of the Apes. American* was more staid and up-scale than *All-Story* or *New Story* and paid much better. Burroughs sent along "Inner World," but reluctantly Phillips sent it back; "too unbridled" was the verdict. Two days later, Burroughs forwarded it to a needier, now somewhat contrite Metcalf, who accepted it immediately.

Once again, Burroughs was at a crossroads. *Gods of Mars* was running in *All-Story*; "Inner World" and "Ape-Man" were due to run in their respective magazines, and *Tarzan of the Apes* was appearing in the *New York Evening World.* At this clip, he could afford to quit his job and write full time. If he had any hesitancy, it evaporated on February 15, 1913, the day his father died.

Even as a grown man and head of his own family, Burroughs had stood in the shadow of his father. He had sought the Major's approval, but until recently had given his father little reason to be proud. His parents had been delighted with *Princess* and *Tarzan* and expressed their hope that their son had finally found his calling. Then, a week before his father's death, Burroughs was able to share the news of *New Story*'s thousand-dollar offer for "Ape-Man," and while this pairing of events was bittersweet, the timing was in a way quite fortunate. For the rest of his life, he took strength from the fact that his father had died knowing that his most wayward son had begun to make something of himself. And every year on Major Burroughs's birthday, he made a solemn point of recording how old his father would have been were he still alive.

In March, Burroughs finally quit his post at *System* and from then on never worked for anyone but himself. "Everyone . . . thought I was an idiot," he wrote in his autobiography, "but I had written five stories and sold four, which I felt was a good average and I knew that I could write a great many more." He was right: between February 1913 and the end of the year, he wrote six more stories, the following year another seven—most of them book-length manuscripts, all of them accepted and serialized.

With experience, Burroughs grew much cagier with editors. When Metcalf was "nonplussed" and aggrieved to learn that he had gone to *New Story,* Burroughs insisted that he meant no hard feelings; it was purely business. "I am not writing stories because of friendship," he reminded Metcalf. "I am writing because I have a wife and three children." Highlighting the increased demand for his stories, he suggested that Metcalf pay him five cents a word for "first refusal" of future work, adding that he would grant only first serial rights.

It was more than a minor point that Munsey had kept *all* the rights to *Tarzan of the Apes* (as well as those to *Princess* and *Gods*); Burroughs had not received any of the fifty dollars paid by the *World* for "second" serialization. By contrast, he had kept the second rights to "Ape-Man" and sold them to the *World* for three hundred dollars, money that went directly into his own pocket. Metcalf was undoubtedly floored by Burroughs's nickel-a-word demand—a rate ten times higher than what he had paid for Burroughs's first story—and insisted that the best he could do was two cents a word for "first refusal of first serial rights." Having played his hand as aggressively as he dared, Burroughs pushed no further and accepted, though with the understanding that the deal was for his "1913 crop" only. Most pulp writers, he knew, didn't make even a penny a word.

At the two-cent rate, and with a family to feed, every word was worth counting. Multiplied by several hundred pages, the difference between 315 words a page and 320 could amount to as much as fifteen dollars. Accordingly, out of need as much as sheer punctiliousness, Burroughs adopted the habit of marking the word count at the corner of each typewritten page and refused to trust his editors to do their own addition. And whenever they asked him to revise a manuscript, he usually *added* words. It upped his take and discouraged editors from arbitrarily meddling with his stories.

No one had ever approached the writing business in quite the way Burroughs did. He brought to bear all the notions of efficiency and productivity that he had learned at Sears, Roebuck and had preached in his advice columns for *System*. As he saw it, the act of writing was only *part* of his job description; marketing, he grasped, could and should be its own fine art. Once a story was on paper, his fundamental strategy was always to get the highest possible fee from the best possible magazine, and then recycle—resell—the plots and characters in every possible way, like a tailor using every scrap from a bolt of cloth. Indeed, he became so immersed in the fine points of syndication and subsidiary rights that he eventually submitted a manifesto that was published in the newsletter of the Authors' League of America. "I am very *recent* in the writing game," he began, "and so, like most *recent* people in any field, feel fully qualified to spill advice promiscuously among my betters. But the very fact of my newness is the strongest argument I have in favor of my propaganda— that writers never part with any of their rights except for value received." There was nothing to lose and a surprising amount to be gained, he advised, citing instances where he had made nearly as much from selling second serial rights to newspapers as he had from the initial sale to a magazine. Besides, no publisher would "permit the question of the ownership of the second serial rights to any manuscript to stand in the way of their acquisition of the first serial rights." Today, such tactics are de rigueur in publishing, but when Burroughs was first espousing them, he was a pioneer and a slightly pushy one at that.

Despite his abundant moxie, he still might never have gained a whit of practical expertise in the field of author's equity had his stories not first been taken on by the *Evening World*—a relationship that was lucrative in and of itself, but also opened even bigger doors of opportunity. In 1912, 1913, and 1914, when Munsey, and then Burroughs, were first trying to sell his stories into a broader market, particularly newspapers, it so happened that the fiction editor at the *World* was Albert Payson Terhune, a storyteller in his own right. Terhune's specialty was dog stories— in the tradition of *Bob, Son of Battle* (1898) and *The Call of the Wild* (1903) and the antecedent of *Lassie Come-Home* (1940). Like Burroughs, Terhune had to keep a day job until his freelancing picked up. He liked everything Burroughs wrote, and with the backing of his boss, J. H. Tennant, paid top rates for second serial rights to "The Ape-Man" (*The Return of Tarzan*), "The Inner World" (*At the Earth's Core*), and the stories that followed: *The Cave Girl,* "A Man Without a Soul" (*The Monster Men*), "The Prince of Helium" (*The Warlord of Mars*), *The Mucker,* and *The Eternal Lover.* Eventually Terhune went on to write *Lad: A Dog* (1919), one of the best-selling dog books of all time. But before leaving the *World,* he did Burroughs a favor of exponential importance. For two years, Burroughs had received lots of courteous responses from book publishers—one had even invited him to enter a story-writing contest—but none had made an actual bid for *Tarzan of the Apes.* When Burroughs griped about their intransigence to Terhune in March 1914, his friend and fan urged him to refer the publishers to him: "[W]e shall be only too glad to testify to the tremendous interest the story has aroused among our readers; and will do all in our power toward urging the advantages of publishing the book." Within a month, Burroughs had a commitment from A. C. McClurg & Company, the Chicago publishing house. It was the next big turning point in his career, and he always credited Terhune's "bully treatment" for having made it possible.

And thanks to the *World's* enthusiasm for Burroughs, and the demonstrable popularity of the stories serialized in its pages, other newspapers grew more interested. With so many papers competing for readership, serialization of stories, including fiction, was one way to keep readers coming back day in and day out. Likewise, with so many cheap magazines, such as those owned by Munsey and Street & Smith, now crowding the newsstands, the dailies saw syndication of serials as a way to fight back. The business of newspaper syndication appeared so fertile, in fact, that in May 1913, Burroughs signed up with a syndication agency, International Press Bureau, which began hawking his stories to chains and individual papers all over the country. The going rate for a paper such as the *Toledo Blade* or the *Tacoma Tribune* was fifty dollars a story—far less than the *World's* two hundred—but the little bits from hither and yon added up to a couple hundred dollars a year at first, and much more in the 1920s. Burroughs's man with International was William Chapman, "a square and decent chap," he estimated. "I hope that I have not made a mistake in placing the matter in his hands," Burroughs wrote to Terhune, a statement that would come back to haunt him several years later.

Burroughs had Chapman handle all newspaper sales and also agreed to let him begin soliciting book publishers, though he continued to negotiate all first serial rights with magazines himself. Throughout 1913, with all of his output committed to Metcalf, he still continued to court Sessions at *New Story,* knowing that at the very least, Sessions would make a useful foil when it came time to renegotiate with Metcalf after the first of the year. At the end of July, Burroughs sent Sessions a copy of the thrice-rejected *The Outlaw of Torn.* Sessions said he would take it and offered the token sum of three hundred and fifteen dollars. Clearly he was currying favor; what he was really after was the next Tarzan. Burroughs, the wily trader, saw through the maneuver and asked a thousand for *The Outlaw of Torn.* He then dangled the figure of three thousand dollars for the next Tarzan. Sessions didn't accept outright, but he was thrilled to be in the hunt. "I am prepared to say that our desire to see [the Tarzan story] is not qualified by the figure you mentioned," he wrote back. In the interim, Burroughs made a pitch that the hungry Sessions now could not refuse: he got him to raise the price of *Torn* to five hundred dollars, securing the additional pledge that if it did well—by what standards he did not specify—*New Story* would kick in more money than that. Burroughs had played his hand masterfully: not only had he succeeded in selling a moribund manuscript for a decent sum, but he had planted the seed for a bidding war when it came time to sell Tarzan No. 3. "You are a blood drinking wretch," a later editor once teased him, and it was true.

Burroughs was now experiencing greater security than he had ever felt. As long as he kept writing, his income was steady and assured. By August he had completed *The Cave Girl,* in which a weak-kneed Bostonian marooned on an uncharted South Sea island must become a he-man to win the comely cave girl; *The Monster Men,* a Dr. Moreau-meets-Frankenstein yarn in which a presumed human experiment turns out actually to be a lovable hero and heir; and *The Warlord of Mars,* completing a trilogy, which, he purported, was all he intended to write about Mars.

Feeling like a "plutocrat" after so much success, Burroughs decided that a change of scenery was in order, and on September 6, 1913, he loaded his wife, three children, and a second-hand automobile on a train bound for California. Since the 1860s, doctors had been prescribing the state's sunshine, clean air, and fresh food as a cure for all manner of ailments, from tuberculosis to neurasthenia. For chill-chapped Midwesterners especially, a West Coast trip had become what the Grand Tour had been for affluent Easterners a generation earlier. And in the wake of the San Francisco earthquake of 1906, many tourists redirected their itineraries from the more cosmopolitan Bay Area to the Spanish-flavored cities of Santa Barbara, Los Angeles, and San Diego. Burroughs stressed that he made the trip for the sake of the children's health—Chicago winters had always meant "a round of sickness and worry"—but his old western wanderlust had to have been a factor as well. He never mentioned why he selected San Diego in particular, but the luxurious Hotel del Coronado, built on a sandbar across the bay from downtown, each room opening onto the ocean, was one of America's best-known landmarks and a radiant symbol of the California good life. Plutocratic avowals notwithstanding, he was not so wealthy that he could actually afford to put his family up at the del Coronado; the best he could do was rent a house nearby. After the first of the year, however, the Burroughses tired of the Pacific dampness that clung to the coast mornings and evenings and moved to a bungalow in the hills above San Diego for the rest of their six-month stay.

It was a tribute to Burroughs's powers of concentration that the trip did not impinge on his work. "We were a long way from home," he wrote in his autobiography. "My income depended solely upon the sale of magazine rights. . . . Had I failed to sell a single story during these months it would have been over the hills to the poorhouse for us, but I did not fail. That I had to work is evidenced by a graph that I keep on my desk showing my word output for year to year since 1911. In 1913 it reached its peak with something like four hundred and thirteen thousand words for the year."

One of the stories he worked on that year was "The Girl from Harris's" (later published as "The Girl from Farris's"). He had begun it in July with the idea of entering it in a novel contest sponsored by the publishing house of Reilly & Britton. The prize was ten thousand dollars and a publishing contract. Because Reilly & Britton was one of the houses that had rejected *Tarzan of the Apes,* Burroughs felt he had to come up with something completely different. And because Reilly & Britton was a Chicago firm, he decided to use a local setting and try his hand at social realism, the school of exposé and uplift exemplified by the Chicago novels of Upton Sinclair, Theodore Dreiser, and Hamlin Garland.

The Farris's of the story's title is a South Side brothel; the "girl" is Maggie Lynch, whose true name is June Lathrop, a small-town innocent ruined by a big-city grandee. She pulls herself up from the demimonde by learning typing and stenography, a profession Burroughs understood much better than prostitution. But just as Maggie is cleaning herself up, her boss, Ogden Secor, is sinking into penury and alcoholism. Perhaps because Burroughs felt the Reilly & Britton judges expected it, he laid on the morality with a trowel: love is more important than money, reformers are not always righteous, and the worst sin of all is to quit when you're down. For some reason, though, possibly because he thought he was out of his depth in terms of genre if not setting, he disobeyed his own credo and set the story aside without finishing it. In a note to Metcalf the day of his departure for California, he acknowledged "the futility of attempting to compete in a field so far removed from my own." Instead, he said, "Have been writing one of my own kind of stories since, and expect to send it on for your amiable consideration soon."

The story was *The Mucker* and like "The Girl from Farris's," it begins on familiar ground. Billy Byrne is a low-class hoodlum—a "mucker" in the underworld argot that Burroughs had been studying— and very much a product of Chicago's ever-coarsening West Side: "From Halsted to Robey, and from Grand Avenue to Lake Street there was scarce a bartender whom Billy knew not by his first name. And, in proportion to their number which was considerably less, he knew the patrolmen and plain clothes men equally well, but not so pleasantly."

In Billy Byrne's Chicago, as in Tarzan's Africa, the fundamental law was survival of the fiercest. In fights between rival gangs, "there was nothing fair, nor decent, nor scientific about their methods. They gouged and bit and tore. . . . No one on the West Side has skilled hands." Rather, "they are equipped by Nature with mitts and dukes. A few have paws and flippers." Billy decides to become the exception, learns to box properly, and begins to show real promise as a legitimate prizefighter. But then a case of mistaken identity puts him crosswise with the law and he is obliged to hop a freight for California. At this point in the writing of *The Mucker*, Burroughs, too, had departed for the coast.

More overtly than any other novel Burroughs wrote, *The Mucker* displays the influence of Burroughs's mentor, Jack London, an affinity that grew stronger once Burroughs arrived in London's home state. Jack London was a year younger than Burroughs, born in San Francisco and educated on the wharves of Oakland, aboard the seal-hunting ships of the Bering Sea, and in the gold fields of the Klondike. Like Burroughs, he wrote his first stories for the pulps; with the success of *The Call of the Wild* and *The Sea-Wolf,* he became the highest-paid, most popular writer in the world, inheritor of the throne once occupied by Rudyard Kipling. In 1913, just before Burroughs began *The Mucker,* London published two novels, *The Abysmal Brute* and *The Valley of the Moon,* both of which had first been serialized in popular magazines, both about prize-fighters who turn their backs on violence in favor of peace and refinement. That summer, as Burroughs was preparing for his trip west, London was completing his lodge, Wolf House, on his ranch, Valley of the Moon, near Glen Ellen, in Northern California. On August 21, a week after *The Mucker* was underway, Wolf House burned to the ground. Reports of the tragedy made headlines nationwide.

Burroughs completed *The Mucker* in California. Like the narrator of *The Sea-Wolf,* Billy Byrne finds himself unexpectedly aboard an outbound ship and impressed into service as a sailor. After an act of piracy and a typhoon, he is cast ashore on a remote Japanese island with Barbara Harding, a version of *The Sea-Wolf's* Maud Brewster, the daughter of a multimillionaire and "scion of the oldest aristocracy that America boasts." Up until this point, Billy has been a menacing, unthinking, if courageous, brute, quick to express his contempt for "pusillanimous highbrows." He and the pure but plucky Miss Harding are set upon by a band of samurais who have interbred with the native headhunters. The result is a colony of "cruel, crafty, resourceful wild men" who have sunk into a state of "aboriginal ferocity" and "primeval ignorance." Combat, capture, near-rape, and escape ensue, and as the Mucker and the maiden claw for survival, they fall for each other. Gradually Billy comes to see himself as two people—not unlike Wolf Larsen of *The Sea-Wolf.* Chivalry is as innate a human quality as brutishness, Burroughs suggests. However, when Billy and Barbara finally make their way back to America, she returns to her drawing room and he to his boxing ring, though the door is left open for a romantic rematch.

Burroughs felt he had written a tour de force. The saga of the Mucker ranges from mean streets to high seas, lost tribes to star-crossed love. But much to his surprise, Metcalf hated it. "I have a feeling that you started to write this story without having doped it out so very carefully," he wrote Burroughs on October 23, 1913. His harshest criticism was of Billy Byrne himself: "[Y]ou work very hard to make perfectly clear the 'Mucker's' character and psychology. You do this almost to the point of tautology. When it comes to a time when the 'Mucker's' character must undergo considerable change you ignore any particular subtleties and jump from one spot to another, and to me . . . the effect is not particularly convincing." In other words, Burroughs was no Jack London.

Sessions of *New Story,* to whom Burroughs next sent *The Mucker* several days later, did not think so, either; nor did *Adventure,* the third magazine he tried. Finally, with nowhere else to turn, he overhauled the manuscript, reluctantly cutting ten thousand money-making words, and resubmitted it to *All-Story* in January. As luck would have it, the revised *Mucker* crossed in the mail with an announcement from Metcalf that *All-Story* was about to become a weekly. Suddenly the formerly picky editor was not so hard to please. "I can use all manner of stuff," Metcalf advised, "novels 30,000 to 40,000 words long, serials and short stories. This is the chance of a life time for a brilliant young author." Once again, the timing was ideal—and not just because of *The Mucker,* which ran from August to October; Burroughs's arrangement with Munsey was up for renewal, and his next Tarzan would be done soon.

He titled the story *The Beasts of Tarzan.* This time Tarzan, wife Jane, and their infant son Jack are wintering in London to escape the rainy season in Africa, where the lord of the jungle is now lord of a "vast estate." Jack is kidnapped by Rokoff and Paulvitch, the Russian rascals introduced in *The Return of Tarzan,* and the evidence suggests that they have spirited him away to Africa. (In the years leading up to the Russian Revolution in 1917, Russian spies, craven anarchists all, made perfect pulp villains.) Tarzan and Jane sail to Africa—separately, it so happens—to save their son. Tarzan, whose time in England had not diminished "the mighty powers that had made him the invincible lord of the jungle," recruits apes, a panther, and finally a native named Mugambi for his search party.

For his generation, Burroughs was not exceptionally condescending in his attitude toward blacks, both American and African. Nor was he particularly enlightened. Having never been to Africa, he swallowed too easily the stereotype of the benighted, violent, superstitious Negro aborigine of that continent. Mugambi, for example, is "a magnificent specimen of manhood," but his fellow natives live in vermin-infested villages, embrace cannibalism, possess "fear-ridden minds," do a great deal of howling and eye-rolling, and turn "almost white with terror" at the appearance of Tarzan's entourage. "Tarzan," Burroughs explained, "had always found that it stood him in good stead to leave with natives the impression that he was to some extent possessed with more or less miraculous powers." Nowadays especially, one of the most virulent and most unshakeable criticisms of Burroughs is his implicitly racist and imperialistic assumption that a Great White Bwana is better equipped to solve the problems of Africa than are Africans themselves.

The sexual assault scene in *Beasts* is Burroughs's most vivid to date. Rokoff captures Jane and vows to make her the wife of a cannibal, but not until he himself is "finished with her." He is in the midst of dragging her to a cot in his tent when she coldcocks him with his own gun and flees into the jungle. The chase is on; Tarzan gets to Jane before Rokoff has another chance to commit the unspeakable. In the final fight with Rokoff, he and his henchmen die "horribly, as they deserved, beneath the fangs and talons of the beasts of Tarzan." Neatly, it is revealed that son Jack had been in London all along, and in closing, Burroughs throws a sappy bone to his readers: "Possibly we shall see them all [again] amid the savage romance of the grim jungle and the great plains where Tarzan of the Apes loves best to be. Who knows?"

Beasts took Burroughs only a month to write, and he sent it to Metcalf in early February 1914. Writer and editor were now on better terms, after Metcalf had snapped up the two stories Burroughs had written since *The Mucker.* One was *The Mad King,* in which he plainly and rather unimaginatively cashes in on the popularity of Anthony Hope's *The Prisoner of Zenda* and the Graustark novels of George Barr McCutcheon. In the "two-by-four kingdom" of twentieth-century Lutha, where cars and telephones meet swords and castles, Barney Custer, an American, is mistaken for the king, and after much swashbuckling and moat-swimming, falls in love with a princess whom, for reasons of breeding and protocol, he cannot marry—that is, until he discovers he is the king's cousin. (Sequel to follow.) In the other story, *The Eternal Lover,* Barney Custer's sister Victoria is visiting Tarzan and Jane's African estate when she finds herself attracted to a Stone Age warrior (shades of Jack London's Big-Tooth) who has awakened from aeonic slumber. Like Jane Porter, she meets her man halfway, seeing virtue and vitality in primitivism. Metcalf scheduled both stories for March publication.

Burroughs had in mind a bidding war for *The Beasts of Tarzan,* but no one wanted to play by his rules. As he had promised the previous summer, he also sent a copy of the manuscript to Sessions at *New Story.* Somehow the manuscript was lost, and Burroughs prevailed on Metcalf to loan his copy to Sessions, knowing full well that the irritation of sharing would sharpen the appetite of both editors. The result was not what he expected, but far from disastrous. Sessions had mentioned a price of three thousand dollars the year before, but having read *Beasts,* which, for all its excitement, was essentially one long metronomic chase, would go no higher than two thousand dollars. Burroughs wisely did not share this information with Metcalf at *All-Story,* instead telling Metcalf that he could have the story for twenty-five hundred dollars, "to demonstrate that I 'have a heart.'" Metcalf accepted his "generosity."

At the same time, Metcalf offered two-and-a-half cents a word for "first refusal" of all Burroughs's 1914 output—a proposal that Burroughs would have welcomed twelve months earlier, but that now made him quite uneasy. "Am still up in the air about that $.025 stunt," he wrote Metcalf. What rankled even more was the clause that allowed *All-Story* to refuse anything it didn't want. "I feel that it would result in selling all my best stuff," he protested, "and not being able to sell what you didn't like at any price, even though it was not entirely rotten, and so I wouldn't have any chance to break into a wider field, and then when I have shot my wad as far as the *All-Story* readers are concerned I shall be just where I was when I first started to write."

On one hand, Burroughs was trying to plot the rise of his star, while on the other he was fretting over its premature descent. "I cannot forget what you once told me about the majority of writers playing out after a couple of years," he continued to Metcalf. "[I]n two years a fellow pretty nearly exhausts his stock of situations, phrases, and the like. I feel that most of mine are already worn to a frazzle."

The burnout factor was quite real; the four hundred thousand words he had written in the past year were still not enough to meet current demand. Metcalf informed him that because *All-Story* was now a weekly, it could use as many as fifty-thousand words a month. At two-and-a-half cents a word, Metcalf calculated, that would mean an income of "considerably over $10,000 a year." In fact, fifty thousand words for twelve months added up to six hundred thousand words, or fifteen thousand dollars a year. How Burroughs, already overtaxed, could increase his productivity by fifty percent, Metcalf did not speculate. He finished his pitch by dangling the possibility that Burroughs might soon graduate to *Munsey's,* the prestigious, high-paying flagship of the chain. (Seven years would go by before one of his stories finally appeared in its pages, a feat he never repeated.) And for his clincher, Metcalf even groveled a bit: "I can only beg of you to come in with us for another year."

Again Burroughs had played his hand as aggressively as he dared and backed off when he felt he could push no further. He took Metcalf's two-and-a-half-cent deal, and at the end of March, having plotted his literary course for the near future, he took his family back to Chicago. "I must have been feeling flush again," he wrote in his autobiography, "for I ordered a new automobile for delivery . . . when we arrived."

In a final flurry before leaving San Diego, he had decided to complete "The Girl from Farris's," though the date for submission to Reilly & Britton's contest had long since passed. He also squeezed out *The Lad and the Lion,* a yarn that all too vividly exposed the cumulative strain of the past couple of years. One more time, a young European heir is lost in Africa, though in this instance he washes ashore, after years of cruel captivity, in the company of a friendly though ferocious lion. Like a man dressing in a hurry, the plot wraps itself in all of Burroughs's favorite devices, including palace conspiracy, an arranged marriage, and a forbidden courtship. None of these elements, however, is as shopworn as the story's pivotal contrivance, the amnesia and sudden reawakening of the hero—a trick perhaps inspired by Burroughs's own head injury while working as a railroad policeman but one he had come to rely on too often in his stories.

His lack of care in his writing showed in other ways, as well. He had written parts of *The Eternal Lover* in the past tense, others in the present, a sure sign of inattention. In *The Lad and the Lion* (and numerous subsequent stories), he made the even more glaring mistake of employing the first person—in effect, introducing himself—in the middle of an otherwise third-person narrative. To be sure, there are worse sins in literature, and Metcalf certainly wasn't upset. If anything, it was the editor who had committed the greater crime of not catching the syntactical errors before they got into print. Like Burroughs, he was in a hurry: as of March 7, 1914, he was frantically trying to fill the pages of the newly named *All-Story Weekly.*

BACK IN Chicago after his extended stay in California, Burroughs's routine was more hectic than ever. Temporarily, he, Emma, and the children lived with Emma's parents on Park Avenue. By May, he felt he could afford to buy his first house (breaking with the family tradition of renting) on Augusta Street, in the respectable suburb of Oak Park. It had five bedrooms, a sleeping porch, two bathrooms, and a garage. But even with so much space, peace and quiet for writing was hard to come by. A short profile of Burroughs prepared that spring by his agent William Chapman for distribution to the newspapers that syndicated his stories describes the commotion that swirled constantly around his desk. "'Were I literary and afflicted with temperament I should have a devil of a time writing stories,'" the ghost-written piece explained, "'for now comes Joan with [her doll] Helen in one hand and Helen's severed arm in the other, strewing a thin line of sawdust across my study floor. . . . Then may come Hulbert with an orange to be turned "insideout." or with a steam calliope announcement that he has discovered a "father long legs," and about the time he has been shunted outdoors with his velocipede Jack tumbles out of his go-cart with a vocal accompaniment that would drive the possessor of a temperament to the mad house.'"

The profile goes on to characterize Burroughs as "a sane, healthy American gentleman, very much in love with his wife and children." It also describes his sudden ascendance as a whimsical lark: "[H]e looks upon it as a huge joke that he and the public are playing on the publishers, for Mr. Burroughs' rates are going up by leaps and bounds—and why not, when every publication that prints his stories is deluged with requests for more?"

Out of cockiness, distraction, resourcefulness, or perhaps all three, Burroughs now mapped out a year of sequels—to *The Cave Girl, The Eternal Lover, The Mad King,* plus a fourth Mars story and a second Inner World. As ever, though, the more settled he became, the more he yearned for change. Despite his growing celebrity and success, he would have traded both instantly for the chance to be a soldier, or at least for the opportunity to witness war. On April 21, 1914, American forces bombarded and occupied Veracruz, Mexico, a preemption of German involvement there and one of the first rumblings of the imminent world war. The day after reading the news of the invasion, Burroughs wired Terhune of the *World*, asking for assignment as a war correspondent. Like every other bid for military adventure thus far, it never came to pass.

Just as well, for in the course of the next few days and weeks, two things happened that dramatically altered his career. The first occurred on April 30, when he finally received a contract from A. C. McClurg & Company of Chicago to publish *Tarzan of the Apes* as a book. McClurg was one of the houses that had rejected *Tarzan of the Apes* earlier, but after Albert Payson Terhune's endorsement, not to mention the success

of the newspaper serials, the firm reconsidered. McClurg was not a prestigious publishing house—certainly not in a league with Scribner's,
Macmillan, or the other venerable New York establishments. Still, beg-
gars could not be choosers, and Burroughs liked the fact that McClurg
was a hometown business. Founded by Alexander McClurg, a local Civil
War hero, A. C. McClurg & Company boasted not only its own imprint,
but its bookstore on Wabash Avenue was by far the biggest and best
stocked in the city.

The book would sell for one dollar and thirty cents, of which Burroughs would receive thirteen cents—a 10 percent royalty, a standard in
the industry even today—for the first five thousand sold. The rate went
higher for the second five thousand sold, higher still—to 15 percent—for
the third five thousand. Additionally, Burroughs would receive a two
hundred and fifty dollar advance. The deal had been brokered officially
by Chapman of the International Press Bureau, to whom Burroughs had
to pay 10 percent of his earnings. It was well worth it, he figured at the
time, for he had been wishing to get into the book business ever since he
first wrote *A Princess of Mars*. A book, regardless of who published it,
was substantial, dignified, permanent, as opposed to a pulp magazine,
which was inherently vulgar and ephemeral. Books would not sell just
for a week or month, but for years and across borders. Two years earlier,
All-Story's cover of *Tarzan of the Apes* had shown a dramatic image of
Tarzan grabbing a lion around the neck, knife poised to plunge into the
lion's chest. By contrast, McClurg's book jacket carried a simple, dark
silhouette of Tarzan seated alertly, but tranquilly, on the limb of a tree.
Tarzan and his author were indeed coming up in the world.

On June 17, Burroughs received advance copies of the first edition.
He had dedicated it to Emma, and he added an additional handwritten
note to the copy he gave to her:

> Do you recall how we waited in fear and trembling the coming
> of the postman for many days after we sent the Tarzan Mss
> to Metcalf?
> And will you ever forget the morning that he finally came?
> Not even this, our first book, can quite equal that unparalleled
> moment.
> That we may never have cause for another such is the wish of
> your devoted husband.

The second important occurrence of that spring was the news that Munsey had decided to merge *All-Story Weekly* with another of its fiction magazines, *The Cavalier*. The new title would be *The All-Story Cavalier Weekly*. Even more significant was the notification that the editorship would be taken over by Munsey stalwart Robert H. Davis. Burroughs had done well enough by Metcalf, but lately they had argued over the secondary rights to *The Beasts of Tarzan*—Burroughs insisting that they were his and Metcalf claiming apologetically but firmly that they belonged to Munsey. Burroughs had threatened to quit writing for Munsey altogether, and implied that he had shelved his next Mars story until the disagreement was settled; meanwhile, letters to the editor were singing his praises and pleading for more of his stories. Suddenly Metcalf was gone, replaced by one of the best magazine editors in the country.

Bob Davis was Burroughs's kind of man. He was the antithesis of highbrow; he had all of the smarts of Thomas Newell Metcalf, with none of the Ivy League arrogance. Like Mark Twain, Davis was born in the Midwest, then had worked as a type compositor in Nevada and California. As a reporter, he covered heavyweight fights and muckraked the beef trust. Joining the Munsey staff as an editor, his journeyman's toughness, folksy sense of humor, and gimlet eye attracted and inspired an impressive list of authors, including O. Henry, Mary Roberts Rinehart, Zane Grey, James Oliver Curwood, and Rex Beach.

Davis grabbed the helm of *All-Story Cavalier* with brisk and cheerful authority, and he took charge of Burroughs in a way no one ever had before. On June 12, he fired off a letter itemizing his priorities: "rehabilitation of Tarzan"; lengthening "The Girl from Farris's"; a new ending for *The Mucker;* more sequels; and the pleasure of meeting Burroughs in person.

Burroughs was flattered. Here was an editor who did not beat around the bush. Ten days after receiving Davis's letter, he was on a train for New York, all expenses paid by Munsey. Davis quickly resolved the rights rift over *Beasts,* giving Burroughs what Metcalf had been so self-righteous in denying. Recognizing the author's obsession with precise word counts, Davis obviated further troubles by agreeing to pay according to Burroughs's totals and declaring that he would not even bother with his own. "You've got old Euclid tied in a clove hitch when it comes to mathematics," Davis joked. "But I forgive you because the brand of words you spill seems to please a large number of readers." With that,

Burroughs had no more bones to pick. Before going to New York, he had complained that he was sick of writing sequels. For Davis, he would tackle them with renewed alacrity.

There was one area in which Davis was no pushover, however: editing. Granted, his new job stressed quantity over quality, story over style, but he was nonetheless determined to turn out the best prose possible. In Burroughs's case, no editor was ever more attentive than Davis, but none was ever more rigorous, either, though it took turning his back on Davis several years later for him finally to appreciate just how good Davis was at his job.

Most of Burroughs's literary peccadillos were attributable to sloppiness and easy enough to rectify. Davis policed his stories for minor characters who came and went for no reason, mistakes of tense and voice, and implausible twists of plot. Nor was he afraid to cut several thousand words if he thought it helped a story, though on one occasion Burroughs complained that his "artistic temperament writhes in contemplation of those fifty-odd bucks going into [the] waste basket." Burroughs even seemed to thrive on Davis's bare-knuckled treatment. "Somebody must step up and bite you or hit you with a stone axe . . . before you really begin to get human," Davis observed, making sure that the money and praise kept pace with the cuffing.

Burroughs welcomed Davis's stick-and-carrot approach for the simple reason that he believed that Davis was keeping him from becoming pedestrian, though both men were careful how they articulated this most delicate of issues. Davis wanted the best pulp fiction Burroughs could write; Burroughs wanted his best pulp fiction to be something even better. The tacit understanding was never to call the end product by its true name. On November 2, for instance, Burroughs submitted "Barney Custer of Beatrice," the sequel to *The Mad King.* Custer is living in Beatrice, Nebraska (hometown of Bert Weston, Burroughs's close friend from Michigan Military Academy), when he receives news that Austria is about to draw Lutha into the world war. He hurries to the European kingdom, but is quickly captured and marched before a firing squad. In the original manuscript submitted to Davis, Burroughs has Custer actually *dodge* the bullet by falling out of the way.

Davis put his foot down—over the near-execution and a number of other scenes, as well. "It is not my habit to quibble with popular novelists," he began, "[but] I hope you won't take it amiss if I make a few suggestions. . . . I will forgive you for having the King and Barney look alike, although it is the oldest device in modern fiction. But it isn't fair for Barney to make his escape by stealing two automobiles in Chapter V and Chapter VI hardrunning. There is no art to that, Burroughs, and no ingenuity. A man can go on writing sequels for the balance of his lifetime if he is permitted to resort to these time-worn stunts."

He wasn't finished. "On page 27 the manner in which your hero escapes the firing squad is nothing short of preposterous. Falling forward on one's face goes on at skating rinks and in the presence of district leaders, but it is beneath you to pull it in fiction." Davis assured Burroughs that he was accepting the story even in its present shape, but pleaded with him to respect his devoted readers: "[G]reat international God, Burroughs, don't hand them a hack story. . . . I don't ask you to break your neck or wear yourself out with this thing. I would much prefer you take your time and do something you are proud of." In closing, Davis had the good sense to apply a little balm to the wound he had just inflicted: "If anything in this letter seems to be peevish, it is not meant to be so. It is just a little man-talk from one to another. You may consider, under all circumstances, old Tarzan, that I am [y]ours to a cinder."

Burroughs took the criticism remarkably well, eliminating the second car theft and creasing Custer's skull with a bullet without killing him. In doing so, he added nine hundred words to his account. In his return letter to Davis, he bristled at the suggestion that he was running out of steam. "Who said I was tired? . . . Nay, I am not, and furthermore seldom have I worked more enthusiastically upon a story than upon this last one. I enjoyed it and really thought that it was better than most of them."

He had good reason to feel bulletproof. The book *Tarzan of the Apes* was receiving lots of attention, nearly all of it favorable. Burroughs's hometown *Chicago Post* called it "highly improbable fiction . . . very odd and very interesting," and lauded its author for his writing and knowledge of ape life. The improbability of the plot was mentioned in nearly every other notice, as well, but usually superseded by praise for the story's ingenuity. The *New York Times* proclaimed *Tarzan* a book of "many marvels" and speculated that "there are few who will not look forward eagerly to the promised sequel."

By the end of 1914, McClurg had sold out its first printing of five thousand and nearly all of the second. A smaller third printing would tide Burroughs and his publisher over until the release of a fifty-cent "popular" edition later in 1915. The author's royalty from these cheaper editions, the forerunners of paperbacks, was incrementally small— roughly a nickel a book—but there was money in the multiples. A. L. Burt, the New York publishing company to whom McClurg had sold the popular edition rights, was poised to print tens of thousands of copies, even millions, as demand grew. And for those book readers awaiting a sequel to *Tarzan of the Apes, The Return of Tarzan* was due from McClurg in March.

TWICE NOW, Burroughs had begun the new year with a fresh Tarzan story. On January 21, 1915, he began *The Son of Tarzan*, his fourth in the series. Fans who know only the MGM Tarzan think of Tarzan's son as the sweet, curly-headed "Boy." The son Burroughs created in 1915 bears little resemblance to the happy-go-lucky sprite played by actor Johnny Sheffield.

The Son of Tarzan opens with Paulvitch, partner to Rokoff, the Russian villain, still alive in Africa, having managed to escape Tarzan and his beasts. He is now a "human derelict," disfigured by smallpox, corrupted by life among cannibals—"the personification of the blighted emotion of hate." After ten years, he captures an ape and takes him to London, where he believes he can make a fortune on the stage. Next Burroughs introduces Lord Greystoke's young son Jack Clayton, who knows nothing of his father's jungle background, but nonetheless has a fascination for wild animals, African explorers, and uncivilized people. He even climbs trees and whoops like an ape. One evening Jack sneaks out to see Paulvitch's ape act at the theater. Greystoke discovers his absence, follows him to the theater, where he recognizes the ape as Akut, his old friend from *Beasts*. After the reunion, father feels obliged to tell son of his life in the jungle as Tarzan.

Son is proof that the Tarzan theme still had plenty of pep. After a botched kidnapping, Jack and Akut run away to Africa and move deep inland. Akut teaches the boy junglecraft, and Jack grows/regresses into a wild state, responding to "the spirit of adventure which breathes strong in the heart of every red-blooded son of primordial Adam." He kills natives in order to acquire weapons and a loincloth. ("There were no after-qualms of conscience. In the jungle might is right.") After killing one tribesman by choking and biting his neck, the son of Tarzan is over-come by a strange urge. "Involuntarily he leaped to his feet and placed one foot upon the body of his kill. His chest expanded. He raised his face toward the heavens and opened his mouth to voice a strange, weird cry." From here on, he is known by his ape name, Korak, the killer.

Korak has long since thrown off all vestiges of gentility when he res-cues a "little nut brown maiden" named Meriem from her Arab captors. At this point, the plot takes a delightful Garden of Eden turn. Korak and Meriem live at first as brother and sister. She learns the life and language of the apes, and in time her body rounds into "the fullness of an early maturity." Korak notices the change and a new light comes into his eyes. "Love raced hot through his young veins. Civilization was but a half-remembered state—London as remote as ancient Rome. In all the world there was but they two—Korak, the Killer, and Meriem, his mate."

In the next twist, Meriem is captured by natives and Korak severely wounded. Eventually she is rescued by Tarzan, who by this time is living with Jane on their African ranch. They have despaired of ever finding their son, and Jane takes Meriem on as a surrogate daughter and teaches her English, sewing, and deportment. Meriem begins wearing dresses and discovers that she somehow knows French. When Korak finally recovers and tracks down Meriem, she is being courted by Morrison Baynes, a suave white hunter. Korak takes stock of his own condition and is ashamed to make his presence known. "Of his own volition he had become a beast, a beast he had lived, a beast he would die." Later, though, he rescues Meriem from a hideous Arab-Negro half-caste. The ending is a grand reunion: Meriem with Korak, Korak with Tarzan and Jane; even Akut shows up. Korak and Meriem are married in an African mission, and shortly after arriving in England, they discover that Meriem is not "an Arab waif" after all, but the daughter of a distinguished French gen-eral, kidnapped by Arabs as a young girl.

UNLIKE most of the previous stories, which Burroughs had been able to finish in a month or six weeks, *The Son of Tarzan* took nearly four months to complete. Stubborn denials aside, his vaunted stamina had finally faltered. The name he put to his affliction was neuritis, though today it might be diagnosed as repetitive motion disorder, the result of too many hours hunched over a typewriter. When the neuritis was at its most painful, he could barely dress himself without assistance; already a fitful sleeper, he often lay awake in agony. Finally he was obliged to inform Bob Davis that he needed to ease up and "devote a lot of time to trying to get well."

Davis was willing to wait for stories, but he remained a stickler for standards. Though he enthusiastically accepted *The Son of Tarzan*—for which he paid three thousand dollars, or three cents a word, a new high for Burroughs—he was disappointed by the stories that followed. Of Burroughs's next four submissions, the rest of his output for 1915, Davis rejected two outright and took the other two only reluctantly.

One of the unacceptable stories was "Beyond Thirty," set in England in the twenty-first century. Britain has fallen into ruins after world war, and nearly a hundred years have passed since any inhabitants of the doggedly isolationist western hemisphere have crossed longitude thirty degrees west to make contact. With little pretense of allegory, the story provides a commentary on current events: two months before Burroughs began "Beyond Thirty," the British steamer *Lusitania* had been sunk by a German U-boat, with the loss of more than a thousand lives, including 124 Americans. Burroughs, a lifelong hawk, was upset with President Woodrow Wilson's reluctance to enter the year-old war and in "Beyond Thirty" predicts the devastation and devolution of England, which by the time the first westerner arrives, is the domain of wild beasts and the descendants of lunatics.

Davis liked the topical conceit of the story, but he panned the end product as "a magnificent piece of scenery with no play." This time he had no suggestions for revision and simply returned it with a short apology. He would handle the next story, *Tarzan and the Jewels of Opar*, the second Tarzan Burroughs had written in 1915, much more delicately.

In *Jewels of Opar*, Tarzan runs short of money and makes another raid on the treasure of Opar, the lost Atlantean city he first visited in *Return of Tarzan*. Before he can get away with the gold, he is struck on the head, suffers amnesia, and is imprisoned by the priestess La, who falls for him madly. She has never been with a man before, "other than the grotesque and knotted men of her clan," and the thought of mating with one of them disgusts her. On the other hand, Tarzan—whose injury has blotted out his Greystoke side and stimulated the savage in him—stirs up "all the pent passions of a thousand generations, transforming La into a pulsing, throbbing volcano of desire."

As Tarzan does his best to thwart La's amorous advances, Jane is falling into a sexually charged predicament of her own. She is kidnapped by the cutthroat slave trader and ivory hunter Achmet Zek and his "horde of renegade Arabs . . . and equally degraded blacks, garnered from the more debased and ignorant tribes of savage cannibals." In all likelihood, Jane is destined for a "black harem" or some "Turkish seraglio." True to form, Tarzan succeeds in finally escaping La and Opar and recovers his memory in time to save Jane from miscegenational depravity and claim a fresh fortune in gold.

Davis was having no problem with *his* memory; he felt like he had read it all before. "I have just finished 'Tarzan and the Jewels of Opar,'" he wrote. "I do not like it nearly as well as 'The Son of Tarzan,' or the previous Tarzan tales. It contains nothing new. You have introduced the old wallop-on-the-bean idea for the purpose of sidetracking Tarzan's intelligence. A good deal of that stuff where the ferocious guy breakfasts on caterpillars, grasshoppers, etc., will have to be cut out."

Davis was wise enough not to repeat the mistake Metcalf had made with *The Return of Tarzan* in 1913; he assured Burroughs that he was accepting the story, but he protested having to pay top dollar for a story he considered barely passable. He asked Burroughs to let him know by return mail what he thought it was worth. "It is your move," he concluded.

Promptly after receiving Davis's gentle challenge, Burroughs left for New York for a face-to-face with his editor. The immediate result was that Davis bought *Jewels of Opar* for twenty-five hundred dollars, but a new edginess, beyond their customary macho give-and-take, now entered the relationship. Burroughs emphasized that he expected five cents a word thenceforth, and he made it equally plain that he was willing to go elsewhere to get it. Davis argued, "I cannot help feel that Tarzan belongs to us," but admitted he had very little leverage: "You're the producer. I'm the consumer. Are we going to get closer together or drift further apart?" Burroughs was no less blunt in his reply: "I would rather write for you than for anyone else. . . . On the other mit[t] I want all I can get for my stories. . . . Why not let things go as they are? I will submit a copy of everything I write to you. What you want you can offer what you know it is worth to you, and I can refuse or accept. . . . It seems to me this is a perfectly he-man way of doing business." To which Davis could only respond, "Spoken like a man." The upshot was that Davis bought Burroughs's next story, a sequel to *The Mucker,* for two-and-a-half cents a word, but then didn't do business with him again for three years.

As a rule, Burroughs never saw a professional relationship that couldn't stand improvement. His other axiom seemed to be, whenever things were going well enough, don't leave well enough alone. He respected Davis and truly felt affection for him; but when he said he was shopping around, he meant it.

His first stop was the Consolidated Magazine Corporation. Founded by a wealthy Chicago hatmaker, Consolidated filled the magazine marketplace with a rainbow of titles: *The Red Book, The Blue Book,* and *The Green Book.* Of the three, *Blue Book* was in the process of changing from a magazine of sedate romances and saccharine theater profiles to one of pulp adventure, a genre with a much more robust audience. Tired of having to sustain novel-length stories and doubtless bothered by neuritis, Burroughs pitched the idea of a series of *Tarzan* tales, each able to stand on its own and the lot adding up to a book. Bob Davis had been ambivalent to the idea, but Ray Long, editor of *Blue Book,* liked the plan and offered three hundred and fifty dollars each for twelve stories—forty-two hundred dollars total. Burroughs was delighted with the price, and the incremental work suited him just then. Among other things, it gave him leeway to work on other projects, the most promising of which was motion pictures.

Burroughs's courtship with the movies had begun in 1914, at roughly the same time he had secured a book publishing contract for *Tarzan of the Apes.* Like millions of other Americans, he was taken with the "flicks," which in the early going filled a similar cultural niche as pulp magazines: they were cheap ("nickel"-odeon) diversion for the masses. As filmmaking technology improved and producers sought to dignify the medium, they looked to books, including such classics as *The Count of Monte Cristo* and Shakespeare, as source for scenarios, the term for screenplays in the silent era. In 1915, when D. W. Griffith adapted an obscure book on the Ku Klux Klan into *The Birth of a Nation,* America's infatuation with the silver screen soared beyond the wildest expectations.

The problem with *Tarzan of the Apes* was that it was considered too difficult to film. No one had ever made a successful movie featuring wild animals. And how to depict a nearly naked man? Even more problematic, how to depict a nearly naked man wrestling and killing a lion? The task was daunting, but Burroughs was eager to test the waters anyway. In June 1914, he contracted with Authors Photo-Play Agency of New York to try and sell the motion picture rights to *Tarzan*; over the next six months, the agency received several bites, but had no takers.

Disheartened but unbowed, Burroughs determined that if *Tarzan* wouldn't sell, perhaps other ideas would. Sure enough, in December, William Selig of the Selig Polyscope Company, Chicago-based producers of "High Class Motion Pictures," expressed an interest in *The Lad and the Lion,* which had been purchased by Munsey but not yet published. It seemed like an ideal fit. In 1910, Selig had made *Roosevelt in Africa,* filmed with a Teddy Roosevelt lookalike on a Chicago set. *The Lad and the Lion* might do just as well, provided Burroughs could deliver a workable scenario.

His scenario was apparently good enough, for in February he struck a deal with Selig: five hundred dollars to make a five-reel feature of *The Lad and the Lion,* one hundred dollars for any reel over five. Selig also paid three hundred dollars for another Burroughs story, "Ben, King of Beasts," which he had first written as a scenario and then as a story that ran in the *New York Evening World.* An enthusiastic Selig hinted that production on *The Lad and the Lion* would begin very soon, and Burroughs persuaded Bob Davis to hold off publication so the magazine story and movie would come out simultaneously.

Over the next few months, Burroughs approached more studios, including Universal, with his stories. As a scenario writer, however, he was a flash in the pan. After his modest successes with "Ben, King of Beasts" and *The Lad and the Lion,* he sent Selig scenarios of *The Mad King* and three original stories: "His Majesty, The Janitor," "The Lion Hunter," and "The Prospector." Selig was underwhelmed, offering sixty dollars for "Lion Hunter" and rejecting the other three. With that, Burroughs's screenwriting career ended almost as quickly as it had begun. He would spend the rest of his life intimately associated with the movie business, and he held strong opinions on how his stories should be adapted for the screen; but he never again attempted a script for one of his own stories.

Nevertheless, he was steadfast in his desire to see *Tarzan of the Apes* made into a movie. In early 1916, still unable to find a willing producer, he briefly considered forming his own company—an early hint of his inclination to self-incorporate—and approached Bob Davis and several others with the idea of investing. Already he had begun to question the trustworthiness of movie producers, a topic on which he would become increasingly vituperative as the years passed. "I believe the time is ripe," he told Davis, "for a producing company that would work on a legitimate basis similar to that of a book publishing house, and give authors a perfectly square deal devoid of even a suspicion of sharp practice." A month later, he scrapped the idea, not because he thought it was unfeasible, but because his neuritis was finally becoming unbearable. "[I]t has come to the point where I must devote practically all of the next year to trying to get back my health," he wrote to one of several producers he was hoping would take a renewed interest in Tarzan.

HIS IDEA of an antidote was anything but conventional. The initial plan was to take a few weeks vacation in Michigan, followed by a car trip to Maine. On its face, it sounded bucolic and relaxing. But in the summer of 1916, despite the popularity of outings, overland automobile travel was an uncommon adventure; most Americans still traveled by train. There were few paved roads, reliable road maps, or tourist camps. No motorist was assured of reaching his destination.

Burroughs wrote to the National Parks Service and *Camp and Trail* magazine, seeking advice on routes, and stockpiled supplies with the care of a quartermaster. On June 14, as recorded in his meticulous and comical diary of the journey, the Burroughs family was ready to depart. Burroughs drove a Packard Twin Six touring car, Emma at his side and Joan, Hully, and Jack (as John Coleman was called), ages eight, six, and three, respectively, in the backseat. The Packard was followed by a three-quarter-ton Republic truck, initially built for hauling ice, that Burroughs had purchased in South Bend, Indiana. It was outfitted with stove, refrigerator, and kitchen cabinet, and pulled a trailer loaded with trunks, tents, bedding, tools, and even a bathtub. Its chauffeur was a brave soul named Louis Zeibs. Filling out the crew were Tarzan, the family Airedale, and a poltergeist affectionately called "the Jinx," whom, according to the diary, "was never to be caught napping."

If the cure for Burroughs's neuritis was the strenuous life, he received a heavy dosage nearly every day. The Jinx took the form of bad weather, boggy roads, and mechanical failure. Getting to Michigan was hard enough, the evening stopovers earning the names Emergency Camp No. 1, Emergency Camp No. 2, and Camp Despair, among others. Eventually the convoy reached Morrison Lake, near Coldwater, where Emma's sister had a summer cottage. A month at the lake did everyone a world of good. A photo of Burroughs shows him lean and jaunty, his pants loose at the waist and his arms tan and muscular. The children thrived on the adventure, and even Emma, who had put on at least forty pounds since becoming a mother, looked chipper and healthy.

In Michigan, word reached them of a polio outbreak in the East, forcing a sudden change of itinerary. Instead of heading for Maine, Burroughs decided they should try a much more challenging journey. Why not California again? After a quick stopover in Chicago, where they switched to a chauffeur named Ray, the Burroughses set out to cross the Great Plains, Rocky Mountains, and deserts of the Southwest. What had begun as a vacation had become a full-fledged expedition.

Burroughs's log of the six weeks is a litany of mishaps: overheatings, breakdowns, washouts, and detours. They camped out nearly every night; unpacking, assembling, cooking, and repacking the mountain of gear was a major feat itself. Some days they made only forty miles; an exceptional day was anything over one hundred. Through it all, the troops bore up admirably. Burroughs would let the two older children take turns sitting on his lap and driving; they took to camping like Indians. Emma received her new circumstances the way she had adapted to Idaho and every other hardship to which her husband had subjected her. "Emma is remarkably game," Burroughs applauded in his diary. "If she feels fear, and I know that she must at times, she never shows it until the danger is past. . . . No man could ask for a better driving companion than she."

Despite the military regimen Burroughs imposed on the trip, he also saw himself as a hobo of sorts, living off the land, choosing his own road—a romantic philosophy that had infected his writing as well. In the sequel to *The Mucker*, which he had completed that spring, Billy Byrne teams up with a hobo poet named Bridge. They wander the West, eventually crossing over into Mexico and embroiling themselves in the revolution there. All the while, Bridge recites the "man-verse" of Burroughs's favorite poets: Kipling, Robert Service, and especially Henry Herbert Knibbs. Burroughs had initially titled the *Mucker* sequel

"Out There Somewhere," in honor of the Knibbs poem of the same name, which he had read in Knibbs's 1914 anthology, *Songs of the Outlands*. The Knibbs poem describes a chance encounter with a very Bridge-like character:

> Says I, "Then let's be on the float. You certainly have got my
>   goat;
> You make me hungry in my throat for seeing things that's new.
> Out there somewhere we'll ride the range a-looking for the new
>   and strange;
> My feet are tired and need a change. Come on! It's up to you!"

The road is Billy Byrne's redemption as well, leading him to exoneration, prosperity, and his beloved Barbara Harding. It was no coincidence that Burroughs chose a similar course for his own adventure, or that he called the thirty-seven-thousand-word diary of the trip "Auto Gypsying." Even in a touring car, freighted with family and a couple of tons of gear, he chased his muse with verve. In Missouri, he made a point of stopping in Hannibal at the boyhood home of Mark Twain and visiting the cave that had inspired *The Adventures of Tom Sawyer*. In Kansas, he called on another one of his literary heroes, Walt Mason of the *Emporia Gazette*, whose "prose poems" praising the simple life and tweaking modernism circulated to millions nationally. Burroughs liked him immensely, especially after Mason said that he had read all of the Tarzan stories.

The Burroughses took another month to reach California. At first they tried to cross the Rockies near Pikes Peak and Colorado Springs, but the severely overloaded truck could not make the climb. They backtracked and crossed over Raton Pass into New Mexico. On September 1, Burroughs's forty-first birthday, he reflected in his diary: "Twenty years ago this Sept. 1st I rode south from Fort Grant, Arizona, with 'B' Troop of the 7th Cavalry after the Apache Kid and his band, and I was about as uncomfortable as I have been on this trip." The family was not in such a state that they could not stop for sightseeing, though often they found themselves the object of curiosity. "Camping out, and, in fact, all forms of touring . . . [are] not the thing among the best families," he noted, "but then again I am usually doing the things that are not done."

Finally on September 23, 1916, they rolled down the final hill into Los Angeles, having added six thousand miles to the Packard's odometer since first leaving Chicago in June. "All are here and all are well," Burroughs wrote in his final journal entry. "Neither Emma [n]or I would undertake such a trip again, nor, on the other hand, would either of us part with the memory of the summer's experiences. . . . [I]f I had the choice of three children from all the children in the world, and one or more wives from all of the wives in the world for another similar trip, I could not find any better than those with which God has blessed me."

He had more to be thankful for that fall: "The trip, which was undertaken in the hope that it would rid me of neuritis, has not been entirely successful . . . but my general health is much better. Last winter I had to have assistance in putting on an overcoat; now I can lift a trunk to my shoulder and perform other Herculean stunts."

It was time to get back to work. The *Blue Book* stories were waiting, and another, even more demanding matter had arisen. Two days before leaving Chicago, Burroughs had been presented at long last with what appeared to be a reasonable proposal to make *Tarzan of the Apes* into a movie. He had signed it, but had not allowed himself to be overly optimistic. Now, however, it looked as if it might happen.

6
MOTION PICTURES

After the release of the movie *Tarzan of the Apes* in January 1918, neither Burroughs nor his jungle hero would ever be the same. The film made Tarzan even more popular, and Burroughs in turn prospered and grew famous. Glory, however, had a price: in expanding his domain from printed page to motion picture, Burroughs lost custody of Tarzan. Not that he was careless enough to give up the rights to Tarzan as a name or literary property; still, he could do little more than sit by as the *image* of Tarzan was gradually appropriated by directors, actors, and an even more inexorable force, the public imagination.

Three years earlier, Burroughs had told his agent that he believed it was "impossible to produce these [Tarzan] stories properly, and, in the second place, I would want more for my rights than anyone would pay me." William Selig's decision to skip over *Tarzan of the Apes* in favor of the *The Lad and the Lion* had only increased Burrough's skepticism. Then, much to his surprise, a producer finally did step forward who was willing to take a chance on Tarzan. On June 12, 1916, Burroughs signed a contract with William Parsons, president of the National Film Corporation of America, a fledgling company located on Forty-second Street in

New York. The deal wasn't as grand as Burroughs once had hoped, but it would surely pay some bills. Besides, he had no faith that another bidder would come along anytime soon. For the film rights to *Tarzan of the Apes,* Parsons offered five thousand dollars in cash, fifty thousand dollars in stock in the company, and 5 percent of the movie's gross receipts.

The project began to unravel almost immediately. Parsons could afford to pay Burroughs only five hundred of the five thousand dollars, the balance pledged for later in the year. To keep an eye on his interests, Burroughs drafted Bob Lay, his old military school friend, now a successful insurance executive, to take the position of vice president, but hesitated to assume the title of president himself.

Shortly after the Burroughses arrived in California, Parsons moved the film company's office to Chicago. By mid-October, Burroughs had lost patience with his new partner. "You told me something of your own ability as a salesman," he wrote Parsons, "yet in four months you raised something like two thousand dollars on a proposition which should have at least fifty thousand in bank before a wheel turns." He criticized Parsons for failing to issue him his promised fifty thousand dollars in stock. As a further expression of his disaffection, he again turned down the presidency, this time once and for all, and refused to participate in fundraising. Parsons tried to win him back by promising great things: "We are going to get out one or two big pictures a year, and we are going to be the biggest operators, I tell you, and we are going to succeed absolutely, and no man will gain as much by this as you." Burroughs was not convinced, nor was Bob Lay, who resigned as vice president.

Burroughs did not allow the consternation Parsons was causing to ruin his time in California. After moving his family into a rented house at 355 South Hoover Street in downtown Los Angeles, he got down to work, writing two stories a month for Ray Long's *Blue Book.* He also found time to type his diary from the cross-country trip, some thirty-seven thousand words, which he eventually sent to Bob Davis, who found it lively reading, but expressed no interest in publishing it.

The longer Burroughs stayed in Los Angeles, the more he felt at home. "I do not know when I have been more contented," he reported to Ray Long. "We have a very pretty little place with many flowers and trees, and a good lawn. There are roses galore. . . . The children are playing out in front with no wraps. . . . Their bicycles and roller skates came a day or so ago, and they are, consequently, quite popular."

Whereas San Diego was still largely regarded as a vacation destination, Los Angeles was increasingly seen not just as a city of sunshine and recreation, but one of substance, as well. The completion of the Panama Canal in 1914 had brought more trade to the city's deep-water port at San Pedro; oil derricks now shared the skyline with palm trees, and both had to make room for the newest growth industry, motion pictures. In myriad ways, Los Angeles was a city of the future, a modern oasis that would attract a million new residents over the next decade—the largest internal migration in the history of the United States. The new immigrants, like the tourists, were mostly from the Midwest, farmers and small-town families who had grown tired of hard winters, hard work, and the repetition of rural life. "At heart," noted humorist Irvin S. Cobb, "Los Angeles is a vast cross-section of the Corn Belt set down incongruously in a Maxfield Parrish setting." Burroughs, while quietly comforted by the link between his new middle-brow neighbors and his old, nonetheless felt compelled to set himself apart. "Am trying to get Walt Mason out here," he told Ray Long. "If I could establish a colony of human beings it would be a nice place to live permanently."

His dream of a new life in California was enhanced, albeit bittersweetly, in late November, when he learned of the unexpected death of Jack London from a drug overdose that may or may not have been accidental. Though the two writers had never met or corresponded, Burroughs was so moved by the news that he wrote to Bob Davis and at least one other magazine editor, proposing that he write a biography of London. He soon learned that another author was already at work on one, but a seed of another sort had taken hold: Burroughs's new ambition was to become a rancher-writer, modeling his own life on the one that Jack London had pursued and then abruptly lost.

Also that winter, Burroughs struck up a friendship with L. Frank Baum, a former Chicagoan and the author of *The Wonderful Wizard of Oz, The Road to Oz, The Scarecrow of Oz,* and other books in the popular series. Baum had moved to the new suburb of Hollywood in 1910 and, like Burroughs, was determined to have his tales adapted to the movies. That year, William Selig had made a hand-colored one-reeler of *The Wizard of Oz.* Then in 1914, Baum had formed his own studio, the Oz Film Manufacturing Company, though the venture had failed after only five films. By the time he met Burroughs—perhaps through Selig— Baum had already completed a full cycle of successes and hard knocks, and he was all too willing to share his insight with an inexperienced fellow Chicagoan nearly twenty years his junior. The two men apparently got along well, for Baum invited Burroughs to join the prestigious men's club he had founded, the Uplifters, which Burroughs described as a "select group of millionaires, clerks, and other celebrities, all members of the Los Angeles Athletic Club, who meet weekly for luncheon and occasionally evenings for dinner and have a heck of a good time." (Baum died in 1919, two decades before MGM, the studio that also made the best and most profitable Tarzan movies, released its classic version of *The Wizard of Oz,* starring Judy Garland.)

MEANWHILE, William Parsons was finally making headway. Much to Burroughs's surprise, National Film Corporation succeeded in paying him the rest of his five thousand dollars and issued him his fifty thousand dollars in stock. Parsons had taken on a sales agent, David Watkins, who had persuaded several wealthy Wyoming stockgrowers to invest in *Tarzan of the Apes.* They were promising to shoot the film in the very near future.

Burroughs considered himself lucky to have received his cash and equity, but he remained less than pleased with the way the deal was being handled overall. Having failed in his own attempts at scenario writing, he had allowed Parsons to hire William Wing, a respected movie writer whose credentials included work with D. W. Griffith. Burroughs and Wing got along well enough, until Burroughs realized what Wing was doing to his pride and joy. "[Wing] has the dyed-in-the-wool movie conviction that every story has to be altered before it can be filmed," he complained to Parsons, "while I am still firmly convinced that to change Tarzan, even though the change made a better story of it, would be to ruin it for the million or so people who have read the story."

The biggest concern was over the conclusion. The original *Tarzan of the Apes* ends with Jane engaged to Tarzan's cousin and Tarzan headed back to the jungle, a finale unpopular with readers and considered too anticlimactic for the cinema. The obvious solution was to have Tarzan and Jane reconcile romantically—except that the actual reunion takes place in *The Return of Tarzan.* Parsons had bought the rights to the first Tarzan only. Strictly speaking, if he borrowed even one scene from the second Tarzan, he would be getting something for nothing, Burroughs felt. Moreover, this would make it impossible to sell the film rights to *The Return of Tarzan.* To resolve the bind fairly, Burroughs suggested to

Parsons that they poll his readers on how best to end the movie, but Parsons was already convinced that a Tarzan–Jane happy ending was the only way to go. The whole affair upset Burroughs so much that he fired off an impulsive letter to agent William Chapman, ordering him to quit shopping his other stories. "I shall never again peddle any of that stuff around," he swore bitterly. "The majority of producers are petty crooks."

Still, he was not so principled that he would kill *Tarzan* as a motion picture. He and Emma were regular moviegoers, and that fall in Los Angeles one of the films they had gone to see was *Intolerance*, D. W. Griffith's next extravaganza after *Birth of a Nation*. Surely *Tarzan* had epic potential, as well. Parsons was now promising "*the* animal classic of motion photography," featuring "the largest and finest specimens of apes to be found, a herd of twenty or thirty lions, plus hyenas, leopards," and "two or three thousand cannibals." Burroughs knew it was possible, but he would believe it when he saw it.

While Burroughs was waiting for Parsons and his crew to arrive in Los Angeles to film *Tarzan*, his other movie colleague, William Selig, announced that he was at last ready to begin shooting *The Lad and the Lion*. Burroughs confided to Bob Davis, who was still waiting for the right moment to publish the story, that Selig would "probably spoil [the movie] anyway." Stubbornly, Burroughs voiced his intention to stay in Los Angeles through the spring in order to keep Selig, as well as Parsons, in line as best he could.

Soon, though, his head was turned by much larger events. In February 1917, Germany began torpedoing American shipping; then on March 1, British intelligence intercepted the infamous Zimmerman telegram inviting Mexico to align with Germany against the United States. If America's entry into the war was inevitable, as it now seemed, Burroughs wanted to be one of the first to serve. "What will a war with Germany do to poor boobs who write fiction?" he queried Davis. "If you have a pull, get me a commission." Davis did not take his request seriously, nor did he offer any help when, several months later, Burroughs asked him for an assignment as a war correspondent. "I don't know that it would improve your style any to go to the front, but it is a certainty that you would improve war," Davis joshed. "Between pronging a Hun and getting his opinion as to how well you executed the job, you could easily subtract enough material to write three serials and then three sequels to those serials."

But Burroughs was not kidding. In March 1917, anticipating Congress's declaration of war, he sought letters of reference from a variety of influential acquaintances touting his qualifications as an officer. Emerson Hough, author of numerous westerns and a friend from Chicago, had vouched, "You will make an excellent officer of volunteers. You ride, shoot, and speak the truth." On the advice of Charles King, now a brigadier general in the Wisconsin National Guard, Burroughs set his sights on the cavalry; toward this end, he secured a recommendation from the head of the Los Angeles Riding Academy, where he had resumed riding after many years away from horses.

He knew that his best chance for winning a commission was in his home state. On March 18, he finished the last of his twelve stories for *Blue Book* and immediately made preparations to return to Chicago. On April 6, the day President Woodrow Wilson signed Congress's resolution declaring war on Germany, Burroughs and the family were unpacking in a three-story brick house he had purchased at 700 Linden Avenue in Oak Park. *The Lad and the Lion* and *Tarzan of the Apes* would have to be made without his guidance. For the rest of the spring and summer, he campaigned relentlessly for a commission.

HIS WRITING during this period was considerably less able-bodied. The *Blue Book* stories, later anthologized as *The Jungle Tales of Tarzan*, were, for the most part, underweight vignettes relating to Tarzan's life in the years before Jane. Among other minor escapades, Tarzan suffers his first nightmare; wrestles glibly with the concept of "God," a term he has found in the dictionary left by his parents; and suffers the jungle equivalent of puppy love, though in this case the puppy is an ape. Overshadowing the general lightheartedness of these tales, however, are the frequent slights against blacks, which even in their day must have been received as mean-spirited. The most generous interpretation of such effrontery would be to accept that Tarzan picked on blacks because blacks just happened to be the humans with whom he, as an adopted member of the ape family, most comes into contact. This, anyway, would excuse Burroughs's observation that the "boy" in "Tarzan and the Black Boy" is "lithe, straight and, for a black, handsome." Likewise, the revelation in "A Jungle Joke" that "[t]he baiting of blacks was Tarzan's chief divertisement." Or the statement later in the same story explaining that, while Tarzan himself has a streak of cruelty, he is not perversely mean-spirited in the manner of blacks; theirs is "the cruelty of wanton torture of the helpless, while the cruelty of Tarzan and the other beasts was the cruelty of necessity or of passion."

A harsher and no less legitimate interpretation of Burroughs's racial characterizations is that he himself was guilty of a form of cruelty that surpassed anything he ascribed to the black Africans in his fiction. To assert that Edgar Rice Burroughs was no more or less prejudiced than many of his white contemporaries or that he was often judgmental of whites, neither negates nor forgives his racism. The very gratuitousness of his remarks in *Jungle Tales*—the implication that his sort of bigotry was fair play and on some level entertaining—is proof enough that the hurt was intentional. Throughout his stories, Burroughs suggests, as Kipling had before, that he was writing "from one white man to another," a racist premise that inevitably leads to racist results. To his credit, Burroughs was an avowed fan of Mark Twain; but while the slave Jim in *Adventures of Huckleberry Finn* is recognizable as an agent of satire, however subtle, Burroughs's blacks are afforded no such complexity. "I felt a certain responsibility for you because you are a white man," a tolerant Tarzan tells a scoundrel in a later novel, but he does not offer a comparable pledge to anyone of color, regardless of their manifest virtues. Except for the black cavalrymen Burroughs met—and praised, though somewhat patronizingly—during his days at Fort Grant, he was resistant to knowing blacks as individuals and especially as equals. In more recent paperback editions of the Tarzan novels, editors have softened much of Burroughs's more egregious language—eliminating the words *nigger* and *smokes*, for instance—but they have done a poor job paraphrasing statements such as the one delivered by Jane's black maid Esmerelda upon arrival on the forbidding African coast: "Ah hoped Ah'd never have to sleep in dis yere geological garden another night and listen to all dem lonesome noises dat come out of dat jumble after dark."

The only other story Burroughs wrote in the spring of 1917 was the forty-thousand-word "Bridge and the Oskaloosa Kid," later renamed *The Oakdale Affair*. The central characters are a group of hoboes, including Bridge, the vagabond poet from *The Mucker*, who again quotes generously from Henry Herbert Knibbs. This time, Bridge is involved in a mystery: a rich girl disappears, a mansion is robbed, a trained bear runs amok, a man is murdered. The story lacked intensity, and Burroughs pronounced it "rotten" even before he had finished it. Bob Davis, to whom he sent the story in June, concurred. "Lord! Edgar," he howled, "how do you expect people who love and worship you to stand up for anything like that?" Davis was particularly offended by the clumsy ruse of making the Oskaloosa Kid a girl in disguise. He rejected the story, and it eventually found its way into the pages of *Blue Book* (and as proof of Hollywood's fickleness, it was made into a movie in 1919). One of its few noteworthy features was the character of Dopey Charlie, a hobo driven to murder because of his morphine addiction. This is Burroughs's first mention of drug addiction, a societal scourge that he had become aware of in California and that would later become the subject of his most personal novel, *The Girl from Hollywood.*

Two other significant developments occurred in the spring of 1917 while Burroughs was trying to get into uniform. One was McClurg's decision to publish *A Princess of Mars,* the first of the Mars stories to become a book. The other event was the completion and release of William Selig's *The Lad and the Lion.* Shot on a low-budget set in Los Angeles, it starred Vivian Reed ("the Girl with the Million-Dollar Smile") as the sheik's daughter and a fake-bearded Will Machin as the lad. By all accounts, it was a tedious five reels, and the toughest review came from Burroughs himself. "They altered the story and I think that they did not improve it," he told Davis after attending the first screening in Chicago on May 13. "The photography is poor in many scenes. I have no pride in it and have not even told the members of my family that it is running here, nor any of my friends." Davis, who had been waiting three years to publish the story, began running it in the June 30 issue of the latest Munsey hybrid, *Argosy All-Story Weekly,* capitalizing on the film with a cover illustration of a movie audience gazing at a screen image of the lad and his lion. At the very least, Edgar Rice Burroughs was now a multimedia phenomenon.

Perhaps because of his disappointment with *The Lad and the Lion,* Burroughs lit into William Parsons in an effort to regain creative control of *Tarzan.* He threatened to take his name off the film if Wing's script was used, which prompted a salvo of irate letters from Parsons. He informed Burroughs that Wing's scenario had already been scrapped and that he was now working from a "composite" script by five writers. He then berated Burroughs for his threatening tone and "ignorance of what is being done." All the while, though, work was proceeding. An item in *The Moving Picture World* reported that Parson's National Film Company had recently moved into a new studio in Los Angeles and that "a corps of assistants are engaged in making costumes which will exactly simulate the ape." Director Scott Sidney, who had worked with the film pioneer Thomas Ince, was making plans to shoot a number of scenes in Louisiana, "where a part of the company will be taken to work among the bayous with large numbers of negro extras." The article said that Gordon Griffith would take the role of young Tarzan. The actor who would play the grown-up ape-man had apparently not yet been chosen.

The feud between Burroughs and Parsons might have escalated further had Burroughs not become even more preoccupied with the war in Europe. On July 19, he finally received a commission as captain in the Illinois Reserve Militia, Second Infantry (not cavalry, as he had initially wished). Exactly twenty years had passed since his discharge from the army, and whatever grudge he had once had toward the military was apparently behind him. He wore his uniform, which he paid for himself, with extreme pride and participated in militia drills once or twice a week. A forty-one-year-old husband and father of three, he had very little chance of seeing active duty. Nonetheless, he announced his readiness to "go over the top and spear a Hun"; short of that, he would pitch in any way he could.

As it turned out, the pen proved mightier than the bayonet. His writing during World War I was not the most polished of his career thus far, but it was some of the most pointed and a harbinger of things to come. If he had been wondering what a "boob" writer should do during wartime, the answer in his case was to become a propagandist. Once America had finally committed itself to war, a variety of domestic campaigns were launched to ensure popular solidarity and to root out the doubters. "Loyalty leagues" and more vigilantish groups such as the American Protective League took an aggressive stance against German-Americans and the home-grown cells of dissent and unrest, labor unions. Congress passed the Espionage Act and Sedition Act and authorized the formation of a Committee on Public Information, essentially an office of agitprop. Newspapers and magazines were urged to accentuate the atrocities of the enemy and to emphasize the "patriotism, heroism, and sacrifice" of American soldiers and citizens working for victory on the home front. "War Issues" courses were taught in schools, and a volunteer corps of seventy-five thousand "Four-Minute Men," most of them drafted from the business and professional establishment, dispersed throughout the land, giving short pep talks in support of the war effort. It is not known if Burroughs delivered any such speeches himself, but the editorials he wrote during the war have an unmistakable Four-Minute tone and may in fact have been ghostwritten for others.

In his first scripts, he promoted enlistment in the state militia and support for the unsung soldiers in the ranks. In a twist on the standard pitch for Liberty Loan contributions, he urged campaigners to solicit money from individuals suspected of being German sympathizers. "Next to sticking a bayonet through a Hun's gizzard," he explained, "you can inflict the greatest pain upon him by jabbing him in the pocketbook, and I can assure those who have never tried it, that a great deal of satisfaction may be derived by watching the home Boche wriggle when you get his purse pinned down."

There is no evidence that this philippic was ever disseminated, either in print or from a soapbox, in Chicago, a city with a sizeable population of loyal, hardworking German-Americans. Still, it was an accurate measure of Burroughs's hard-edged patriotism. Frustrated (or perhaps inwardly embarrassed) that he could not serve overseas, he railed against those who would not volunteer and berated clergymen who advised against military drilling on the Sabbath. He aimed particular calumny at union members who were reluctant to join up. (The army had a history of strike-breaking and violence against workingmen. After the war, Burroughs urged that the reserve militia be maintained to put down the "street-corner orators of the I.W.W. and Bolshevik types.")

He also wrote three essays about the roles women should play in the war effort. "To the Mother" urges American homemakers to look after lonely soldiers on leave in strange cities. "To the Home Girl" asks young women to uphold the "ideal of home, mother, sweetheart . . . an ideal to fight for, to die for." Both mothers and home girls were the first line of defense against the subject of his third essay, "To the Woman of the Town." He had made clear in "The Girl from Farris's" that beneath the breast of every whore beat a heart of gold. Surely prostitutes would put patriotism ahead of promiscuity, he exhorted in his essay to America's soiled doves: "I know you as well as you know yourself. I know the sweetness, the self-sacrifice, the generous impulses which are innately yours by virtue of your sex and proven by your profession, for it is always just these impulses, unguided and uncontrolled, which recruit your ranks. . . . You have made a great sacrifice in the past—the greatest that a woman can make. . . . Now you are called upon to make a slight sacrifice of pleasure and money for a nation. . . . We cannot thrash the Kaiser with a diseased army. Since you [first] gave your all you have been giving, giving, giving. Now you have your chance to redeem yourself in the eyes of God and man. . . . If you believe yourself to be unsafe, then shun a boy in uniform as you would the devil, for the devil, who is the ally of the Kaiser, is looking for you through the eyes of the boy."

ULTIMATELY Burroughs decided to wage war in the one forum in which he knew he could inflict the most damage and cut the most heroic swath. In September 1917, he commenced work on a trilogy about the mysterious island of Caspak in the South Pacific. In the first part, "The Lost U-Boat," an American, Bowen Tyler (Tyler was the middle name of Burroughs's father), is en route to Europe to join the ambulance corps when his ship is sunk by the Germans. Rescued by a tugboat, he and his new crewmates succeed in capturing a U-boat. After diverse travails, the U-boat lands on the remote island of Caspak, where the crew is challenged by dinosaurs and a pecking order of primates at all stages of evolution. (When a reader noted the similarities between Burroughs's lost world and Conan Doyle's *Lost World*, he deflected the charge by saying that he had started Conan Doyle's novel but had never finished it. Yet in a letter to Bob Davis three years earlier, relating to *The Cave Girl*, which also features dinosaurs, he hinted that he *had* read *The Lost World*, and very carefully at that.) In the course of the next two installments, "Cor Sva Jo" and "Out of Time's Abyss," it is revealed that every Caspakian climbs the evolutionary ladder from ape (Ho-lu) to human (Galu, the golden race) during a single lifetime.

From a purely science fiction standpoint, the trilogy—released in book form as *The Land That Time Forgot*—stands out as some of Burroughs's cleverest work. His apparent knowledge of paleontology ("[F]or around us there had sprung up a perfect bedlam of screams and hisses and seething cauldron of hideous reptiles . . . a veritable Mezozoic nightmare") and whimsical treatment of anthropological theory ("I now knew that I was looking upon the last remnant of that ancient man-race—the Alus of a forgotten period—the speechless man of antiquity") prove that he had done considerable reading in recent years and make for especially wonderful adventure. In a strictly political context, though, the saga is ham-handedly laden with anti-German hyperbole; as frightening and fascinating as the Caspakian creatures may be, they are not as low-down or loathsome as the German submariners who abandon Tyler and his mates on the savage island. Nothing could be "more truly Prussian than this leave-taking," Bowen Tyler observes. "[D]amn the Kaiser and his brood."

Burroughs was just warming up. A month after completing "The Lost U-boat," which ended up in *Blue Book* the following summer, he wrote "The Little Door." The German army is marching toward Paris like "a huge grey snake . . . its fangs bared against the heart of France that later it might wind its folds about a world." Jeanne, a young French girl, witnesses the brutal murder of her father and, to avoid being raped, pretends to seduce her Prussian assailant. She lures him through a little door in her house, then rushes out, locking him within. Muffled, terrifying sounds are heard from behind the door, and the officer never reemerges. The story is meant to be a nifty puzzle but succeeds only as a blunt instrument. Jeanne steers a parade of Germans through the little door, and not till the end of this mercifully short story does Burroughs reveal that she has been routinely feeding the soldiers to her pet lion Brutus.

Of all the magazines to which he could have first sent the story, he picked *Collier's,* despite the fact that it catered to a much more genteel audience than the pulps. Not surprisingly, the story was turned down. He finally submitted it to Bob Davis, and when he, too, rejected it, Burroughs wanted to know why. "There is nothing the matter with 'The Little Door,'" Davis answered sarcastically, "except that behind it is a tidal-wave of bloodshed, horror, and suggestion." Davis then counseled Burroughs to leave the war alone; the public did not need further morbid stimulation.

In August 1918, Burroughs attended a training camp with his Oak Park militia at Geneva Lake, Illinois, and relished every minute. Promoted to major of the First Battalion of the Illinois Reserves upon his return, he was more patriotic than ever, as his next group of stories would prove. A year and a half had passed since he had written a Tarzan adventure, and Ray Long, who had considered the Caspakian trilogy "a corker," was keen for him to get back to his jungle tales. This time he wanted them for *Red Book,* the big sister of *Blue Book,* and was offering a hundred dollars more per story than he had for the last bunch of Tarzans. Like Davis, Long begged Burroughs to ignore the war. Burroughs, however, could not resist unleashing his ultimate weapon on the Germans.

Virtually everything he knew about the German presence in Africa he had extracted from a book Joseph Bray had sent him, *Marching on Tanga*, by Francis Brett Young, a military memoir of the 1917 British campaign against German East Africa (now Tanzania). In cautioning Burroughs to tred carefully in his fictional treatment of the subject, Bray pointed out that, as colonialists, the Germans in fact had a better record than most. To which Burroughs responded: "I have learned enough about the Germans in the last four years to know that there aint no such thing as a good German record." He vowed to put the "wickedest kind of Germans" in his next serial "and let Tarzan chew their hearts out."

The series of related stories he wrote that fall (the first dozen chapters of *Tarzan the Untamed*) delivered on the promise. The chronology begins in 1914. Tarzan is hurrying home to his East African farm from Nairobi, where he has just heard the news that England and Germany are at war. Meanwhile, Hauptmann Fritz Schneider, a German officer, is lost in the jungle, along with several junior officers and a retinue of native soldiers and porters. By chance, Schneider's party wanders onto the Greystoke estate. "We have come upon the English schweinhund long before he can have learned that his country is at war with ours," Schneider tells a subordinate. "Let him be the first to feel the iron hand of Germany."

Tarzan has not yet arrived, leaving Jane and the family's loyal native staff that much more vulnerable. When he finally reaches home, he beholds a gruesome scene. The barns and outbuildings are in ashes. Vultures circle the bodies of his livestock and Waziri retainers. Entering the house, he discovers Jane's personal bodyguard crucified on the living room wall. Then, picking his way through more bodies, he enters the bed chamber. Sprawled across a couch is the lifeless body of Jane. Tarzan's heart plummets to "the uttermost depths of grief and horror and hatred."

Short of sacrificing Tarzan, there was no shriller way for Burroughs to express his disdain for Germans. In the end, though, the murder of Jane was more than despicable; it was unthinkable—or so said the editors who read the first draft of the story, and they beseeched him to alter, or at least muddy, the plot. In the first version he submitted to *Red Book*, Burroughs indicates quite plainly that the body in the bungalow is Jane's. However, after the roar of protest from editors, he changed the wording so that the body is "charred beyond recognition," thereby introducing the possibility of mistaken identity. By and by, Jane does turn up alive, but not before Tarzan has meted out unholy revenge: "[I]t was a sublime hate that ennobled him . . . hatred for Germany and Germans. . . . [H]e cursed their progenitors, their progeny and all their kind. . . . After he had accounted for [Schneider] he would take up the little matter of slaying *all* Germans."

Tarzan tracks down Schneider and leaves him in a tree, his imminent death ensured by a lion circling below. He then joins a battle between British and German forces, first picking off Germans with a sniper's rifle, then turning a ravenous lion loose in the German trenches. Tarzan himself becomes a wild animal, snapping the neck of one soldier with his bare hands. He then "placed a foot upon the carcass of his kill and, raising his face to the heavens, gave voice to the weird and terrifying victory cry of the bull ape."

The *Untamed* stories also pick up where *Jungle Tales* leave off in respect to racism. In particular, Tarzan reiterates his love for "blackbaiting—an amusement and a sport in which he had grown ever more proficient," and he goes out of his way to make numerous other demeaning generalizations about African natives. "It is a happy characteristic of the Negro race, which they hold in common with little children, that their spirits seldom remained depressed." Similarly, "[t]he blacks are so unprincipled themselves that they can imagine no such things as principle or honor in others." Burroughs apologists frequently promote "The Black Flyer," the story in the *Untamed* series in which a native learns to fly an airplane in two days, as evidence of the author's enlightened view of black Africans. More accurately, "The Black Flyer" is the exception that proves a more unpleasant rule.

THE DISTRACTIONS of the war did not prevent William Parsons from filming *Tarzan of the Apes*. He overcame financial setbacks and Burroughs's truculence and completed it by mid-January of 1918. Many of the scenes, including those of the Claytons' African cabin, were filmed in Griffith Park in Los Angeles. For better jungle foliage and shadow, director Sidney also took the crew to Morgan City, Louisiana, where recruits from a New Orleans athletic club cavorted in monkey suits. Some footage was even shot in the Amazon, though by whom is not clear. Brief glimpses of South Americans paddling dugouts and a dramatic scene in which an entire village of reed huts is set afire lend a jungle-primeval effect, however anomalous.

The original version of the film was two hours and ten minutes long and divided into three chapters. Sadly, the only prints that survive are barely an hour long, with immense amounts of the most explicative footage excised. As well as can be judged today, the plot, while departing from the novel, does not betray it wantonly. After a mutiny aboard ship, Lord and Lady Greystoke are set ashore on the African coast. A kindly crewman named Binns (who is not in the novel) is also marooned and quickly captured by Arab slavers. The scene in which the apes kill Clayton is grim and convincing, and the picture of hairy Kala with a soft, white baby in her arms is tender and heartwarming. "Talkie" technology was still nine years off, but none is needed to communicate the instinctive, primal bond between the gigantic but gentle ape mother and the helpless infant. Today one can only guess at the effect these images must have had on 1918 audiences. In the brief history of motion pictures, not even the most cultured viewer had seen anything like *Tarzan of the Apes.*

The second part of the movie focuses on young Tarzan, played by ten-year-old Gordon Griffith—unwashed, unkempt, and unself-consciously naked until he steals the loincloth of a native. Tarzan frolics gayly with Kala, delights at the alphabet primer he finds in his parents' cabin, and pounds his chest and grins impishly after killing a rival ape with his newly acquired knife. Meanwhile, Binns escapes after ten years in Arab shackles and finds the boy. Before attempting the long journey back to England, he teaches Tarzan to read, write, and converse—a development that is much more plausible than the self-education Tarzan pursues in the novel.

By the third episode, Tarzan is an adult, played by a hulking Elmo Lincoln. Finding just the right actor to play Burroughs's superman had been the hardest part of making *Tarzan of the Apes.* Lincoln, born Otto E. Linkenhelt in 1889, was nobody's first choice. As a physical specimen, he was impressive: nearly six feet tall and well over two hundred pounds. Yet he was everything Burroughs's had wished Tarzan *not* be. If Lincoln fit an ideal, it was that of the abysmal brute. He had an enormous chest, arms, and thighs, but not only was he as strong as an ox; he *looked* like an ox, too. He was not hairy, which would have been unforgivable, but his beefy build belied the grace, suppleness, and refinement of the literary

Tarzan. D. W. Griffith had more appropriately cast him as a blacksmith in *Birth of a Nation,* and he was given the role of Tarzan only after New York actor Winslow Wilson walked off the Louisiana set to join the army. As Tarzan, Lincoln wears a furry breechcloth and a headband around shoulder-length hair. He does some laborious hand-over-hand tree-climbing, but no vine-swinging or swimming. He pounds his chest with his fists to celebrate victory, though of course his bull-ape yell must be left to the imagination. For the most part, his mightiness has to be taken as an article of faith, at least until Jane and the rest of her party arrive.

Due to the loss of nearly half the film's footage, the characters of Jane Porter, Archimedes Porter, Samuel T. Philander, and William Cecil Clayton understandably have little depth. Cousin Clayton is unchivalrously pushy; Porter and Philander are citified, though not dithering, and wear pith helmets and jodhpurs instead of their comedic top hats and long-tailed suits. The mammy-ish maid Esmerelda provides negligible comic relief. More frustrating still, the movie's most harrowing scene ends almost before the audience can make out what is going on. Jane and Esmerelda are in Tarzan's old cabin when a lion attempts to jump through the open window. Tarzan arrives in the nick of time, grabs the lion by the hind quarters, and stabs it to death, all in the blink of an eye.

The precise details of the lion-killing and how it was filmed remain a topic of conjecture to this day. In 1934, helping pull together promotional material for MGM, Burroughs wrote to Lincoln, asking for exciting stories about the early Tarzans. Lincoln described the cabin scene: "You recall that as the lion was part way into the window I leap upon him and stab him with my knife, then I throw him to the ground, placing my foot upon his chest I give Tarzan's killing cry." Lincoln claimed that he had truly killed the lion with his knife, and when he placed his foot on its lifeless chest, its lungs expelled a loud growl. "Yes we killed the lion," Lincoln insisted, "and he was placed in the lobby of the Broadway when the picture opened in New York."

Perhaps, but it seems preposterous that an actor would stab a full-grown lion to death on camera, even in the unregulated early years of moviemaking. In 1934, when Lincoln wrote his letter, he was down on his luck and could easily have stretched the truth in order to curry favor. Too, the publicist whom William Parsons had hired in 1918 was notorious for his attention-grabbing stunts. For example, before the movie's premiere, he had dressed up as an ape and attempted to register at New York's Knickerbocker Hotel. The circulation of a lion-killing story and the display of a stuffed lion in the theater lobby were just his style. Adding to the conundrum is the spotty memory of Enid Markey, the actress who played Jane in *Tarzan of the Apes.* Though she gave scores of interviews throughout her long career (she enjoyed a brief second career in television in the 1960s) and recounted many wild moments from her silent film days, she had no vivid recall of Lincoln killing the lion.

Regardless of Lincoln's credibility as a cat-killer, his romantic interplay with Jane is convincing and quite touching. Jane is abducted by a large black native (striking the familiar chords of threatened rape and miscegenation). Tarzan catches up with them and kills the native in a wrestling match. As in the novel, he endeavors to soothe Jane and make her comfortable by bringing fruit and building a nest in a tree, and the image of a half-naked man with a fully clad woman deep in the forest is even more provocative on film than on the printed page. "I remember Mother had that dress made," recalled Markey, who was twenty-one and a veteran of a dozen movies when she first played Jane. "It had a plaid skirt and a green jersey top with white flannel collar and cuffs and a patent leather belt . . . and of course low-heeled white buck shoes and white stockings." At the opposite sartorial extreme, Lincoln looks as though he had scavenged his brief outfit from a taxidermist's floor.

Somehow, though, the jungle chemistry works, and the screen captions make doubly sure that the audience gets the message: "The nearness of the clinging form, the warm touch of the first woman he had ever known, thrilled Tarzan with a new emotion, and every throbbing pulsebeat spurred him to take her for his own." He puts his big arm around her and puffs out his chest. Jane recoils, then relaxes and gets a dreamy look in her eye. To demonstrate that he is a gentleman, Tarzan offers to let her sleep with his knife. She is honored, but hands it back trustfully. After all, the screen reminds, "Tarzan is a man, and men do not force the love of women."

Tarzan guards her through the night against lions and in the morning gives her a tour of his paradise. Finally he escorts her back to the cabin. He prepares to leave her, sad and unfulfilled. "Tarzan!" she cries. He raises one arm, whoops, and runs to her. The movie ends with their warm embrace.

Tarzan of the Apes opened at the Broadway Theatre in New York on

January 27, 1918. The following day's *New York Times* commended it for its "stirring" realism and, of all things, its "touch of educational value." Four days later, *Variety* took a more jaded view. As Tarzan, Elmo Lincoln was "all that could be asked for," and Gordon Griffith as young Tarzan was "wonderful," but because the movie spent so much time on the back story of Lord and Lady Greystoke, the pursuit of Jane by a skirt-chasing (and false) heir to the Greystoke title, and the revelations of Binns the sailor, "mystery, suspense, etc." were in short supply. The reviewer was also frustrated by the fact that the movie ended without resolving Tarzan's true identity as the rightful Greystoke.

Such quibbles, most of which focused on the choice of actors, were soon obliterated by a deluge of ticket stubs. "I never thought of Tarzan as a movie," Joe Bray confessed to Burroughs. "I went to see the picture and I did not think much of it. Coming out from the theatre, however, I found people in clusters talking about it. There was not a dissenting voice, most of the audience thought it the greatest picture they had ever seen. . . . I awoke right then, realizing that I had been on the wrong track. I had been measuring the picture from my own ideas of what a picture should be and I had not gotten down to the public point of view." Soon the press had reached an enthusiastic consensus. "Do you remember how you sat up most of the night to finish your first real adventure story?" the *Chicago Tribune* asked. "Well, it's better than that! And do you remember your first love story? Well, it's better than that!"

Burroughs did not see the film before its New York opening. He also declined an invitation to the Broadway premiere and in fact did not get around to seeing it until June 7. Reports from confidants who had previewed it had been so upsetting that he had written the Authors' League of America, looking for a way to disassociate himself from what he now considered a bastard production. "The story is not mine," he blurted. "For instance, in my story the psychology, interest, and action depended to a considerable extent upon the fact that Tarzan was reared by a she-ape and never saw a human being until he was ten or twelve years old. . . . He taught himself to read and write English from some books left in his father's cabin. He thought he was an ape. He did not see a white person until he was about 19 or 20. Now in the film version they have an English sailor with him during his boyhood."

The fact that his story had not been translated meticulously was a blow to more than just his ego. "I derive an income of some $15,000.00 a year from this one character," he explained to the Authors League. Believing that Parsons and the National Film Corporation were about to injure his reputation and reduce his income, he wanted to know if there was any way he could take both his name and Tarzan's off the picture. In a postscript, he noted that he had sold his fifty thousand dollars in National stock for five thousand dollars.

But he was too late to distance himself, and, ironically, it was not the failure of the film that he now had to endure, but its success. In many cities, theaters were obliged to schedule more screenings and held the movie over for additional days or weeks. *Tarzan of the Apes* was on its way to grossing a million dollars, one of the first movies to do so. If that was indeed the case, Burroughs was due forty-five thousand dollars—5 percent of the gross receipts exceeding one hundred thousand dollars. Yet by summer, he still had not received a dime beyond his initial five thousand advance and a second five thousand for selling his stock.

For the time being, he was uncharacteristically patient about finances, accepting Parson's explanation that money was slow to trickle in from distributors. Once he finally saw the movie, he was politic enough to say that he had liked it "immensely," though he must have been standing in the glow of the box office when he issued his review. Quite honestly, he deeply hated the choice of Elmo Lincoln as Tarzan, confiding to his brother Harry that the actor had all the grace and intellect of a "prize bear." He didn't like Enid Markey as Jane any better. He joked to old friend Bert Weston that the reason he had slain Jane in the first pages of *Tarzan the Untamed* (written in August 1918) was because, "[a]fter seeing Enid Markey . . . , I was very glad to kill her."

Perhaps the best indication of the success of *Tarzan of the Apes* was National's decision to produce a second movie based on the final chapters of the novel. Burroughs first learned of the sequel from a Chicago gossip column. Flabbergasted, he immediately tried to quash the project, only to be advised by his lawyer that there was nothing he could do. The contract with Parsons gave National the film rights to the book; nowhere did it specify *how many* movies could be made. Burroughs had no choice but to let Parsons proceed, though he managed to extract a twenty-five hundred dollar advance for the new picture. This time, he was not consulted about the script or production.

The Romance of Tarzan was made in a hurry on a budget of less than twenty-five thousand dollars. Lincoln, Markey, and most of the original cast were back, though this time the director was Wilfred Lucas. No prints of the film are available today, but reviews and records indicate that it was as big a flop as *Tarzan of the Apes* was a hit. Aside from the names of the characters, it bore no relation to the first Tarzan novel or any other, for that matter.

Picking up where the first movie left off, Jane and her party, including her father, the devious Cecil Clayton, and fearful, faithful maid Esmerelda, are attacked by natives. Tarzan helps them escape to their ship. After Cecil, who has designs on Jane and the Greystoke title, reports that Tarzan has been killed, the ship sails off. Tarzan, very much alive, tries to swim after them; his attempt fails and he winds up on an island where he learns the ways of civilized man from a priest. He then stows away on a ship and lands, quite by coincidence, on the very stretch of California coast where Jane is now living. He arrives just in time to rescue her from outlaws, but their troubles are not yet over. Tarzan, who has traded loincloth for evening clothes, is pursued by a vamp named La Belle. He has eyes for Jane only, but Cecil Clayton, who has failed in every attempt to kill his rival, convinces Jane that Tarzan has been untrue, and she calls off their engagement. Despondent, Tarzan returns to Africa, but finds that the jungle has lost its appeal. When Jane learns the real story from La Belle, she and her father set out for Africa to find her ape-man.

The *New York Times* labeled the decision to remove Tarzan from the jungle a "literary crime." If Elmo Lincoln was too stiff and brutish to play the lord of the apes, he was even less convincing as a drawing room gent, and the public apparently stayed away in droves. After wishing for years that Tarzan would become a movie, Burroughs now felt manhandled and vulnerable. The promise of a substantial royalty from the first film had mollified him somewhat, but if this was the way Parsons and National were going to operate, then it was time to consider other options.

In May 1918, just as Burroughs got the news that National intended to make a sequel to *Tarzan of the Apes*, he had received a letter from a man by the name of Pliny Craft, head of Monopol Pictures, asking about the film rights to other Tarzan novels. Burroughs responded bitterly: "[M]y experience with motion picture producers has been of such a nature that I am not at all interested in disposing of the rights to any more of my [stories] for motion picture purposes." Craft was undeterred. "There is money in your books!" he argued. "And any motion picture man who knows his business can extract it from them . . . and my integrity, or lack of it is something readily ascertainable." Craft continued to lobby Burroughs throughout the summer; having read about National's follow-up movie in *Variety,* he warned Burroughs that it was an "outright steal." Further, he suggested that, to protect himself, Burroughs ought to "dispose of the picture rights of your works or arrange to have the stories produced without necessary delay."

By August, Burroughs had softened. He advised Craft that he would consider selling the rights to his next title, *The Return of Tarzan,* but only under certain conditions. He wanted a financial arrangement similar to the one he had with National—certainly no less and hopefully better. He wanted assurances that the movie use scenes from *Return* only. Furthermore, he wanted a voice in the direction. "I realize that . . . producers feel that an author is more or less of a nuisance around a studio, yet on the other hand I feel that the knowledge of the taste of my readers who are also the same class of people who attend the motion picture theaters . . . might be used profitably by a tactful director."

Negotiations went smoothly throughout September, especially after Burroughs hinted that National was also interested in making the film. Craft offered him a salaried position as assistant director, and Burroughs conceded that two pictures could be made from the novel. By the end of the month, he and Craft had signed a memorandum of agreement, and articles of incorporation were on the way. All was well until Craft saw *The Romance of Tarzan.*

The movie was released at the end of September, though Craft did not get around to seeing it till sometime in mid-October. Suddenly he displayed an entirely different side of his personality, this one volatile, greedy, vengeful. In Craft's eyes, *The Romance of Tarzan* was an "outright infringement" of his rights to *The Return of Tarzan.* He claimed that *Romance* had not used scenes from the concluding chapters of *Tarzan of the Apes* as promised; instead, he had recognized "at least three very important ones" from *Return.* Both Parsons and Burroughs begged to differ with Craft, pointing out that, if anything, *Romance* bore no relation to *any* Tarzan novel. To head off a lawsuit against National and its distributor, Parsons agreed to pay Craft three thousand dollars, and then, for some reason, Parsons demanded that Burroughs reimburse the company for the unplanned expense.

Whether he made a movie or not, Craft was determined to make money from Tarzan. At first he suggested that Burroughs buy back the allegedly tainted rights to *The Return of Tarzan,* but then changed his mind and allowed that he would make the movie on the condition that Burroughs guarantee him an option on the next three novels. Burroughs wrote back, assuring Craft that if he made a good film of *Return* and otherwise fulfilled his contractual obligations, then by all means he would be given the opportunity to bid on other Tarzans.

Had Burroughs known how his relationship with Craft would turn out, he never would have been so generous. A year and a half would go by before *Return* became a movie, and Craft's legal quarrel with Burroughs lasted until March 1923. Along the way, the agreement to have Burroughs participate as an assistant director fell by the wayside, and he never again considered a similar position in one of his movies.

Meanwhile, his relationship with Parsons was deteriorating, as well. He was outraged to learn that National was deducting the expense of prints and distribution from the films' income before calculating his royalty; his contract clearly stated that he was to receive 5 percent of the gross. It took the threat of a lawsuit for Parsons to give him a fair accounting of *Tarzan of the Apes* and *The Romance of Tarzan.* Early on, Burroughs had anticipated making as much as a hundred thousand dollars from the two films, but the figure fell far short of that. The records available today are sketchy, but a letter from Burroughs to his attorney suggests that he settled for as little as fifty thousand dollars. How he and Parsons worked out the three thousand dollars paid to Craft is not known.

THE MONEY wasn't what he had expected, but it was enough to get him where he wanted to go. Burroughs had left Los Angeles reluctantly (though hastily) in the summer of 1917, and because of his militia obligations, he had been unable to get back. Now, with the war over and so much of his energy devoted to motion pictures, he announced that he and the family were going to move to Southern California for good.

Before leaving, he had a number of loose ends to tie up in Chicago, including resigning from the militia, selling his house and two other properties, and storing the furniture. This time, the family would travel by train and ship the Packard touring car.

The community gave Burroughs quite a send-off. There were

farewell parties for the children, and Burroughs was roasted fondly by the White Paper Club, a downtown fraternity of newspapermen, authors, and publishing types who had taken him in after his books had begun to sell. At a banquet at the LaSalle Hotel, they worked him over in a skit entitled "Tarzan, the Monkey Wrench," and club president Emerson Hough, unexpectedly absent, sent in a written jab: "I don't see why any man should want to leave Chicago and move into a mission building ... where you have to climb a tree for water, dig in the ground for wood and spell Hickory with a J. Still, I have always noted primordial tendencies in Edward [sic], and for some reason, don't blame him for wanting to move out closer to the movie studios so he can exercise his well marked prehensile tendencies." The printed program for the evening's proceedings was decorated with numerous ape caricatures by J. Allen St. John, who also illustrated Burroughs's books for McClurg.

In retrospect, at least, Burroughs had shaped up as quite a local celebrity. The Oak Park paper recapped the career of a "versatile genius" and reported that the film royalties to Tarzan of the Apes had brought him a "small fortune." The item also indicated that his dream for California was already well developed: he expressed his ambition to buy a ranch near Los Angeles where he would raise purebred Berkshire swine.

Just before departing on January 31, 1919, Burroughs received a curious note from William Parsons, who was already established in Hollywood. "Delighted to hear you are coming to California," Parsons said cheerily. "Trust that I may continue to produce your stories in motion pictures. I did so enjoy Tarzan and my young lady friend equally enjoyed the parties I gave out of the profits."

Burroughs's scribbled reply was a succinct: "Go to Hell."

7

TARZANA

Few of the recent arrivals to California had as much momentum as Edgar Rice Burroughs. His forays into the motion picture business had been frustrating, but they were starting to reap rewards, both direct and indirect. Joe Bray reported that book sales had been "wonderfully expanded" due to the movies, and he informed Burroughs that he could expect royalties of well over thirty thousand dollars in each of the next three years. Bray's firm, A. C. McClurg, had settled into a rhythm of publishing a Tarzan and a non-Tarzan book annually and A. L. Burt Company of New York was churning out fifty-cent "popular" reprints. Burroughs books were also published in Europe and Latin America, where they were catching on well. (There was one hitch with the British edition, published by Methuen & Company of London: agent William Chapman, who had received a commission for his perfunctory role in negotiating Burroughs's original deal with McClurg, claimed he deserved a cut of the British royalty, also. Burroughs considered Chapman lazy and greedy and had separated from him in 1917. Chapman eventually sued him, and the case dragged on till 1926.)

Everyone, it seemed, wanted a piece of Tarzan, though not all were as dollar-minded as Chapman. One measure of Tarzan's broad appeal was the formation in Virginia of the first of what would eventually become scores of Boy Scout–like fan clubs—"tribes" of boys who emulated Tarzan's woodcraft and virtues. Burroughs's hero was now a role model on a par with Daniel Boone or Teddy Roosevelt.

Such good tidings, combined with the rampant optimism of Southern California, were intoxicating. Arriving in Los Angeles the first week of February 1919, the Burroughses lived first in a hotel, then a rented house, while Burroughs looked for the right place to raise his children and, he hoped, a herd of swine. Initially he had in mind a small farm, but frugality was forgotten the minute he set eyes on the San Fernando ranch of Harrison Gray Otis, the recently deceased publisher and owner of the *Los Angeles Times.* Burroughs had to have it, and by the first of March he did. Thenceforth, the 550-acre estate would be known as Tarzana.

No other name would have fit as well. Tarzan had paid for Tarzana, of course. More than that, Tarzan and Tarzana would prove to be an apt match metaphorically, for if the career of Edgar Rice Burroughs is a case study in the mushrooming of popular culture in the twentieth century, then Tarzana is the story of Southern California's very similar explosion from sleepy Spanish land grants to pell-mell suburbia. Then, too, Tarzana, like Tarzan, was born of an impulse and, also like Tarzan, would soon prove to be more than its master could manage easily.

The San Fernando Valley is a basin of 175,000 acres, connected to downtown Los Angeles, twenty miles east, by Cahuenga Pass and separated from the Pacific Ocean, fifteen miles south, by the Santa Monica Mountains. In the century following the founding of the pueblo of Los Angeles in 1781, only a handful of Anglos had settled in the valley; most simply passed through on the old road that linked Los Angeles to Santa Barbara. Then in 1869, two partners, Isaac Lankershim and his son-in-law Isaac Van Nuys, purchased the southern half of the valley, formed the Los Angeles Farming and Milling Company and commenced growing dryland wheat. Several other farmers soon followed their lead, though on a somewhat smaller scale.

The shortcoming of the greater Los Angeles area had always been water. A brief rainy season was not enough to support most crops, and the only other sources of water were the fickle Los Angeles River and a shallow aquifer. Natural beauty and plenty of sunshine, plus a good port and rail service, augured well for the prosperity of the region. But by the turn of the century, experts speculated that unless more water was found, Los Angeles's growth would be permanently stunted. Outlying farms were in an even worse fix; because the city controlled the water rights to the Los Angeles River and the aquifer, farmers could provide only enough irrigation for small groves, gardens, and pastures. Even raising a drought-hardy variety of wheat was a struggle in this desert by the sea.

How Los Angeles solved its water shortage is now one of the sagas of American public policy, civil engineering, and personal aggrandizement. It is a story that has been recast as biblical parable and filmed as Gothic whodunit. In all versions, the fate of the San Fernando Valley is tied inexorably to that of Los Angeles. And as chance would have it, there are few greater monuments to the tumultuous events of those early years than the ranch Burroughs bought in 1919.

The story first began to heat up in 1904, for that was when William Mulholland, city engineer for Los Angeles, and Fred Eaton, a former mayor and the man most responsible for municipalizing the city's water system, returned from a clandestine trip to the Owens Valley, at the foot of the Sierra Nevada, confident that Los Angeles's thirst could be quenched by diverting the snow-fed Owens River through a colossal aqueduct that would snake across 240 miles of desert and mountains. The proposal Mulholland and Eaton submitted to the city's powerful Water Commission specified the San Fernando Valley, rather than Los Angeles proper, as the terminus for the man-made flood. A number of high-elevation reservoirs were envisioned to capture excess flow, which was greatest in spring and early summer. But the biggest and best storage tank of all, Mulholland argued, was the valley's underground water table; unlike the reservoirs, the aquifer would require no dams and would not evaporate.

Yet there was another, even more compelling reason for ending the aqueduct in the valley, and it had less to do with hydrology than self-fulfilling prophecy. At Los Angeles's present size of three hundred thousand, it could not support the municipal bonds required to fund the estimated twenty-five million dollar aqueduct. By annexing the San Fernando Valley, however, the tax base would expand accordingly. And why would taxpayers in the San Fernando Valley want to share the city's enormous financial burden? Because Los Angeles would not share—or even sell—its water until the valley joined the city. How could there possibly be enough taxpayers in the valley to make a difference? Because the valley was about to have an abundance of water and therefore would be ripe for subdivisions. And who would develop those subdivisions? The answer, of course, was the same civic leaders who had promoted the aqueduct in the first place. Asked to articulate how important the Owens River aqueduct was to the future of Los Angeles and the San Fernando Valley, the ever-pragmatic Irish-born William Mulholland told his fat-fingered superiors: "If you don't get the water, you won't need it."

No one had a greater vested interest in the aqueduct than Harrison Gray Otis. Indeed, no one played a larger role in the shaping of modern Los Angeles than the man known by admirers and enemies alike as "the General." Otis was born in a log house near Marietta, Ohio, in 1834. A printer by trade, he moved from job to job throughout the Midwest. He was one of the first to join Lincoln's Republican Party and one of the first to enlist in the fight against the Confederacy. Wounded twice, he nevertheless saw four years of nearly continuous action and left the army a brevet major. After more years in government jobs and as a newspaperman, he and his family settled in Los Angeles in 1882, where he bought an interest in the *Times*. Throughout his career, he was a fierce, unforgiving publisher and powerbroker. He fought unions, rival papers, and anyone else who got in his way or did not agree with his agenda of bold capitalism and tacit oligarchy. Six feet tall and more than 250 pounds, Otis was a formidable figure even as he aged, and it was his sheer bellicosity (as well as his longstanding friendship with President William McKinley) that won him command of a brigade of Philippine Expeditionary volunteers in the Spanish Civil War. Unlike most of the superannuated officers who served in the Philippines and Cuba, Otis actually led his men into combat and was breveted major general for his "meritorious conduct."

Not surprisingly, General Otis saw the growth of Los Angeles in military terms as well. If, for instance, the city needed water, the solution was to go out and seize it. And as with most conquests, the spoils were not necessarily divided evenly. In Otis's case, increased circulation and advertising for the *Times* were only two of the most obvious benefits of growth. To anyone who knew that the Owens River was about to take a radical detour, as Otis surely did, the price of San Fernando real estate was an outright steal.

In real estate especially, timing is everything. In October 1903, a year before Mulholland and Eaton had made their historic trip, a syndicate that included Otis and several other wealthy, well-informed Southern Californians purchased an option on the sixteen-thousand-acre Porter Ranch in the northern part of the valley. In 1905, three days *after* the city Water Board approved Mulholland's plan for the Owens River project— and four months *before* Otis's newspaper shared the news with the rest of the world—the syndicate exercised its option, paying a very modest thirty dollars an acre. When the details and timing of the transaction were eventually discovered, Otis and his partners were roundly excoriated for inside dealing, but were never officially charged with a crime or censured for breach of public trust. Otis, in fact, had so few qualms about his combined role as publisher/speculator that in 1909, with construction of the aqueduct in full swing, he joined a second syndicate to buy Van Nuys's wheat ranch (including present-day Tarzana) on the other side of the valley. This time he could not be accused of cheating. Cornering the real estate market in the San Fernando Valley was simply good business. So was using his paper to remind Angelenos of the salubrious effect the aqueduct would have on Southern California.

The syndicate formed to buy the Van Nuys ranch was named the Suburban Homes Company, and its five biggest investors, known as the Board of Control, were some of the most powerful men in Los Angeles. Otis was joined by his son-in-law Harry Chandler, active in real estate as well as the *Times*; Moses Sherman, member of the city Water Board and builder of the region's interurban streetcar system, popularly known as the Red Cars; Hobart Whitley, the developer of Hollywood and a series of railroad towns in the Midwest; and Otto Brand, general manager of a local title company. Together with thirty other investors, they paid $2.5 million for 47,500 acres, virtually the whole southern half of the valley. At the time, it was said to be the largest private real estate deal in the history of California. The rate of fifty-three dollars an acre was more than twice that which Otis's other syndicate had paid for the Porter Ranch four years earlier. But with construction of the aqueduct already quite far along, the valley was that much closer to booming. Over the next two years, the same land, subdivided, would go on the market at ten times that rate.

Now more than ever, real estate was the true business of Southern California, and the Suburban Homes syndicate was the most formidable player of all. In 1909, the valley was served by the Southern Pacific Coast Line, and along its right of way the Board of Control platted three towns: the westernmost, Owensmouth (now Canoga Park) was named for the terminus of the aqueduct; in the middle they established Marion (now Reseda), named for Otis's daughter (and Chandler's wife); and to the east, Van Nuys, named after the rancher who had sold his land for what now seemed like a song. Within two years, Sherman's Pacific Electric had extended a Red Car line from Los Angeles over Cahuenga Pass, and it would eventually stretch as far as Owensmouth. Simultaneously a boulevard was laid along either side of the interurban track, with macadam lanes for horse-drawn vehicles and paved lanes for automobiles. The entire route was lined with palm trees, oleanders, and other exotic flowering plants. The trip from downtown via Red Car took approximately an hour. For automobiles, there was no speed limit on Sherman Way, as the boulevard was christened, and a daring motorist could make the commute in thirty or forty minutes.

The dawn of California suburban sprawl had arrived. The Board of Control hired a canny sales manager by the name of William Whitsett, who was the prototype for all tract hustlers to come. Anticipating the completion of the interurban line (which would be finished two years before the arrival of the aqueduct), Whitsett staged a series of dazzling events that were part picnic, part circus, part auction. Each town had its own grand opening; Van Nuys opened for business on Washington's Birthday, 1911; a year later, Owensmouth had its turn; then Marion. Enticed by a "Monster Free Spanish Barbecue," a race between a car and an airplane, and cheap fares on special trains, thousands came out from the city to join in the hoopla, and many went home with a real estate contract, or at least a brochure, in their pockets. Whitsett claimed that at the Van Nuys auction, a lot sold every three minutes. Some paid as little as one hundred and fifty dollars an acre; others paid five hundred dollars or more. Not all bought residential lots; with water soon to be plentiful, many took enough land to grow alfalfa, beans, melons, potatoes, vegetables, and citrus.

But before any of the Suburban Homes land went on the market, each member of the Board of Control got to set aside a choice piece for himself. Brand chose 850 acres at the western end of the valley (now Woodland Hills) and stocked it with the world's largest herd of Guernsey milk cows. Sherman reserved a thousand acres at the eastern end, which he eventually developed into the suburb of Sherman Oaks.

For his share, Otis chose land that was more picturesque and somewhat less arable than that of his partners: 550 acres against the foothills of the Santa Monica Mountains, just south of Marion. He leveled off fifteen acres of hilltop and erected a handsome 4,500-square-foot hacienda, with deep, shady porches, white stucco walls, and twenty spacious rooms surrounding an inner courtyard. Around the house he planted elaborate flower beds and an arboretum of trees and shrubs that he imported from around the world. Appropriately, he named his retreat Mil Flores— "Thousand Flowers."

In 1912, with construction of Mil Flores nearing completion, General Otis donated the Bivouac, as he called his in-town mansion, to Los Angeles County to be turned into a fine arts museum. Thereafter he lived at the ranch. He took pleasure in superintending his gardens and overseeing the raising and shearing of a thousand Angora goats, which grazed in the rugged Santa Monica Mountains to the south. When cronies would come out from town, they would often repair to the Koonskin Kabin, a rough-hewn vestige of *rancho* days that Otis had lovingly restored. Or else they would sit on the veranda of the main house and enjoy the magnificent view of the valley. By all measures, it was Otis's kingdom that now sprawled before him, just as Mil Flores was his castle.

On November 5, 1913, the official day of completion of the Owens River aqueduct, Harrison Gray Otis was seventy-six years old. He and the Board of Control were given seats of honor before a crowd of forty thousand wide-eyed celebrants as the first water gushed ceremoniously from an enormous spigot. William Mulholland, who over the past nine years appeared to have sweated nearly as many drops as were now spewing from the aqueduct, turned to the exuberant crowd and pronounced with a note of relief and pride, "There it is—take it."

General Otis and his syndicate members had already taken plenty. By the time the aqueduct water began flowing, they had realized millions from the development of the old Van Nuys ranch, though in a way the boom was just beginning. In May 1915, 105,000 acres of valley land—including most of the Suburban Homes tracts—were annexed by the city of Los Angeles; a week later, aqueduct water was finally made available to valley residents. With the stroke of a pen, the city had more than doubled in area (though it had increased by only a few thousand in population); likewise, the value of the syndicate's remaining land, now amply watered, doubled in value and would soon double again. Now when Otis sat back and surveyed his valley, he did so in the knowledge that he and his partners had tripped a flood of growth that had no foreseeable end.

GENERAL OTIS died in 1917, and the following year Mil Flores was put up for sale. There is no record of how Burroughs first learned of its availability, but he could not have missed the copious ads for San Fernando Valley land in the local papers. One can picture him motoring over Cahuenga Pass in his Packard touring car. It had been the dead of winter when he left Chicago. As he descended into the valley, the sun would have been shining, and he might well have had the top down as he sped along the concrete boulevard. Perhaps he looked at a few small places in the valley, and when he expressed an interest in raising pigs, perhaps he was shown the Adohr Dairy, located next to the Otis ranch, as an example of a well-run agricultural operation. By whichever means he first came to Mil Flores, it must have seemed like Xanadu, its mission walls and Moorish cupola gleaming through a grove of lush greenery.

The salesman would not have had to say much—perhaps fill Burroughs in on General Otis and his legacy, explain the elaborate underground irrigation system already in place, push the potential for crops and livestock. Mostly, though, Burroughs would have sold the place to himself. He could see the entire valley from the front porch; on every horizon were mountains, set against a clear blue sky. (This before the advent of smog.) The house was cool and comfortable and not too formal; it was a home and headquarters all in one. He could work here, in and out of doors, as a writer and as a rancher, much as Jack London had intended to do in Northern California. He could ride again; Emma and the children would, too. They had moved so often; this at last would be home. Even Tarzan had settled down on an estate in East Africa. In Burroughs's mind's eye, everything fit.

He paid $125,000 for Mil Flores, which, for 550 acres, a 4,500-square-foot-house, gardens, orchards, fields, and a herd of goats, seems like a bargain today. In 1919, though, it was a stretch for Burroughs's budget. Royalties from the movie *Tarzan of the Apes* and book sales, plus cash from the sale of Chicago real estate, allowed him to make an acceptable down payment but left him with a stout mortgage and not a great deal of working capital. He rationalized his extravagance with the prediction that, if run efficiently, the ranch would eventually pay for itself. Besides, he fully expected to be earning one hundred thousand dollars a year, and if all else failed, he could subdivide and sell a few acres. No matter what, he would find a way to make it work.

He moved the family into Tarzana the second week of March and immediately threw himself into the task of taming the ranch. "My brain, if it ever was in a rut, has certainly been dynamited out of it," he wrote to Joe Bray on March 21. "I have to think about Angora goats, sheep dogs, draft horses, plows, cows, chickens, Fresnos, tractors, cooks, foremen, ranch hands, goat-herders, a keg of ten penny nails, coyotes, cotton-tails and several hundred other things." It was obvious he was enjoying every minute of it. "I believe that [this] is one of the loveliest spots in the world," he wrote to his Chicago lawyer that same day.

Within a month, though, the utopian fabric began to show signs of wear. In Chicago, Burroughs had used a secretary named Grace Onthank. He had persuaded her to move with him to California and had promised her husband, Fred, an Oak Park policeman, a bungalow and a job at Tarzana as well. By the middle of April, the Onthanks had quit in a huff, apparently over something Emma had said or done. In an angry letter written after they had returned to Chicago, Fred Onthank insisted that they would have stayed on if only Burroughs and Emma had treated them "like white servants should be treated and not niggers." Several other employees either quit or were fired in the first month, including the ranch foreman, two goat herders, the cook, and Emma's maid Theresa, who, like the Onthanks, had faithfully made the move from Chicago.

Some friction was doubtless inevitable, as everyone adjusted to new duties, new bosses, and a new location. But innuendo suggests that Burroughs and Emma might have allowed themselves to become a bit overbearing as the lord and lady of Tarzana. Totally inexperienced at ranching, Burroughs had begun by running the place like a military post. He rose before dawn and reviewed the work assignments of the staff. He posted schedules and rules in the barn and even ordered his staff to observe a moment of silence for the Unknown Soldier on Armistice Day ("Bulletin No. 27"). In Emma's case, she was at last living more in the manner to which she had been accustomed as the daughter of a hotel proprietor. She, too, became starchier in her treatment of the rank and file.

Managing so many employees was only half the problem. Paying them—as well as the rest of the bills—was a separate challenge. By the end of March, Burroughs was overdrawn on his account at Illinois Trust and Savings, where he still did his banking. "The initial expense here is appalling," he wrote to Bray, explaining his urgent need of an advance of "five thousand iron men" to carry him through till July 1. "Just now everything is going out and nothing coming in. I have had to buy new machinery and my pay roll is large." The future still looked bright, he assured his publisher, "yet in the meantime I am worrying my fool head off—can't sleep and all that rotten stuff. I guess I bit off a hell of a hunk."

For the time being, the plan to raise Berkshire hogs would have to wait. The purchase of the ranch had included five hundred Angora goats, which needed constant attention. On his lower ground, barley and hay were ready to be harvested, and beans, corn, and fruit trees needed weeding and watering. Pens for pigs and a barn for horses would take time and money that he did not have at the moment.

THE IDEA from the beginning had been to make Tarzana self-sufficient, and as soon as Burroughs realized just how much it would take to make agriculture pay, he began to consider another scheme. One of the reasons he had come to Southern California in the first place was to be closer to the movie business. Pliny Craft had moved to Los Angeles not long after Burroughs and was plugging away on *The Return of Tarzan,* though he still had not done much more than pull together a synopsis of the scenario he intended to produce. Burroughs thought it was lousy, though he tried not to rile Craft any more than need be. "I wish you could find it possible to go the limit on this picture," he encouraged tactfully. "If you are right in believing that *The Romance of Tarzan* may have injured the possibilities of future Tarzan pictures there is only one way to overcome this and that is to present a picture that will absolutely command favorable attention." Burroughs proposed that the movie be shot at Tarzana, where he could keep his eye on it and make sure the plot of the movie stayed true to the book. "Furthermore," he suggested, "I have a friend who owns twenty-three of the finest lions you ever saw in your life who is anxious to bring his whole herd over and will do so if I will furnish the cages." The lion man's name was William Beckwith, and Burroughs even nominated him for the role of Tarzan.

Yet Burroughs was obviously looking far beyond Craft's picture.

More and more studios were establishing themselves in and around Los Angeles, and he believed his ranch had great potential. "There is a small canyon on my property that is almost a natural amphitheater in which all the buildings could be located without interfering in any way with my tillable land," he explained to Bray. "My plan . . . is to make a specialty of wild animal productions and . . . to control the business end of the proposition personally."

Control was becoming one of Burroughs's bywords, and it meant eliminating the middle man whenever possible. He had fired William Chapman as his agent, taken over syndication of his stories himself, and done much better. It had made economic sense; beyond that, he saw it as a way to circumvent the shabby dealings that always seemed to stand between him and the greater success he believed he deserved.

Even so, he was wise enough to understand that he couldn't declare complete independence. There was no getting around editors, for instance; he certainly couldn't publish his own magazines. And his book publisher was doing a good job, for the time being anyway. The only real problem was with movie people. "I have been jipped [*sic*], insulted and robbed by motion picture producers to such an extent," he ranted to Bob Davis, "that I have made up my mind that the only way that authors can get a square deal is by having authors in a position to look after their interests from the inside."

His model was United Artists, the film company recently incorporated by director D. W. Griffith and actors Charlie Chaplin, Douglas Fairbanks, and Mary Pickford. Tired of distribution companies gobbling up a huge percentage of the revenues from their lucrative motion pictures, the principals of United Artists, four of the most powerful figures in Hollywood, had simply taken over production and distribution themselves. Burroughs decided he would call his company United Authors, and it would be made up of "a number of the best known writers in the country." As his ideas coalesced, he tried them out on the people whose advice he respected. One of his first letters was to Eric Schuler of the Authors' League of America, an organization founded in 1912 (Winston Churchill was its first president, Theodore Roosevelt its first vice president, and Jack London, Hamlin Garland, and Booth Tarkington councilors) for the protection and advocacy of authors' rights. "I . . . have felt for some time that something should be done to obtain for writers the same honorable treatment in the filming of their stories that is usually accorded them by magazines and book publishers," Burroughs told Schuler. As head of United Authors, he would issue a standard contract giving an author not only approval of the screenplay made from his story but also a say in the selection of the actors in the film. The contract would also stipulate that the movie company "use the author's knowledge of his characters, scenes and incidents for the purpose of following his story as closely as the limitations of the screen permit."

Everybody wished him a lot of luck but they were quietly pessimistic about his chances. "No industry that has ever been developed in the United States has succeeded in building up such a nation-wide hatred for its methods [as the movies]," Bob Davis commiserated, but he had no particular suggestion for how to proceed. In the end, Burroughs never took any firm steps toward forming United Authors, though it was the same urge for autonomy that would eventually lead him to form his own publishing company twelve years later. In the meantime, he resolved to do a better job negotiating with film companies. Toward this end, in July 1919 he hired John Shea, who had been assistant to the general manager at Universal studio and possessed a good working knowledge of all phases of the industry. One of Shea's first successes as Burroughs's secretary and assistant was to rent Koonskin Kabin as a set for a Wallace Reid picture. And in appearance at least, Burroughs looked very much the Hollywood player; not only did he wear jodhpurs, the signature costume of directors, but for a while he even wore a toupee in a bid to look more dashing.

As MUCH as Burroughs and Shea would have liked to devote their full time to the movie business, sooner or later Burroughs had to get back to his mainstay, writing. The previous December, before leaving Chicago, he had sent a letter to the Justice Department, asking for information on the activities of Bolsheviks and the International Workers of the World (IWW) in the United States. He explained that he was considering "a novel of the future showing conditions one or two hundred years from now, presupposing a worldwide adoption of Bolshevism. . . . I may be entirely wrong but I believe that the success of such a movement would eventually stop all commercial and social progress and precipitate the world into a period similar to that which followed the decadence of Greek and Roman civilization."

Burroughs's bias against organized labor was longstanding, dating back to the Pullman strike and the Haymarket bombing in Chicago. With the end of World War I a year earlier, socialism, anarchism, and union violence were perceived as the new global threat by Main Street Americans fed up with foreign entanglements and wary of any further challenge to the prewar—and, in effect, pre-twentieth-century—status quo. Each day's paper conveyed some form of Red hysteria or decried the IWW's perceived hooliganism in California; the *Los Angeles Times,* which had been bombed by strikers in 1910, was particularly virulent. An important benchmark in the campaign against radicalism occurred two months after Burroughs had moved to Tarzana. On April 30, 1919, the governor of California signed into law the Criminal Syndicalism Act, which made it a felony, punishable by a stiff prison sentence, to advocate violence for the sake of effecting industrial or political change. Perhaps it was coincidence, but on the same day, April 30, Burroughs began writing the story he had outlined to the Justice Department. The title he gave it was "Under the Red Flag."

The story takes place in the twenty-second century, following another war and a subsequent "peace-at-any-price" policy that has led to global disarmament. As a result, Earth had been easily conquered by an invading force of moon men, known as Kalkars. Julian 9th, able-bodied descendant of the "rapidly diminishing intellectual class," now lives in the ruins of Chicago and tends his herd of Angora goats. The totalitarianism of the Kalkars has "sapped the manhood from American men" and civilization has regressed to preindustrial gloom. Marriage is outlawed, taxes are worse than those of a "Roman occupying army," and religion, a vague, post-Christian pantheism, has been driven underground. Julian's father, Julian 8th, who keeps an American flag in a secret hiding place, remarks that "once the world was happy—at least, our part of the world; but the people didn't know when they were well off. They came from all other parts of the world to share our happiness and when they had won it they had sought to overthrow it." In particular, he blames this immigrant working class for having "flirted with the new theory of brotherhood the Kalkars brought with them from the moon."

More egregious still, they had interbred. "The pure Kalkars were the worst," Julian observes, "but there were millions of half-breeds and they were bad, too, and I think they really hated us pure bred earth men." While the mixed-blood men were degenerate, the mixed-blood women were "low-browed, vulgar, bovine." It is in this context that Julian 9th comments that "[n]o stock can be improved, or even kept up to its plane, unless high grade males are used."

Julian soon marries one of his own, Juana—an Oak Park girl, no less—and after he and his family suffer numerous indignities, including sexual assaults, at the hands of the Kalkars, he foments a popular uprising. "We looked for no perfect form of government," Julian reflects, "for we realized that perfection is beyond the reach of mortal men—merely would we go back to the happy days of our ancestors." Astride his fiery bay stallion Red Lightning, he leads his Yanks, as the purebred natives are known, into battle against the moon men and their mongrel spawn. Their rebel yell: "On to Chicago!"

The irony that under the new California law against political agitation, a similarly patriotic exhortation could send a man to prison did not occur to Burroughs. He sent the manuscript to Ray Long in June 1919, purporting that he had not written it for any higher purpose than to entertain. Clearly, though, it was intended as inflammatory. Long, who had gladly published Burroughs's accounts of lions in the German trenches, rejected "Under the Red Flag" under the pretense that it was too unrealistic: "In spite of all we know about what bolshevism does and has done, it seems incredible that anything of the sort could happen to America." The truth was that *Red Book* and *Blue Book* had just been acquired by the publishers of *Cosmopolitan,* and Long was feeling less daring. Bob Davis, who was still on friendly terms with Burroughs, even if he hadn't accepted one of his stories in nearly three years, was at least frank in his rejection of "Red Flag." "It wouldn't do intelligent people a particle of harm to read the story," he leveled. "On the other hand the Pharasees [sic] would raise hell with any magazine that resorted to fiction designed to point out the obvious truths. It's all right to stir the populace up, but it isn't good ethics and it isn't good business for magazines."

Burroughs was disappointed for the usual reasons relating to ego and money, but also because every rejection of a story such as "Under the Red Flag" drove him back toward Tarzan or Mars. "I have just about reached the point where I cannot write Tarzan stories," he moaned to Joe Bray. To Bob Davis, he confessed, "I have long since said everything there is to be said about the characters and used all the incidents and situations that I am capable of evolving. For the last few years it has been a case of re-arranging and camouflaging thread-bare situations. If it wasn't for the lure of the filthy lucre I should never write another Tarzan or Martian story."

He put off beginning his next Tarzan for another year and instead wrote "The Efficiency Expert," a story he hoped Shea could sell to the movies. Also noteworthy was the letter he sent to the editor of *American Boy* magazine, proposing to write "a series of stories around an Apache Indian boy during the period before the Indian country had been encroached upon by whites. I think that I could make the boy almost as interesting a character as Tarzan, because I have lived for a while among the Apaches." *The War Chief,* the first of Burroughs's two Indian novels, was already gestating, though he would not sit down to write it for another six years.

BY THE beginning of 1920, life at Tarzana had become more manageable. Burroughs was acting as his own foreman, keeping eight employees busy at ranch chores, including construction of a piggery for fifty newly purchased Berkshire swine. Emma had charge of the house and children, who, at ages twelve, ten, and six, were totally absorbed by their new surroundings. Burroughs noted with pleasure that they had little interest in toys anymore and now begged for riding boots, spurs, and books on stars, flowers, and natural history. In early March, Burroughs's mother, seventy-nine and suffering from kidney disease, came for a visit and was greatly comforted by the tableau of ranch life. "All I can think of is an English estate," she wrote to son George, still living in Idaho. "The family life too is not unlike what one reads of English life. Ed and the three children are up early and take a long ride over the hills every morning followed by their dogs. And you should see the abounding health that such a life has brought to them."

Mary Burroughs knew that her own condition would never improve and had chosen Tarzana as the place she wanted to die. When she finally succumbed on April 5, Burroughs was saddened but took comfort in the fact that she had spent her final days in such a pleasant setting. "Emma and I are both thankful for the four weeks that we had with her," he wrote to his brother Harry the day after their mother's death. "She loved Tarzana and one of the last things that she said, and she said it twice— once to me and once to Emma—[was] 'I am so glad I am here.'" He proposed building an aviary on the ranch in her memory.

Burroughs's mother's death was a cloud over an otherwise sunny time. The previous year, *The Oakdale Affair* had been made into a movie, starring Evelyn Greeley. Both of his Tarzan movies, *Tarzan of the Apes* and *The Romance of Tarzan,* were still being shown in theaters in the United States and abroad, and royalty payments were now arriving regularly. William Parsons had died unexpectedly, but Burroughs's relationship with the new president of National Film Corporation, Harry Rubey, was off to a surprisingly good start. Still not prepared to form his own company, he had sold Rubey the rights to make a fifteen-part serial of *The Son of Tarzan* for a five thousand dollar advance and 5 percent of gross returns. Burroughs's prediction that the deal would lead him into the "same slough of despond" as his "other ventures screenic" did not come true. He would have to wait a full year for the film to be made, and he had his usual amount of gripes about the script (which he had initially proposed writing himself), credits, and distribution; but at least Rubey proved to be a responsive, if not entirely acquiescent, man to do business with.

There was progress on other fronts. In May, Burroughs sold to Arthur Gibbons of London the rights to produce a stage version of Tarzan. The ape-man had been burlesqued on vaudeville for several years without Burroughs's authorization, but this would be the first attempt at legitimate theater. The play opened in Brixton in October with favorable notices, though it never did make the expected leap to London. (A New York production, with members of the British cast and two live lions, was short lived as well.) Even so, the play was one more measure of Tarzan's universal appeal, and at the outset, anyway, the deal with Gibbons had looked promising.

The prospects for the film adaptation of *The Return of Tarzan* were not quite so rosy, but Burroughs was thankful that the movie was finally going to be made. Pliny Craft had been a thorn in his side for two years, to the point that Burroughs chose to communicate with him only through his lawyer. As a result, he had to learn secondhand, and rather belatedly, that Craft had impulsively sold the rights to *Return* to Numa Pictures, owned by three brothers from New York, the Weisses.

The good news, from Burroughs's perspective, was that the Weiss brothers had decided against casting Elmo Lincoln as Tarzan. The bad news was their bizarre decision to give the role to a totally inexperienced New York fireman, Gene Pollar (real name, Joseph C. Pohler). Pohler happened to be upstairs in his fire station the day the Weisses showed up, looking for young men with athletic builds. Six foot two, 185 pounds, and twenty-five years old, Pohler fit the bill. "I slid down the poll," he recalled years later, "and I heard one of the men say, 'That's our man.'" He took the job for a hundred dollars a week.

For all of Elmo Lincoln's physical bulk and thespian shortcomings, he had defined Tarzan in the mind of moviegoers and for that reason alone was a tough act to follow. Pollar was much leaner and considerably more dapper in his over-the-shoulder leopard skin. In the early scenes, he knocks about Paris in white duck trousers or formal evening wear, but he eventually returns to Africa, where he wrestles a lion—"they didn't tell me about that in advance"—and rescues Jane, played by Karla Schramm.

All along, Burroughs had insisted that the movie be called *The Return of Tarzan,* in part because it would boost book sales. As the July release date neared, exhibitors expressed concern that the word *Return* might be misconstrued as a reprise of an old Tarzan, and so at the last minute Burroughs relented and the film was retitled *The Revenge of Tarzan.* (To confuse matters even further, the Weisses sold their rights to Goldwyn Pictures, which cut nine reels down to seven.) Yet despite the orphan odyssey of *Return /Revenge,* and the small ration of novelty it finally delivered to the screen, it did surprisingly well. Even Pollar got fair marks (though he never acted in a movie again). If nothing else, his performance rebuked Burroughs's theory that all it would take is one more imperfect Tarzan to sink the entire franchise. Tarzan, he discovered, was much more resilient than that.

Audiences did not have long to wait for their next encounter with the ape-man. National Film shot its fifteen episodes of *The Son of Tarzan* throughout the summer and fall of 1920 and released them to theaters as they were completed. In the era before television, serials (along with newsreels and cartoons) were a welcome prelude to a theater's main attraction, the "feature." These twenty-minute episodes of *Son,* for example, were meant to draw audiences back to the same theater time after time. Filmed entirely on the West Coast, *Son* was Burroughs's closest association with one of his movies so far. He did not end up writing the scenarios, but he reviewed each one before it went into production, rewrote some of the subtitles, and was welcome on the set.

Perhaps because of Burroughs's guiding hand, the serial is more faithful to the original story than any of the three previous screen adaptations, and it is arguably the best of the silent Tarzans. The scenario follows Lord and Lady Greystoke's son Jack and his (artificial) ape companion Akut from England to Africa. In the jungle, Jack, who is now Korak the Killer, rescues Meriem, the kidnapped daughter of Tarzan's friend Jacot. They live as brother and sister for a while, but after a wholesomely erotic scene in which young Korak, played by Gordon Griffith (who had played young Tarzan in *Tarzan of the Apes*), observes Meriem (Mae Giraci) taking a bath in a jungle pool, it becomes obvious that childhood can last only so long. Accordingly, we soon meet the mature Korak, played by the exquisitely clean-limbed Kamuela Searle, and the full-grown, minimally costumed Meriem (Manilla Martan). From here on out, the action—the sustaining pulse of serials—never slows, and the various escapades of Korak and Meriem are paralleled by those of Tarzan (ex-opera singer P. Dempsey Tabler) and Jane (Karla Schramm, fresh from her role as Jane in the Weisses' *Revenge of Tarzan*), who have returned to Africa in search of their son. If one is not wrestling a lion or Arab slavers, then another is in the grip of cannibals or unscrupulous ivory hunters.

Burroughs and twelve-year-old Joan were on the set for one of the lion scenes, when one of the lions jumped over a barrier very close to where they were standing. "I knew enough about lions to stand still," Burroughs explained many years later, "but I had also learned from experience that they seem to be particularly fond of small children. . . . As the lion came toward us, I edged Joan behind me and aged ten years; but he passed by us and jumped back again onto his own side of the fence. . . . It's a great life if you don't weaken."

From the standpoint of cineasts and Burroughs buffs, the most significant incident in the making of *The Son of Tarzan* occurred during the shooting of the climax, in which Korak is about to be burned at the stake. As the flames lick higher, Korak calls for his jungle ally Tantor the elephant, who arrives at the last possible moment. Wrapping his trunk around Korak's waist, Tantor lifts him and the stake to which he is bound and hurries from the village, spear-wielding natives in hot pursuit. After reaching safety, the elephant sets the butt of the stake on the ground, then lets go. The precise details are important because almost every published discussion of this movie in later years states that Kamuela Searle was badly hurt during the filming of this stunt and soon died from his injuries. A typical recap of "the grim tragedy" asserts that a morbidly curious public "flocked to the theaters for the final install-ments, in anticipation of seeing the scene."

Curiously, though, there is scant evidence to prove this fatal out-come. When the elephant drops Searle, he falls perhaps three or four feet, landing on his side—hardly a killing blow. As the scene continues, Korak struggles gamely at the ropes that still bind his arms. Then Tarzan and Meriem arrive and untie him, and the three walk off arm in arm, with no signs of trauma apparent. The only suggestion that anything at all is amiss comes in the final scenes, when Korak, in suit and short hair, reunites with his mother. Though he never turns his face to the camera, it is clear that the actor who closes the episode is not Kamuela Searle. Per-haps he had been shaken up after all, at least sufficiently to keep him from appearing in the last scene.

That very little is known about Searle only adds to the mystery. He was born Samuel Cooper Searle on the island of Hawaii. (Kamuela is the Hawaiian nickname for "Sam.") Around 1915, when he was twenty-five, director Cecil B. DeMille spotted his bronzed, athletic physique on the beach and invited Searle to Hollywood. His acting career was just getting underway when World War I broke out; he volunteered, was sent to France, and was apparently wounded, though where or how is not clear. After the war, he won a part in *Male and Female,* DeMille's tale of a low-born butler and a high-born lady shipwrecked on a desert island. His big break came in *The Son of Tarzan.*

In 1932, Burroughs wrote a series of letters to former Tarzans, asking them for colorful anecdotes from their respective films. P. Dempsey Tabler mentioned three from *Son,* one of which was the elephant incident. Time apparently had muddled Tabler's memory, for he did not describe it the way it happened on film; he even led Burroughs to believe that it was he and not Searle who had been tied to the stake. "I managed to wriggle out," he testified, "was dropped, and fortunately not stepped on." If Searle had been seriously injured, Tabler would surely have remembered (as Burroughs would have, too), and it seems unlikely that even a decade later he would have stolen the scene from its battered victim.

Another document that more explicitly contradicts the fatal finale scenario is a letter written by Searle's brother in 1950, in which he states that after returning from France "cancer developed, which finally took his life." This would explain why Searle was able to appear in at least one other movie (*Fool's Paradise,* 1921) and why he died in 1924—at far too young an age, but still four years after *The Son of Tarzan.* In the end, the real significance of the Searle intrigue is not that a scandal is buried somewhere in the jungle of Hollywood, but that ardent Tarzan aficionados prefer their myth in the strongest dosage possible. *The Son of Tarzan* was an excellent serial, made all that more memorable by the story behind the story.

IN AUGUST 1920, with *The Son of Tarzan* still in production, Burroughs tackled a task he had been postponing for some time: the writing of another Tarzan story. The pressure to produce was greater than it had ever been. More daunting than the motivation of mounting expenses at Tarzana was the seduction of increased public demand for his work. In 1919 and 1920, McClurg had published 63,000 copies of *Jungle Tales of Tarzan,* and Grosset & Dunlap, which had replaced A. L. Burt, was about to release a popular edition of 100,000. The latest book, *Tarzan the Untamed,* would do even better. The British market was booming, also; Methuen & Company, Burroughs's publisher in London, sold 175,000 copies of *The Beasts of Tarzan* in 1920. Even the four Martian novels, always in the shadow of Tarzan, were performing gamely; combined, they had sold more than 100,000 copies so far. That summer, when Burroughs finally sat down begrudgingly to write his next book, *Tarzan the Terrible,* he had eleven titles in print. The total number of books sold was well into the millions. (The top sellers of 1919 and 1920, Blasco Ibanez's *The Four Horsemen of the Apocalypse* and Zane Grey's *The Man of the Forest,* respectively, sold more than half a million copies, a mark Burroughs never attained with a single title in a single year.)

No particular book was going to make him rich; he had to keep producing. McClurg now paid Burroughs a 20 percent royalty for each $1.95 book, or 38¢, but McClurg kept a title in print for only a year or so. Grosset & Dunlap, the publisher for the long haul, paid him only five and a half cents for each seventy-five-cent popular edition sold. The result was that, after a year, the income from a title tended to go down even as the number of books sold went up. The answer, not surprisingly, was not simply to sell more books, but to write more books; the more titles, the more money. It was a harsh rule to live by, and Burroughs was not sure if he could.

After two months, he had not made very much progress on *Tarzan the Terrible.* "I can't tell you what awful hard work it is," he confided to Joe Bray. "If it were any other sort of story I think I could turn it out in a hurry. I fully appreciate what you say about the necessity for writing Tarzan stories but I really doubt if I can ever write another one, and it is very possible that I shall never be able to finish this."

His fear that he was falling into a rut was not exaggerated. Too often, Tarzan could be counted on to go up against a despot or corrupt high priest, and every fortress or temple has its dungeon, sacrificial altar, and labyrinthine secret passages. Inevitably, a princess or slave girl falls for Tarzan and abets his escape. And often a fifth column of decent men, sparked by Tarzan's heroics, rallies to take back the country. This is the case in *Tarzan the Terrible* as well, though despite the purported duress under which it was written, it somehow managed to rise above the commonplace.

The *Terrible* chronology picks up where *Tarzan the Untamed* leaves off. Jane, who was saved from death by Burroughs's publisher, is now the captive of another German, Obergatz, who rather than accept defeat, has fled with her into the depths of the Congo. When Tarzan learns that his wife still lives, he vows to track her to the ends of the Earth. After months of searching, he crosses a vast morass and enters a "beautiful but forbidding" land which, due to its inaccessibility, has become a refuge for otherwise extinct species and unknown hybrids. Tarzan encounters saber-toothed tigers and triceratops, called gryfs, which he eventually learns to ride. More intriguing still, he discovers the missing link between man and ape.

The strange province, called Pal-ul-don, is populated by creatures who possess the hands, feet, and tails of monkeys, but in nearly every other respect appear human. Their language, which Tarzan soon masters, is complex; they use weapons, wear clothes, and adorn themselves with gold and jewels. Burroughs identifies the "man-things" as pithecanthropine, though whether they are "some strange race or . . . but an atavism" he cannot tell. In Pal-ul-don, there are two races of pithecanthropus, the Waz-don and the Ho-don. The former are white and hairless, the latter black and hirsute, and though Tarzan gets along with both, Waz-don and Ho-don have a history of mutual enmity. "Not even the fact that they appeared to be equals in the matter of intelligence made any difference—one was white and one was black," Burroughs explains in one of his more equitable digressions on human nature. "[I]t was easy to see that the white considered himself superior to the other—one could see it in his quiet smile." Besides hair and color, they also differ in their religious beliefs: one believes that God has a tail, the other believes He does not.

In a letter written to Bob Davis two years later, he explained that the idea for Pal-ul-don had been partially inspired by a British fan who had sent him "clippings relative to purported encounters between white and native hunters, and some huge creature of prehistoric appearance in the swamps of central Africa." The exact articles are unknown, but in the nineteenth century, a number of European travelers had returned from Africa with rumors of men with tails. One story that Burroughs's fan might have shared is recounted in *Savage Africa: Being the Narrative of a Tour in Equatorial, Southwestern, and Northwestern Africa* (1864) by W. Winwood Reade, a member of the British Anthropological Society. As Reade tells it, a group of Arabs venturing deep into the African bush came upon a group of "wild Niam-Niams"—hairy black men with long tails. The Niam-Niams, like the Waz-dons, lived in caves, used weapons and tools, and though cannibals, were much more highly evolved than apes.

As inspiration for the saber-toothed tigers, gryfs, and the morass near which they live, Burroughs did not need to look any farther than downtown Los Angeles. In the late nineteenth century, workers attempting to extract asphalt and oil from a bog just off Wilshire Boulevard had stumbled upon an astounding collection of prehistoric remains, including the fossils of saber-tooths, dire wolves, mastodons, and mammoths. Twenty years later, when Burroughs began work on *Tarzan the Terrible*, the tar pits of Rancho La Brea were generally considered to be the largest fossil deposit in the United States.

Several other of *Tarzan the Terrible*'s distinguishing twists are worth mentioning: an enigmatic stranger doggedly stalks Tarzan, even as Tarzan searches for Jane. Meanwhile, Jane, in a refreshingly progressive subplot, eludes Obergatz and other male assailants and proves that, in terms of woodcraft and wits, she can be her own Tarzan. Goring the ox of organized religion is a perennial Burroughs pastime, but in this instance, having Tarzan pose as the son of (a tailless) God in order to gain entree into the Ho-don stronghold makes for particularly nifty satire.

Like most Tarzan stories, *Terrible* is full of appreciation of pristine wilderness and bitterness toward the human forces that would trample it.

Yet Burroughs's deepening affection for his California surroundings now applies fresh ardor to what had become a stock jeremiad. "What a paradise!" Tarzan remarks to himself as he surveys Pal-ul-don. "And some day civilized man would come and—spoil it! Ruthless axes would raze the age-old wood; black, sticky smoke would rise from ugly chimneys against the azure sky." (Was he already imagining the smog and sprawl of the San Fernando Valley?)

The dark mood passes, however, and the novel ends with a miraculous reunion. The mysterious tracker turns out to be son Jack—Korak—who has returned from soldiering in the trenches of France in time to save his long-separated parents. Having doubted he could finish the story at all, Burroughs had managed to pull off one of his best ever.

HE COMPLETED *Tarzan the Terrible* on December 16, 1920. The highlight of Christmas that year was a gift from Harry Rubey of National Film to the Burroughs children: two lion cubs and two monkeys used in *The Son of Tarzan*. At first they were a big hit. "The lions are very cute and we can all go into the cage with them safely enough," Burroughs wrote to his brother Harry. But the chore of cleaning up after the monkeys in particular quickly overshadowed the novelty of wild animal ownership, and he gave them away shortly after New Year's.

Given the amount of other pleasurable distractions at Tarzana, the cubs and monkeys were hardly missed. Under Burroughs's urging, the family had fallen into the routine of rising before daylight and riding one of the many primitive trails that led into the Santa Monica Mountains. On January 1, Burroughs began a diary which, though short-lived, conveyed how good life could be at Tarzana. "Rode this morning," he jotted on January 25. "A wonderful morning & a wonderful ride. The moon was almost full and still several hours high; the first signs of dawn were showing in the east. . . . The Colonel was all ears and eyes and nervous startings as though each bush and tree concealed some terrifying monster. I love to ride and I love The Colonel and some day when I am very old, with nothing but memories, I shall go through the daily record and live again the happiest days of my life."

The children and Emma seemed to enjoy Tarzana just as much. Joan was a pretty, energetic thirteen-year-old, and clearly her father's pride and joy. Disappointed by the local public school, Burroughs and Emma had enrolled her in a parochial school in Alhambra the previous September; after the Christmas holidays, she transferred to the Hollywood School for Girls, where many movie people sent their children. Joan enjoyed riding and the life at Tarzana, but, of the three children, she was the one whose head would be turned by the bright lights of the city and the studios.

Hully and Jack took to Tarzana like a pair of desert rats. If they were not riding, they were pestering the livestock, climbing on trucks and tractors, capturing small creatures, or exploring the outback. In the best photos of them, they are as brown as Indians, slightly mussed, and grinning like Penrod and Sam. Hully, three and a half years older, was the easygoing one, Jack the more sensitive. Living so far from other children, they were always boon companions. In September, they had enrolled together as day students at Page Military Academy in Los Angeles, where Hully had adjusted better to the strict regimen than Jack had. A chauffeur drove them and Joan in and back each day.

Burroughs's relationship with his sons was much more complex than the one he had with Joan. He was enough of a martinet to want his boys to taste some of the discipline to which he himself had been exposed as a student and soldier. Yet when eight-year-old Jack begged not to be sent back to Page in January, his father relented and agreed to tutor him at home for the rest of the year. As the boys grew older, he softened even further and became more of a coach than a commanding officer. He was always young at heart, and macho enough to think that he could keep up with his very athletic offspring, whether the sport was swimming, riding, tennis, or wrestling. The intergenerational rivalry was always wholesome and the joshing that accompanied it never mean. For a man who had very few friends, his sons were his two closest. At the end of his life, there is no question that he considered his well-crafted bond with Hully, Jack— and Joan as well—his greatest achievement by far.

All indications were that his relationship with Emma was fine in the first years at Tarzana. The brief 1921 diary, for instance, mentions Emma and him motoring and horseback riding together and celebrating their anniversary. Even knowing that their marriage would one day end in divorce and that Emma would tumble into alcoholism, the seeds of unhappiness are as yet indiscernible in Burroughs's behavior or writing. Emma pitches in energetically around the ranch and is received as a trusted confidante in business matters. Does Burroughs take her for granted? Perhaps somewhat, but his failure to mention her in correspondence, for instance, cannot be interpreted as incipient disaffection. Did he find her unattractive? She certainly was not the model for the shapely, minimally clad heroines of his stories; yet even if she was big-boned and significantly overweight, she had been that way as long as he had known her. In a letter to brother Harry on January 11, Burroughs jokingly compared himself to a neighbor who had gone into the hog business, gone broke, and then divorced his wife. In almost the next breath, however, he described Tarzana as heaven on Earth: "It took God millions of years to get Tarzana and me together . . . and I have to give Him credit for pulling off at least one very successful job." From remarks such as these, one can only surmise that, for the time being, he viewed the Burroughses as one big, happy family.

He had many reasons to believe that the coming year would be as good or better than the last. Though the ranch had lost seventeen thousand dollars in 1920, Burroughs had made an unprecedented one hundred thousand dollars. Expecting more of the same, he continued with his improvements on Tarzana. Most notably, he added a crude, nine-hole golf course, a swimming pool, and a split-level outbuilding behind the main house. The golf course soon dried up and reverted to pasture, but the pool, despite having no filtration system, was a great success and the centerpiece for parties and family fun for years. The new building included a three-car garage (one Packard was not enough for Burroughs), upstairs office and servants' quarters, and on the lower level, a combination ballroom and movie theater. Burroughs took great pleasure in showing two-reel comedies and westerns to family, neighbors, and ranch employees.

For all of his misgivings about motion pictures as an industry, he still loved them as entertainment. He and Emma frequently drove into Los Angeles to take in the latest release at Grauman's Million Dollar Theater, the Rialto, or another one of the new theaters opening up downtown. Such outings further whetted his desire to form his own production company, and he and secretary John Shea even drafted a prospectus for a business to be called Burroughs Films Incorporated. Burroughs pitched the idea informally to editors, agents, and friends, but for some reason his endeavors were left-handed and desultory.

As always, another story beckoned. He had completed *Tarzan the Terrible* before Christmas and at the first of the year diligently launched into his next Martian tale, *The Chessmen of Mars.* At the time, he and

Shea were apparently in the habit of playing chess after dinner, and this is precisely how *Chessmen* begins.

The narrator, who is presumably John Carter's nephew, and Shea, now a fictional version of himself, have just finished their game: "Shea had gone to bed and I should have followed suit, for we are always in the saddle here before sunrise; but instead I sat there before the chess table in the library, idly blowing smoke at the dishonored head of my defeated king." Suddenly, a figure is standing in the living room doorway, "a bronzed giant, his otherwise naked body trapped with a jewel-encrusted harness from which there hung an ornate short-sword and at the other a pistol of strange pattern. The black hair, the steel-gray eyes, brave and smiling, the noble features—I recognized them at once." Who could not? The man is John Carter. The warlord of Mars makes himself comfortable in his nephew's chair and, upon eyeing the chessboard, proceeds to talk until dawn about an equivalent Martian game, jetan, played with real men on an arena-size grid.

It is plain from reading *The Chessmen of Mars* that Burroughs was more enthralled with inventing a new game than with crafting a fresh story. He painstakingly explains the field, pieces, and moves of jetan, and before he ever finished the manuscript, he approached Joe Bray with the idea of selling a board version of jetan along with the book. (The game was never mass-produced, though a number of readers, including one unusually diligent prison inmate, eventually worked up homemade versions and corresponded with Burroughs about the fine points of the strategy and rules.) But in terms of sheer action, *Chessmen* reads too much like the gladiator sequences in *A Princess of Mars*.

The most original feature of *Chessmen*—and the one that tells the most about Burroughs's state of mind—in fact has nothing to do with jetan. Before John Carter sets foot on the jetan board, he must first elude the kaldanes and rykors, the bodiless heads and headless bodies of Bantoom. These ghoulish, disassembled Martians are of a race that has evolved to the point where the mind and body have become distinct and separate. The kaldanes are merely heads with little spider feet who attach themselves to the rykors, whose witless, well-formed physiques stop at the neck. Kaldanes, naturally, are the masters; rykors are the slaves or, worse, beasts of burden.

With no particular subtlety but with a delightful amount of dark wit, Burroughs shakes a finger at modern man and makes a pitch for what a generation or two later would be called holistic living. "Their theory of development is wrong, for it does not tend toward a perfectly balanced whole," a character who is of one indivisible piece lectures a symbiotic friend. "You with your kaldane brain and your rykor body, never could hope to achieve in the same degree of perfection those things that I can achieve. Development of the brain should never be the sum total of human endeavor. The richest and happiest peoples will be those who attain closest to well-balanced perfection of both mind and body, and even these must always be short of perfection." Such talk echoed the philosophy of the Physical Culturists; it also happened to describe the lifestyle of mental and physical exercise that Burroughs had prescribed for himself and his family at Tarzana.

He did not complete *Chessmen* until early November; construction at the ranch had demanded a great deal of attention. On November 12, he sent the manuscript to Bob Davis, who had recently left Munsey and was now operating as an independent literary agent. Burroughs had urged Davis to try to place the story with *Collier's, The Saturday Evening Post,* or *The Popular Magazine.* These magazines routinely paid up to twenty thousand dollars for a serial, often more. But when Burroughs told Davis that he would like to get seventy-five hundred dollars from one of these weeklies, Davis told him he was dreaming; his best chance was with *Argosy-All Story Weekly,* and the most he could expect would be thirty-five hundred dollars. (And this was precisely how it ended up.)

Burroughs was beside himself. He felt trapped in a genre that limited his income in at least two ways. First, the pulps would never pay top dollar, despite his popularity; second, he was certain that the appearance of his stories in "decent magazines" would have "considerable effect on the sale of a man's books."

Money wasn't the only reason for his frustration, though with the mounting expenses at Tarzana, it was the biggest. He had been tired of Tarzan and Mars before he had written *Tarzan the Terrible* and *Chessmen;* now he was absolutely exhausted. He would never come right out and say as much, but he wanted to graduate: not only did he desire to get paid the same as authors of "grown-up novels," but in his heart of hearts, he yearned to be considered a qualitative peer of those authors. Ironically, now that he was the laird of Tarzana, he worried that he would one day be remembered merely as the man who wrote Tarzan yarns and nothing else. Not surprisingly, when a fan in Georgia wrote to say that he was contemplating a trip to Africa, Burroughs replied that although he had once hoped to see the continent he had described in so many stories, at present such an adventure did not appeal to him in the slightest. Everything he wanted was in Tarzana, and like the character in *Chessmen,* he idealized a life that was one organic piece.

He also felt it was time that his writing more nearly express what he was seeing and feeling in his home and outside his window, not some world across an ocean or in outer space. On December 1, he informed Bray that he had begun working on something "which is entirely different from anything I have ever written and more in line with what I, possibly in my ignorance, imagine is an American novel." He insisted that he was doing it only in the hopes of getting it into a "high-class" magazine and making more money, but as usual his wallet was a shield for his ego. Don't worry, he assured Bray, "I am not going to try any Ibsen stuff," but he vowed never to go back to his old stock-in-trade, either. "I think I shall never write another Tarzan or another Martian story, so if the dear public cannot stand my other stuff I shall have to make reservations in the poorhouse."

Specifically, the "other stuff" was *The Girl from Hollywood,* in which a wholesome ranching family finds itself hemmed in by dope fiends, bootleg liquor, and the wickedly seductive subculture of motion pictures.

8

IMAGINATION
WITHOUT TRUTH

urroughs had wanted to call it *The Penningtons,* a dignified title for a story he hoped would transcend pulp appeal. The year is 1922, and the setting is Rancho del Ganado ("livestock ranch") in Southern California. Colonel Custer Pennington is a Virginia gentleman who had come west at the turn of the century to recover from a wound received in the Spanish-American War. "I have been looking at it for twenty-two years," he says of the ranch, "and each year it has become more wonderful to me." He sees the canyons and mountains as God's masterpieces and his domain a blessed sanctuary from "the wholesale districts of humanity." His wife, Julia, loves the lifestyle as much as he, and it has been a perfect place to raise their children, Custer Jr. and Eva—or so the initial testimony suggests. The whole family rides expertly. After a day of ranch work, everyone takes a refreshing plunge in the pool, father and son playfully dunking each other. ("Though there was twenty-six years' difference in their ages, it was not evidenced by any lesser vitality or agility on the part of the older man.") Dinner conversation ranges from grand opera to stockbreeding. Afterward, everyone dances for an hour in the ballroom. Then to bed, "for they rose early and were in the saddle before sunrise, living their happy, care-free life far away from the strife and squalor of the big cities, and yet with more of the comforts and luxuries than most city dwellers ever achieve."

No such paradise can last forever, and the seeds of disharmony are soon sprouting. The Colonel wants his son to follow in his footsteps, but young Custer feels trapped, repressed, and he drinks too much. His misery increases when his girlfriend, Grace, moves to Hollywood to pursue an acting career. Meanwhile, Custer's sister, Eva, a perky, flapper-talking teenager, becomes engaged to Guy Thackeray Evans, a struggling writer who has become mixed up with a gang of bootleggers whose whiskey is cached on the ranch.

Next the focus shifts to Gaza de Lure, an actress turned morphine addict. Her real name is Shannon Burke; raised in a small Midwestern town, she has come to Hollywood with an innocent's dream of becoming a movie actress. Instead, she is seduced by Wilson Crumb, a salacious and smooth-talking actor-director who, though he cannot quite take her virginity, succeeds in enslaving her through cocaine and finally morphine. As it happens, Gaza/Shannon's mother is a neighbor of the Penningtons, and when Mrs. Burke dies suddenly, Shannon—the girl from Hollywood—is offered succor by the Colonel and his family. They know nothing of her drug addiction, but thanks to the fresh air and wholesome regimen of Rancho del Ganado, she is able to kick her habit on her own.

Meanwhile, the fortunes of the Penningtons and the Evanses continue to sour. When the bootlegging scheme is discovered, Custer Pennington takes the fall for Guy Evans and is sent to jail. In a bizarre twist of fate, Hollywood heavy Wilson Crumb, who was the man behind the bootlegging all along, seduces Grace and introduces her to morphine; she winds up dying of an overdose. Later, Crumb, who has not yet been linked publicly to either Shannon or Grace, arrives at Rancho del Ganado to film a western. When his body is later discovered in the hills, Custer and Shannon, now lovers, are arrested for murder. Learning the truth about Guy Evans's cowardice in the bootlegging affair, fiancée Eva attempts suicide, and Guy is driven insane by grief and guilt. Mrs. Pennington's health also shatters under the cumulative stress, and the Colonel must do his best to live down the stains on his escutcheon. The story brightens somewhat in the final pages—the Penningtons survive—but there is no promise that they will live happily ever after.

The sordidness that envelops *The Girl from Hollywood* is actually no darker than the headlines of the time. In September 1921, three months before Burroughs began his chronicle of the Penningtons, popular comedian Roscoe "Fatty" Arbuckle was arrested for the brutal rape and murder of model Virginia Rappe in a San Francisco hotel room. The crime made headlines nationwide, and though Arbuckle was ultimately acquitted, the public never accepted his story that a ransacked hotel room and battered corpse were the unfortunate result of exuberant but consensual sex. Corpulent, cheeky Arbuckle was the perfect metaphor for the sinful appetites of the country's new elite, the movie community. Then in February 1922, while Burroughs was still at work on his manuscript, prominent director William Desmond Taylor was found murdered; subsequent investigation, again played out in detail in the papers, uncovered a lover's triangle (or possibly even quadrangle), a secret identity, a collection of pornography, and a narcotics ring. A year later, matinee idol Wallace Reid, whom Burroughs had met when Reid filmed a movie near Tarzana in 1919, would die in a sanitarium after a long addiction to drugs and alcohol.

Burroughs never intended *The Girl from Hollywood* as a roman à clef, though there was no mistaking certain connections. Rancho del Ganado is Tarzana to the last detail; the descriptions of roads, trails, topography, and architecture verge on the encyclopedic—and thus have great historical value for anyone trying to picture the original Tarzana before it became suburbia. Just as explicitly, Colonel Pennington embodies Burroughs's habits and ideals, with a little Harrison Gray Otis thrown in, and to a certain extent, the Pennington children are a reflection of Burroughs's worry that his own daughter would be mesmerized by Hollywood and that his sons would grow bored with Tarzana.

He finished *The Girl from Hollywood,* more than 100,000 words, in less than two months. Doubtless he was at first excited to be describing the world he knew best. But as the narrative progressed, his healthy enthusiasm was replaced by dyspeptic impatience, and by the end, judging from the clattering pace of the final chapters, he seemed anxious to have the novel over and done with—as if he knew it had gotten away from him, which plainly it had. Despite Burroughs's professed aim to write a story about "a family whose life exemplified, possibly in a slightly idealized form, that of thousand upon thousands of American families," *The Girl from Hollywood* devolves into broad melodrama, more gruesome than wholesome, more voyeuristic than enlightening. Characters are most compelling when they are drugged or drunk or when rape or death are imminent; the rest of the time they are merely cutouts blotting the landscape of Rancho del Ganado. In its topicality, *The Girl from Hollywood* bears a certain likeness to *The Beautiful and Damned,* F. Scott Fitzgerald's novel of that same year about a disinherited blue blood reduced to writing "wretched and pitiable" stories for the "well-known" monthlies. But stylistically, *Girl* lacks Fitzgerald's offhanded poignancy, and despite the Jazz Age themes of the novel, it is absent the nimble irony of the postwar era.

Indeed, Burroughs was metabolically and psychologically still incapable of narrative subtlety, modern or otherwise. A short attention span was the accepted meter of his life. Speed guaranteed productivity, but hasty writing also begot mediocrity, and haste provided a built-in excuse for mediocrity, as well. And so in the midst of crafting his "American novel," Burroughs essentially bolted, either from lack of confidence or lack of concentration, and *The Girl from Hollywood* came to resemble not so much Fitzgerald as cliché-fraught *Love Story Magazine,* the country's first romance pulp, which had debuted several months earlier.

Sensing the novel's shortcomings, Burroughs decided against offering it to *Cosmopolitan,* as he had initially intended, and instead submitted it to Bob Davis, who had recently returned to the Munsey organization. In a sarcastic, sour-grapes letter to his old friend, he asserted that there was nothing about the slicks he admired anyway, except of course for the money they paid. "I tried to [read a few slicks] this month but in the first story I tackled[,] a woman sixty years old was in love with a young man, and in the next story two married men were engaged in a drunken jazz party with two shop girls. . . . I am afraid I am not sufficiently highbrow." As shrewd as he was chivalrous, Bob Davis offered thirty-five hundred dollars for the wounded story and slated it for *Munsey's,* which, though not quite as sophisticated as rival *Cosmopolitan,* was a cut above *Argosy All-Story* and was read mostly by women. Burroughs accepted gratefully and with an almost audible sigh of relief. He had hoped for more money, but *Munsey's* was a better placement than he had come to expect. When Davis declared that *The Penningtons* was too staid a title for this sort of tale, he gave in and volunteered *The Dope Fiend, The Snow*

Slave, The Wages of Sin, and *The Girl from Hollywood.* After only slight changes to the manuscript, Davis scheduled it for June publication and turned to a more important matter. Specifically he wanted to know how soon Burroughs could write another Tarzan.

After *The Girl from Hollywood,* there was no point in running from the jungle. Burroughs assented to Davis's request, though his heart was not in it. Compared with *Tarzan the Terrible,* written two years earlier, *Tarzan and the Golden Lion,* as the next novel was titled, seems almost perfunctory, mechanical. Actually, it was not *written* (or typewritten) at all, but dictated into an Ediphone.

The story has several clever touches, but not enough to make a satisfying whole. After the world war and after the long and arduous rescue of Jane in Pal-ul-don, Tarzan realizes that the expense of repairing his estate has put a dent in his finances. His solution is to make yet another trip to Opar, the land of lost Atlanteans whose gold he had appropriated in *The Return of Tarzan* and *Tarzan and the Jewels of Opar.* Treachery and palace intrigue force Tarzan and Opar's Queen La, who still has a crush on the ape-man, to flee through the mountains to the land of the Bolganis, a fierce and furry invocation of the myth that in precolonial Africa blacks and gorillas had often interbred. Less objectionable and more engaging are the characters of Esteban Miranda, an actor who impersonates Tarzan in order to steal the Oparian gold, and Jad-bal-ja, the golden lion Tarzan trains as a hunting and fighting companion. Both, it seems, were inspired by the Weiss brothers' newly completed film, *The Adventures of Tarzan.*

By the terms of the original contract the Weisses had bought from Pliny Craft, the filmmakers had the right to produce a second movie from *The Return of Tarzan.* Their first film from the book, *Revenge of Tarzan,* had not lived up to expectations, but envying the enormous success of National's serialization of *The Son of Tarzan,* the Weisses decided to produce a serial of their own. This time they brought back Elmo Lincoln, whom they billed as "the Tarzan of Tarzans." Since starring in *Tarzan of the Apes* and *The Romance of Tarzan* in 1918, Lincoln had parlayed his celebrity into two serials, *Elmo the Mighty* and *Elmo the Fearless,* and was now an established box office draw. Burroughs had never liked him as Tarzan and was disappointed that he had been given the role once again. Watching Lincoln on the set did not improve his opinion. In a letter to his brother Harry, he complained that "Elmo Lin-

coln is a big, overgrown boy . . . [and] in many respects, a physical coward, requiring the use of a double or a dummy in practically every dangerous situation." (The stunt man was Frank Merrill, who would get his
own chance to play Tarzan in the late 1920s.) Accordingly, when Burroughs sat down to write *Tarzan and the Golden Lion,* he used Esteban
Miranda to tweak Elmo Lincoln indirectly: "Of jungle craft [Esteban]
had none, and personal combats with the more savage jungle beasts caution prompted him to eschew."

The one real strength of *The Adventures of Tarzan* is the lions. Burroughs had been fascinated by lions and lion trainers ever since first visiting the Selig movie zoo in 1916. After moving to California, he had
become good friends with two of Hollywood's best trainers, Walter
Beckwith and Charlie Gay, and his own lack of patience for training lion
cubs only reinforced his high opinion of those who made it their profession. The lion stunts in *Adventures* are spectacular and some of the best
to appear on film thus far. Lions jump through windows, onto branches,
and at one point Tarzan (presumably not Lincoln) lassoes one and hoists
it into a tree. The fights between Tarzan and a succession of lions—in one
instance, two at a time—are stunning in their ferocity and realism. During the filming of the fifteen episodes, several crew members barely
escaped serious injury by excited lions departing from the scenario. Burroughs was so impressed by the action in *Adventures* that he wrote a
short article for the movie magazine *Screenland,* which appeared the following summer. "[T]he fact remains that a lion is always a lion—a savage,
flesh-eating beast of prey," he explains appreciatively. "However, the
results obtained with some of them are little short of marvelous, more
especially those animals that have been trained by humane masters who
have felt and demonstrated an actual affection for their charges."

Naturally Tarzan makes the best lion trainer of all, and in *Tarzan
and the Golden Lion,* he teaches Jad-bal-ja obedience without sapping
the animal's wildness. Man and beast make a perfect team, and Jad-bal-ja
deservedly earns a permanent place in the menagerie of Burroughs characters, as conspicuous in the printed stories as Cheetah the chimpanzee
would soon become in the movies. Unfortunately, Jad-bal-ja's debut in
Tarzan and the Golden Lion does not do for the novel what the Hollywood lions had done for *The Adventures of Tarzan.* The serial was a
smashing success in 1922; the novel, which Burroughs submitted in May,
was, in his own estimation, "rotten."

If Bob Davis concurred with this low opinion of *Golden Lion,* he did not say so. A month earlier, he and Burroughs had struck an agreement whereby Munsey would have the right of first refusal to all of Burroughs's output for the next two years, including 180,000 words of Tarzan; the rate was five cents a word. *Golden Lion* was the first story under the new contract, and Davis was confident that it would sell magazines, regardless of its quality. Publicly he declared it "a new and magnificent masterpiece."

Burroughs received no such praise from Joe Bray, to whom he had just sent *The Girl from Hollywood.* Bray rejected it, explaining that while he had enjoyed the novel personally, he was certain that publishing it would damage Burroughs's reputation. "[Y]our readers expect lively stories of adventure from you," Bray advised. "I do not think you are fitted to write stories in which very little happens. . . . You are too much of a he-man for that sort of thing."

Burroughs was more demoralized than angry. McClurg & Company was by far his steadiest source of income, and Bray had been generous and timely with advances. But to be told that his publisher wanted only the same old Tarzan and Mars stories—and that he was not worthy of writing anything else—was a bitter pill to swallow. "I am simply written out on Tarzan," he told Bray, "and it would seem to me that it would be better for me to write mediocre stories in another vein than to attempt to put poor Tarzan stories on the market."

To which Bray responded: "I do know that a man, if he wants to get anywhere, should find out first the things that he can do best and then work hard along that line."

Criticism was forthcoming from other directions, as well. In December 1921, the *Iowa Library Quarterly* published an essay, "Stepping Stones to Correct Taste," which originally had been presented as a speech to the state's annual convention of librarians. "Helping pupils to distinguish a good book from a poor book is an important service," lectured A. B. Noble, professor of English at Iowa State College. "If pupils are interested in trash, how can we lead them to appreciate something better?" Professor Noble defined trash as "imagination without truth" and singled out *Tarzan of the Apes* as a glaring example of "mere bosh." Borrowing brimstone from a Prohibitionist sermon, he warned that "books of the Tarzan type are simply literary dramshops, intoxicating their readers while they linger there, and weakening their power to reflect and to reason. . . . Let no one consider that books like 'Tarzan' are harmless. If [a reader] loves 'Tarzan' and dreams of 'Tarzan,' his fate is sealed."

Always quick to disparage his stories himself, Burroughs claimed not to mind when others piled on. "I would rather have them roast me than ignore me," he once remarked to his British agent Curtis Brown. Even so, he rarely allowed a negative review to go unchallenged. In a letter to the editor of the *Wisconsin Library Bulletin,* in which the Noble article was reprinted the following March, he accused the professor—and nearly every other critic of his work—of missing the point. "My royalty reports indicate that many millions . . . have been entertained by Tarzan," he elaborated, "and though I receive letters from readers in all parts of the world, I have yet to learn of any greater harm resulting from the reading of Tarzan than an injury sustained by an English boy who fell out of a tree while attempting to emulate him." The trouble with Professor Noble, Burroughs suggested, was that he had been "attempting to treat seriously something that was never intended to be serious."

It was a gracious letter, especially considering the damning tone of the Noble essay, but on the advice of Joe Bray, Burroughs decided not to send it. This was no time to stir up the hounds of reform and censorship, not when Bray was reporting a recent downturn in book sales.

Bray could not explain exactly why the slump was occurring, which made Burroughs all the more uneasy. At the beginning of 1922, he had told his publisher that he was so far behind on his bills that he was "hanging . . . by the skin of my teeth." By summer, he was no better off. "It looks very doubtful now whether I will be able to pull through until the next royalty payment," he informed Bray on July 11, "and my mind is so much obsessed with financial worries that it is hard for me to concentrate upon writing." Bray urged his anxious author not to panic. "You have no fear going to the poorhouse or anything of that sort," he assured. "I am aware you have been living at a very expensive rate recently and you will probably have to cut down some. In fact," he counseled, perhaps having just glanced at the latest sales reports, "if I were you, I would start in right away."

Actually, Burroughs already had. Despite his observation in *The Girl from Hollywood* that "[t]here isn't a rancher or orchardist . . . in the valley who couldn't make more money year in and year out if he'd keep a few brood sows," in March 1922, three months after expressing such great confidence in his husbandry, he decided to sell his entire herd of hogs and to lease most of his irrigated fields.

And at the end of the summer he took an even more momentous step. In the three years since he had purchased Tarzana from General Otis, quite a few of the neighboring ranches had been subdivided. Most recently, a developer named Charles L. Daniels had purchased 320 acres directly to the north of Tarzana, just across Ventura Boulevard, the old valley highway, and had begun selling one-acre poultry and truck farms. Following Daniels's lead, Burroughs decided to carve off the hundred acres of his ranch closest to Ventura Boulevard and "start a town called Tarzana." Custer Pennington had worried that if Rancho del Ganado "were wiped off the face of the earth tomorrow," his father would "never be happy again." Yet when it came time to cannibalize his own dream, Burroughs was remarkably phlegmatic. He consoled himself with the fact that he was selling off only a fraction of Tarzana; in his mind, he pictured an "artists' colony."

By mid-October, the business lots along Ventura Boulevard were selling briskly but the residential property remained torpid. Clearly the artist colony pitch was not doing the trick. "I did not mean it in the way people seemed to choose to interpret it," he explained to friend Bert Weston. "I wanted decent people in here, not a bunch of roughnecks, [but] the majority of people are just about as crazy to live with a bunch of authors and artists as I should be." Taking a less snobby tack, he invited P. Dempsey Tabler to a special Sunday reception for prospective buyers. "Tarzan of the Apes to Sell Lots in Tarzana" trumpeted a press release to the *Los Angeles Examiner.*

But the Tarzan promotion didn't work much better. Come November, the residential lots were still not selling, and another get-rich scheme—drilling for oil on the ranch—had come to naught as well. "I can make money in but one way, and that is writing stories," he lamented to his brother Harry. "Everything else that I attempt flivs."

The two final stories he wrote in 1922 were clearly written by a man with too much on his mind. "The Moon Maid," dictated into the Ediphone over a period of a month, is a companion to "Under the Red Flag," relating the adventures of Julian 5th, Julian 9th's great-great-grandfather, on the moon during the late twentieth century. This time around, the bad guys are Thinkers, quasi-intellectual liberals who are slow to work but quick to criticize democracy and capitalism. Burroughs was no more pleased with the result than he had been with *Golden Lion.* Somehow, though, "The Moon Maid" passed the muster of Bob Davis—which was not the case with his next story, "Beware!," about an exiled European prince, Macklin Donovan, who, ignorant of his true identity, grows up to become an agent for the United States Secret Service. Taking to heart the recent criticism that a story so "un-Burroughs" would hurt his name, he submitted "Beware!" under the byline "John Tyler McCulloch." Bob Davis declared it "the closest thing to mediocrity" that Burroughs had ever written and refused to publish it no matter who the author was. "Beware!" fared no better at *Blue Book* and two of the lesser pulps, *Detective Tales* and *Weird Tales.* (In typically stubborn fashion, he never let it die and finally sold it to *Fantastic Adventures* in 1939 for two hundred and forty-five dollars.)

By the end of 1922, the string of disappointments and the pressure of trying to sell Tarzana had begun to affect Burroughs physically. His neuritis had flared up again, the first time in years, and to help relieve his stress and discomfort, he increased his drinking in open defiance of the Volstead Act. "History narrates that under the regime of prohibition drunkenness was common," he wrote in the futuristic "Moon Maid," though in respect to his own conduct, he apparently didn't see any cause for concern. "'A Pennington never drinks more than a gentleman should,'" the Colonel tells his wife in *The Girl from Hollywood.* "'[My] father and . . . grandsires, on both sides, always drank, but there has never been a drunkard in either family.'" Surrounded by fruit trees and removed from public scrutiny, Tarzana was a good place to make beer and brandy, and before the laws had changed, Burroughs had also stock-piled a reserve of commercially distilled spirits. He took pride in both the quantity and quality of his private inventory and laughed dismissively when his son Hully, just turning thirteen, tried to get him to comply with Prohibition. "It makes a good combination," Burroughs wrote to Bert Weston, "for Hulbert can do the temperance act and I can do the drinking for the family."

He was not drinking alone, however. Emma enjoyed liquor at least as much as he. And though there is no direct anecdotal evidence that she had begun her slide into alcoholism by then, in light of her tragic future, the sentiments expressed by Colonel Pennington and young Hully are perhaps revelatory. In boasting of the Colonel's inherited ability to hold his liquor, was Burroughs distancing himself from Emma, whose blood was not as sturdy? In backing universal temperance, was Hully in fact trying to sound an alarm in his own home?

BY THE beginning of 1923, Burroughs was scrambling, which was what he did best. With very little going according to plan in his career and at Tarzana, he threw himself into a dozen things at once. In a well-publicized auction on January 15, he sold off most of his farm equipment and livestock, including dairy cattle, several saddle horses, and his beloved Berkshire swine, which he had not been able to unload the previous year. Immediately after the auction, he redoubled his effort to rent the ranch as a movie location; a printed circular sent to all the major studios announced, "Your own sets may be erected, while Koonskin Kabin, an artistic log cabin, constitutes a permanent 'set.'" Rates were fifteen dollars a day, seventy-five dollars a week, and, he noted, "We also control the location rights to some 3000 acres adjoining Tarzana." A number of studios expressed immediate interest, and over the next few years, at least half a dozen pictures were shot at the ranch, although Burroughs was disappointed when Goldwyn decided to shoot *Ben-Hur* elsewhere.

In February, he made a quick trip to New York to testify in a lawsuit Pliny Craft had filed four years earlier which had at long last been put on the docket. The whole affair turned out to be little more than a costly distraction—the judge threw the case out before it ever got to a jury—and Burroughs was home within a week. But while in New York, he had found the time to meet with the Howells Sales Company, which now controlled the rights to *The Son of Tarzan*. Both Howells and Burroughs were interested in squeezing more income out of the already proven serial, and at their meeting, Burroughs volunteered to cut the fifteen episodes down into a feature. Upon his return to Tarzana, he shut himself up in the ranch theater and, with no previous experience, set to snipping and gluing. Four weeks later, he had edited the serial down to seven reels, rewritten the titles, and delivered the finished product to Howells—who, much to everyone's surprise, pronounced it "a very good job." Burroughs had never done more than run his own projector before.

His next move, though just as unprecedented, was in a way far more predictable. On March 26, he formed Edgar Rice Burroughs, Incorporated. He had always approached writing as a business, as evidenced by his negotiation of secondary rights and use of the latest office technology. And for years he had entertained the idea of banding together a group of writers for mutual protection and profit. Modifying this long-gestating concept, he issued stock to himself, Emma, and the children and became an employee of his own company.

He was not, as some have claimed, the first to think of such an arrangement, but he was surely in the vanguard and one of the authors for whom incorporation made the most sense. For one thing, it lowered his personal income taxes, which in recent years had taken a sizable bite out of his six-figure earnings. For another, the formation of Edgar Rice Burroughs, Inc., more properly defined his professional evolution since arriving in California. He was not just another by-the-word author; he now oversaw syndication, ranching, real estate, and he was still ambitious to make his own movies. More grimly, incorporation also codified his status as slave to his own assembly line. He had been treating his stories as products for some time. As a company man, he would come to treat them with even greater dispassion.

Business, though, was not what it once had been. In January, Burroughs had been obliged to sell the book rights to *The Girl from Hollywood* to the Macaulay Company of New York for a five hundred dollar advance, much less than McClurg usually paid. Chillier still was Joe Bray's news that the popular editions of many of Burroughs's titles, including the normally robust Tarzans, had fallen off by a third or worse. *Tarzan and the Golden Lion*, McClurg's latest release, would likely be the poorest performer ever. As a result, Burroughs's royalty check for the first three months of 1923 was twelve thousand dollars, roughly half of what it had been the previous year. "I have been expecting it for a long time," he admitted when he received the bad news from Bray. "Well, I had a damn good run for my money, established a few precedents, got into fifteen or sixteen languages and made a lot of good friends," he exaggerated morbidly. "If I never do anything more I'll have lots to remember between checker games in the poor-house."

Because of the slump, he was even less enthusiastic than usual about writing another Mars or Tarzan story and jumped at the chance for postponement. The previous fall, his British publisher, Methuen & Company, had urged him to try his hand at a western, a genre popular since the days of the dime novels and reinvigorated by the proliferation of cowboy movies starring actors such as William S. Hart and Tom Mix. Burroughs had tucked Methuen's suggestion away, and in March, when he took up writing again, there was no question where he would begin. "I have never written a wild west story," he had told his British agent, "although I think I could do it, since I have spent a great deal of time in the West, punching cows and mining in Idaho and Oregon, and serving in the Seventh Cavalry many years ago."

Firsthand experience, which had never mattered to Burroughs before, was the one advantage he had in breaking into the already crowded western market, for the writers who ruled that range had no dust on their boots to speak of. Owen Wister, author of one of his all-time favorite novels, *The Virginian,* was at heart a Philadelphia fop; Zane Grey, Burroughs's closest rival for sales between the world wars, had been a dentist in Ohio; Frederick Faust, who wrote prolifically under the name Max Brand, was a Berkeley bohemian; and Clarence Mulford, creator of the Hopalong Cassidy series, lived in Brooklyn. Burroughs was quite familiar with the work of all of these men and in fact shared the same publisher and editor with some of them: Bob Davis had edited Zane Grey (though he had rejected *Riders of the Purple Sage*) and had virtually discovered Max Brand; Joe Bray had published both Grey and Clarence Mulford.

The idea of competing with them head-on, in their own genre, struck Burroughs as a welcome and not so formidable challenge. In a way, he had been writing westerns for years. *A Princess of Mars* actually begins as a western, and John Carter is essentially Wister's Virginian transported to another planet. Tarzan, too, is an equatorial equivalent of the lone rider—blue-blooded, red-blooded, and cold-blooded when he has to be.

Burroughs endeavored nothing terribly daring in his first western novel, choosing to stay within the bounds of cowboy convention in order to please Methuen & Company and its British audience. Bull, the hero of *The Bandit of Hell's Bend,* bears more than a passing resemblance to Hopalong Cassidy—the rugged, hard-drinking pulp Hoppy, not the debonair screen version played by William Boyd. Bull is the foreman of the Bar Y, a ranch owned by well-bred Elias Henders and his daughter, Diana. Once again, the plot twists around a case of mistaken identities: Bull is accused of being the outlaw, while the true outlaws—who are not only robbing the stage, but also conspiring to take the ranch and its gold away from the Henderses—hide behind a mask of effete propriety. Bull eventually exposes them as craven crooks and wins Diana, who blurts, "I don't care, Bull, what you are. All I care or know is that you are my man"—an ending Burroughs uses in at least half a dozen other stories.

"I have made no effort to write a historical novel, but just to spin a yarn which I hope will prove entertaining," Burroughs explained to Curtis Brown upon completing *Hell's Bend.* Clearly, though, he had mined his own personal history. The name Bar Y is borrowed from the Idaho ranch run by his brothers and their Yale classmate. And while the Bar Y of *Hell's Bend* is in Arizona, an equally familiar locale, many of the characters there are modeled on real people Burroughs knew when he was cowboying for his brothers and Lew Sweetser. Two poems, "The Passin' of My Pal, Bill" and "The Bad Hombre," verses of which are interspersed throughout the text, are yarns within a yarn, recollections of Burroughs's favorite Idaho stories.

Methuen & Company agreed to publish *The Bandit of Hell's Bend* but preferred to wait until it had appeared in an American magazine and as an American book, a feat that was more difficult than Burroughs had originally anticipated. When the idea of a western had first come up, he had run it by Davis for a second opinion and received unqualified support. "You seem to be pretty well equipped to handle rough men, wild animals, and coarse country," Davis responded cheerfully. "I would print a western story from you in a minute. Let 'er go." When the story came in, however, he could not hide his disappointment. Cowboy yarns, unlike Tarzan yarns, were easy to come by—every month a new magazine seemed to be popping up with names such as *Ranch Romances* or *Western Story*—and Davis had expected something beyond the tried and true from Burroughs. "You have . . . drawn little on your imaginative powers," he scolded gently. "I can't understand how a bean as active as yours could refrain from butting in and slamming a few novelties into the good old powder-burned frontier." He did not come right out and say that he never wanted Burroughs to write another story like *The Bandit of Hell's Bend,* but he got his message across just the same. "Don't blame me if the million people who love and revere you start to howl," he needled. "There comes a time in the life of an author when he can do anything he wants and get away with it. That time has come in your life. What do you think of yourself?"

In response, Burroughs acknowledged that *Hell's Bend* would never be a classic, but begged for better treatment: "Say something nice to me sometime, Bob—I need encouragement." Davis finally accepted *Hell's*

Bend for *Argosy All-Story,* but from then on he felt free to offer his own story ideas. For starters, he tendered, how about Tarzan versus an army of pygmies?

That Bob Davis was now inventing his own Tarzan plots was a fair indication of how Burroughs felt about having to think them up himself. Before Davis had suggested the pygmies, Burroughs had briefly considered sending Tarzan to Abyssinia "where there is a real emperor surrounded by real warriors, with a system of religious rites already established." But after reading a couple of books on the region, he had lost interest, which was fine by Davis. "I am glad you have gone cold on Abyssinia," the editor wrote at the end of April 1923. "From what I can gather, it is a low-down section of Africa, on the east coast, flooded with Ethiopians and saturated with dice-chuckers."

Davis then spelled out his own idea at great length. There was no question that he had in mind a remake of *Gulliver's Travels,* but his version of the Lilliputians would have sent Swift into a swivet. Davis saw the pygmies as a "self-governing, battle-scarred bunch of little fellows, who, like the black bass, are game to the core. . . ." Having read and edited thousands of pulp stories over the years, he felt free to let his imagination gallop: "The thing that fortifies them against destruction is a manufactured odor which they have discovered and perfected. If a man loses his stench, so to speak, it is like any other person losing a cartridge belt of ammunition. . . . I suppose your golden lion will come into this story. Why not have the golden lion serve as a mount for the brigadier-general of the pigmy army[?]" He wasn't through: "In order to give full play to your well-known affection for throw-backs among the species, you might have one branch of them albino." Finally Davis urged Burroughs to introduce some women warriors and twist the plot in such a way to take "a cynical belt at feminism": "Turn the women into archers because of their accuracy and indifference to pain."

Burroughs did his best to please his editor, but it wasn't easy. Throughout the summer and fall, he worked on *Tarzan and the Ant Men* in spurts of ambivalence, interrupted by stints as a real estate salesman. "I could write faster if I enjoyed it more," he explained to Davis. Still, he promised he would not turn in a lousy story.

The manuscript he sent off in November was both good and bad. Tarzan, who has just learned to fly an airplane, crashes in an unexplored region of Africa known as the Great Thorn Forest. In the ensuing tale, as in so many others, Burroughs is at his best at the beginning, plunging into a new world as if he himself is the one penetrating the thicket and discovering the next mysterious land. But once the stage is set, the actors costumed, and the curtain raised, his authorial excitement diminishes, and the drama settles into a churning sort of action, recycled and predictable. Capture, escape, capture again, rebellion, freedom—perhaps it is a formula no more shopworn than the plot of *The Odyssey*, but by 1923 Burroughs, by his own accounting, had "said all there is to say about Tarzan seven or eight times." (He would have shuddered then to know that he would do it at least a dozen times more.) "Don't get the idea that you're through with a basic plot when you've written one story from it," Burroughs advised beginning authors in *The Writer's Monthly* several years later. "Keep it and sprout another—or three or four. It's easy!" However, he did not bother to tell the would-be writers just how stale he felt his plots had become.

Despite the off-the-rack sameness of the basic narrative, *Tarzan and the Ant Men* does have some unforgettable characters. The first strangers that Tarzan encounters in the Thorn Forest are the Alali, a primitive, speechless race whose women, enormous and cruel, are sexually dominant and whose men, timid and dull, are sexual prey to be hunted down with slings and clubs. (The Alali are similar to the "Alus" that Bowen Tyler encounters in *The Land That Time Forgot*; both, in turn, are a fanciful interpretation of *Pithecanthropus alalus*—"speechless ape-man"— which was the name given to a missing link that had been hypothesized, but never actually discovered, by German biologist Ernst Haeckel shortly after Darwin had published *The Descent of Man*.) Tarzan teaches the Alali men to fight back. At first they do so merely in self-defense, but then, with confidence bolstered, they learn that they can force women to do their bidding. In a scene which Burroughs undoubtedly intended to be comical, an Alali man seizes a woman by the hair and disarms her. "'Why do you not kill her?'" his comrade asks in the sign language of their people. "'I am going to keep her,'" the first man replies. "'I do not like to cook. She shall cook for me.'" After striking her with his spear and kicking her, she crawls to him and embraces his legs in a gesture of "doglike adulation and devotion." "'You will cook for me!'" he demands again. "'Forever!'" she signals obediently.

The Alali are soon upstaged by the ant men—the Minunians. Tarzan first observes them as they fight to free one of their comrades from the

Mary Evaline Burroughs and Major George Tyler Burroughs,
Edgar Rice Burroughs's parents.

Burroughs *(left)* with two of his classmates at the Michigan Military Academy in
Orchard Lake, Michigan. After a rocky start at the school, Burroughs learned to
appreciate the disciplined life. "I love everything military," he announced.

In May 1896, Burroughs *(second from left)* enlisted in the army and was assigned to the Seventh Cavalry at Fort Grant, Arizona Territory. It was, Burroughs was assured by his recruiting officer, "absolutely the worst assignment in the United States Army."

On January 31, 1900, Burroughs married Emma Centennia Hulbert, his childhood sweetheart, whose father managed several Chicago hotels.

Emma, Burroughs, Jack, Hully, and Joan "auto-gypsying" in California.

Burroughs around 1912,
the year he wrote his first
Tarzan story.

The cover of *The All-Story* featuring the first Tarzan story.

The first film Tarzan was Elmo Lincoln, who appeared in the 1918 version of *Tarzan of the Apes*. Physically, Lincoln was everything Burroughs had wished Tarzan *not* be.

Burroughs at Tarzana, circa 1919.

In March 1919, Burroughs bought the 550-acre San Fernando ranch of Harrison Gray Otis, the recently deceased publisher and owner of the *Los Angeles Times*. Burroughs named it Tarzana.

In 1920, Gene Pollar, a New York fireman who had never acted before, was hired to star in *The Revenge of Tarzan*.

Burroughs next to his Tarzana pool. He believed in the benefits of exercise and passed on his athletic enthusiasm to his children.

Because of the mounting costs of running the Tarzana ranch, Burroughs eventually turned the land and house into the El Caballaro Country Club, while he and his family moved into a bungalow in a subdivision he developed on some of the Tarzana land.

The Burroughs family. From left: Burroughs, Jack, Emma, Joan, and Hully.

Jim Pierce, who became Edgar Rice Burroughs's son-in-law, as Lord Greystoke and Tarzan in the movie *Tarzan and the Golden Lion*.

The redoubtable Ralph Rothmund, who began work as a secretary in 1927 at Edgar Rice Burroughs, Inc., but oversaw the day-to-day workings of both the company and the entire Burroughs family.

Frank Merrill, a former world-class gymnast, starred in *Tarzan the Mighty*, a fifteen-chapter silent serial loosely based on *The Jungle Tales of Tarzan*.

To millions of moviegoers, Johnny Weissmuller and Maureen O'Sullivan defined the characters of Tarzan and Jane. They appeared together first in *Tarzan the Ape Man*, which became one of the more popular films of 1932. The role of Tarzan turned out to be a natural for Weissmuller: though he speaks very little in the movie, he manages to convey a wide range of emotions.

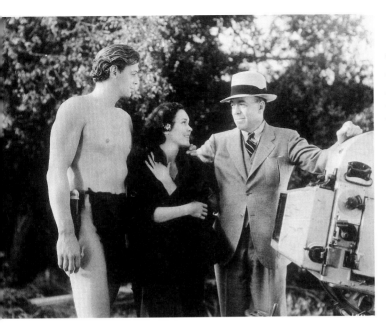

Weissmuller,
O'Sullivan,
and Burroughs
on
the set.

The two "Johnnies":
Weissmuller and
Johnny Sheffield in
Tarzan Finds a Son.

Ashton Dearholt was having an affair with co-star Ula Holt during the filming of *The New Adventures of Tarzan.*

Emma Burroughs, near the end of her life. As she aged, she fought a losing battle with alcoholism, and she and Burroughs drifted apart. Burroughs eventually became involved with Florence Dearholt, a friend of his daughter's, and moved out of the Burroughs house in 1934.

Burroughs with Florence Dearholt and her children, Caryl Lee and Lee. The public announcement of their marriage came in Walter Winchell's gossip column.

As Tarzan, Buster Crabbe never enjoyed the success in the role that Weissmuller did.

Burroughs learned to fly, shortly before his separation from Emma.

Glenn Morris, the 1936 Olympic decathlon gold medalist, was perhaps the worst Tarzan of all. In *Tarzan's Revenge,* he speaks a total of four words and is out-acted by Eleanor Holm, herself a gold medalist in the backstroke.

The Tarzan character was a natural for publicity stunts, such as Herman Brix playing golf in Tarzana to promote *The New Adventures of Tarzan.*

During World War II, Hully served as an aerial photographer in the Pacific while Burroughs wrote a short-lived column for the *Honolulu Advertiser* called "Laugh It Off," served in a civilian guard, and eventually became the oldest war correspondent to serve in the Pacific.

Burroughs at his desk at ERB, Inc. He had the foresight to incorporate himself, and today his descendants continue to oversee a very robust franchise of books, movies, and merchandise.

clutches of an Alalus. Mounted on tiny antelope, they bound in and out of harm's way with an agility and daring superior to that of the best cavalryman. "It was a pretty sight and an inspiring one, and however unreal it had first appeared to [Tarzan] he was not long in realizing that he was looking upon a race of real pygmies—not members of the black tribe with which all African explorers are more or less familiar, but with that lost white race of diminutive men reference to which is occasionally to be found in ancient manuscript." To Tarzan's discerning eye, the eighteen-inch-tall ant men were "the perfect warriors, the perfect heroes."

Tarzan befriends the Minunians and is welcomed in their city of anthill-like domes, multistoried mazes, each large enough to house fifty thousand Minunians but none of a scale to admit a human of Tarzan's proportions. Inevitably, Tarzan is captured—swarmed, like Gulliver—in a battle with a rival city and, by means of a secret potion, reduced to Minunian size.

At this point, the story becomes quite conventional, at least by Tarzan standards. Tarzan leads his fellow Minunian slaves in an uprising (in a Burroughs story, slavery is typically on the Roman, rather than Old South, model), and after a predictably perilous flight through the labyrinth of the ant dome, he escapes with his brave accomplice Komod-oflorensal and the Minunian's sweetheart, Talaskar. The shrinking potion wears off just after Tarzan has scrambled through the outer barrier of the Thorn Forest, en route to the Greystoke estate.

Bob Davis loved the story. The ant men were just what he had hoped for—not too leprechaunlike—and the gender wars of the Alali far exceeded his misogynistic wishes. Burroughs had ignored Davis's suggestion to include the golden lion and had wrinkled the plot by inserting Tarzan's old impostor, Esteban Miranda, into a sequence of non-Minunian scenes. But for the most part, he had followed orders with flair and exceeded even his own jaded expectations. "Sometimes I don't think you are aware of how great you are," Davis congratulated in a letter that accompanied a check for three thousand seven hundred and fifty dollars. "You love to pour yourself into these stories. Don't ever think of stopping."

It had been a while since Burroughs had received such high praise from anyone, though he must have winced when Davis requested an encore. Earlier that fall, Burroughs had vowed to Joe Bray that *Tarzan and the Ant Men* would be "absolutely the finish. . . . I feel now that I would just as soon spend the rest of my days on the back steps of the poor house as write another Tarzan story, as much as I admire the old boy, and as grateful as I am to him." He had made the same pledge—and sentenced himself to the poor house—a dozen times by now, but with each threat he seemed much closer to meaning it. The only thing that kept him coming back, he said, was the money. When asked to write a few words on "Why I Wrote 'Tarzan and the Ant Men,'" he dared his publisher to print the truth: "I might tell you that I was prompted by an artistic urge that would not be denied expression, or that clamoring readers from . . . Patagonia . . . to Oshkosh insisted upon another classical interpretation of jungle life, but the truth of the matter is that [my daughter] Joan is sixteen and loves to dance, which is an expensive pastime with shoes at eighteen dollars a pair, and that Hulbert blossomed forth in long trousers . . . the same year, while the demands of Jack for rifle ammunition, marbles and kite string threatened to exceed the supply. It must be wonderful to be able to devote one's life to art for art's sake, a luxury which I have never been able to afford."

While contemplating his status as both creator and captive of Tarzan, Burroughs was pleasantly surprised to hear from the publisher of *The Girl from Hollywood* that the book was selling well. The Macaulay Company had chosen a suggestive illustration of a young woman disrobing before a movie camera on the dust jacket and a sketch of an opium pipe on the front cover—imagery that appealed to the scandal-hungry readers of the romance pulps but made Burroughs blush. "The story is intended to be clean, while [the] advertising suggests that it is rotten," he complained to agent Curtis Brown. "I hate nasty stories, and I did not intend 'The Girl from Hollywood' to be such" (though that in fact was how it had turned out). Still, he could not knock success, and it surely took the sting out of the reviews, which were some of the nastiest of his career. "The curse of Hollywood," chided the *Chicago Daily News*, "is too dangerous to be played with by men of small talents."

Ever since the *Iowa Library Quarterly/Wisconsin Library Bulletin* attack the previous year, he had become more aggressive, and more thin-skinned, toward his highbrow detractors. He had not mailed his rejoinder to the librarians, but several weeks later he was invited by the book editor of the *Los Angeles Times* to submit an essay of his choosing. "Sometimes reviewers waste whole columns [explaining that my books] are not classical literature. This is misspent energy," he advised. "The only standard by which I judge the fiction that I enjoy is whether it has the punch to hold my interest and is able to deliver the k.o. for dull care and worry." In a letter to old Chicago chum Charles Miller, written at about the same time as the *Times* article, he again tried to shrug off his misguided critics by belittling his own achievement: "It seems to me that . . . the purpose of the work being reviewed should be thoroughly understood by the reviewer, in which case fiction might fall under several heads, among which would be historical novels, novels . . . which deal with questions of vital economic, social or political situations . . . , novels written merely to entertain, and so on. . . . To attempt to measure my stories, for instance, which fall in the last class, with the same rule that one would use against *really great novels* [emphasis added] . . . is not only unfair, but ridiculous."

Modesty continued to be one of Burroughs's most admirable qualities, but like his handling of *The Girl from Hollywood*, the assertion that he did not belong in a category with the "really great" novelists had a distinctly defeatist undertone. By demanding dispensation as a pulp writer, he resigned himself once again to the fact that he would probably never be more than that. If he couldn't be Colonel Pennington, he would be Bull, the rugged ranch foreman. Diversion (and remuneration) had always been goals; now they were his only goals. He tried tirelessly to dignify them, though of course the person he most wanted to convince was himself.

AFTER completing *Tarzan and the Ant Men* in November 1923, he did not begin another story for nearly five months. He spent the rest of the fall and winter almost exclusively on the development of Tarzana. Having had so little luck selling the residential lots on his own, he made a deal with a veteran broker, H. B. Currier, to handle the razzle-dazzle that the real estate business now demanded. More than a million people had moved to Los Angeles in the past decade, and nearly three hundred thousand automobiles now traveled its roads. To attract some of these freewheeling newcomers, Currier put on a "jungle barbecue," gave away a Ford, and handed out autographed photographs of Burroughs. Southern California's chief selling point in those days was its atmosphere of sunshine-drenched egalitarianism—the notion that a man's bungalow was his castle, every truck farm a yeoman's paradise. Currier's tasteful brochure invited the public to "Live Under Your Own Fig Tree and

Prosper." "Tarzana offers more than just a homesite," the text elaborated. "Its broad fertile acres spell independence and happiness." Writing in a local real estate magazine, Burroughs offered an effulgent testimonial to the abundance of good water and air, the fertility of the land, the wholesomeness of country living, and the proximity of schools, mountains, beaches, and Hollywood. "Tarzana is where I have lived with my family for five years," he attested. "Now I want others to enjoy this glorious country and location with me. . . . I love it here, and I believe you will love it. . . . My profession is such that I can live anywhere in the world that I choose . . . and I hope and expect to live here the rest of my life." An acre lot in this "favored place" cost three thousand dollars, a half acre went for fifteen hundred dollars. But hurry, he urged his future neighbors, "The city is rapidly going out Ventura way."

But even as he was expressing his desire to live at Tarzana forever, he was hatching a plan that would roust him from his hacienda on the hill within a year. At the beginning of 1924, he and a group of investors formalized an agreement to develop El Caballero Country Club on 120 acres of Tarzana and 100 acres of the ranch to his west. Plans called for an eighteen-hole golf course that would take advantage of the "sporty" topography; bridle paths linking a system of trails that ran from Beverly Hills, through the mountains, all the way to the ocean at Santa Monica; plus polo, trap shooting, croquet, and swimming. The Burroughs house, billed as the "Otis mansion," would make an ideal clubhouse, and the gardens and view were as lovely as those of any club in Southern California. Memberships, of which there would be approximately five hundred, would begin at a thousand dollars.

It is not clear why he made the decision to give up the hilltop at Tarzana, especially after having pledged such undying devotion to it. Perhaps he had not been exaggerating about the direness of his financial straits, or maybe the club prospectus was simply too good to turn down. In a letter to Joe Bray, with whom he shared all of his financial confidences, he fairly salivated at the thought of his imminent windfall. "The contract price for the subdivision and the club property will net me about $350,000 and I will have left some 335 acres of hill land between the club and the summit of the Santa Monica mountains," he calculated, "at which point [my land] will be touched by the new Mulholland Scenic Drive, giving me property that is estimated will be worth within the next three to five years close to a million dollars." The point of the letter, however, was that despite such rosy prospects, he was still strapped for cash.

The need to sell and the promise of great wealth notwithstanding, the Caballero deal was an odd fit. Burroughs and Emma had joined the Hollywood Country Club when they moved to California, but he was not a natural clubman, nor was he a habitual golfer. Nevertheless, he threw himself into the project with his usual intensity, talking up the club's luxurious amenities and distinguished backers, including several real estate men, bankers, and, most delicious of all, the head of the Los Angeles office of the Internal Revenue Service. Burroughs anticipated no tax worries thenceforth.

In early June 1924, to make way for the country club, he moved the family from Tarzana to a rented house on South Gramercy Place in downtown Los Angeles. Surprisingly, no one seemed particularly sad. "When we first contemplated leaving Tarzana I thought that I should feel very badly about it," he wrote to Harry Burroughs, "but as a matter of fact I am much more contented here than there. I will have less responsibility, and infinitely less detail to think about, and my expenses will probably be cut in two. Emma likes it very much here, and the children seem to be happy." Their residence at Tarzana had lasted precisely five years, which, though less than an epoch, was about as long as Burroughs had lived at any one address since he was a child.

The family welcomed the convenience of the city. The house was within two blocks of a grocery store, and a streetcar stopped at the corner. Nor did they have to give up their Tarzana lifestyle entirely. Burroughs stabled several horses at a Hollywood riding club, and he and the children were regulars on the nearby bridle paths. "The only objection to our living here that I can see will be upon the part of our neighbors," he reflected, "as five years of isolation and independence have resulted in a rather loud family."

Contrary to his statements in the Tarzana promotional literature, he and Emma had never been fans of the public school nearest to Tarzana, in Marion. They had chauffeured Joan, Hully, and Jack to various private schools in or near Los Angeles and had kept them home with private tutors at different times. But as the children had grown older—Joan turned sixteen in 1924, Hully fifteen, Jack eleven—they came to crave friendship and stimulation beyond the ranch, just as Burroughs had anticipated in *The Girl from Hollywood*. Unlike Colonel Pennington, however, he was not resistant to having them broaden their horizons. "They are growing up fast," he lamented to his friend Bert Weston, "and pretty soon I won't have any children at home at all." Even so, he was proud whenever they showed initiative and independence, two qualities no Burroughs should be without. He was elated when Joan showed talent in singing and acting; she took voice lessons throughout the summer and in the fall entered the Marta Oatman School of the Theatre in Los Angeles. And for all Burroughs's misgivings about Hollywood and its morals, he hoped that his daughter would one day make a movie, and the following year, even helped arrange a screen test with Metro-Goldwyn-Mayer. In the case of the two boys, the conversion to city life chafed a bit at first. Hully squirmed and sulked when he had to don his first tuxedo and attend a school dance, but as the studious one, he quickly settled in at Los Angeles High School. Jack, the most spoiled, chafed at junior high, but muddled through with little hardship.

As usual, Emma's disposition was not recorded, though having lived in a house boat, cabin, tent, various apartments and houses, and a mansion on a hill, she was undoubtedly able to take the latest move in stride. "Emma has not changed, which leaves me in the apparent position of having robbed a cradle," Burroughs remarked to Bert Weston after the family had been in the Gramercy Place house several months. The following spring he inscribed a copy of *The Cave Girl* tenderly, "To Emma From her Cave-man."

IN APRIL 1924, Bob Davis notified Burroughs that their two-year agreement was about to expire. Burroughs proposed new terms whereby he would accept five cents a word from Munsey, but only on the condition that the company accept *everything* he submitted. Davis refused, advising Burroughs, "I have no guarantee that you won't fly off in a tantrum and cut loose in directions unknown to man." Instead, he proposed paying six cents a word for the right of first refusal. Burroughs accepted and blithely commenced a story that he knew Davis would not like. It would be the longest story he ever wrote.

Encouraged by the unexpected success of *The Girl from Hollywood* and disappointed by the sales of his latest Tarzan book, *Tarzan and the Golden Lion*, he conceived another "realistic" story along the lines of his other two "Girl" stories, *The Girl from Hollywood* and "The Girl from

Farris's." Like these previous heroines, Marcia, the central figure of *Marcia of the Doorstep,* is a good girl flung into life's cruel whirlpool by moral indiscretion. Her mother was a fallen woman, her father the son of United States Senator John Chase. After her father commits suicide to escape being blackmailed and exposed by a scoundrel attorney, Max Heimer, Marcia is left on the doorstep of hard-luck stage actor Marcus Aurelius Sackett and his wife, Clara. When Marcia makes her entrance, she is sixteen (the same age as Joan Burroughs), beautiful, and the possessor of a lovely singing voice. The oily Max Heimer reappears to help Sackett with a legal matter relating to his struggling theatrical company and, guessing Marcia's true parentage, proceeds first to shame her grandfather Senator Chase into setting up a secret trust fund for his long-lost bastard grandchild, and next to bilk Sackett out of the money he receives from the senator and the theater. Marcia, meanwhile, departs on a cruise to the South Seas, during which she falls in love with—who else?—Jack Chase, the senator's grandson, her putative brother, though neither is cognizant of the blood connection. Inevitably, in a twist borrowed from *The Return of Tarzan, The Cave Girl,* or *The Mucker,* the ship is wrecked and Jack and Marcia are marooned on a desert island. After their rescue, Marcia learns her true identity, boards a San Francisco–bound steamer, where she is "discovered" by a film director—in this case, an upstanding one—and becomes a Hollywood star. In an ending not unlike that in "The Girl from Farris's," information comes to light that suddenly makes it possible for Marcia to marry Jack; the Sacketts prosper, and Max Heimer gets his just desserts.

At 117,000 words, *Marcia* is half again as long as most other Burroughs novels, thanks to a plot that rumbles out of control. Like *The Girl from Hollywood,* the tale is topical, but this time instead of deriding Prohibition, dope, and Hollywood morals, Burroughs grinds a more personal ax. While tinkering with the manuscript, he briefly considered changing Max Heimer's name to Louis Kosch. Kosch was the real-life attorney for Numa Pictures, and someone Burroughs had come to loathe. In April 1924, as he was beginning *Marcia,* he was also contemplating suing Numa for delinquent royalty payments on *The Revenge of Tarzan* and *The Adventures of Tarzan.* In the final draft, Kosch became Heimer again, but throughout the story he is the stereotypical Shylock— or in Burroughs's crueler shorthand, "the Jew" or "the kike."

Another goal of *Marcia,* this one more laudable, was to pay tribute to Emma, who is clearly the model for long-suffering Clara Sackett. She endures the "erratic fortunes" of her husband with stoicism and grace. "To be young and broke presents, oftimes, elements of comedy, but to be broke and old is tragedy, unadulterated." In this last, he was referring only to himself.

Burroughs sensed that *Marcia* was foredoomed. "All the time I was writing it I was positive that you would refuse it," he wrote to Davis. He pleaded with him to "stretch a point in my favor," and Davis, in rejecting the story, had tried to let him down easily, arguing that because of the length, complexity, and number of characters, it would be "fatal" to publish *Marcia* in serial form. "I commend your efforts to escape the perfume of the jungle and the star-dust of Mars," Davis consoled before administering stronger medicine: "You have acquired fame writing about the jungle and the moon and the unsurveyed centers of the earth. You have a remarkable ability for making it possible for your readers to visualize those remote, mysterious, hitherto unexplored quarters. Nobody can compete with you in those realms, but when you begin to tamper with everyday life you are no better than the average."

Burroughs answered bluffly, "I presume that having been pushed back into my rut I should stay there," but warned that he probably would not do so. "I cannot afford to stop writing entirely . . . between Tarzan and Martian stories," he complained, "and I do not believe that I can do my best work if I devote myself exclusively to this type of fiction." He joked that he was considering writing a story about "organizing a country club," except that he knew it would be unprofitable and "barred from the mails." In the end, he accepted defeat. He never even bothered to send *Marcia* to Joe Bray, knowing that he would like it no better than *The Girl from Hollywood,* and he never attempted another "realistic" novel. The story has yet to be published.

SOMEWHAT chastened, he turned his attention back to El Caballero Country Club. By November he had taken on the title of managing director and had moved into the club's downtown sales and development office. "I am giving up my writing and practically everything else to put this Club across," he wrote brother Harry. He noted that fourteen of the eighteen greens were completed and expected the course to be ready for play the following July.

Little else was going as well. He had made several more unsuccessful runs at starting his own production company during the past year and had pitched several ideas for movies to Hollywood studios, again to no avail. Book sales, too, were continuing to sag. The one bright spot besides the country club was the overseas market. Curtis Brown of London, which handled all of Burroughs's foreign rights, reported that Tarzan was now being read in seventeen different languages, including Icelandic and Arabic, and Burroughs was the agency's best performer by far, exceeding the novels of Britain's immensely popular John Galsworthy. Specifically, Curtis Brown noted, Tarzan was a smashing success in Germany and Russia.

"Russians Prefer 'Tarzan' to Marx" announced the *New York Times* on April 17, 1924. Quoting a Moscow newspaper, *Times* correspondent Walter Duranty noted that young Russians preferred reading cheap editions of American novels over Marxist pamphlets. The preferred authors were O. Henry, H. G. Wells, Jack London, Sir Arthur Conan Doyle, and Upton Sinclair. Topping all of these, however, was Edgar Rice Burroughs. "Six books of Tarzan's adventures have already appeared here," Duranty observed, "and been eagerly snapped up . . . at the price of sixty cents a piece to the number of 250,000. 'Yet the supply is inferior to the demand,'" the publisher told Duranty. "'We could easily sell a million. They read it [Tarzan] in offices, read it in street cars, read it in trains, read it in factories. Go to the villages and you find the educated young soldier reading "Tarzan" to a circle of peasants with mouths agape.'"

Seeking to understand the Tarzan craze, Duranty interviewed the head of the Russian poets soviet. "'Our revolution killed the fairies,'" the poet explained, "'just as education killed them in Western countries. But if you dress up Jack the Giant Killer in a sufficiently modern guise to give him at least a semblance of probability the masses will love him as did their fathers and grandfathers.'"

Burroughs, an ardent anti-Communist, was tickled by his unexpectedly warm reception in the enemy camp. Thanking Bob Davis for passing along the *Times* clipping, he noted wryly, "It is evident that Tarzan is overthrowing the Soviet government."

Unfortunately, though, the Cyrillic translation of Tarzan was not earning him a dime. "Burroughs is the rage from one end of the country to the other," exclaimed *The Saturday Review of Literature*. "If the Russians were paying royalties he would become a millionaire in a short time." But the Russians did not abide by international copyright law and Burroughs went unrewarded financially. "[S]uch is life and Bolshevism," he chuckled.

Assuredly he would have been far more frustrated if he weren't beginning to make money in Germany. For several years, the Tarzan novels had been published in that country as part of the Tauchnitz Collection of British and American Authors—English-language editions distributed on the continent by Leipzig publisher Baron Christian von Tauchnitz—from which Burroughs had received royalties. Then in July 1923, Curtis Brown had arranged with the German publisher Dieck & Company of Stuttgart to publish a German-language edition of Tarzan. By the following summer, Burroughs was pleased to report to Joe Bray that "Tarzan is doing wonderfully in Germany. My first royalty check was for over 1800 pounds Sterling, and as my royalty is not very high [10 percent] this would mean quite a number of copies." By the end of the year, Dieck had released four Tarzan novels and Burroughs was able to brag that he had received "the largest royalty check ever paid to a foreign writer for a similar period of time."

Little did he realize that five months later his sales in Germany would fall to zero and his books would disappear from German shelves. Jealous of Dieck's success with the Tarzan books, rival publishers dug up the World War I-era *Tarzan the Untamed*, which Dieck had been wise enough to exclude from its list. Suddenly Burroughs found himself in a tempest of controversy that turned all the good news to bad. It hadn't helped that someone in the German press chose to brand *Tarzan the Untamed* as *Tarzan the German-Eater*.

9

EVOLUTION ON TRIAL

After World War I, Germany struggled to regain its national pride, and Tarzan, as presented in Dieck & Company's new German-language editions, was the ideal hero for the time. "[I]n our present position . . . we are strengthened manyfold" by Tarzan's example, one former German soldier observed, speaking for his thousands of recently demobilized brothers in arms. Tarzan's "courage and self-confidence," he said, "awaken the desire to bring German work and skill back again into the world." By the fall of 1924, Tarzan novels were conspicuous in every book stall from Cologne to Berlin, Hamburg to Munich. "[N]o good workman starts his daily work without taking a Tarzan pill in the form of a Tarzan book," remarked another German editorial.

Yet the same nationalism that had first drawn Germans to Tarzan would turn them against Burroughs once they became aware of *Tarzan the Untamed.* The precise chronology of the German scandal is now unclear, though Dieck apparently saw it coming as early as October, when other publishers began grumbling that the Burroughs books were eroding literary taste. When Dieck passed the criticism on to Burroughs, he dismissed it as more sour grapes and another echo of the prudishness expressed by American librarians.

There was more to it than that. Later in the fall, a German writer, Stefan von Sorel, published a scathing criticism of Burroughs under the title *Tarzan der Deutschenfresser (Tarzan the German-Eater),* accompanied by several excerpts from *Tarzan the Untamed,* which Burroughs and his agents had never released in Germany. The German press, already intrigued by the Tarzan phenomenon, exploded. "It is not possible that a greater insult to the German reading public could be written," huffed one Berlin paper. The New York correspondent for the Frankfurt *Zeitung* called *Untamed* "one of the most repugnant products" to come out of the war. "Burroughs is so full of lies about the German nation that there is no excuse to be found for it."

By early February 1925, the furor had risen to such a pitch that Charles Dieck telegraphed Burroughs in a state of near panic: "Tarzan editions now much attacked by our press. Give us please quickly good notices that your book 'Tarzan the Untamed' is born during war-bitterness and most of all that you are fond of German people. Otherwise your German business will diminish." In fact, the situation was already out of hand: many people were now calling for the complete banishment of all Tarzan books and movies from Germany.

Burroughs's response, an open letter "To My German Readers," composed the same day he received Dieck's wire, was brave, but fundamentally spurious. He began by comparing the friction between America and Germany to that which had existed between the North and South after the Civil War. "[T]he children of the South were taught to believe that the Yanks grew horns and were the authors of hideous crimes and atrocities, but even in my childhood we were being taught to respect and love the people of the South, and today there is none of the old animosity left." In regard to his characterizations of Germans in *Tarzan the Untamed,* he chose not to softpedal his "honest convictions" during "the height of the bitterness of an extremely bitter war," yet insisted that he had not intended to villify *all* Germans—only "cruel, ruthless, arrogant" German officers such as Hauptmann Fritz Schneider, the villain in *Untamed.* "I never knowingly offend honorable and decent classes of society," he clarified and expressed his confidence that most Germans shared his dislike of this "negligible minority" of the "worst type" of human menace exemplified by Schneider.

He blurted one excuse after another, like a sticky-fingered child trying to fast-talk his way out of a candy store. He assured Dieck that the Kaiser had always been one of his heroes. Moreover, Burroughs vouched, he was practically German himself, or the next thing to it. "One of my brothers-in-law is a German, a native of Hamburg and a member of a great ivory importing family of that city. . . . Both of his daughters have recently been my guests in Los Angeles, one of them remaining with us some seven months. My brother-in-law and his family have, I believe, read all my Tarzan stories and I am quite sure that I do not dislike the German people." In closing, he dismissed the entire affair as a "tempest in a tea pot."

Charles Dieck thanked Burroughs for his letter, but chose not to circulate it to the German press for reasons he kept to himself. Meanwhile, the teapot continued to hiss. Throughout the winter and spring, editorial writers mauled Tarzan. All the reasons for once having liked Burroughs's hero were now the reasons for loathing him. "The yell . . . which Tarzan utters whenever he has killed a victim, in its affected crudeness . . . was not heard by the watchman of our good ethics," lectured the *Nieue Freie Presse* of Vienna. "Still, it seems strange that a race which has scarcely escaped the horrors of war, who is still living under its terrible consequences, could give itself to this thirst for blood as celebrated in the orgies of Tarzan."

In the first six months Tarzan had been available in German, Dieck had sold more than half a million books. But by April 1925, the publisher informed Burroughs that Tarzan had vanished from the German book market entirely. Distributors and bookstores had returned thousands of books to Dieck, afraid that their stores would be boycotted if customers spotted Tarzan novels on their shelves. And they were refusing to pay for the books that they had already sold.

By turns, Burroughs's reactions now ranged from blithe to angry, contrite to conniving. "Of course the circulation of my books is but a trivial matter," he averred at first. But then in an effort to forestall further controversy, he suggested withdrawing *Tarzan the Untamed* and *The Land That Time Forgot* from all countries, all languages, and he promised to introduce a sympathetic German character in a forthcoming story. At one point, he even proposed using a German pen name, on the theory that "it is I whom the Germans dislike and not Tarzan." Throughout the whole ordeal, however, he never acknowledged that he had made a mistake. "To assume a spineless attitude and retract and apologize ad nauseam is something that I cannot do," he wrote to Curtis Brown, who had negotiated the Dieck deal. "The whole thing is stupendously asinine and the attitude of the German press has nothing whatsoever to do with patriotism or injured German sensibilities but it is quite evidently prompted by jealousy of German publishers who did not have the business foresight and sense of values possessed by Mr. Dieck."

By summer, though, he permitted a circular to be distributed to German papers and booksellers, announcing that " 'Tarzan the Untamed' is being exterminated"—discontinued in all markets worldwide. Few papers took notice, and few booksellers consented to restock the four existing German-language Tarzans. A year after the first alarms had been sounded, Dieck & Company reported that the effort "to make Tarzan again beloved" was still a "thankless task." The best the German publisher could report was that a local circus was exhibiting two trained monkeys named Tarzan I and Tarzan II.

THE GERMAN controversy was a constant source of irritation through 1925, but a small matter alongside the task of completing El Caballero. Unlike so many other previous projects, the country club had held Burroughs's interest beyond the first few weeks of brainstorming. As a publicity stunt, on New Year's Eve of 1924, he had begun a round of golf on the unfinished course; playing under jury-rigged electric lights, he completed the round shortly after midnight and, by beating L. W. Craig of Los Angeles, claimed to have won the first United States golf tournament of 1925. By March, he was boasting to his brother Coleman that "we are over the worst of the obstacles now" and that the course would still be ready for legitimate play in July. "I am not a golfer, but disinterested experts tell us that we are going to have one of the finest courses in the United States." For the moment, real estate was not a chore, but an adventure. "The work . . . has been interesting and highly instructive," he said, "and has brought me into association with a great many of the best men in Los Angeles."

He was so bullish about the real estate climate and his new role as wheeler-dealer that he made several more plays in and around Los Angeles. He took back the unsold Tarzana subdivision lots and resumed selling them himself. He and Emma bought their own lot in Beverly Hills and began drawing up plans for a new house there. And with El Caballero looking so promising, he bought an option on 120 acres of land just north of downtown Los Angeles with the idea of developing another eighteen-hole public course.

On top of all that, he wrote to brother Harry, "Bob Davis wants me to write a sequel to the Moon Men. Joe Bray wants another Tarzan book, another Mars story, and is also waiting for a sequel to the Moon Men. Between times I am trying to exercise five saddle horses, keep up my reading, and work for the interest of the . . . bridle trail promotion here. All this in view of the fact that Dr. [Egerton] Crispin told me last October to drop everything and go away for a long rest. Being naturally a lazy man, there is only one explanation for my behavior—that I am what the English would call a bit balmy."

His reference to his health was not insignificant. Despite his generally youthful outlook and regimen of vigorous exercise, he was not as resilient as he once had been. The previous summer, he had taken his sons on a pack trip into the Sierras, where the altitude had bothered him much more than he at first had wanted to admit. He returned home thoroughly drained and was slow to regain his strength. Summoned for jury duty later that fall, he had Dr. Crispin advise the judge, "Edgar Rice Burroughs has been . . . under treatment for pain in his heart following a severe strain of over-exertion last summer, and many anxieties since." Besides being chronically high-strung and reluctant to relax, he was also a smoker; numerous photos show him with either pipe or cigarette in hand. So far, he had suffered no major illnesses or setbacks, but on the eve of his fiftieth birthday, he was facing the prospect that his body might not keep up with his mind indefinitely.

Aging and transience were clearly in his thoughts throughout 1925, as evidenced by the two stories he wrote that year, "The Red Hawk" and *The Master Mind of Mars.* "The Red Hawk" is the sequel to "The Moon Men" that Bob Davis and Joe Bray had expressed an interest in. Three hundred years have passed since Julian 9th's uprising against the Kalkars, tyrannical invaders from the moon. The Americans ("Yanks") have long since fled the cities of the East and are living much as the Indians had once done in the plains and deserts of the West. They tend their herds, paint their faces, fight with lance and shield, and adorn their blankets with the scalps of fallen Kalkars. Julian 20th is now Chief of Chiefs, known as Red Hawk for the feather he wears in his hair. After generations of warring westward and living as nomads, he and his clan are poised to raid the lush Kalkar strongholds of the Pacific Rim.

During a gory, all-day battle in which the Yank warriors "hacked until our tired arms could scarce raise a blade," Red Hawk is captured and led through the derelict "tents" of what must have been downtown Los Angeles. ("How long and at what cost had the ancients striven to the final achievement of their mighty civilization? And for what?") Escaping, he makes his way first to the beach at Santa Monica, and then, following a canyon inland again, he arrives at what is obviously Tarzana. "Never had I looked upon a place of such wondrous beauty," Red Hawk sighs. "Through the trees I could see the outlines of the ruins of one of the stone tents of the ancients sitting upon the summit of the low hill." He marvels at the variety of trees, shrubs, and flowers—hearty holdovers from Harrison Gray Otis's original gardens and orchards.

The next story Burroughs wrote in 1925 offers a much harsher view of aging. The hero of the tale, Ulysses Paxton, is wounded in World War I. As he lies bleeding on the battlefield, he wills himself "to throw off the hideous bonds of my mutilated flesh"; he opens his eyes to discover that he is on Mars. Soon he is taken on as the apprentice of Ras Thavas, a thousand-year-old scientist of the Moreau–Jekyll school and a moral descendant of the mad professor in Burroughs's *The Monster Men* (1913) who has perfected the art of transplanting limbs, organs, glands, and even brains from one body to another. He has put male brains into female bodies, ape brains into human bodies. Much to the regret of Ulysses Paxton, who now goes by the Martian name of Vad Varo, Ras Thavas has transferred the brain of the wicked and aging queen Xaxa into the beautiful, young body of Ulysses's beloved Valla Dia. Vad Varo eventually learns that the reason Ras Thavas has taught him his secrets is so he can transplant the superannuated scientist's brain into a young body. Vad Varo agrees to perform the operation if he'll promise to give Valla Dia her original body back.

The details of the operations in *Master Mind* are gruesome, especially for their day, though they are no more vivid than the description of the eating habits of headless creatures in *The Chessmen of Mars* or many of the accounts of brains splattered and jugulars slashed in other Burroughs stories. Still, the matter-of-fact depiction of blood and guts was apparently too much for Matthew White, the Munsey editor in charge while Bob Davis took what was supposed to be a six-month leave of absence. "[T]he present vein you are writing in does not suit the *Argosy*," wrote Davis's surrogate. In passing, White indicated that even though Davis had already accepted "The Red Hawk" before leaving on vacation, he himself would have turned it down.

Burroughs was flabbergasted, and the most stunning news of all was that Bob Davis was not simply on leave but had decided to leave his editor's job for good to write a column for the Munsey newspaper, the *New York Sun*. Burroughs would continue to do business with the Munsey magazines on and off over the next decade, but the peculiar pact of respect and allegiance that had existed between an "entertaining" writer and his equally entertaining editor was no more. In one of his last official letters to Burroughs, Davis had teased, "You could take any one of the psalms, make it 100,000 words in length, and then leave a string dragging for a second verse." Now the string was unraveling. Of the three stories Burroughs had written in the past two years—*Marcia of the Doorstep*, "Red Hawk," and *Master Mind*—Munsey had turned down two. "[T]hey can go to hell as far I am concerned," Burroughs vented to Joe Bray after the final incident with White, the stern successor. Later, though, he himself acknowledged the "rottenness" of *Marcia* and *Master Mind*, explaining them away as "a reflection of my mental attitude at the time I wrote them." Borrowing an image from one of his own manuscripts, he confessed to Bert Weston on December 29, "I have had one hectic year, during which time I have been vainly attempting to handle several bushels of ideas in a three pint head."

ONE OF those ideas was evolution, a perennial interest of Burroughs which lately had been making front-page headlines. Six decades after the publication of *On the Origin of Species*, Charles Darwin's theory of biological determinism had gained widespread acceptance, to the point that it was now imbedded in the curriculum of nearly every high school and university in the country. Meanwhile, the supporting evidence continued to mount. The most recent big discovery had come in 1925, while Burroughs was in the middle of writing *The Master Mind of Mars*. Anatomist Raymond Dart, upon examining a skull dug from a South African cave, declared that it had belonged to a child who, judging from the way the spinal cord had joined the brain, had stood upright and walked on two feet, a characteristic of *Homo sapiens*. He named the new species *Australopithecus africanus*—"southern ape of Africa"—and estimated its age as two and a half million years, making it the oldest missing link to date. His pronouncement created a stir worldwide, though not everyone was ready to believe Dart's data or date. Leading the chorus of doubters were American religious fundamentalists, who estimated the Earth's age at something closer to two thousand years.

Fundamentalism had first taken hold in the nineteenth century as a conservative response to the rapid changes brought on by the industrial age. By the 1920s, as homespun values were challenged by bobbed hair and bathtub gin, fundamentalist fervor grew proportionately. Prohibition was perhaps the most conspicuous fundamentalist cause, though creationism—"Adamism," as opposed to "Darwinism"—was a close second. In 1924, a number of smaller anti-evolution movements joined to form the Anti-Evolution League of America. Its members preached their doctrine from church pulpits, challenged "modernists" to public debate, and launched a state-by-state campaign to outlaw the teaching of evolution in any school that received public tax dollars. Their first victory was in Tennessee. In March 1925, the Tennessee legislature made it illegal "to teach any theory that denies the story of the Divine Creation of man as taught in the Bible, and to teach instead that man has descended from a lower order of animals." Immediately liberals, humanists, and scientists sounded their own call to arms.

The so-called "Scopes monkey trial" was not a witch hunt, as many have come to believe, but in fact was a test case in which a small-town high school science teacher by the name of John Scopes agreed to plead guilty to teaching evolution in his biology class as a way to challenge the constitutionality of the freshly minted state law. The plan, as laid out by the American Civil Liberties Union, was to invoke the sacred American principle of separation of church and state and head off the fundamentalist juggernaut before it could overrun other state legislatures. Though the issues were unquestionably grand and the ensuing debate grandiloquent, few predicted that the Scopes trial would end up being one of the most closely followed courtroom dramas of the era, along with the trials of Sacco and Vanzetti in 1921; Bruno Hauptmann, kidnapper of the Lindbergh baby, in 1935; and alleged Communist Alger Hiss in 1948. With William Jennings Bryan orating for the fundamentalists and Clarence Darrow for the evolutionists, everyone in the country sat up and took notice. And soon enough, everyone had their own opinion to offer, including the father of Tarzan.

By 1925, Burroughs had improved his layman's grasp of anthropology somewhat. He kept up with recent archeological revelations in journals such as *Popular Science* and *National Geographic* and even perused monographs from the Smithsonian Institution. So far, though, he had treated the subject of evolution rather undogmatically in his writing. The Waz-dons and Ho-dons of *Tarzan the Terrible,* the Alali of *Ant Men,* and the Bolgani of *Golden Lion,* along with the Stone Age atavisms of Pellucidar, the Tree of Life races of Mars, and the seven tiers of Caspakian beast-men, were for the most part intended merely as fictional amusements. And his various musings on breeding, racial hierarchy, and natural law in the Tarzan stories could best be described as a grab bag. In the garden of evolutionary thought, Burroughs seemed satisfied with merely wandering around, doing no heavy spadework of his own, and gathering whichever fruits dropped randomly along his path.

Nevertheless, when he was asked by the International Press Bureau to prepare a commentary on the upcoming Scopes trial, he saw it as his duty to share his cumulative insight. As the creator of Tarzan, he believed that his opinion was worth as least as much as that of H. L. Mencken, the most famous of the scores of journalists covering the proceedings. Yet as the essay he submitted made plain, having to articulate his thoughts on Darwin was not nearly as simple as sending a fictional he-man into the jungle. Beneath the self-consciously convoluted rhetoric, his main point seems to be that God and Nature are one and the same, and regardless of which omniscient power one believes in (Burroughs's own preference is clear), the universe they created is manifestly a work in progress. "It is immediately obvious, even if we go no further back than the Cro-Magnon," he argues, "that nature did not produce the finished product originally, but something that was susceptible of improvement, and if that is not an heretical admission then there is nothing heretical in the whole theory of evolution, which simply goes back a little further—to the beginning—and tried to follow out the workings of one of Nature's laws, one of God's laws, which men who had not progressed as far as we have tried to interpret some two thousand years ago. It is not strange that they made mistakes. They were ignorant and superstitious."

The article ran in the *New York American* on July 6 and perhaps other papers, as well, though Burroughs's normally thorough records do not specify how many. His opinion had no apparent effect on the trial's outcome; Scopes was found guilty and fined one hundred dollars, a verdict that was later reversed by the state supreme court. But from that moment forward, Burroughs became increasingly pointed, and political, in his treatment of issues relating to evolution and human development.

AFTER WRITING his Scopes piece and after the rejection of *The Master Mind of Mars* later in the year, he turned away from writing for several months. Once again, he allowed himself to be seduced by Hollywood. Four years has passed since the release of *The Adventures of Tarzan* and six years since *The Revenge of Tarzan,* the most recent feature. In the interim, movies had become much more sophisticated and even more popular. Epics such as *Ben-Hur* (1925) were now the norm and Al Jolson's blackface crooning in *The Jazz Singer,* the first "talkie," was only a year in the offing. On February 15, 1926, Burroughs signed a contract with Film Booking Offices (FBO) to produce and distribute a movie adaptation of *Tarzan and the Golden Lion.* Having failed in several previous attempts to strike a deal on the novel, he was especially pleased to receive a ten thousand dollar bonus for selling the rights. More exciting still was the knowledge that FBO was backed by one of the shrewdest money men in the country, Joseph P. Kennedy.

After making a fortune in the stock market in the early 1920s, Joe Kennedy was eager to invest in motion pictures. He and many others on Wall Street were attracted by Hollywood's impressive cash flow, not to mention its obvious glamour. In February 1926, Kennedy had bought the Robertson-Cole Company (R-C), a small, debt-hobbled studio that produced adventure films and melodramas, which were distributed mainly to small towns by its subsidiary, Film Booking Offices. One of Kennedy's very first acquisitions as the new head of the recapitalized, reenergized studio—now called simply FBO—was *Tarzan and the Golden Lion.* The man who would one day make a president out of a son had little doubt that he could make a hit out of the next Tarzan picture.

Burroughs seized the chance to start over, to bring the movie Tarzan back in line with the original Tarzan of the novels. Once again the hunt was on for the ideal physical specimen. And as luck would have it, he didn't need to look any farther than his own backyard, where a trap had been baited by his eighteen-year-old-daughter.

In the summer of 1926, Joan Burroughs had her heart set on a career as an actress. She had graduated from the Marta Oatman School in May and had played the lead role in the spring production of *Enter Madame,* for which she received excellent reviews. Her aim was to join a repertory troupe and, with luck and perhaps some parental pull, break into movies. That summer, however, she was caught up in the social whirl of early womanhood. In June, she threw a pool party at Tarzana, now officially the El Caballero Country Club.

One of the guests that day was twenty-five-year-old James Pierce, a law student and former all-American center on the Indiana University football team. Pierce remembered the day as one of the greatest in his life: "We were all swimming, so I was in trunks when Joan took me over to meet [her father]. . . . About two weeks later, I received a phone call from the Film Booking Office (FBO) casting director. He said, 'We are in search of a man to play the lead in an upcoming production of *Tarzan and the Golden Lion* and Mr. Burroughs thought you would be a good bet.' "

That same summer, FBO had cast football legend Red Grange in *One Minute to Play.* Along with boxer Jack Dempsey, Grange was one of the first celebrity athletes to transfer his fame directly to the screen. Pierce was no Dempsey or Grange, but what mattered to Burroughs was that he was no Elmo Lincoln, either. The guest who had stood dripping wet beside the Tarzana pool was six foot three and a lean 190 pounds. He was clean-limbed—the most essential requirement—with the suppleness of a natural athlete and the poise of a gentleman. Even so, he was still a surprising choice for the role of Tarzan, for he was a bit on the gangly side, and he looked more like a club tennis pro than a jungle hero. His hair was blond and wavy, unlike Tarzan's, which was black. He was unquestionably handsome, with blue eyes and a strong jaw, but there was nothing inherently primal in his mien. Somehow, though, he was just the man Burroughs was looking for. FBO claimed that it auditioned ninety-two actors before selecting Jim Pierce to play Tarzan, but the result was never in doubt. "We have at last found a man who really *is* Tarzan," Burroughs exclaimed when he finally got his way, and for the next several years he would continue to vouch that Pierce came as "near to being Tarzan of the Apes . . . as any man I have ever seen."

ALL IN ALL, 1926 was shaping up to be one of the good years. Most sectors of the national economy were booming, and that was especially true in California. Burroughs and his fellow conservatives still manned the rhetorical ramparts against labor unrest, the Red Scare, and the immigrant underclass, though in fact the likelihood—or at least the *imminent* likelihood—of anarchy had subsided with the enactment of tough new legislation restricting the comings and going of these perceived troublemakers. A revolution of sorts had occurred in the twenties, but it was a revolution of women's suffrage, jazz, and Babbitry, not of Bolshevik bomb throwers. After World War I, President Warren Harding had promised a "return to normalcy" but wound up engulfed in the Teapot Dome scandal and rumors of sexual turpitude; by 1925, however, the country was in the hands of a dyed-in-the-wool puritan, Calvin Coolidge. And though small-town life and the family farm were beginning to wither beneath the incandescence of the cities, the nation felt unified—by highways, by radio, and by national brand names. To be sure, America was more complex, more uproarious, and its future still uncertain. But for the time being, there was a contagious sense that most of its problems were solvable.

In June, shortly after Joan Burroughs's graduation and introduction to Jim Pierce, Burroughs had made a quick trip to Chicago to settle a long-stewing lawsuit pressed by agent William Chapman, who claimed that Burroughs had cheated him out of royalties on foreign editions of *Tarzan of the Apes*. Burroughs took Joan and they had a wonderful time with old friends; even better, he was able to settle the suit for the reasonable sum of one thousand dollars.

Earlier in the year, he had decided against building a new house in Beverly Hills and instead had sold the lot and begun constructing a modest house in his Tarzana subdivision. Though located less than a quarter mile from the Otis hacienda—now the El Caballero clubhouse—the new place bore little resemblance to the sturdy mansion on the hill, which, according to "The Red Hawk," had been built to last for centuries. Burroughs's four-page list of specifications for the builder called for "the cheapest thing that can be built that won't fall down under ten years"— something along the lines of the kit houses sold by Sears, Roebuck. Completed in July, the new residence was a typical Southern California bungalow with clapboard siding and striped awnings. Several years earlier, he had written a song, "My Own Tarzana Ranch," the chorus of which urges:

Pine no more my lassie
My little lad be gay!
For we're going back
To our own Tarzana Ranch
To our own Tarzana Ranch far away.

Now such lyrics only seemed mawkish and passé.

Remarkably, Burroughs didn't seem to mind living below and within sight of his former dream house. He was glad to be back in the Valley, and a smaller house meant less upkeep and fewer worries all around. When sixteen-year old Hully made a hole in one on the El Caballero golf course in the first month the course was open for play, it was taken as a small sign that fortune was again smiling on the family. Now was as good a time as any, Burroughs figured, to undertake a story he had been contemplating for years: a novel about the life of an Apache warrior.

He had been weighing the Apache idea since 1919. Then in the fall of 1925, H. C. Paxton, an editor at *The Country Gentleman,* a sister publication to *The Saturday Evening Post,* had written an unsolicited letter complimenting him on *The Bandit of Hell's Bend,* which had just come out as a book. Paxton wished to know if Burroughs planned to write any more westerns. He wrote back that he had in mind setting a story during the "Geronimo campaign" of the 1880s. "I [see] the possibility of a romantic character that might be likened to an Apache Tarzan," he informed Paxton. He also announced that he would research the subject carefully before sitting down to write, a stark contrast to his traditional approach. Besides mining his own firsthand experiences in the army in Arizona, he made an effort to read "every book on the subject." He selected real-life Apache chiefs Geronimo, Victorio, and Juh as characters and endeavored to ground "nearly every incident, battle and raid" in "a more or less authentic history of the times." Even so, he cautioned Paxton when he submitted his manuscript to *Country Gentleman* in November, "the spottiness of the available literature," as well as the "biased and one-sided" impressions of his youth, had prompted him to take considerable license. "I hope that you will like the story," he told Paxton. "I have tried to make it, first and above all other considerations . . . entertaining."

The historical event on which *The War Chief* is based was well known throughout Apache country, and over time its bloody details and mysterious outcome had lent themselves to local legend. On March 28, 1883, a small band of renegade Apaches surprised a buckboard driven by Judge H. C. McComas outside Lordsburg, New Mexico, east of Fort Grant, where Burroughs would serve in the cavalry thirteen years later. The Apaches shot and bludgeoned the judge and his wife to death and kidnapped their six-year-old son, Charley. Newspapers in Arizona, New Mexico, and Mexico carried a picture of the boy and offered a thousand-dollar reward for his return. In the ensuing weeks and months, young Charley McComas became a national cause célèbre, a cautionary tale of the country's still unresolved Indian "problem." Despite a rigorous search by civilians and the United States Cavalry, the boy was never found. Many who followed the case came to accept that he, too, had been murdered by Apaches, but well into the next century the rumor persisted that Charley McComas was alive—that a fair-haired, blue-eyed American had been seen living among a small group of "Lost Apaches" in the Sierra Madre of Mexico. Hearsay even suggested that he had assumed leadership of this last group of reservation holdouts.

In Burroughs's recasting of history, Charley McComas becomes Andy MacDuff and ultimately "the Apache Tarzan." His father is of Scottish stock, a descendant of "Caledonian savages," and his mother is one quarter Cherokee. Her Indian genes have expressed themselves volubly in baby Andy, who "looked more an Indian than she, with his round face, his big, dark eyes, his straight, black hair." Early in the story, father and mother are murdered by Apaches in McComas fashion, and young Andy is abducted and raised as an Indian, ignorant of his origins. "Back and forth across New Mexico and Arizona, beneath blistering sun, enduring biting cold, drenched by torrential rain, Andy jounced about upon the back of Morning Star [his Kala] and laughed or crowed or slept as the spirit moved him." At the age of ten, he kills a black bear and takes the bear's name, Shoz-Dijiji, as his own.

Shoz-Dijiji grows up to be an exemplary warrior, though a faint (white) voice in the back of his mind keeps him from torturing his victims or harming women and children. Like Tarzan, he is naked except for a G-string. He knows every rock and wrinkle in southern Arizona and northern Mexico and can move through the rugged landscape swiftly and invisibly. He has a rival in Juh, an intratribal version of Terkoz, and ultimately falls for a white woman, Wichita Billings.

Wichita lives with her father on a remote ranch in what has historically been Apache country. She is initially enamored of Lt. Samuel Adams King (the surname a likely salute to Burroughs's mentor, Charles King), a West Pointer who wishes she was as refined as she is pretty. Shoz-Dijiji rescues Wichita from a group of brutish white assailants and takes her back to his people. In his broken English, which he had acquired during a three-month stay on the reservation, he tries to explain the integrity of Apache life and make clear the effrontery of white civilization: "Before [the pindah lickoyee, the white man] came there was plenty for all, but like a fool he set out to kill every living thing that Usen [the Great Spirit] has put here. . . . He is trying to take away from us the ways of our fathers—our dances, our medicine men, everything that we hold sacred; and in return he gives us whiskey and shoots us wherever he finds us. I do not think the pindah lickoyee are such good men that they tell the Indian how to be good."

In the final chapter, Shoz-Dijiji returns Wichita safely to her ranch. They kiss, and she begs him to stay. Instead he rides over the hill. Unlike Tarzan, no telegram has informed him of his true parentage. "You are white—Shoz-Dijiji is Apache," he says, fighting the lump in his throat. "White girl could not love Apache. That is right. . . . Shoz-Dijiji sorry. Good-bye!"

Burroughs's nostalgia for traditional Indian lifeways jibed with his view of Africa as a paradise lost—though, ironically, he does not portray African natives with the same sensitivity that he shows toward North American natives. This inconsistency was doubtless lost on him, and he was not alone in his selective progressivism. At the end of the nineteenth century, once the last Indian uprising had been put down and the last tribe assigned to a reservation, the stereotype of Indians as enemies was to a large extent replaced by the notion of Indians as noble but vaguely quaint exhibits. Geronimo was allowed out of prison to appear at the St. Louis World's Fair in 1904, where he signed autographs and sold bows and arrows. Railroads, the instrument of the Indians' undoing, now enticed tourists to the West with posters of war-bonneted braves, illustrated by some of America's most accomplished artists. Indians performed their traditional dances and told stories in sign language at the gateways to national parks. Folklorists such as Burroughs's contemporary Charles Lummis, founder of the Southwest Museum in Los Angeles, led campaigns to collect and preserve Indian artifacts and oral histories. Indians were still bad guys in countless movies and pulp sto-

218 -+- JOHN TALIAFERRO

ries, but in 1926, exactly fifty years after Custer's last stand, a growing number of whites were expressing at least a modicum of remorse over the passing of the First Americans.

Unfortunately for Burroughs, the sympathies of *Country Gentleman,* "the oldest agricultural journal in the world," were at best perfunctory. "Most people who give any thought to the subject now see clearly that one of the most shameful chapters in American history is that which sets forth our dealings with the Indians," H. C. Paxton wrote Burroughs after reading *The War Chief.* But in Paxton's judgment, it did not necessarily follow that Americans wanted to read a story told from the "the Indian's side." James Fenimore Cooper's "redskin characters" had been an anomaly, Paxton explained, and for most readers—or at least *Country Gentleman* readers—"the most effective use of savage peoples in fiction is where the red or brown or black man is shown as the staunchly loyal follower of the white leader." Paxton wished Burroughs luck in selling his story elsewhere.

As badly as he had wanted to break into the genteel and potentially more lucrative pages of *Country Gentleman,* Burroughs did not take an entirely submissive tone in responding to the racist and patronizing Paxton. He was proud of *The War Chief* and unusually protective. He had been "a little bit fearful" about writing from an Apache point of view, he told Paxton, but insisted that to do justice to the topic he could not write any other way. He then politely rubbed in the fact that he had no difficulty in placing the story elsewhere—though he did not mention that it was with the more plebeian *Argosy All-Story.* Later, when book publisher Joe Bray expressed concern over the vivid descriptions of scalpings and other atrocities, Burroughs stood his ground again: "I anticipate a great deal of adverse criticism . . . but I was very careful to have some sort of authority for every statement I have made and every Indian word that I have used." When the book was published in fall 1927, he sent an early copy to Charles King, the old Apache fighter, now eighty-three and living in Milwaukee. *The War Chief* "comes nearer being a worth while book than any I have written," he allowed in a rare moment of self-congratulation.

He was already planning the next story in the series and was even contemplating a Shoz-Dijiji trilogy, though Bray, pleasantly surprised at the healthy sales of *The Bandit of Hell's Bend,* was urging him to write a more conventional ranch romance. "I hate to start in on a series of western cowboy stories as it would seem like encroaching on Zane Grey's preserves," Burroughs replied. "However, I see no reason why I should not continue my Indian stories, if they prove popular, in which case I can have my Indians kill Zane Grey's cow-punchers."

The rivalry with Zane Grey was more than just a cue for a joke. Throughout the 1920s, Grey was far and away America's most popular writer. He had long since broken out of the pulps and was now the object of bidding wars between slick magazines such as *The Saturday Evening Post, The Ladies Home Journal, Collier's, Cosmopolitan,* and *American,* none of which had ever accepted a Burroughs story. *Country Gentleman,* his latest disappointment, routinely paid Grey fifty thousand dollars for the serial rights to a novel; in Burroughs's entire career, he never made more than ten thousand dollars for a serial, and that only once. In 1921, Grey had formed his own film company and over the next seven years produced no fewer than two films from his novels each year. His annual income rose to nearly half a million dollars, which amply underwrote his passion for deep-sea fishing around the world. (At his level of success, he needed to work only part of the year.)

Though Grey and Burroughs had much in common and lived less than an hour apart (Grey in Altadena), the two were not acquaintances, and according to Burroughs's records met only once, and then only in passing. Burroughs had good reason to be jealous of Grey, which probably explained his aloofness. Grey, who was from the Midwest also, had accomplished everything Burroughs had hoped to do when he had come to California and had eclipsed him at nearly every turn. If anyone can challenge Edgar Rice Burroughs's ranking as America's best-selling writer of the first half of the century it is Zane Grey, who sold an estimated twenty-seven million books by the time of his death in 1939.

BURROUGHS did not get around to writing a sequel to *The War Chief,* which sold respectably, until later in 1927. In between, he wrote a children's book, *The Tarzan Twins,* for the P. F. Volland Company of Joliet, Illinois, which despite its handsome design and illustration, did poorly. He also finally succeeded in selling *The Master Mind of Mars.* The pulp market had continued to splinter and specialize during the 1920s, first with the westerns, then detective and romance magazines, and finally, in 1926, with the appearance of the first all-science fiction magazine,

Amazing Stories. In recent years, Hugo Gernsback, president of Experimenter Publishing Company, had been running what he called "scientifiction" in his how-to magazines, *Modern Electronics* and *Electronic Experimenter* (later *Science & Invention*). Unlike scientific romances such as Burroughs's Mars stories, published by *Argosy All-Story, Blue Book,* or *Popular,* the stories Gernsback featured tended to be more technology-based—adventures that played off current knowledge of radiation, rocketry, astronomy, and the like. Though Burroughs had little interest in the nuts and volts of scientific invention and tended to finesse the details of such gizmos as David Innes's subterranean "mole" or Barsoomian spaceships, he had made a point of cultivating Gernsback, who had reprinted *The Land That Time Forgot* in the January 1927 issue of *Amazing.* "A magazine such as [yours] which publishes highly imaginative fiction . . . is worthy of support," he wrote after receiving the debut issue. "I shall watch with interest the results of your worthy experiment." In May 1927, Gernsback agreed to pay twelve hundred and fifty dollars for *Master Mind,* a puny sum by Burroughs's current standards, but he was grateful to find any home at all for his gory tale of surgical transplants. The story appeared in an immensely popular special edition of *Amazing* in July, after which Joe Bray agreed to bring it out as a book.

In a ten-week period between May and July, Burroughs willed himself to write another Tarzan. In an escapade derivative of Mark Twain's *A Connecticut Yankee in King Arthur's Court,* Tarzan comes to the rescue of a natty, slang-talking New York photographer named Blake, who has stumbled upon the descendants of English crusaders in a remote corner of Africa. The latter-day knights have lost all track of time, still favor castles, chain mail, and jousting, and fill their speech with "ye," "thou" and "Ods blud!" Initially Blake assumes that he has wandered onto a movie set, gives the knights the "raspberry," and makes inside jokes about the Knights of Columbus and Knights of Labor. The story's lighthearted tone, not unlike that of *Connecticut Yankee,* is a welcome change from recent Tarzans. In *Tarzan and the Ant Men,* Burroughs had created a fantasy world too dense for its own good, first introducing the primitive Alali and then the diminutive ant men. Likewise in *Tarzan and the Golden Lion,* Tarzan becomes entangled in Opar and then with the mongrel Bolgani. At seventy thousand words, *Tarzan, Lord of the Jungle,* as the new story was eventually titled, is not much shorter than most other

Burroughs novels, but thanks to generous levity and limited gimmickry, it feels like a much leaner story and for that reason is a very readable one. It was immediately snapped up by *Blue Book* for five thousand dollars, the first time he had sold anything to that magazine (or its sister, *Red Book*) since the *Tarzan the Untamed* stories. A year later, as McClurg was preparing to publish the book version of *Tarzan, Lord of the Jungle,* Burroughs wrote to express his surprise at how well the story had gone over with magazine readers: "From comments I have heard, I am commencing to believe that this is going to rank as one of the best." The lesson was clear: he need not try to outdo himself with each new adventure, and he would never overwork a Tarzan story again.

Meanwhile, the opposite was occurring in the filming of *Tarzan and the Golden Lion,* the most elaborate Tarzan film so far. He had had such high hopes for the picture, his optimism stoked by the money FBO was lavishing on the project; he was additionally grateful to the studio for allowing him to help in choosing Pierce as the new Tarzan and for giving him a say in the development of the script. He had come away from visits to the set with the conviction that the picture was going to be a "knock-out." But when he saw the final version in May 1927, he pronounced it a "silly mess." For the sixth time, Tarzan had fallen on his face.

He never blamed Jim Pierce, though even if he had been let down by Pierce's acting, he could not have said so openly. After their first meeting at the Tarzana pool party, Pierce and Joan Burroughs had become inseparable to the point that Joan had walked away from a promising job with a repertory company in Utah in order to be with Pierce in California. Yet despite the increasing likelihood that Pierce would one day be part of the Burroughs family, his performance in *Tarzan and the Golden Lion* did not bode well for his future as a movie Tarzan. Dressed in an over-the-shoulder leopard skin similar to that worn by Gene Pollar in *The Revenge of Tarzan,* he gamely attempts several aerial stunts, including some swinging, shinnying, and a hand-over-hand traverse of a "vine" stretched between two trees. But in none of these does he demonstrate extraordinary agility or even proficiency. He looks much more natural ensconced in Greystoke's African estate in dinner jacket, bow tie, and white duck trousers or when trotting at the head of his squad of trusty Waziri warriors.

FBO had spent freely on sets, especially the Greystoke bungalow and the bejeweled temple of the Tangani, which Tarzan reaches just in time to save Jane's sister from being sacrificed to Numa, the sacred lion. The action scenes, however, are few and for the most part disappointing. Tarzan has his own lion sidekick, Jab, but like a dog, the creature does little more than run, jump, and stay. The lion's obedience is a reflection of the excellent skills of his trainer, Charlie Gay, but the movie could have benefited from more of the unruly roughhousing between man and beast that were so spellbinding in *The Adventures of Tarzan*. The climactic fight in the temple amounts to little more than a shoving match, and Burroughs, for one, was upset that Jim Pierce was given so little leeway. "I cannot understand why [you] did not take advantage of Pierce's great strength," he grumbled to FBO. "[He] is able to lift a man above his head and throw him, and the only instance when he was allowed to do anything of the kind was cut after a brief flash." He closed his letter by wondering how different the picture would have been if he had directed it himself.

But the time for wishful thinking had passed. When he had first gone into business with FBO, he had imagined the company making a series of Tarzan movies and adapting several of his non-Tarzans. Then, when *Golden Lion* earned only half of what had been expected—probably no more than two hundred thousand dollars—he accused FBO of cheating him out of royalties. The studio was outraged by the accusation and never considered doing business with Burroughs again.

EVEN AS one professional relationship was sputtering, another was sprouting. In July 1927, two months after the release of *Golden Lion*, Burroughs made the acquaintance of Joe Neebe, a family friend who worked for an advertising agency in Detroit. As would soon become apparent, Neebe was a man of diverse talents and extraordinary energy and in his spare time had written a play which enjoyed a brief run in Los Angeles. Neebe invited Burroughs to see the play with him, and the next night took him to dinner and pitched an idea that instantly lit a fire under his fellow author. Neebe had in mind forming a company to develop and syndicate comic strips based on famous books. He wanted *Tarzan of the Apes* to be the first.

Since the turn of the century, comic strips had become a mainstay of American newspapers. Beginning with *The Katzenjammer Kids* in 1897, most "comics" were, as the name implied, of a humorous bent, with a punchline typically falling in the last frame of each day's installment. Favorites included *Mutt and Jeff, Barney Google,* and *Moon Mullins.* By the mid-1920s, so-called "continuity" strips, those with a stronger narrative thread, such as *Little Orphan Annie,* were catching on, but so far no one had ever attempted to translate a full-blown adventure story into the medium.

As radical as Neebe's idea was, he had little difficulty convincing Burroughs of the feasibility of shoehorning an entire novel into three hundred pictures. The money was even easier to visualize. A very fair rate for syndication was one dollar and fifty cents per day per ten thousand newspaper readers. Assuming the strip could reach, say, four million readers, and multiplying by fifty-two weeks, the total income came to one hundred eighty-seven thousand dollars a year, half of which would go to Burroughs. And four million was a conservative number, Neebe advised; the Hearst chain of papers, which had already expressed interest in Tarzan, reached five million readers alone. Then, too, the strips could be compiled and published in book form, and once the strips and strip books gained momentum, why not go beyond Tarzan? "I decided not to do any [more] figuring," Burroughs wrote to Neebe, "as I have a weak heart, for with some twenty eight titles in book form, I can see where we would soon make Mr. Ford take a back seat in the financial world." He was kidding, of course, but it didn't hurt to dream.

Actual creation of the comic strip took much longer than either Burroughs or Neebe had anticipated. While still hanging onto his job at the Detroit ad agency, Neebe found time to incorporate as Famous Books and Players and put Burroughs on the advisory board. Searching around for a worthy artist to draw the strip, Neebe finally settled on thirty-six-year-old Hal Foster, who did advertising illustration for Neebe's agency. The task of signing up newspapers was trickier, and Neebe and Burroughs finally had to hire the Metropolitan Newspaper Service of New York as a broker. Sales did not take off at quite the rate they had originally hoped, either; for instance, the Hearst papers would not handle a strip for which the movie rights had already been sold. But Neebe and Burroughs were confident that more papers would sign the strip up once it debuted. They set a date of January 1929.

With the disappointment of *Tarzan and the Golden Lion* fading and the comic strip to look forward to, Burroughs was back in good spirits. A regimen of regular exercise and limited socializing had worked wonders on the "anxieties" that had previously worried his doctor. In fact, the entire family was "disgustingly healthy," he boasted. Joan's marriage to Jim Pierce in August 1928, under an arbor swagged with blooming asters at El Caballero, was a joyous affair. And the boys were beginning to settle down after years of switching schools and tutors and falling behind. Hully was headed for Pomona College in the fall of 1929; Jack would follow the year after.

Burroughs hit a good stride in his writing as well. In the fall of 1927, perhaps inspired by Joe Neebe's play, he had tried one of his own: *You Lucky Girl!*, about an actress torn between her career and the strictures of marriage. He clearly wrote it with Joan in mind as the lead and gave it a strong feminist slant. Ironically, though, Joan never got a chance to act the part before quitting the theater to marry Pierce, who still believed his screen career was about to soar.

That same fall, Burroughs finished a sequel to *The War Chief.* Even though *Argosy All-Story* had published his first Apache story, he had no particular loyalty to the Munsey magazines since Bob Davis's departure. Accordingly, he submitted the new story, *The Apache Devil,* to *Blue Book,* which had been so complimentary in its acceptance of *Tarzan, Lord of the Jungle.* But *Blue Book* editor Edwin Balmer was not interested in an Indian story, and so *Apache Devil* landed back at *Argosy All-Story.*

The further adventures of Shoz-Dijiji and Wichita Billings are set against the history of Geronimo's final days. Again Apaches are defended and whites demonized. After Shoz-Dijiji saves Wichita's life again and avenges the murder of her father, she confesses that she loves him even though he is an Indian. Shoz-Dijiji, who has learned his true ancestry from Geronimo, tells her on the final page that he is white, nimbly sidestepping the unspeakable eventuality of miscegenation, a well-exercised Burroughs taboo.

The following spring, Burroughs wrote another Tarzan, *Tarzan and the Lost Empire.* This time he approached Street & Smith's *Popular Magazine,* though it had already rejected *Marcia of the Doorstep* and his two most recent Martian stories. Editor Charles MacLean was eager to read the new Tarzan and mentioned that he might pay ten cents a word if he liked it. Armed with *Popular*'s pitch, Burroughs quickly fired off a letter to Balmer of *Blue Book,* bragging that a certain magazine had just "ordered" a story "at the highest rate that I have ever been offered."

Given the recent demand for his work, he added casually, he couldn't imagine selling a future Tarzan to *Blue Book* for less than fifteen cents a word. Just out of curiosity, he inquired, how much *would* Balmer be willing to pay for a commissioned Tarzan?

He was running a bluff, trying to trick *Blue Book* into bidding higher than *Popular's* tentative ten cents a word—a clever enough strategy, even though it did not play out quite the way he had hoped. In June, *Popular* rejected *Tarzan and the Lost Empire*, a fact Burroughs did not disclose when he sent the manuscript on to *Blue Book*, which was all too pleased to have it fall in its lap, the first Tarzan to run in its pages since *Jungle Tales* eleven years earlier. Burroughs didn't get anything close to fifteen cents a word, or even ten; in fact, Balmer paid only seven and a half cents, but he likely would have offered even less if Burroughs had not played his cards so shrewdly.

Tarzan and the Lost Empire is essentially *Tarzan, Lord of the Jungle* with a mothballed legion of Roman centurions in place of English crusaders and a well-mannered German archeologist in place of an American photographer. Throughout his writing career, Burroughs had borrowed heavily from classical history and mythology; in *Lost Empire,* he takes even greater liberties with these familiar sources. Inevitably, Tarzan must fight a lion in an arena beneath the scowl of a Roman emperor, and the story's archaic vocabulary—with a heavy sprinkling of terms such as *impedimenta* and *cohort*—invokes a schoolboy's translation of Caesar's *The Gallic War.* Tarzan, who like all Burroughs heroes, has a knack for languages, learns to speak Latin in three weeks.

But not all of *Lost Empire* is so easygoing. In one of the many digressions on ancient civilization, Burroughs makes a curious aside about law and order under the emperor Honus Hasta. To rid the land of crime, the emperor calls for the execution of not only criminals but their family members as well, "so that there [will be] none to transmit to posterity the original inclination of a depraved sire." Such harsh punishment had little to do with ancient, or even latter-day, Roman law, but was in fact an expression of Burroughs's ongoing and escalating fixation on eugenics.

In January, just before beginning *Lost Empire,* he had intentionally thrust himself into the thick of the debate over social and biological degeneracy by arranging with the Hearst-owned *Los Angeles Examiner* to cover the murder trail of William Edward Hickman. The heinousness of the crime—Hickman had hacked young Marion Parker to pieces with a butcher knife—was sensational in and of itself; but what made the story of particular interest to Burroughs was the fact that Hickman's attorney had entered a plea of not guilty on the grounds of insanity, a rarity in those days. Burroughs was so fascinated that he agreed to write a daily column for free.

IF CREATIONISM was the antithesis of Darwinism, then eugenics was Darwinism taken to extremes. In the nineteenth century, Darwin and his more outgoing spokesman, Herbert Spencer, had declared heredity the guiding force in the world. All physical and mental traits are determined genetically, they asserted, meaning that all humans are entirely creatures of "nature"—as opposed to being shaped by the cultural influences of "nurture." For ardent Darwinists, there was no middle ground. Not only did they believe that characteristics such as skin color, facial features, and skull size were inherited, but they also attributed the abstract qualities of intelligence, "feeble-mindedness," ambition, sloth, honor, and criminality to heredity.

After Spencer, the next Darwinist in rank was Francis Galton, a British doctor and cousin of Darwin. In the year's following the publication of *On the Origin of Species,* Galton extrapolated that certain bloodlines were, by the law of natural selection, more highly developed than others. He then went on to assert that certain larger genetic pools—races—were more advanced than others, a hypothesis that also happened to mesh neatly with prevailing social and political doctrine. Galton endeavored to prove his argument by studying the pedigrees of eminent Englishmen and discovered that they had a much greater proportion of "outstanding" forebears than did individuals who were "average" or not so eminent. Today, his deduction seems at once specious and ludicrously obvious, given what we now understand about cultural advantages. But when Galton's *Hereditary Genius* was published in 1869, it was applauded as a work of great brilliance.

Galton did not stand on anecdotal evidence alone, however, and he soon became a pioneer and proponent of anthropometry and standardized mental testing—the forerunner of IQ tests—to measure where an individual stood on the ladder between savagery and civilization. He was also one of the first scientists to speak out on the practical applications of biological determinism. By practicing "judicious mating," he advised, the fit could become even fitter. And through a broader policy of procreative planning, "race improvement" was feasible and the world would be that much farther down the road to perfection. More draconian but just as crucial to the refinement of the gene pool was the importance of discouraging certain bloodlines. In 1883, Galton gave his doctrine of biological engineering the name "eugenics."

Eugenics had a ready audience among the American establishment, which, even as it prospered, continued to be alarmed by the blurring of racial, ethnic, and social demarcations across the country, particularly in cities. That there might be a scientific explanation for, and solution to, the problems of crime, poverty, and the other epidemic forms of moral decay was welcome and reassuring news.

In 1874, an ambitious member of the New York Sociology Club by the name of Richard Dugdale paid visits to thirteen county jails in upstate New York, where he was surprised to discover six relatives under lock and key at the same time. Over subsequent months, he dug up the family tree of Max Juke, the pseudonym he gave to the patriarch of this unfortunate clan, and determined that out of 709 relatives and persons married to relatives, more than two hundred had been on relief at some time in their lives, 128 had been prostitutes, eighteen had kept brothels, and seventy-six had been convicted of other crimes. Dugdale's report on his findings, *The Jukes: A Study in Crime, Pauperism, Disease, and Heredity,* which appeared in 1877, was the most influential work on American heredity and criminology in the nineteenth century and a seminal document in the American eugenics movement. Dugdale had provided statistical proof of what was already common knowledge in drawing rooms and corner offices everywhere: bad blood only makes more bad blood.

By the first decade of the 1900s, followers of Dugdale's and Galton's doctrine were vocal and well organized. In 1910, Charles Davenport, a geneticist and member of an organization ominously named the American Breeders Society, published *The Science of Human Improvement by Better Breeding,* advocating that ten million dollars spent on eugenics would go a lot further than the same amount given in charitable relief of "vice, imbecility, and suffering." In July 1912 (on the eve of publication of *Tarzan of the Apes*), Davenport led an American delegation to the First International Eugenics Conference in London; upon his return, with financial assistance from the likes of John D. Rockefeller, George

Eastman, and Mrs. E. H. Harriman, he began accumulating a list of "America's most effective blood lines" for a private agency called the Eugenics Record Office. By 1914, scores of American universities offered courses or lectures on eugenics, and literature on the subject grew increasingly inflammatory. Madison Grant's *The Passing of the Great Race* (1916) and Lothrop Stoddard's *The Rising Tide of Color* (1920) preached a doctrine of racial supremacy that anticipated the 1930s exterminationist policies of the Nazis.

Since more than half the states in the country already had laws against interracial marriage, eugenicists did not actively deploy on that front, though they did join the lobby in favor of tighter immigration laws. Another eugenicist cause was sterilization of certain undesirable denizens of mental hospitals and prisons. Indiana was the first state to pass such a law, in 1907, and more than thirty more states would follow over the next quarter century, the most prominent sterilization case occurring in Virginia in 1924. Eighteen-year-old Carrie Buck, a patient in a state mental hospital was said to be "the daughter of a feeble-minded mother . . . and the mother of an illegitimate feeble-minded daughter," and so became the first person selected for sterilization under Virginia's new law. Those who felt that the severing of Buck's fallopian tubes was cruel and inappropriate eventually had their day before the Supreme Court in 1927. Justice Oliver Wendell Holmes, applying the bluntest of instruments, patriotism, upheld Virginia's right to take away Buck's fertility. "We have seen more than once that the public welfare may call upon the best citizens for their lives," said Justice Holmes, himself a twice-wounded Civil War veteran. "It would be strange if it could not call upon those who sap the strength of the state for these lesser sacrifices. . . . Three generations of imbeciles are enough."

BY THE time of the Buck ruling, eugenics had plenty of critics (most notably Columbia University anthropologist Franz Boas, the father of "cultural determinism," and his promising young disciple Margaret Mead), but Burroughs was definitely not among them. It is true that in *The Monster Men* (1917), he pokes fun at the pirates who, upon opening the treasure chest of human experimenter Arthur Maxon, discover that it contains nothing more than a dreary collection of books on eugenics. But ever since editorializing on the Scopes trial, he had become an enthusiastic proponent of genetically driven social policy.

At the end of 1927, he was between stories, having completed *The Apache Devil* the previous month and not wishing to begin his next Tarzan *(Lost Empire)* till after the Christmas holiday. On December 15, William Edward Hickman, an eighteen-year-old former honor student from Kansas City, kidnapped twelve-year-old Marion Parker, the daughter of a bank clerk, from her junior high school in Los Angeles. After strangling Marion in his apartment, Hickman, who had once held a job disemboweling and disjointing chickens, performed a similar operation on the girl, using his bathroom as an abatoir. Next, he painstakingly applied makeup to her cheeks, tied her hair in a bow, and fixed her eyes open by running picture wire through her lids. His handiwork complete, he propped Marion up in the front seat of his car and on a dark Los Angeles street, succeeded in convincing her father that she was still alive. Arrested in Oregon five days later with most of the fifteen hundred dollar ransom money in the back of his Hudson, he revealed that all of his actions had been guided by "Providence." Asked why he had requested only fifteen hundred dollars, he explained that it was the precise sum he needed to pay his tuition to divinity school.

Hickman made a full confession to Los Angeles District Attorney Asa Keyes on Christmas Day. One month later, his trial began in the Hall of Justice in downtown Los Angeles. His attorneys did not dispute that he had killed Marion Parker, but instead entered an insanity plea and prepared to prove that Hickman was schizophrenic and thus could not be held accountable for the ghastly crime.

Burroughs attended all thirteen days of the trial, joining a hundred other reporters and the occasional movie star in the gallery. He paid scant attention to the blow-by-blow details—he left that to the others—and instead used his daily inches, which were syndicated to Hearst papers across the country, to criticize the judge, the circus atmosphere in the courtroom, and the testimony of the various "alienists," whom he considered much crazier than the defendant. In his first dispatch, he took a dim view at the insanity defense. "Hickman is a moral imbecile, and moral imbecility is not insanity," he expounded. "[I]f he is crazy, I am Professor Einstein." Armed with a font of eugenic jargon and a novelist's knowledge of psychiatry, Burroughs asserted that Hickman was perfectly capable of discerning right from wrong; he simply did not care what the results of his actions might be "so long as he may gratify his abnormal egotism or his perverted inclinations." Such abnormality, he averred, was genetic—an "inborn brutality of will"—which was the best reason of all for giving Hickman a death sentence. "If we hang him we have removed . . . a potential menace to the peace and happiness and safety of countless future generations, for moral imbeciles breed moral imbeciles, criminals breed criminals, murderers breed murderers just as truly as St. Bernards breed St. Bernards."

What made Burroughs's pronouncement so bold was that he gave it before he had heard a word of testimony. "[H]e is of minor importance," he said, treating a guilty verdict and death sentence as foregone conclusions and moving on to an even more important issue: Hickman was not the only one who deserved execution. "[W]e should not stop with Hickman; in fact, we need not wait to begin with him," Burroughs wrote after the first day in court. "The city has plenty of moral imbeciles that we might well dispense with."

Once he was able to study the countenance of Hickman more closely, he was even more sure of his own verdict. "To me, he is but a type—a type of a different species that numbers countless members and is daily growing larger." The name he gave to the new strain was "instinctive criminal." "I was not looking at a human being—I was watching for reactions in some species of beast that does not react to the stimuli that affect human beings." To Burroughs, Hickman appeared to be "a representative of a new species of man that has been evolving through the ages, and only when society awakens to the fact that species may be differentiated by something other than anatomical divergencies . . . it will realize that the members of this new species may not be judged by the same standards that hold for us. . . . Destruction and sterilization are our only defense and we should invoke them while we are yet numerically in the ascendancy."

Each day Burroughs's byline was accompanied by the phrase, "Noted writer of 'Tarzan' and author of 'The War Chief,' " as if these somehow credentialed the audacious statements that followed. No doubt the plug of his name and books was a payment from Hearst in lieu of cash, but not all the attention he received worked in his favor. "From the standpoint of anyone who is at all familiar with normal and abnormal psychiatry," one professor wrote, Burroughs's views were "preposterous"—except in one sense: "[Y]our deductions concerning human 'imbecility' show just that in your own personal case." A number of other letters suggested that Burroughs was out of his mind or at least out of his depth. Yet the virulence of his remarks was a fair indication of the number of citizens whom he expected would agree with him. "The show is almost over," he preached in his final column, while the jury was still out. "Whatever the verdict may be, our battle must go on. There are more Hickmans in the world. There always have been Hickmans—there always will be Hickmans. The best that we can do is to discourage the uncaught Hickmans from plying their chosen profession and destroy those whom we do catch."

The jury did its part: it found Hickman to be sane at the time of the murder, and he was eventually hanged. A month after the Hickman trial ended, Burroughs began his Tarzan novel about a latter-day Roman empire in which undesirables and their blood relations are systematically destroyed. Meanwhile in Germany, Adolf Hitler's *Mein Kampf* (1925), in which the author envisions his homeland as the natural continuum of the "First Reich"— the Holy Roman Empire—was already a best-seller. In 1933, Hitler's Third Reich would enact its own Eugenic Sterilization Law.

ONCE HE had said his piece at the Hickman trial and in *Lost Empire,* Burroughs turned his attention to other less controversial matters. The previous summer, he had switched secretaries again and by sheer good fortune had hired Ralph Rothmund, a thirty-one-year-old Minnesotan who, if anything, was even more of a stickler for logic, order, and efficiency than Burroughs. After serving in the army during World War I, Rothmund worked as paymaster and foreman at an iron mine in northern Minnesota. He moved to California in 1925 and took a job with a company that made ice machines. In June 1927, he had answered Burroughs's newspaper advertisement, believing he was applying for an opening at the Burroughs Adding Machine Company. Though the position being offered was that of secretary, it was clear from the start that the responsibilities would be much broader.

A month after Rothmund began, Edgar Rice Burroughs, Inc., moved into a new office that Burroughs had built on one of his commercial lots along Ventura Boulevard. From the low-slung, Spanish-style building, Rothmund oversaw the transcribing and typing of Burroughs's manuscripts; did the bookkeeping; handled his voluminous business correspondence; and kept up with all contracts and royalties relating to magazines, books, movies, and eventually comic strips and radio. He was also active in real estate sales and promotion and published several issues of a brochure entitled *Tarzana Bulletin* in August and September of 1927. Married but childless, Rothmund took on not only the company, but the entire Burroughs family as his life's work and became intimately involved in every aspect of their personal lives.

Thanks to Rothmund's talents and work ethic, many more things were possible. With Rothmund assisting, Burroughs resumed dictating his stories on the Ediphone and this time became much more proficient. On good days he could dictate as many as five cylinders, or more than four thousand words. He grew so confident in Rothmund's ability to turn out an accurate typescript from his unpunctuated ramblings that he did not always read over the pages carefully before they were mailed. Under the new system of dictation and delegation, 1928 was a productive year. After completing *Lost Empire,* Burroughs dictated two hollow-earth stories, *Tanar of Pellucidar* and *Tarzan at the Earth's Core,* both of which he sold to *Blue Book.*

But even though Ralph Rothmund was unquestionably a godsend, he was no miracle worker. Despite all the positive things that had occurred during 1928, the year ended on two low notes. In the fall, Universal Pictures released *Tarzan the Mighty,* a fifteen-chapter silent serial loosely based on *The Jungle Tales of Tarzan.* After visiting the set and seeing a few of the daily rushes, Burroughs was so disgusted by the license taken with the original story—most egregiously, Jane is replaced by another love interest—that he briefly considered suing Universal to prevent the serial's release.

The one thing the serial had going for it was Frank Merrill, who looked and moved more like the "paper" Tarzan than did any of his predecessors. Universal had originally given the part to circus strongman Joe Bonomo, but when Bonomo shattered a leg on the third day of shooting, thirty-year-old Merrill was the obvious next choice. He was a world-class gymnast with a slew of medals and a broad chest to pin them on. Retiring from sports, he had parlayed his fine, expressive face, superb athleticism, and exquisite physique into stunt and stand-in jobs in Hollywood. He had appeared in both *The Son of Tarzan* and *The Adventures of Tarzan* and finally won starring roles in films such as *Perils of the Jungle.* Wearing an over-the-shoulder leopard skin outfit, he took vine swinging and climbing to a level that shamed all of his predecessors. Future Tarzans would scrap Merrill's corny costume, but hereafter each would be expected to live up to his acrobatic standard.

Despite Merrill's prowess and the eventual success of *Tarzan the*

Mighty at the box office, Burroughs was not impressed. He called Universal's adaptation "just another serial" and refused to see any of the completed episodes. Adding insult to injury, the following year, Universal released a fifteen-chapter sequel bearing the alliterative title *Tarzan the Tiger.* Clearly no one had bothered to ask Burroughs about Tarzan's embarrassing history with tigers in Africa.

The second disappointment of the fall, this one much more serious than *Tarzan the Mighty,* was the default of El Caballero Country Club. The club had shown great promise in 1925 and 1926, and in 1927, after El Caballero has hosted the ten thousand dollar Los Angeles Open, it was praised as one of the best courses in the country. Sportswriters joked that there was nothing "missing" from its "links," though, in fact, El Caballero was lacking in one important category: membership.

In November 1928, the club of which Burroughs was a director, announced that because of insufficient revenues from dues, it was no longer able to make payments on the 125 acres (including the Otis mansion) it had bought from Burroughs four years earlier. He had no choice but to take the property back through foreclosure, which triggered a whole new set of worries. The club had financed construction of the golf course and the remodeling of the clubhouse with a two hundred fifty thousand dollar bond—a bond that was secured by a mortgage on the club itself *and* on Burroughs's remaining 350 acres of Tarzana property. In other words, by foreclosing and taking over ownership of El Caballero, Burroughs was now personally responsible for paying off the bond. If he did not, he stood to lose all of Tarzana.

Suddenly he had to rethink his finances. Edgar Rice Burroughs, Inc, had grossed approximately sixty thousand dollars in 1928, enough to meet expenses and turn a small profit. Burroughs's salary was a modest fifteen thousand dollars, and by moving into the Mecca Avenue house and selling off all of his livestock except for a few horses, he and Emma had assumed a much more modest lifestyle—though they were still able to afford a maid, chauffeur, stableman, gardener, and half a dozen automobiles. That, however, was as much belt-tightening as he cared to do. To pay for El Caballero, he would simply have to make more money.

The daily comic strip was one new source of income, but in spite of its obvious potential, it was not the immense and immediate source of revenue that Burroughs, Joe Neebe, and Metropolitan Newspaper Service had anticipated. Hal Foster had done a terrific job with the illustration; his renderings of Tarzan were truer to the original than that of any film director, and his detailed but uncluttered panels were superior to most movie scenes in terms of composition and perspective. Instead of a typical text balloon in each frame, a paragraph from the novel ran beneath each panel, creating the effect of a movie with subtitles. Yet even with such an innovative format—or perhaps because of it—only thirteen papers chose to carry the Tarzan strip when it debuted on January 7, 1929. Until more newspapers picked it up, Burroughs had little choice but to badger his book publisher and magazine editors for better terms. Knowing that some writers now made more than a dollar a word, he brazenly demanded sixty thousand dollars for *Tarzan at the Earth's Core*, insisting that it was worth that much in the current market. Eight thousand was as high as *Blue Book* would offer, and Burroughs accepted, but not without a final gripe: "Compared with these [dollar-a-word] plutocrats, I am only a Chinese laundry man. Ten cents a word seems to be nothing."

He lodged a similar complaint with Joe Bray at McClurg: "The last royalty statement shows about two hundred and fifty thousand copies for half a year and yet my income is measly compared with that of many other writers. . . . Zane Grey, the only other writer probably who tops my sales, owns yachts and beautiful summer homes." Bray responded by advising Burroughs that sales of Grey's popular reprints were beginning to slide, while Burroughs's were holding steady. His only advice was for Burroughs to watch his expenses.

By the end of April, Burroughs had had enough of Bray's excuses and patronizing tone; he wanted more money, and to get it he knew he would have to end their fifteen-year relationship and become his own publisher. Over the next few weeks, Bray was able to disabuse him of the idea of going on his own, but he could not keep him from quitting McClurg. Looking around for an alternative, Burroughs immediately thought of Metropolitan Newspaper Services and its energetic manager, Max Elser, who was working very hard to make the comic strip a winner.

Joe Neebe had thought up the idea for the Tarzan comic strip, Hal Foster had drawn it, but it was Max Elser who had sold it. The comic version of *Tarzan of the Apes* had run for ten weeks—five panels a day, six strips a week, sixty strips total—and though only a handful of papers had carried it, the response had been overwhelmingly positive. As the first installment neared the end, readers began clamoring for more, and papers who had hesitated in January were now eager to subscribe.

The second series of strips was not ready until June. Hal Foster had returned to advertising illustration (but would later return to comics with his even more successful *Prince Valiant*), so Elser gave the job to a less accomplished artist, Rex Maxon, who had done feature illustration for several New York papers. Although Maxon was a poor second to Foster, the change didn't seem to matter. By the end of the summer, more than seventy papers had bought Tarzan, and Elser had arranged with Grosset & Dunlap to publish a book of the first series of strips. Better news still, the strip's popularity had increased the sale of the existing Tarzan novels, making the next step seem both logical and synergistic: why not have Metropolitan be the first-edition publisher of all of Burroughs's future books and handle his syndication as well?

Metropolitan Books was formed in June 1929; its sole author was Edgar Rice Burroughs. The first title published was *Tarzan and the Lost Empire,* followed by *Tanar of Pellucidar,* and then by *Tarzan at the Earth's Core.* Like the newly forged relationship between author and publisher, *Earth's Core* was one of a kind in that it is the only instance in which the hero of one Burroughs series (Tarzan) crosses over into the world of another (David Innes of Pellucidar).

The story actually begins with neither of these characters, but with Jason Gridley, whom Burroughs had first introduced in the previous hollow-earth story, *Tanar of Pellucidar.* Gridley, like many of the readers of *Electronic Experimenter* and the other pseudoscientific pulps, is a radio buff. In his infinite fiddling, he has discovered a new wave—"the Gridley wave"—that can "pass through all other waves and all other stations." (Today *The Gridley Wave* is also the name of the newsletter of the Burroughs Bibliophiles.) In another of Burroughs's surreal wrinkles of plot, Gridley's radio set is located in what readers clearly understand to be Burroughs's office in Tarzana. Faintly, Gridley picks up a signal from Pellucidar reporting that David Innes is imprisoned in a dungeon at the Earth's core. He realizes that the only man who can save Innes is Tarzan.

Tarzan's escapades in Pellucidar are truly perilous but exceptional only in the otherworldliness of the creatures who stand, or slither, in his way. More thrilling is the route by which he arrives at the Earth's core. Whereas David Innes had originally penetrated the Earth's crust aboard an iron "mole," Jason Gridley and Tarzan enter via a vast aperture at the North Pole.

Since writing his first Pellucidar novel in 1913, Burroughs had made a point of collecting center-of-the-Earth stories. In creating *Tarzan at the Earth's Core* (as well as *Tanar of Pellucidar*), he borrowed freely from accounts of the so-called Symmes Hole, one of the great scientific fallacies of the nineteenth century. In 1818, Captain John Cleves Symmes, a retired infantry officer from St. Louis, posited that there were large openings at the Earth's poles and that the Earth's antipodes simply curved inward to a hollow interior. Another ninety years would pass before a human would visit the poles; until then, the circumstantial evidence remained intriguing. "Well, for example," Jason Gridley explains, summarizing the Symmes theory for Tarzan, " warm winds and warm ocean currents coming from the north . . . reported by practically all arctic explorers; the presence of the limbs and branches of trees with green foliage upon them floating southward from the far north. . . ; and then there is the phenomenon of the northern lights. . . . And in addition to all this is the insistence of the far northern tribes of the Eskimos that their forefathers came from a country to the north."

By 1825, Symmes's theory had stirred up enough public curiosity that Congress actually considered funding an expedition to determine its veracity once and for all. Edgar Allan Poe gave Symmes new life in his 1838 novel, *The Narrative of Arthur Gordon Pym of Nantucket*. As recently as 1873, the *Atlantic Monthly* had published an article defending Symmes. And even after Robert Peary's putative "discovery" of the North Pole in 1909 and Roald Amundsen's arrival at the South Pole two years later, the hole-in-the-pole theory was still cherished by a few diehards. In 1913, writer Marshall Gardner published *A Journey to the Earth's Interior,* in which he is even more explicit about the size, location, and nature of the polar openings and the world within our world. In *Tarzan at the Earth's Core,* Jason Gridley obliquely acknowledges having studied an expanded edition of Gardner's treatise, published in 1920.

Getting Tarzan and Jason Gridley to the polar opening is simple enough: they order a dirigible to be built in Germany, and with a crew that includes three German officers (Germans now being Tarzan's friends), ten Waziri warriors, and two Filipino cabin boys, they reach the North Pole in two days. The dirigible is called o-220, which happened to be Burroughs's Tarzana phone number; the idea of giving the ship a number for a name may also have been inspired by Rudyard Kipling's *With the Night Mail* (1906), a tale about No. 162, a dirigible that carries mail around the globe. Kipling's story goes into great technical detail about the construction and operation of No. 162, though Burroughs had likely conducted his own study of the dirigibles that had recently begun flying around Los Angeles and the San Fernando Valley. (Dirigibles would become even more topical after the 1931 release of Frank Capra's film *Dirigible*, about a dirigible flight to the South Pole.)

BURROUGHS had been fascinated by flying for years, and after Charles Lindbergh's celebrated Atlantic crossing in 1927, there was no question that the airplane had become the new American chariot. Burroughs was still several years away from owning and flying his own plane, but in 1929, as he was completing *Tarzan at the Earth's Core,* he decided to participate in the construction of a new airport at nearby Van Nuys.

Where he got the money to invest in Metropolitan Airport is not clear. The comic strip money was coming, but it hadn't come yet. RKO had leased part of the ranch for the set of the musical comedy *Rio Rita,* but the rent was less than a thousand dollars. Otherwise, Burroughs's income was about the same as it had been the previous two years. Nevertheless, in February he invested ten thousand dollars in the airport, and shortly thereafter acquired stock in a second company that was developing two new aircraft engines. He was sanguine enough about both that he got his longtime friend Bert Weston to invest as well. "[I]t is impossible to prophecy to what heights this stock might soar in view of the increasing air-mindedness of the entire nation," he wrote to another investor in the airport. His role in the development of the engines was so influential that the company took the name Apache Motor Corporation, and its first engine model was christened the Apache Devil.

As the summer of 1929 came to an end, Burroughs seemed if not carefree, then at least relatively unfettered by the nitty-gritty concerns of his life. In particular, he refused to let the El Caballero imbroglio get him down. Various legal maneuvers had apparently forestalled worse financial burdens relating to the club, and rumors circulated that Paramount Studios might buy it; for the time being, El Caballero stayed open as a public course.

In August, he and his sons took a car trip to Baja, before Hully entered college and Jack his senior year of high school. That fall he did little writing, assuring himself that he was so far ahead he could afford to take a couple months off. He worked around the ranch, rode horseback, and kept close tabs on work at the Apache plant, which was proceeding splendidly. His health, he exclaimed in a letter to Hully, was superb. His weight was down to 165, the lowest it had been in many years, and he and Jack were even doing a little boxing—not bad for a man who had just celebrated his fifty-fourth birthday.

He was so at ease during this period, in fact, that he hardly batted an eye when the stock market crashed on October 29. "We are going to have a great year," he wrote to Bert Weston after Christmas. And even as global depression loomed and more and more Americans struggled to make ends meet, Burroughs was one of the few who genuinely thrived—with the help of Tarzan, of course, whose domain would soon expand from magazines, books, and comics to radio, fan clubs, bread, ice cream, gasoline, and, last but not least, to movies in which the ape-man's jungle yell could finally be heard.

10

"JANE . . . TARZAN"

In July 1929, shortly after signing the contract that created Metropolitan Books, Metropolitan's manager Max Elser asked Burroughs to think up ways to promote the new venture. Burroughs's response, via telegram, was both impulsive and unorthodox: "I might be induced to accept commission correspondent Russo-Chinese scrap. How about it?" His old hankering to go to war had not entirely left him, although when Elser advised Burroughs that such an assignment was out of the question, he was plainly relieved. "I felt that if I could go it would be wonderful publicity and might tend to increase the value of my book rights," he wrote Elser, "but the idea of leaving Tarzana left me cold."

Elser didn't expect him to do anything so dramatic. In the end, all he wanted was for Burroughs to write a brief account of his life that could be sent around to newspapers and magazines. Again, Burroughs's response was not exactly what Elser had hoped for: he drafted a twenty-thousand-word "Autobiography," which he submitted to Elser in installments between July and September.

Some of the reminiscences are whimsical and verge on stream of consciousness, while others indicate that Burroughs had carefully sifted through his personal records for dates, names, and other details. The tone throughout is humorous and self-effacing, but the very fact that he carried on for so many pages suggests that he was taken with his own life story more than just a little—though, as with everything he wrote, he was unsure how it would be received. Initially he had informed Elser that the manuscript, which had been transcribed by Ralph Rothmund from Dictaphone cylinders, was merely an "outline for fuller and more complete treatment later." Then, like the self-conscious host who suddenly realizes he has monopolized conversation for too long, he quit writing altogether, just at the point in the narrative where McClurg has accepted *Tarzan of the Apes* and his career is about to take off. "[T]his damn thing bores me to extinction," he snapped. "How could anyone have endured fifty-four such dull and dreary years and still remain sane, I cannot conceive."

Elser found merit in the rambling autobiography nonetheless, and after boiling it down to two thousand words, succeeded in placing it in several newspapers, including the *New York World,* the first paper that had syndicated Burroughs's fiction. The headline read, "Made Wealthy by Sale of 8,000,000 Books, Creator of Ape Man Can Joke About Days When He Turned to Writing After Failing at Everything Else."

Burroughs was apparently pleased enough with the published result that he cooperated promptly when Elser requested another personal essay later that fall, also for the purpose of publicity. As before, the piece he submitted was not exactly what Elser had wished. "My Diversions," as the essay is called, was supposed to be about recreation and hobbies, but Burroughs quickly abused the premise by stating that if a hobby is the thing a man thinks about most, then his was money. "[N]ot that I care particularly about money in itself, nor do I care particularly about any power which may be derived from the possession of money. I think about what I can do with money, and outside of those things which we all wish to do for our families, our friends and for the less fortunate, my greatest desire for money is that it will permit me to carry out a cherished ambition, which is to own a vast tract of land somewhere—land on which there are hills and streams and trees and rolling meadows." He did not mention that he had once owned such a tract of land, that he had been forced to develop and sell a large portion of it, and that he was now about to get it back under burdensome circumstances.

Nor did he mention that his former ranch had recently become the town of Tarzana. In August 1928, the four hundred residents of the Tarzana subdivision and the adjacent subdivision of Runnymede had gathered in the Reseda Masonic Hall and voted to unify under the name "Tarzana." Where a decade earlier there had been open fields and a handful of modest homes, now there was a proper American suburb. One of the first initiatives of the newly formed Tarzana Civic Improvement League was to petition the U.S. Postal Service for official recognition; two years later, in December 1930, Tarzana could finally boast its own postmark, as well as its own post office, located in the rear of a grocery store.

Burroughs, who had been one of the area's leading boosters and was still very much in the real estate business, was thrilled to have a town named for his ranch and literary creation. On the other hand, he was nettled by the encroachment of neighbors, houses, and traffic. In *Tarzan at the Earth's Core,* as in so many of his Tarzan stories, he expresses his (and Tarzan's) outrage at "the atrocities with which man scars the face of nature," a complaint that grew more pointed—and ironic—as the town of Tarzana continued to press in around him.

Being hemmed in by bungalows, backyards, orchards, and vest-pocket farms was only one bother; even more irksome was the actual invasion of his privacy. Burroughs had long ago sworn off hunting and in fact had developed a philosophical aversion to it, after reading the sentimental, pseudo-scientific books of popular nature writer William J. Long. He and his sons still enjoyed shooting at targets, and on their daily rounds at the ranch, they had always armed themselves against rattlesnakes and coyotes. But now they rode the hills and fence lines with pistols on their hips and eyes peeled for trespassers and poachers. Among his neighbors, Edgar Rice Burroughs, the avuncular founder of Tarzana, soon earned a reputation as one of the valley's curmudgeons. In "My Diversions," he describes his ideal home not as an arcadian retreat but as a scowling fortress, "with a single gate leading into my grounds and this gate would be fastened with a padlock which could not be picked or broken, and I should have a sign on the gate that would doubtless be both rude and profane, but it would inform the world that I was minding my own business and suggest that it do the same."

To Max Elser, Burroughs's brand of honesty was alarming and certainly inappropriate—the article was never published—though the Burroughs of "My Diversions" is not without charm. Here was a celebrity who didn't brag about mingling with the smart set. Instead, all he apparently wanted was time alone. As for actual diversions, he avowed a routine that bordered on the ascetic. "I . . . spend a considerable part of my waking time in keeping strong," he wrote in his essay, explaining that he rejected trendy "systems of physical culture" and instead began each day with his time-tested military "setting-up" exercises in order to preserve his "girlish figure." After breakfast, "I get on my horse and ride up into the hills. . . . As soon as I get inside my own pasture gate, I strip to the waist, combining a sun bath with my exercises." In the afternoon, upon finishing his office work, he sought the sun again, often hauling a load of manure in the hills on the bed of a flatbed truck and returning with a load of gravel or flagstones for improvements on the house. "The road up into the hills skirts a golf course," he elaborated with Thoreauvian beatitude. "I know that the golfers I see would, if they knew what I was doing, think me crazy." But it is the golfers who are crazy, he suggested: "Imagine a pastime that utterly ruins a man's entire holiday if he chances to hook or slice his first drive. . . . Up on my hillside, where I have a flagstone quarry, if something goes wrong with one flagstone . . . my afternoon is not ruined." If such a regimen sounded simple, then so be it. "An English reviewer stated that I had the mind of a child of six. I hope he is right and if he is I thank God, for if so it may always be active and interested in . . . simple things, from which, I believe, we derive the truest happiness."

Another of the simple pleasures was grandfatherhood. In January 1930, Joan had given birth to a daughter, Joanne. In his diary—the first he had kept since 1921—Burroughs pronounced the baby a "darling" and his own daughter "a perfect little mother."

With the Depression deepening and the nation's mood turning glum, he counted himself among the fortunate. Negotiations with the bank over the El Caballero settlement looked promising; he had hopes that he would soon be getting a large chunk of the ranch back, free and clear. And the Apache airplane motors were coming along so well that he reported to Bert Weston that he was considering buying a yacht. Instead he bought a thirty-eight hundred dollar Cord Cabriolet roadster, a middle-age plaything if there ever was one. All the while, the comic strip was growing in popularity—more than a hundred papers now carried it—and the four books that had appeared in strip form so far—*Tarzan of the Apes, Return of Tarzan, Beasts of Tarzan,* and *Son of Tarzan*—were enjoying a modest bump in sales, despite the general decline in book publishing nationally. Burroughs was proud to report that all of his books were still in print, though it always vexed him that his public had never liked anything better than *Tarzan of the Apes.*

He set his newest story, *Jungle Girl,* in the ancient Cambodian ruins of Angkor Wat and made no secret that it had been inspired by Robert J. Casey's 1929 archeological travelogue, *Four Faces of Siva.* He was optimistic enough to think it might sell to one of the slicks, but received rejections from both *Liberty* and *Elks.* He then accepted seven thousand dollars from his old standby, *Blue Book,* which had recently been acquired by the McCall Company. He had hoped that at the very least the story could have been serialized in *Red Book,* which had a slightly more fancy (and more feminine) audience, but his mood at the time was sunny enough that he did not pitch his usual fit when the story was demoted.

THEN, suddenly, at the first of March, he hit a streak of bad luck. Of all things, it was his health, which he had looked after so fastidiously, that faltered first. On March 2, he awoke with a pain in his chest that he called "a touch of pleurisy." The acute symptoms went away after a few days, but he felt fatigued for much longer. On March 19, he nearly passed out in his doctor's office. The diagnosis was stress, and the doctor recommended a vacation.

As if he needed any clearer warning of his mortality, two days after his collapse, he received word that his brother Coleman had dropped dead from a heart attack. He took the news stoically—his diary entry for the nineteenth records, "Hung new gate at entrance to Jack Knife Canon and worked on new Tarzan story in canon, out in the sunshine"—but in the weeks that followed, his best efforts to put grief and illness behind him were interspersed with bouts of feeling "rotten" and "very tired."

Soon his business dealings in and around Tarzana began to falter, as well. The El Caballero settlement was taking much more time and energy than he had expected, though his attorney assured him that everything was still on track, which was not the case with his investment in the airport and airplane motors. In May, he was advised that tests on the two-hundred-horsepower Apache had been unsatisfactory, and by July the company was moribund. With the economy in such bad shape, there was no point in trying to recapitalize or start over. Not only did Burroughs lose his ten thousand dollar investment, but he bore the additional burden of having to inform Bert Weston that he had lost the same.

The two stories he completed in 1930 were a direct reflection of his listlessness and distraction. "That Damn Dude," written in four weeks, is a murder mystery set in Arizona. Cowboy Buck Mason is accused of murder and poses as a tenderfoot at a dude ranch, where he succeeds in solving the crime and winning the girl of his dreams. Burroughs professed to Donald Kennicott of *Blue Book* that the story was in "an entirely different vein from anything that I have done before." His aim, he said, was to write something "more lady-like in the hopes of getting it into some hermaphrodite publication like *Red Book*." Accordingly, he had cut down on the number of killings, but "That Damn Dude" was deadly anyway. Kennicott would not consider it for *Red Book, Collier's* rejected it, too, and not even *Argosy* was interested. The story was so lackluster, in fact, that it did not find a home for another nine years, when *Thrilling Magazine* bought it for a token five hundred dollars.

The Tarzan of 1930, eventually titled *Tarzan the Invincible*, is not much better. Burroughs wrote it in fits and starts between March and June. The villain, Peter Zveri, is a Russian Communist with an elaborate scheme to foment world revolution. His coconspirators include an Italian, an East Indian, a Mexican, and a Filipino—all of them revolutionaries who await his signal to start popular uprisings in their respective homelands. Ostensibly an agent of Stalin, Zveri harbors his own secret plan to become king of Africa. He envisions that simultaneous eruptions in Mexico, the Philippines, and India will distract Britain and the United States from even more insidious developments elsewhere. Disguised as French soldiers, a force of Zveri's men will invade Italian Somaliland, thus triggering a war between Italy and France, which will presumably lead to an Italian Fascist conquest of Europe. Meanwhile, Zveri will stage a coup in Abyssinia and seize control of colonial Africa. The whole affair depends on one thing: gold, which Zveri intends to steal from the lost city of Opar. The deviousness of the plotters is no match for Tarzan's bravery; when push comes to shove, Burroughs quips, Reds prove to be "yellow." "If you find food for thought" in any of this, "so much the better," he counsels his readers in the opening chapter of *Invincible*, though in hindsight he regretted that he had not been more subtle in his treatment of current events. He was relieved when *Blue*

Book agreed to pay eight thousand dollars for what was arguably his most convoluted Tarzan to date.

By August, he was ready to heed his doctor's advice to take a vacation. He had written two books so far that year, and his publishers could handle no more, especially in the slow market of 1930. He had in mind an expedition reminiscent of the family's cross-country trip in 1916. He purchased two trailers—one a sleeping car and lavatory, the other a kitchen and dining room—which he hitched to his Packard roadster and Ford pickup truck. Accompanied by their cook and cook's wife, he, Emma, Hully, and Jack motored north to the redwood forests of Northern California, getting as far as Grant's Pass, Oregon, before turning toward the Pacific and then south.

In October, he and Emma took a second car trip, this time just the two of them. On the thirty-first of the month, Burroughs jotted in his diary: "Breakfast at 5:30. Emma & I left in Cord for Tucson, Arizona. Arrived Tucson 7 P.M. (Pac Coast Time). Elapsed time 12 hrs, 55 min, running time 12 hrs 15 min. Distance 535 miles." He had good reason to boast, especially since the route was almost entirely unpaved. How relaxing the trips had been—and how well they had suited Emma—was a separate matter entirely. In "That Damn Dude," written four months earlier, one of the characters asks, "Haven't you often wondered lots of times what some married people saw in their mates that would have caused them to select the one they did above all others in the world?" It was a question Burroughs was apparently beginning to ponder himself.

The Arizona trip was the last bit of fun he had for some time. On November 16, the El Caballero Country Club property was finally turned over to him, "but the fly in the ointment," he explained to Bert Weston, "is caused by the question as to whether it is not going to be too much of a burden for me to carry, in addition to which I can see anywhere from fifteen to twenty-five thousand dollars expense in rehabilitating the property, which was permitted to run down badly." His intention was to sell it as quickly as possible, though the current market was less than robust.

Yet El Caballero was not the worst of his problems. Ten days before he had regained ownership of the property, his doctor had discovered an obstruction in his bladder. On November 25, he checked into the Hollywood Hospital and underwent surgery the following morning. The operation was initially deemed a success, and he was sent home after ten days. His recovery was unsatisfactory, however, and shortly after the first of the year, he had to return for more surgery. The two operations and the long period of fever and discomfort that followed left him as weak as a baby. "Had a hell of a time," he noted flatly on February 3, his first diary entry since entering the hospital in November.

All told, he made four different trips to the hospital, incurred twenty-five hundred dollars in medical bills, and was off his feet for nearly ten weeks. "I lay in bed so long I couldn't walk," he wrote to his brother Harry, "and for weeks I could get no relief from pain or [get] rest without taking dope." Finally, by the end of February, he was able to report to Harry that he was once again feeling "first rate." He was even able to ride a horse.

While Burroughs was recovering from his operations, Ralph Roth-mund had written to McClurg & Company, inquiring about the size of the next royalty check. Even after Burroughs had given his first-edition business to Metropolitan, McClurg had continued to handle the Grosset & Dunlap popular reprints of the books it had originally published, though lately business had been poor. Joe Bray had to report that the Depression was finally catching up with Tarzan and the other titles, despite the boost provided by the comic strip.

The news was disheartening enough that Burroughs decided to take a step he had been contemplating for several years. Thenceforth, Edgar Rice Burroughs, Inc., would publish all of Burroughs's first editions itself (cutting out Metropolitan), and Grosset & Dunlap would continue to distribute the popular editions (though McClurg would still take a cut of the popular editions of the titles it had first published). What mattered to Burroughs was that neither Metropolitan nor McClurg would get a cut of the royalties from any future editions, either original or popular. "[W]hile I may not expect to make very much profit on the original edi-tion and do not expect to make anything over my twenty percent roy-alty," he explained to brother Harry, "we shall [nonetheless] save the cream of the profit by hanging on to all of the popular copyright royal-ties. . . . [A]ll that [Metropolitan and McClurg] have been doing in the past is collecting a share of my profits on this popular copyright edition after permitting the original edition to languish for a year."

The plan was for ERB, Inc., to publish two books a year, one Tarzan and one non-Tarzan. The first title would be *Tarzan the Invincible*. Joe Bray warned that he had chosen the worst possible time to go into the publishing business, but to Burroughs's way of thinking, he had no choice. If total sales were down, he needed to make even more money per book sold. "Perhaps at the end of the year we shall be wiser and sadder," he wrote to Max Elser of Metropolitan Books, "but I know of no other way in which we can get the bug out of our system."

Fortunately, the portents of doom issued by Elser and Bray were off the mark, and Burroughs had absolutely no regrets about his declaration of independence. If anything, his timing had been just right. Throughout the 1930s, while the rest of the country suffered, ERB, Inc., bore up better than most businesses.

The decision in February to publish his own books was only the first of several entrepreneurial advances. On March 15, 1931, two years after the debut of the Tarzan daily comic strip, a color Sunday page appeared for the first time, also drawn by Rex Maxon. Meanwhile, plans were underway to launch a Tarzan radio show. And the biggest development of all occurred on April 15, when Metro-Goldwyn-Mayer contracted with ERB, Inc., to make the first Tarzan "talkie."

THE THREAD of MGM's *Tarzan the Ape Man* actually begins in 1929 with the making of another MGM movie, *Trader Horn.* MGM's Irving Thalberg had bought the film rights to the 1927 best-seller of the same name—a memoir by African adventurer Alfred Aloysius Horn—and had put it in the hands of director W. S. "Woody" Van Dyke. Van Dyke had in turn convinced the studio that the only way to shoot a credible movie about an African safari would be to send actors and crew on a safari of their own. And so in March 1929, Hollywood had invaded East Africa. The expedition was made up of thirty-five whites, two hundred natives, three sound trucks—for this would be MGM's very first talkie— and ninety tons of equipment, including a complete laboratory for developing and printing film.

The plot of *Trader Horn* is no more elaborate than that of an early Tarzan tale and vaguely reminiscent of a novel by H. Rider Haggard. Trader Horn (played by veteran cowboy actor Harry Carey) and a wealthy South American named Peru (Duncan Renaldo, who would later star as the Cisco Kid) are on safari in Africa when they learn of a missionary's daughter who has been kidnapped by natives as a child and who is now worshipped as a White Goddess (blonde up-and-comer Edwina Booth). They set out to rescue her, but are themselves captured and sentenced to death. The goddess, who has fallen for Peru, intervenes, and the threesome then must survive a gauntlet of crocodiles, rhinos, hippos, and lions in their flight to civilization.

The travails of the film crew quite nearly equaled those of the characters in the script. During seven months of shooting, the MGM safari traveled nine thousand miles and filmed in four different African colonies: Kenya, Tanganyika, Uganda, and the Belgian Congo. Van Dyke, who had learned his craft at the elbow of D. W. Griffith and had recently completed *White Shadows in the South Seas,* was regarded as Hollywood's premier nature cinematographer. In Africa, he shot more than a million feet of film. He had Carey and Renaldo charge lions, dodge rhinos, and swing Tarzan-like across a pool of agitated crocodiles. He immersed Edwina Booth in an eddy of the upper Nile near Murchison Falls, while armed crewmen kept the crocs at bay. His obsession for authenticity went far beyond the script, and he spent an enormous amount of time and effort documenting dozens of species of wildlife, native ceremonies, and every detail of the African interior that came within range of his cameras. Even then, a number of scenes had to be shot or reshot later in California and Mexico.

Needless to say, the production ran way over budget, but Van Dyke's fanatical effort paid off. *Trader Horn,* released in 1931, was an enormous hit, to the point that it rekindled a huge public interest in Africa. (Ernest Hemingway reportedly told Duncan Renaldo that the movie had first given him the Africa bug.) MGM immediately began looking around for another African story that could make use of the fantastic footage left over from Van Dyke's safari. Inevitably, someone suggested Tarzan.

In early discussions with MGM, Burroughs had demanded seventy-five thousand dollars for the movie rights; eventually he settled for forty-five thousand dollars. For the first time, Hollywood did not attempt to follow the plot of a specific Tarzan novel, but simply purchased the right to make a movie based on the Tarzan character. An early draft of *Tarzan the Ape Man* has Trader Horn leading a safari in search of a lost civilization; in the final version of the script, Horn is replaced by trading post owner James Parker, who, along with partner Harry Holt and daughter Jane, ventures into the interior in search of a legendary elephant graveyard and its motherlode of ivory.

Van Dyke was the only choice for director. This time, though, he decided to shoot the entire movie in and around Hollywood, using bits of his African footage to lend realism. Casting, as always, was crucial, and Van Dyke was especially difficult to please. Clark Gable and Joel McCrea were considered for the Tarzan role but instantly rejected. "I want someone like Jack Dempsey, only younger," Van Dyke purportedly barked. At one point, Douglas Fairbanks suggested that the studio consider Herman Brix, who had been an all-American football player at the University of Washington and a gold medalist in the shotput at the 1928 Olympics. But before Brix could don a loincloth, he broke his shoulder making another film, *Touchdown,* and Van Dyke was back to square one.

According to movie legend, one day Cyril Hume, the script writer of *Tarzan the Ape Man,* was exercising at the Hollywood Athletic Club. Because the club had one of the best swimming pools in the area, it had become the favorite training spot for twenty-seven-year-old Johnny Weissmuller, the world-renowned swimmer who was now earning his living modeling bathing suits for BVD. Hume did not recognize Weissmuller at first but was impressed by the dark eyes, wavy hair, and magnificent physique of the seminude athlete he saw sauntering to the pool. Learning Weissmuller's identity, Hume hastened to invite him to a meeting with Van Dyke.

The director knew at once that he had found his man. Weissmuller's figure was indeed impressive, but what really struck Van Dyke was his total lack of self-consciousness. In an era when most men still wore two-piece swimsuits, Weissmuller had posed for an advertisement wearing nothing but a fig leaf. And it didn't matter that he had very little experience before a motion picture camera. The script Hume and Van Dyke were working on didn't call for him to speak much at all.

In terms of pedigree, Weissmuller had little in common with John Clayton, Lord Greystoke. John Peter Weissmuller was born in Romania in 1904. The following year his parents immigrated to Pennsylvania, where his father found work in a coal mine. In the bigoted slang of the day, the Weissmullers were "honyockers"—Eastern European Catholics who, along with the Irish, Jews, Italians, and other minorities, were scrambling for a second chance in America. (Later, to qualify for the United States Olympic team, Johnny switched birth certificates with his Pennsylvania-born younger brother, Peter John Weissmuller; later still, as a celebrity, he gave his nationality as Austrian.)

After one or two years in Pennsylvania, the Weissmullers moved westward to the melting pot of Chicago and found an apartment in the ethnic warren of Cleveland Avenue, on the city's near North Side. His father ran a beer hall but lost his money and then his health. He died of tuberculosis shortly after World War I. To support Johnny and his younger brother, Elizabeth Weissmuller took a job as a cook in a German social club. When Johnny was old enough, he worked as a bellboy in the Plaza Hotel. On the Oak Street Beach of Lake Michigan and in the pool at the local YMCA, he discovered he had a gift for swimming, and by the time he was seventeen, he had pulled himself from poverty with a stroke powered by a passion for a better life.

Up until the 1920s, swimming was an unrefined science. The world's fastest swimmer of the day was Hawaiian Duke Kahanamoku—also remembered as the father of modern surfing—whose untutored style had won him gold medals in the 1912, 1916, and 1920 Olympics. By the time Weissmuller was sixteen, he was six foot three and 165 pounds, with the streamlined figure that would become the prototype of all champion swimmers to come. When coach "Big Bill" Bachrach first observed him swimming at the Illinois Athletic Club in 1920, Weissmuller already had formidable speed, despite very inefficient mechanics. Bachrach worked with Weissmuller over the next year; he was both relentless and protective, like a fight trainer aiming to sneak up on the world with a sure thing. On August 6, 1921, Bachrach entered Weissmuller in the American Athletic Union national championship, his very first official swim meet. Using his signature arched-back, heads-up stroke, Weissmuller won the fifty-yard freestyle in 23.2 seconds, just one fifth of a second short of a world's record.

From that day forward, Weissmuller never lost a race. Between 1921 and 1928, he won fifty-two national titles, held every freestyle record, and broke his own dozens of time. He defeated Duke Kahanamoku in the 1924 Olympics in Paris, taking three gold medals, and won two more in the 1928 Amsterdam Olympics. He was the Jack Dempsey or Babe Ruth of his sport, an international superstar and heartthrob.

In the Roaring Twenties, as Americans tossed aside their late-Victorian prudishness, they viewed Johnny Weissmuller as the least inhibited man alive. Previous movie Tarzans had been muscle*bound;* Elmo Lincoln and Frank Merrill wore their physiques like garments, muscles armoring the inner man. Other Tarzan actors, when they wore loincloths and leopard skins, seemed merely undressed. Weissmuller, by contrast, was clean-limbed in every sense. He gave the impression that he could have sold Bibles door to door wearing nothing but a G-string. Like Adam himself, he was naturally ideal and ideally natural. There was no hint of either embarrassment or braggadocio in his comportment. A certain eroticism could not be denied, but he radiated no suggestion of bawdiness. In future generations, a parade of athletes would sell their bodies to Hollywood, but none would have the benignly provocative impact that Johnny Weissmuller had in his day.

Burroughs had no say in the selection of MGM's Tarzan. To those who wondered why he didn't make even a token push for his son-in-law Jim Pierce, whom he had once considered the best of the five actors to have played the role, the answer soon became embarrassingly apparent. Over the past fifteen years, Burroughs had railed against the underhandedness and unprofessionalism of motion picture studios. Now, just as the MGM project was getting underway, he found himself in a movie squabble in which *he* was the alleged bad guy.

In January 1929, ERB, Inc., had given permission to producers Jack Nelson and Walter Shumway to make a feature or serial entitled *Tarzan the Fearless,* provided that the producers released the film within seven years and cast Jim Pierce in the role of Tarzan. Since making *Tarzan and the Golden Lion* and marrying Joan Burroughs, Pierce's career had not taken off; he'd picked up a few bit parts in westerns, but no star billings. Burroughs had done what he could to help Pierce out, and at one point, when film work was particularly slow, he had set him up in business, investing in a company that made chicken feed out of dehydrated oranges. Writing Pierce into the *Tarzan the Fearless* contract was the ultimate show of faith in his not-so-confident son-in-law.

For two years, *Tarzan the Fearless* had seemed to be going nowhere. ERB, Inc., had not received the ten thousand dollars stipulated in the contract, and Burroughs had come to the conclusion that the project was a dead letter. It was not. Not long after signing the contract with MGM, he learned in a roundabout way that producer Sol Lesser and several partners had bought out the original *Fearless* contract and were intending to produce a fifteen-chapter serial. At one point, a rumor even circulated that Lesser was intending to shoot—heaven forbid—a Tarzan parody. Meanwhile, MGM had made clear its intention to spend upward of a million dollars on its feature; the last thing Burroughs wanted was for Sol Lesser to pollute the market with a trifling comedy. Even more perturbing was the fact that Jim Pierce was still slated to play the leading role.

In the fall of 1931, as MGM proceeded with the filming of *Tarzan the Ape Man,* Sol Lesser filed suit, claiming that Burroughs had reneged on his promise and was now trying to suppress *Tarzan the Fearless.* MGM, which Burroughs had led to believe was the only studio with the rights to a Tarzan movie, could just as easily have filed a suit of its own, but fortunately did not. Instead it bore down on Lesser, who eventually accepted a sum of money to postpone—but not abandon—the making of *Fearless.* James Pierce would have to wait for his second chance at stardom. For the time being, the jungle belonged to Johnny Weissmuller alone.

Having dodged what could have been a doubly disastrous calamity, Burroughs was profusely cooperative with MGM. He seemed not to be upset that *Tarzan the Ape Man* bore little resemblance to his Tarzan stories; the contract had never stipulated that it should. In February 1932, a month before the movie was to be released, he wrote a letter to Woody Van Dyke that was clearly intended to be circulated to the public: "[N]ow that I have seen the picture I wish to express my appreciation of the splendid job you have done. This is a real Tarzan picture. . . . Mr. Weissmuller makes a great Tarzan. He has youth, a marvelous physique and a magnetic personality." To Bert Weston he noted that MGM had changed his pronunciation of "Tarzan"—which he had originally intended as *TAR-zn*—to *Tar-ZAN,* but he was long past quibbling. "I don't give a damn what they call him," he said, "as long as their checks come regularly."

And the checks did indeed arrive at a happy clip; *Tarzan the Ape Man* was one of the most popular movies of 1932. Among the reasons for its success, first and foremost was the performance of Weissmuller, who was received as a blend of Gable and Nijinsky. He didn't do all of his own stunts—the stupendous "vine" swinging was done by circus aerialist Alfred Codona—but two different swimming scenes were inserted expressly to show off Weissmuller's Olympic prowess. The biggest surprise of all was Weissmuller's acting, which was unpretentious and, like everything else about him, entirely natural. Though he speaks very little in the hundred-minute movie, and then mostly in monosyllables, he still manages to communicate a wide range of emotions, including wit and tenderness, with his eyes and gestures. Most of his body language is directed at Jane, and their chemistry is just right. She does the majority of the talking and sparks most of their shared scenes, but Weissmuller deserves praise for accomplishing the more subtle dramatic task of *allowing* O'Sullivan to draw out the nuances of his personality.

Twenty-year-old Maureen O'Sullivan had completed six movies in rapid succession for Twentieth Century-Fox, her last being *A Connecticut Yankee* (1931), before signing with MGM, where she took the role that seemed to have been made just for her. As Tarzan's ingenue, she is cute and bold, petite without seeming fragile. Her Jane Parker arrives at her father's trading post with umpteen trunks ("just the necessities of life"), blithely strips to her slip, then announces to her pipe-smoking père, "I'm through with civilization. I'm going to be a savage just like you." Unlike every other member of the forthcoming safari to the elephant graveyard, she loves Africa the more time she spends there. Not until the safari scales the bewitched Mutia Escarpment does she appreciate the true dangers of her new world, at which point her fate is nearly sealed. Tarzan, who has never known whites before, happens to be nearby when warriors attack the Parker party; he snatches Jane from harm's way and takes her to his grass-padded nest in the treetops.

The initial tension between Weissmuller and O'Sullivan approximates that which existed between Elmo Lincoln and Enid Markey in the very first Tarzan movie—that is, the threat of rape is unspoken but palpable. Yet in this case the image of a fully clothed woman struggling in the arms of a man whose only garment is two skimpy flaps of hide somehow seems so . . . acceptable, even to 1932 audiences. If anything, Tarzan's nakedness makes obvious that he has not a malicious bone in his body. When he first touches Jane, even roughly, she flies into hysterics, but her blood does not run cold. And more often than not, it is she who clings to him.

As in the 1918 Tarzan, their first day together ends with Tarzan tucking Jane into his lair. He then curls up chivalrously outside her door with his enormous knife unsheathed and stuck in a timber at his side. He spends the night like a picketed stallion, dispelling even the faintest suggestion that he might turn his plainly phallic instrument on the damsel within. In what would become one of the most famous scenes in motion picture history, Tarzan awakens Jane on their first morning together by pulling her from the nest by the ankle. "Thank you for protecting me," she says.

"Me?" Tarzan responds, groping for the meaning of her strange tongue.

No, she says, "Me." She points to herself and indicates, "Jane."

He pushes her with apelike force, an energetic pupil: "Jane." Then he taps his own chest: "Tarzan." Contrary to public memory, he does *not* say, "Me Tarzan, you Jane." Instead he pokes his chest, her chest, his chest, her chest, repeating, "Jane . . . Tarzan. Jane . . . Tarzan. Jane . . . Tarzan."

And so beauty and the beast become acquainted with each other's bodies well before actual sparks of love ever fly. If Jane is not in Tarzan's arms, if he is not carrying her, dunking her, swinging through the trees with her, then his lithe body is only inches from hers. Their sybaritic nearness suggests much more than primitive sexuality, however. It plays out on the screen as distinctly modern intercourse—cozy, casual, and unapologetically promiscuous. At one point, as Jane floats in a jungle pool, held up by Tarzan's strong swimmer's arms, she ponders with a giggle, "I wonder what you'd look like dressed." Later, as Jane reflects on her unchaperoned interlude with Tarzan, she surprises herself with how terrific she feels. "What am I doing here—alone, with you? Perhaps I'd better not think too much about that. It's enough just to be here alone, happy—and I *am* happy. Not a bit afraid. Not a bit sorry." And, she might have added, not a bit stigmatized by what "society" might say or think.

Amazingly, few of the reviews of *Tarzan the Ape Man* commented on its sexual frankness, except to flutter over Weissmuller's delectable physique. The biggest stir initially was over the wilderness action, animals, and other exotic embellishments. When the movie debuted in March 1932, *Variety* described it as a "jungle and stunt picture." Similarly, the *New York Times* called attention to its humor, action, and most especially its cinematic "trickery." Director Van Dyke had made sure that *Tarzan the Ape Man* had something for everybody.

And the trickery was spell-binding. Several early scenes were shot against rear-projected *Trader Horn* footage of tribesmen dancing and parading their finery. Though obviously contrived, such interludes are nonetheless strongly redolent of the true Africa. The key wild animal scenes—Tarzan outswimming the crocodiles, the safari rafts set upon by hippopotami—were shot in Hollywood but are adroitly laced with footage of crocs and hippos in their African habitat. In several scenes, Van Dyke employs a dummy hippo, and in several others he tries to get by with actors in ape suits, but for the most part, his menagerie is authentic and spectacular. When a herd of elephants stampedes the native village to save Tarzan and the Parker safari from sure death, it is easy to forgive the fact that they are Indian elephants wearing large artificial ears to make them look African. The unchecked mayhem they wreak is leagues ahead of the elephant rescue in the 1920 *Son of Tarzan* and a cinematic tour de force by the standards of any era. And for good measure, Van Dyke has Tarzan (actually a stand-in trainer) wrestle *two* lions, one after the other, and pits him against a leopard as well.

Yet for all the histrionics of the hippo, croc, and lion scenes, the animal who steels the show is Cheetah, the chimpanzee, who like Nkima, the monkey in numerous Tarzan novels, serves as confidant, spy, messenger, and comic relief. The only person who didn't seem to care for the chimp was Maureen O'Sullivan. Cheetah, a female, was deeply jealous of her human rival for Tarzan's attentions and would attempt to scratch or bite O'Sullivan every chance she got. "I always had the same average— one fresh bite, one about half-healed, and one scar," the actress recalled years later.

Other injuries inflicted by *Tarzan the Ape Man* did not heal so easily. The scenes in which white safari "bwanas" whip stereotypically superstitious black porters—played by extras recruited from the black neighborhoods of Los Angeles—must have provoked a healthy amount of outrage even in 1932; more egregious still is the scene in which a heavily laden porter slips while scaling the cliffs of Mutia. "What's in the pack, Parker?" one of the whites asks as the African plummets to a certain death. Humor only makes things worse: later on, as the safari is encircled by a tribe of short, black savages—actually white little people wearing black makeup—a panicky Jane asks, "Are these pygmies?" "No, they're dwarves," quips her traveling companion, denigrating two constituencies in a single blow.

Perhaps Woody Van Dyke could have made a better movie, but the public didn't seem to think so. When Bert Weston wrote Burroughs to tell him how well *Tarzan the Ape Man* was doing in Nebraska, he fired back an exuberant report of his own: "It opened at Loew's State [in Los Angeles], and according to their advertisements is breaking all records. The rush was so great Saturday and Sunday that they advertised in this morning's paper that they are forced to put on seven shows a day starting at about nine in the morning." The acclaim was the same nationwide and overseas. MGM had spent nearly a million on the movie, and made nearly that in net profit, making it the most successful Tarzan film by far.

Burroughs was naturally thrilled to learn that the studio was contemplating a sequel. "I have not seen or heard a single adverse criticism," he wrote to the movie's producer, Bernard Hyman. "It seems to me that we have a splendid property . . . which should continue to be profitable for years, if no mistakes are made and if the pictures are not produced too often. We have found that once a year is often enough for Tarzan books, and I believe that the same will hold true for the pictures." He was sorry that Van Dyke was not going to make the next one but was confident that MGM had in its stable any number of worthy replacements.

THE SUCCESS of *Tarzan the Ape Man* had a pronounced ripple effect, increasing the popularity of the daily and Sunday comic strips and propping up sales of Burroughs's books, which were feeling the pinch of the Depression. In January 1932, three months before the release of *Ape Man,* Joe Bray had offered another friendly word of caution to Burroughs, who had just released *Tarzan the Invincible,* the first title bearing the ERB, Inc., imprint. "The book business is flopping worse than ever," Bray lamented. "Don't forget that we have an unresponsive public. People are frightened stiff, and they are hoarding. I just want to say, be careful." But in June, with the public lining up to see the Weissmuller movie, Burroughs was able to inform Bray that ERB, Inc., had made a profit on *Invincible,* which wasn't even a very good book, and expected to the same with the next title, *Tarzan Triumphant.*

With the rising tide lifting all boats, the time was ripe to launch one more. The notion of a Tarzan radio show had been gestating for a couple of years; principle credit for the idea belonged to Joe Neebe, father of the Tarzan comic strip, who had recently left his Detroit ad agency to work for a Detroit broadcasting company. Through Neebe, Burroughs contracted with the American Radio Features Syndicate of Los Angeles to adapt the Tarzan stories into a series of fifteen-minute programs.

Radio had come a long way since the first scheduled public "broadcast" in Pittsburgh in November 1920. Independent stations had combined into "networks," advertisers became "sponsors," and improved technology made it so nearly every American household could afford a reliable "set." Over the next decade, listeners attached themselves to favorite programs more passionately than they had to any comic strip or motion picture. (Until 1927, radio had a monopoly on sound.) The most popular show of the era by far was *Amos 'n' Andy,* the Pepsodent-sponsored serial in which two white comedians impersonated a pair of black simpletons. (Radio made black "face" unnecessary.) Forty million listeners, roughly one-third of the population of the United States, tuned in nightly. Variety shows, such as those hosted by Rudy Vallee and Eddie Cantor, were hits, and dramatic series—*Stella Dallas*, *The Shadow*, and *Sherlock Holmes*—were soon vying successfully for the public's ear. (Radio coined the term *soap opera*.) Of particular interest to Neebe and Burroughs was the debut of *Little Orphan Annie*, a spinoff from the comic strip, in April 1931. By the time MGM's *Tarzan the Ape Man* was released a year later, American Radio Features had already completed a number of Tarzan episodes. And in April and May of 1932, with *Ape Man* leading all other movies in box office returns, the signing of sponsors for the radio show and its syndication to stations became almost a foregone conclusion.

The shows, produced at a sound studio in Hollywood, were considered state of the art for their day. Each episode was transcribed onto phonograph records, which were then sent to subscribing stations. As with the comics, Burroughs went over every installment, and no scripts were recorded or records circulated without his approval. He nixed "cawing" vultures; vultures, he lectured, do not caw. Likewise, he vetoed any scene that called for Tarzan to laugh; in print, Tarzan might smile on occasion, but he was no bon vivant. In general, though, Burroughs was thrilled by the results. "They have injected all the jungle noises," he wrote to a niece in Michigan, "including the roaring of Numa the lion, the screaming of Sheeta the panther, the cries of the bull apes, the laughing of the hyenas, the rustling of the leaves, the screams and shouts—you can almost hear the blood gushing out of jugulars." An even more pleasing aspect of the radio shows, to Burroughs anyway, was the choice of actors to play Tarzan and Jane. Press releases from American Radio Features declared that they had been selected from a broad pool of able candidates, though, in truth, there was never any doubt that the roles would go to Jim Pierce and Joan Burroughs Pierce.

The show debuted on September 12; initially five fifteen-minute episodes were scheduled per week. The first two important sponsors were Foulds Milling Company, a Chicago noodle manufacturer, and Signal Oil Company of Los Angeles. Later sponsors included H. J. Heinz, Southern Dairies, and, in Australia, Pepsodent toothpaste. To kick off an elaborate promotional campaign, Signal Oil hosted a "World Premiere

Radio Show" at the Fox Pantages Theatre in Hollywood, where three thousand guests greeted Burroughs, the Pierces, and the biggest draw of all, Johnny Weissmuller, who delivered his famous Tarzan yell.

Weissmuller's yell had nothing to do with the radio show—Jim Pierce had his own holler—but of all the stirring elements jammed into the movie *Tarzan the Ape Man,* the one that summed up the new Tarzan craze best was Tarzan's yell, specifically Weissmuller's Tarzan yell. For years kids had been swinging from branches and pounding their chests; now their aping had a sound track, and every boy who won a snowball fight or outraced his mates to the top of the hayloft became a jungle soloist. Weissmuller was not actually the first to shatter the air of the nation's theaters; Frank Merrill had warbled in his second serial, *Tarzan the Tiger,* which had a partial, rudimentary sound track. But the fact that Merrill's movie career ended as the sound era began is a fair indication of how effective his efforts must have been. By contrast, Weissmuller's yell was a thing of primal virtuosity. And when MGM realized how popular his eerie aria had become, it concocted a story that the sound was actually the invention of engineers, who had blended Weissmuller's own voice with a hyena's howl played backward, a camel's bleat, the pluck of a violin, and a soprano's high C. It was a commentary on the mystique of talkies and the bizarre singularity of the yell itself that the public accepted the studio's fib as fact. Actually, the noise was nothing more than Weissmuller's own yodel, which he had acquired, after a fashion, from the German beer halls and immigrant picnics of his youth.

The sound of Tarzan was now nearly as important as his image, and the radio program, even without Weissmuller, was an instant hit. Another reason for the show's success was the web of promotional gimmicks that quickly surrounded it. Radio, more than any other medium to date, appreciated the synergy between content and advertising, and Tarzan proved to be a superb drawing card and sales vehicle. Signal Oil, sponsor of the *Tarzan* show throughout California, worked him into all manner of lucrative tie-ins and premiums. Over the air, kids were invited to visit their local Signal filling station to pick up a Tarzan pin, enter a Tarzan jigsaw puzzle contest, or join a Tarzan Club, "organized with the purpose of furthering the principles and ideals of Tarzan." Since the formation of the first official Tarzan fan club in Virginia in 1916, individual clubs had sprung up sporadically. But in the first three months of the Signal Oil campaign, more than 100,000 children joined the new club—and while the kids were taking the Boy Scout–like "Tarzan Pledge," their parents were swearing their own fealty to Signal gasoline and motor oil. In the East, Southern Dairies traded Tarzan booklets and novels for the lids to ice-cream cups: twelve Southern lids earned a booklet, ninety-two a novel. Before the radio show had ever aired, ERB, Inc., had ordered sets of clay statuettes of Tarzan and various jungle animals from the Gem Clay Forming Company of Sebring, Ohio, the same company that had made figures for the *Our Gang* radio show. The statuettes were then wholesaled to sponsors, who offered them as premiums to customers. In the first eighteen months that Tarzan was on the air—and two generations before anyone had ever heard of Barbie, G.I. Joe, or Ninja Turtles—half a million miniature Tarzans, Janes, Numas, Kalas, witch doctors, pygmies, and cannibals had been passed out to the consumers of Heinz rice flakes, Foulds macaroni, and flour from the Collins County Mill & Elevator Company of McKinney, Texas. The list of Tarzan products soon grew to include bows, arrows, spears, knives (rubber, of course), bathing suits, masks, costumes, pith helmets, games, and jungle maps. Eventually there would be Tarzan bread, Tarzan ice cream, and Tarzan chewing gum.

With such a proliferation of products, Burroughs came to realize that he needed to be more protective of the Tarzan name than he had been thus far. Stuffed "Tarzan" monkeys had first appeared in 1922. Since 1927, the wry pleasure of submitting his manuscripts on "Tarzan" bond paper had kept him from clamping down on the piratical manufacturer. In the mid-1920s he had offhandedly permitted cowboy star Ken Maynard to name his horse Tarzan, a favor that came back to bite him when Maynard decided to title a 1932 movie, *Come on, Tarzan.* Finally, however, with the launching of the radio show and its related promotional campaigns, he decided to hire a middleman, Stephen Slesinger of New York, to oversee the licensing of products and to make sure that ERB, Inc., was duly remunerated for every toy that bore the Tarzan brand.

Oversaturation, though, was not one of his worries. He ignored the Cassandras who had predicted that the radio show might compete against the syndication of the *Tarzan* comic strip, and his conviction that one medium would nurture, not harm, another was borne out when newspaper royalties increased by 24 percent during the first nine months the radio show was on the air. "Tarzan is a rather unusual property," he remarked to an MGM executive. "By all the rules . . . the Tarzan idea should have been dead as a door mat years ago, but instead its popularity is steadily increasing."

Though nowhere near as lucrative as the movies, books, and comics, the radio show was a steady moneymaker. The weekly fee paid by the three best sponsors, Foulds Milling, H. J. Heinz, and Signal Oil, was thirty-five hundred dollars. At the height of popularity, the show might have grossed as much as five thousand dollars a week. Even assuming that production costs—studio time, talent, distribution—absorbed half of the gross, and that ERB's royalty was less than 50 percent, the net return was nothing to scoff at, especially during the Depression.

The other reward derived from the radio show was the fresh opportunity it provided Jim and Joan Pierce. To Joan, who had traded her dream of a stage and screen career for marriage and motherhood, the role was a welcome and workable compromise. As for Jim, his prospects as a radio Tarzan were better than anything else he had going, including *Tarzan the Fearless,* which at last was going to be made.

Sol Lesser had stood aside while MGM had made a huge splash with *Ape Man,* but his desire to shoot his own Tarzan remained undiminished, and if anything, it had increased. The Tarzan boom was on, and he felt that it was his rightful turn to have a go. His only hitch, and a rather delicate one, was what to do with Jim Pierce. The contract with ERB, Inc., still called for Pierce to play Tarzan, but it was now quite obvious that he had outgrown the job. He was no longer the trim letterman who had caught Burroughs's eye at El Caballero. Since starring in *Tarzan and the Golden Lion* five years earlier, he had gained at least fifty pounds. It was doubtful he could do a single chin-up, much less swing on a vine.

Once again, Lesser proved to be a deft diplomat and businessman. In 1931, he had won Burroughs's respect and gratitude by defusing what could have been a devastating three-way fracas involving Burroughs, MGM, and himself. Now the triangle included Burroughs, Lesser, and Pierce.

Confidentially, Burroughs accepted that Pierce was in no shape to play Tarzan in Lesser's movie, though outwardly he insisted Lesser stick to the terms of the contract. Lesser had never been keen on Pierce, and he was even less interested now that Johnny Weissmuller had set a new acme in ape-man appeal. And Pierce, who was exercising frantically at the Hollywood Athletic Club, surely must have known that he was unfit for jungle duty, unless Lesser acted on his earlier notion to make a Tarzan farce.

Lesser's solution was clean and decisive: he brought Pierce in for a screen test; he then invited Burroughs to view the test; Pierce saw it, as well. Next Lesser drafted a euphemism-rich letter stating that the role he had in mind would require a "different type" of actor than Pierce. Pierce did not take issue with Lesser's appraisal. Rather, he announced that he wasn't *available* for the part anyway. Pity, but his commitment to the radio show took precedence. That his loyalty to radio had been reinforced by a five thousand dollar check from Sol Lesser was not something the public needed to know. In the end, Pierce saved face, Burroughs came off as a loyal father-in-law, and Lesser was free to hire the Tarzan he wanted: Clarence "Buster" Crabbe, America's latest Olympic hero.

Sol Lesser was smart enough not to try to reinvent Tarzan, and the role he created in *Tarzan the Fearless* and the actor he chose to fill it were more a nod to MGM than to the original Burroughs character. Buster Crabbe was even a friend of Johnny Weissmuller. They had both swum on the 1928 Olympic team (though Crabbe had not won a medal); Weissmuller had followed Crabbe's athletic career at the University of Southern California and had been poolside when Crabbe won the gold medal in the 400-meter freestyle in the 1932 Olympics in Los Angeles. Crabbe continued in Weissmuller's wake, playing the part of Kaspa the Lion Man in Paramount's 1933 Tarzan knockoff, *King of the Jungle* (yet another indication of how big the Tarzan phenomenon had become). If Lesser couldn't have Weissmuller himself for *Tarzan the Fearless,* then Crabbe was the next best thing.

Yet Lesser's Tarzan was a lesser Tarzan in nearly every way. As director, Lesser installed Edward Kull, who had directed Elmo Lincoln's swan song, *The Adventures of Tarzan.* As leading man, Buster Crabbe is unquestionably handsome, but he looks more like a lifeguard than a feral god, with none of Weissmuller's smouldering sexuality. And while Weissmuller comes across as curious, bemused, and instinctively wise, Crabbe exudes only a jugheaded ignorance. He utters fewer than twenty-five words in the entire movie, and sin of sins, when Mary Brooks (a Jane alternative, played by Jacqueline Wells) first asks, "Are you Tarzan?" he grins goofily and emits a manic, high-pitched giggle. His Tarzan yell, which he vents after slaying obligatory lions, falls far short of the Weissmuller standard.

The thread of the *Fearless* plot, as one reviewer noted drolly, is thinner than any jungle vine. Mary Brooks, her hubby, Bob, and a pair of loutish white hunters are on safari in search of Mary's father, a scientist who has fallen into the hands of a lost tribe, whose icons are imbedded with priceless emeralds. The white hunters lust for jewels and blonde Mary and stalk Tarzan for the ten thousand dollar bounty on his head. Tarzan prevails, the scoundrels are vanquished, Mary's father is saved, Mary dumps Bob for Tarzan, and beauty and her rippling, grinning idiot set up housekeeping in his den.

Though *Fearless* opened in August 1933 to uniformly horrible reviews, it at least deserves credit for taking a couple of chances. The vine swinging is the best of any Tarzan picture thus far, and Buster Crabbe, besides outswimming a crocodile, as Weissmuller had done, actually fights one—a realistic scene that caught the jealous eye of MGM. The biggest innovation backfired, however. Lesser had conceived the movie as a hybrid: a sixty-minute feature to be followed by eight two-reel serials, the idea being that audiences would get hooked on the entrée and come back for snacks later. Trouble was, most theaters ran only the feature without informing their audiences that there were more episodes to come. Worse, some theaters never ran the serials. Nevertheless, *Tarzan the Fearless* did well enough at the box office, especially overseas, where Tarzan was, if anything, more popular than he was at home and where paucity of dialogue was actually advantageous.

Even with the success of the recent movies, Burroughs did not dare ease up. With Ralph Rothmund's assistance, he kept close tabs on the comic strip, radio show, the product spinoffs, and his publishing company.

For a while, he had run El Caballero as a public course, but couldn't meet expenses, and by August 1933, he was so far behind in his payments that he reluctantly handed it over to the bank. The Otis mansion, seriously run down, had been demolished two years earlier. He assuaged his remorse by buying a house on the beach in Malibu, the renovation of which he supervised assiduously. And somehow between May 1931 and May 1933, he managed to find time to write seven book-length stories and an array of other articles and essays. In terms of the variety and quantity of tasks undertaken and completed, this was quite possibly the most productive period of his career.

His output was, as usual, of varied quality, but with demand for his work at an all-time high, he no longer wrote with teeth clenched, swearing to his editors that he would never send them another Tarzan. Who could he complain to anyway? As the publisher of his own books, he had committed to providing ERB, Inc., two novels a year, one of them a Tarzan.

Between February and September 1931, he wrote back-to-back Tarzans: *Tarzan Triumphant* and *Tarzan and the Leopard Men.* In *Triumphant,* the characters include an Amelia Earhart-like aviatrix who crashes in the African mountains; a handsome, highbrow geology professor; a displaced Chicago gangster; an Italian Communist now engaged in the slave trade; and Stalinist Leon Stabutch, bent on getting even with Tarzan for foiling the plot of Peter Zveri, villain of *Tarzan the Invincible.* They all come together in the land of the Midians, a lost tribe of Christians zealots who, due to inbreeding, are stricken by the genetic curse of epilepsy.

Reviewers found *Triumphant* inbred in its own right. "[Each Tarzan story] seems to be just a bit more absurd . . . than the preceding one," clucked a Dallas critic. Sensitive to complaints that *Triumphant* had become too caught up in political commentary, Burroughs vowed that his next book, *Tarzan and the Leopard Men,* would adhere more closely "to the stark realism of the untouched forests of Central Africa." *Leopard Men* does deliver ample jungle scenery, and the plot, in which Tarzan rescues an American girl from a secret society of cannibals (the Leopard Men), has its share of thrills. But once again, Burroughs succumbs to the weary devices of amnesia and mistaken identity, and even the bloody parts somehow seem banal. "By the end of the third rescue," noted a Georgia review, "the reader is not at all worried, for he realizes that as the savage hand draws back to plunge the fatal knife, an arrow would come to pierce the would-be murderer's heart. . . . If Mr. Burroughs would let the knife fall just once, the reader would be terribly amazed." Ironically, the new surge of interest in Tarzan had created a jaded, more judgmental audience. After being spellbound by Tarzan in the movies, another writer observed, "it is difficult to admire him in the limitations of cold type."

WITH TARZAN under such intense scrutiny, not all of it flattering, Burroughs decided it was a good time to expand his portfolio. He had first contemplated writing about Venus in 1929, the year distinguished British astronomer Sir James Hopwood Jeans had identified Venus as "the only planet in the solar system outside Mars and the earth on which life could possibly exist." Though pulp writer Otis Adelbert Kline had beaten Burroughs to the punch with his Venusian novel *Planet of Peril* later that year, Burroughs still considered the field wide open. The fact that he knew much less about Venus than about Mars—James Jeans had not been as descriptive as Percival Lowell—hardly seemed to matter, either. Before embarking on this new literary journey, he drew his own map of the planet—"Amtor," he named it—and invented a Venusian alphabet, just as he had done for Mars twenty years earlier. In creating a new hero, however, he was less inventive: Carson Napier, the blond-haired, blue-eyed, independently wealthy descendant of Virginian and British stock, is cut from virtually the same romantic cloth as John Carter and David Innes.

To get to Venus, Napier flies a rocket car from an island off the west coast of Mexico, spins past the moon, and then bails out after his ship has penetrated the Venusian cloud cover. To send back his tales of encounters with tree men, bird men, and Duare, the scantily clad virgin daughter of a Venusian jong (king), Napier uses mental telepathy he learned from a Hindu in India.

Burroughs found the Venusian atmosphere particularly conducive to allegory. Long ago, Duare's people, the Vepajans, had belonged to a society made up of a benevolent professional class, diligent merchant class, and contented working class. That is, until a laborer named Thor formed a secret society ("Thorists") and led an uprising against the happy status quo. Thanks to Thor and his fellow barbarians, "The people exchanged the beneficent rule of an experienced and cultured class for that of greedy incompetents and theorists." Those Vepajans fortunate enough not to have been killed or enslaved by the Bolshevik-inspired Thorists now live in tree cities.

Three months after completing *Pirates of Venus*, as the first Carson Napier venture was titled, Burroughs embarked on a very different pirate tale, *Pirate Blood*, a 34,000-word chronicle of two genetically cursed souls: John Lafitte, descendant of the infamous pirate Jean Lafitte, and Daisy Juke, who carries "the blood of old Max Juke," the patriarchal subject of the 1875 survey on American degeneracy. Early in the story, before Lafitte begins his inevitable slide into crime, a friend asks, "Johnny, you don't believe in all this heredity bunk, do you?" Lafitte responds sadly that he does: "Science may not be able to prove *how* it is done, but it certainly has proved that it *is* done—that germ cells carry

certain characteristics down through a line for generation after generation, physical, mental, and moral." (August Weisman had said as much in
The Germ Plasm: A Theory of Heredity in 1893.)

Toward the end of the story, Lafitte, a cop turned criminal, finally
tracks down his beloved Daisy, now a prostitute in Singapore. "It's the
blood, the curse of the blood," she tells him. "It made you a pirate; it
made me—what I am." He tries to console her, saying, "We'll get out of
this and start over again somewhere." Daisy shakes her head. "I wonder
if we can. I wonder if we can ever escape our putrid blood streams, either
here or hereafter." She leaves him and a moment later a pistol shot is
heard. She has chosen the hereafter.

Having once again climbed on his favorite high horse, eugenics, Burroughs was not in any hurry to dismount. In his second Venus novel,
Lost on Venus, which he commenced shortly after completing *Pirate
Blood,* Carson Napier visits the city of Havatoo, where eugenics is the
law of the land. Previously, Havatoo had been ruled by a self-serving
aristocracy, which had relegated half its population to live "in direst
poverty, in vice, in filth; and they bred like flies." Over time, the "better
classes" refused to bring children into such a world and their numbers
shrank rapidly. "Ignorance and mediocrity ruled." Then along came a
wise and persuasive jong who, with the backing of the warrior class,
"encouraged the raising of children by people whom [his committee of]
scientists passed as fit to raise children, and he forbade all others to bear
children." Likewise, he made sure that "the physically, morally, or mentally defective were rendered incapable of bringing their like into the
world; and no defective infant was allowed to live."

This policy ultimately resulted in "a race of rational people who
know the difference between right from wrong" and who are governed
not by "man-made" laws but by "natural" laws. There are still a few bad
people left, Napier is informed, "for there are bad genes in all of us," and
on the rare occasion that a resident of Havatoo commits a crime, he is
exterminated as "a menace to the race." As an outsider, Napier must be
approved by a panel of scientists before he is permitted to live and move
freely in Havatoo. His physical characteristics, he is told, "approach perfection"; intellectually he is deemed "alert"; but psychologically he is
apparently "the unfortunate victim of inherited repressions, complexes,
and fears." He is complimented for the extent to which he has risen
above these "destructive characteristics"; nonetheless, "the chromo-

somes of [his] germ cells are replete with these vicious genes, constituting a potential menace to generations yet unborn." Only after Napier convinces the panel that he is from another planet (and that he possesses valuable knowledge of aeronautics) is he permitted to live.

In the end, Carson Napier must flee Havatoo in order to save his beloved Duare, who has been sentenced to death for allegedly having been "contaminated" against her will by a rogue scientist known for his ghoulish human experiments. But unlike Professor Arthur Maxon of *The Monster Men,* who sees the folly of attempting to engineer a perfect race, Carson Napier, even in flight, does not reject the principles on which Havatoo was built. He is advised that "it is better to do an injustice to a single individual than to risk the safety and welfare of many. Sometimes that policy is a cruel one, but results have demonstrated that it is better for the race than a policy of weak sentimentalism." Napier does not argue with the righteous logic of such a statement. As interlopers, he and Duare simply withdraw, leaving Havatoo for the Havatoovians.

As events abroad were already making clear, eugenics and fascism were made for each other, and in "I See a New Race," written at roughly the same time as *Lost on Venus,* Burroughs applauded the marriage. From the vantage point of the future, he describes a remarkable revolution that occurred during the twentieth century. "Every one knew that there was something quite wrong with the way in which man utilized the powers that evolution had given him. He was not far from perfect, but he did not appear to be improving as the centuries unrolled. There were many, in the 20th Century, who believed that the masses were less intelligent than the Cro-Magnon race of Paleolithic times. But, even worse, it was apparent that as the stupid multiplied without restriction the whole world was constantly growing stupider."

As evidence of this devolution, Burroughs offers the Depression of the 1930s: "There were bread lines; there was a tremendous increase in crimes of violence; there was a system of vicious racketeering protected by an unwilling police under orders from city officials who were obligated to the political bosses who profitted by the various rackets." But then, in the darkest hour, a reform movement caught fire in a "small city." Its scientists formulated a series of intelligence tests; all political candidates were required to take them, and the results were publicized. Those with the highest IQs qualified to fill the highest posts, and so on. Slowly the idea caught on in other cities, counties, and states, and "[i]ntellect commenced to come into its own" once again. As a result, "precedent, superstition, and maudlin sentimentalism became minor rather than major factors in molding the destiny of the nation."

With the brightest people in charge, sensible policies followed. Widespread dissemination of birth control and public instruction in eugenics, along with sterilization of "criminals, defectives, and incompetents" resulted in a rapid rise in the national intelligence after two generations. With crime and other aberrant behavior now obsolete, "[l]aws, law courts, and lawyers were no longer necessary. The aims of justice were directed toward a single end—the future of the race. . . . The citizen whose acts might retard the advancement of the race because of their anti-social nature was considered merely as a problem of eugenics."

Nowhere in "I See a New Race" or in his personal records and correspondence does Burroughs explicitly mention Adolf Hitler or the policies of sterilization and persecution that was then unfolding in Germany, but they surely were on his mind. In the early 1930s, with the national economy in a shambles and the social fabric fraying, many Americans (including Henry Ford, Joseph Kennedy, and Charles Lindbergh) had begun to regard the Nazi agenda as a model for recovery on this side of the Atlantic. In the ensuing years, when Hitler's pragmatic means produced such abominable ends, it was hard to find anyone who would own up to having ever been seduced. "I See a New Race" was never published, but there can be little doubt that at the time he wrote it, Burroughs believed in both the end *and* the means.

As IF TO offset his ponderous discourses on eugenics, Burroughs also kept up a steady output of lighter fare. In 1932, he wrote a 6,500-word murder mystery, "Calling All Cars" (which was rejected by *The Saturday Evening Post* and elsewhere), and three short "Murder Mystery Puzzles," which ran in a local Beverly Hills magazine, *The Script.* His main outlets were still *Argosy* and *Blue Book,* and he had little difficulty placing his recent output with one or the other. All the while, though, his desire to sell a story to one of the slicks remained undiminished. A higher fee was one obvious motive, and the prestige mattered twice as much. Moreover, he now saw everything in terms of synergy, and he knew that there was no better plug for a forthcoming book than to have it first serialized in a well-regarded magazine. Too, he realized, with the success of

MGM's Tarzan, his chances of selling a story to a slick—something he had not been able to do in twenty years—were as good as they were ever going to get.

In April, Burroughs hired a sales agent named Michael S. Mill to represent the ERB, Inc., line of books to East Coast distributors. The following year, he asked Mill to double as a literary agent and try peddling his stories to upscale New York magazines. It was the first time he had ever put anyone between himself and an editor; anything Mill accomplished with the good magazines had to be an improvement on his own track record. Most recently, *Pirate Blood* had been rejected by *Collier's*, *Cosmopolitan*, and *Liberty*. (It never did appear in a magazine.)

In the spring of 1933, he tried one more time to crack the slicks. This time he sent Mill door to door with his newest Tarzan, *Tarzan and the Lion Man*. After numerous rejections, finally in October Mill got a nibble from *Liberty*. Burroughs was so flabbergasted that he had no notion what to ask for the story. Twenty-five thousand dollars wasn't too much to expect from a magazine such as *Liberty*, was it?

In fact, it was. In the end, Burroughs settled for ten thousand dollars, of which he paid Mill fifteen hundred. Even so, it was the biggest magazine sale of his career, and, other than *The Girl from Hollywood*, the only time he ever succeeded in placing a story in anything other than a pulp magazine.

If there is one Tarzan story that deserved to appear in a slick magazine, it is *Tarzan and the Lion Man*, for it provides, in effect, an inventory of all the essential Tarzan elements: tenderfooted whites, bloodthirsty cannibals, swarthy Arabs, lost treasure, a secret civilization of genetic mutants, lion killing, tree swinging, cliff scaling, escape from dungeons, an ape Dum-Dum, near rape, the pall of miscegenation, mistaken identity, and, of course, romance. In addition, *Lion Man* is a Tarzan story about the Tarzan phenomenon itself.

The plot centers on a Hollywood film crew that has ventured into the heart of Africa to shoot a jungle picture about a white man who has been raised by a lioness. The play on *Trader Horn* and *Tarzan the Ape Man* is deliciously satiric. In place of Woody Van Dyke is Tom Orman, who has just returned from directing a film in Borneo. For the part of the lion man, the studio has chosen Stanley Obroski, whose Polish name is possibly a zing at Johnny Weissmuller's Eastern European heritage. Obroski has never acted before, but he is a world-champion marathoner. "Marathon dancer?" someone asks. "No, marathon runner," comes the answer, "and he's got a physique that's goin' to have all the girls goofy." The "Jane" character, the girl who tames the lion man, is played by Naomi Madison, a vain Hollywood vamp whose survival skills seem to extend no further than the casting couch.

Not surprisingly, the safari turns into a disaster as trucks laden with tons of equipment break down and crew members collapse with fever and heat prostration. Director Orman proves to be a drunken tyrant, whipping the natives hired to clear the path and pull the trucks from the mud. Stanley Obroski turns out to be a layabout and a coward. The situation progresses from bad to worse when the safari is attacked by cannibals, who kill many natives and crew members and capture Obroski. Not long thereafter, Naomi and her plucky stand-in, Rhonda Terry, are kidnapped by Arabs. The plot twists nicely with the arrival of Tarzan, who turns out to be a dead ringer for Obroski.

Thereafter, all trails lead to London, except London in this instance is the name of the mountain sanctuary of a rogue English scientist who claims to have solved "the mystery of heredity." He has stolen the "germ cells" of English nobility from the tombs in Westminster Abbey and produced a race of gorillas who, save for their unavoidable knuckle dragging, fang baring, and diet of celery and leaves, are true replicas of Henry VIII and his sundry wives, dukes, guards, and sixteenth-century minions. The scientist is known to one and all as "God."

Tarzan does plenty of rescuing throughout, though everyone in the Hollywood crew assumes that their savior is Obroski, miraculously emboldened to fill the loincloth of his character, the Lion Man. Tarzan chooses not to disabuse them of their perception and is amused by the fact that they believe anyone but Tarzan could perform his feats of strength and bravery.

He becomes so curious about movie people and their ways that a year later he makes a trip to Hollywood and checks into the Roosevelt Hotel under the name John Clayton. At a party, he is spotted by a producer who has a contract to make a Tarzan movie. "You think I might file the role of Tarzan of the Apes?" the dapper Clayton asks. "You ain't just what I want, but you might do," the producer answers. The next day, though, Clayton is informed that he is "not the type at all" and a famous adagio dancer is cast as Tarzan instead. As a consolation, Clayton is given a bit part of the white hunter whom Tarzan rescues from a lion. On the set, the lion runs amok and an alert Clayton tackles it and kills it with a knife. "Clayton leaped erect; he placed one foot upon his kill and raised his face to the heavens; then he checked himself and [a] slow smile touched his lips." At which point the production manager rushes onto the stage, apoplectic. "'My God!' he cried. 'You've killed our best lion. He was worth ten thousand dollars if he was worth a cent. You're fired!'" It is the last day's work the real Tarzan ever does in Hollywood.

AFTER completing *Tarzan and the Lion Man* in May 1933, Burroughs did not begin another story for five months—the longest hiatus in several years. But he was far from idle. He still attended to the details of the comics, radio, and book publishing, and throughout the summer he made a concerted but unsuccessful push to sell the El Caballero golf course, which was losing money at a rate of a thousand dollars a month. He did a lot of traveling, as well. In April, he, Emma, and the boys had taken a trip to Death Valley. In June, they all attended Hully's graduation from Pomona. In September, they took a boat to New York via the Panama Canal and Cuba.

The most noteworthy trip, however, was one Burroughs made by himself to Arizona in July. Apparently he had no goal other than to get away. He did no writing, not counting letters home, and had no inclination to read. Mostly he just drifted, visiting ancient Indian sites, riding horseback, motoring through the deserts and mountains of southeastern Arizona, not far from the location of Fort Grant, where he had served in the cavalry. "If I stay here much longer," he wrote to Emma, "I shall forget how to worry."

His letters give no indication that anything in particular had prompted him to leave his wife and family for the first vacation he had taken alone in thirty-three years. Certainly nobody deserved time off more than he. Yet something *was* worrying him—and it was more than just the usual knot of concerns over publishing or real estate. While staying with a ranch family near Springerville, at the headwaters of the Little Colorado River, he wrote Emma, "This family life is very beautiful. They are all pals." Given that in seven months he would be irreparably separated from Emma and at odds with his children, this casual observation about close-knit families resounds with wistfulness.

11

THE NEW GIRL
FROM HOLLYWOOD

or years Burroughs had kept his troubles with Emma private, and even when he was no longer able to keep them a secret, he was not entirely forthright in his version of what had gone wrong. He found it much easier to blame Emma's drinking than to admit that he had become preoccupied with his own aging and indifferent to his wife of thirty-three years—a state of mind that had in turn exacerbated Emma's own insecurity and made the bottle that much harder for her to resist. Above all, he endeavored to soft-pedal the role that another woman, Florence Gilbert Dearholt, had played in the split.

Apparently the wheels did not begin to come off until sometime in late 1931. For Christmas that year, Burroughs had given Emma a diamond wristwatch, though whether he did so as an expression of affection, guilt, or appeasement is not known. A more telling artifact is a letter he wrote to Jack several weeks earlier, describing a recent dream. Burroughs's trouble sleeping had worsened over the years, and he continued to wake the house and himself with his noisy nightmares. Yet there was something about this particular dream that had moved him to share it with his son. "Last night . . . I dreamed that Mamma and I were in a bedroom that was unfamiliar to me," he began. The rest of the reverie concerned an intruder, Burroughs's paralysis in the presence of danger, a mysterious key, and a vague but pressing sense of estrangement.

Looking back, the Burroughs children could surmise only that their parents had "drifted apart." None could claim to have seen the end coming, although when Burroughs finally left home on the evening of February 19, 1934, no one seemed to regard his action as a lightning bolt from a clear sky. Hully, in writing to break the news to Jack, who was away at Pomona, noted, "I have seen for years, as I suppose you have too, that they have been far from happy together." Still, neither Hully nor the rest of the family had appreciated the degree of that unhappiness. In his own letter to Jack several days later, Burroughs tried to explain the "countless hours of hideous suffering I have endured for thirty years." And to Hully he wrote: "Mamma must remember that she told me ten years ago that she did not like me anymore. Perhaps now she and you children can realize what that did to me, and I had no one to talk to about it." Both statements were made in the days immediately following the separation and bespeak a need to inflate his grievances in order to justify himself to his children, who had for the moment rallied around their mother.

Emma's drinking had been a problem for some time. When she and Burroughs went to parties together, they both drank, but it was Emma who got drunk. Burroughs was proud of the fact that he could hold his liquor and disappointed that Emma could not. He urged her to cut back and for a while they accepted fewer invitations and did not stay long at the gatherings they did attend. The result was that Emma, who had no tolerance and no ability to moderate, drank at home, with or without her husband. And as is the case with many alcoholics, she drank secretly, though of course it was really no secret at all.

Burroughs's response to Emma's affliction can be best measured by the evolution of his own attitude toward alcohol in the years before the breakup. Early on, he had come out against the Volstead Act and had pledged his support to an organization called the Association Against the Prohibition Amendment. But beginning in 1929, his tune began to change. In "My Diversions," written in October of that year, he declared primly that, after a day's work, he did not need a drink. "I have no sorrows to drown," he asserted. In a radio interview the following spring, he warned against liquor's wicked side: "Like a Ford, a brain may run faster on alcohol, but it is likely to run around in circles for a while and then lie down beside the road to rest." And in "Entertainment Is Fiction's Purpose," published in *Writer's Digest* in June 1930, he pronounced that "temperance is essential to good work."

His brief on the dangers of drinking carried over into his fiction, as well. "My business is fighting, not drinking," John Lafitte announces in *Pirate Blood,* written earlier in the winter of 1932. "By God! You are right," responds a shipmate. "There are many times we need a sober head on board." In *Tarzan and the Lion Man,* written a year later, director Tom Orman learns Lafitte's lesson the hard way. Scotch turns him into a slave driver, literally, and he nearly loses his movie crew as a result. But with a smash of the bottle, he turns his life around. By contrast, Daisy Juke, John Lafitte's childhood sweetheart in *Pirate Blood,* is unable to resist the lure of strong drink, though she is the first to acknowledge that it had caused "a lot of suffering in her family's history."

Presumably Burroughs hoped that his editorializing and abstemiousness would have an effect on Emma, but clearly they did not. Nor did even more histrionic gestures. The children recall the time he flew into a rage and poured all the booze in the house into the El Caballero swimming pool. (The pool, which had no filtration system, surely benefited from the alcohol's sterilizing effect.) The incident had occurred years earlier, when the family still lived in the house on the hill, but Burroughs made a very similar demonstration again in November 1932, when he called police to remove several gallons of wine that he had discovered cached on the ranch. That he allowed the story to run in local and national papers shows how far he had come since the days when he had waggishly called the law that had dried out America a "wet blanket."

Clues to Burroughs's larger disaffection with Emma likewise could be found between the lines of his stories. Over the years, any number of rich and beautiful vamps had worked their charms on Tarzan (as well as on John Carter, David Innes, and Carson Napier), with no success. Indeed, no Burroughs hero is ever unfaithful. On the other hand, in the years leading up to Burroughs's and Emma's divorce, Jane is totally, conspicuously absent from Tarzan's life, to the point that one begins to wonder if Tarzan, albeit a celibate Tarzan, is married at all. Jane does not exist in *Tarzan the Invincible* (written in 1930), *Tarzan Triumphant* (1931), *Tarzan and the Leopard Men* (1931), or *Tarzan and the City of Gold*

(1931). One possible explanation is that Burroughs had simply run out of ways to accommodate both Tarzan and Jane within the same ripsnorting plot. Curiously, though, in *Tarzan and the Lion Man* (1933), he has plenty of time and space to rhapsodize on the "profound attraction that the blond female has for the male of all races."

He was gentleman enough not to say that he no longer found Emma physically attractive, but if she had been a dumpling when he married her in 1900, she had expanded considerably since then. Burroughs, whose obsession with his own weight intensified as he aged, apparently did not nag Emma about her own, which was well over two hundred pounds. Yet without his ever saying a word, she knew how he felt about her figure. She read every one of his stories; the breathtakingly voluptuous, minimally clad heroines whose "seductive languor" drove men to traverse planets and fight gargantuan beasts bore no resemblance to the thick-waisted, multiple-chinned matron she herself had become.

In the first years of the 1930s, Burroughs spent less and less time at home. The children were married or at college, and between comics, radio, movies, magazines, and books, he had plenty to keep him busy at the office. That left Emma alone too often, and when Burroughs would finally arrive at the end of the day, he never knew in what condition he would find her. Sometimes everything would be fine, he explained in his letter to Jack, "but always in the background was the specter of fear of what would inevitably come the next day or the next. I dreaded always to come home. . . ." Inexorably, their relationship assumed a vicious cycle: she drank more, and he found more reasons to stay away, and because he stayed away, she drank more still.

As his marriage was sinking, Burroughs resolved to act on his long-standing urge to take up flying. He had been fascinated by airplanes, dirigibles, and all things related to aeronautics ever since flying machines had existed, and his failed investment in Apache Motors and Metropolitan Airport had not dampened his enthusiasm. He had made John Carter and Carson Napier master airmen; Tarzan had learned to fly in *Tarzan the Untamed*; finally it was his turn. As best he could, he tried to conceal from Emma the fact that he was taking lessons—a deception that suggests that he had more than just a hobbyist's motive for trying out his wings.

He took his first lesson at Clover Field in Santa Monica on January 5, 1934, at the age of fifty-seven. He was tense at first, as was to be expected, but by the third lesson he found it "lots of sport." After ten lessons and before he had ever soloed, he bought his own plane, the *Doo-Dad*, which was also the name of the calligraphic colophon ERB, Inc., stamped on all of its books. It did not take long for Emma to learn of his new diversion, and perhaps to prove to Burroughs that she was not a stick in the mud, she insisted on being taken up for a ride herself. A few days later, Hully, who had moved back home and gone to work overseeing the radio show, got the bug and took his first lesson. Jack was soon taking lessons on weekends home from college.

Then suddenly the horizon tilted. The events of mid-February, as recorded in Burroughs's diary, all seem related, though without any clear ties of cause and effect. On the twelfth, Burroughs soloed for the first time: "Got my wings. Great thrill." But on the sixteenth, Hully cracked up the *Doo-Dad* while attempting to land at Clover Field. He was thrown from the cockpit, but fortunately received only minor cuts and bruises. Then, three days later, on the nineteenth, came another calamity. "LEFT HOME AT DINNER TIME," Burroughs wrote in deliberate capitals. The next day's entry notes matter-of-factly, "Came to live at the Garden of Allah, Villa 23," a residential hotel in Hollywood owned by silent movie star Nazimova and favored by many of Hollywood's actors and actresses.

His new address sounded like something out of a pulp confessional, and his next diary entry was no less evocative: "Went to Palm Springs with Florence. . . ." He mentioned nothing about what had finally prompted him to walk out on Emma and did not attempt to articulate his feelings at the time. The record reflects only that three days after leaving his wife, he and a blonde half his age departed for a desert resort together.

His best efforts to put an innocent shading on his acquaintanceship with Florence were not entirely successful. "Blame for the separation is being placed on the shoulders of Mrs. Florence Dearholt most unjustly as she had nothing at all to do with it," he wrote to his brother George after his split with Emma had become common knowledge. "At the time Emma and I finally separated, Mrs. Dearholt had no reason to believe she would be separated from her husband or that he would give her any grounds for divorce. It was a mere coincidence that their separation and divorce followed so soon after my separation. Mrs. Dearholt and her husband have been two of my best friends for years and it was natural that we should be thrown together when I was alone."

None of which came close to explaining why he and Florence drove to Palm Springs three days after he walked out on Emma.

It is true that Burroughs had known the Dearholts for quite some time, and it is likewise true that among thousands of pages of his private papers there is not one shred of proof suggesting that he and Florence had ever acted on any amorous impulses before he left Emma. Taking Burroughs at his word, their romance may well have been a case of all the pieces falling in place serendipitously. Then again, the very order of events tells its own story—not necessarily contradictory to Burroughs's, but not entirely corroboratory, either.

Ashton Dearholt was a thirty-three-year-old Hollywood journeyman when he first visited Tarzana in 1927 to present his ideas for making a series of pictures based on some of Burroughs's non-Tarzan stories. Dearholt had come to California from the Midwest in 1911 and over the next fifteen years had acted in three dozen movies, most of them westerns. When sound arrived in 1927, he quit acting and became a production manager. That same year he met and married actress Florence Gilbert, twenty-three, and, like Dearholt, a creature of the silent era.

Florence's mother had wanted her daughter to be the next Mary Pickford; Florence even looked a bit like "America's Sweetheart," with her curly, fair hair and peppy winsomeness. In 1918, Mrs. Gilbert sent photos of Florence to Pickford, and the star encouraged Florence to leave her hometown of Chicago and come to Hollywood. Her first parts were as Pickford's double, which quickly led to her own roles in a series of two-reel comedies for the Mack Sennett Studios. Though still a teenager, she became the sole breadwinner for herself, her mother, and younger brother. (Her father, who was Burroughs's age, had stayed behind in Chicago and lost touch with the family.) Beginning in 1924, Florence played the female lead in the popular "Van Bibber" comedies, based on the magazine stories of Richard Harding Davis. She quit acting when she met Dearholt in 1927—though perhaps talkies were likewise to blame. Their fist child was born in 1929.

Nothing had come of the first meeting between Dearholt and Burroughs, except that the two men had liked each other's style and struck up a friendship. When Burroughs needed advice on movies, he felt comfortable calling Dearholt, and over the years, Dearholt, who never stuck with one job for very long, was always pitching new schemes to Burroughs. By 1930, the Burroughs and Dearholt families were seeing a lot of each other. Dearholt and Florence would drive out to Tarzana, or Burroughs and Emma would join them for dinner in town. In addition, Florence and Joan Burroughs had had babies within months of each other, and the two mothers became close friends. They were so kindred, in fact, that in November 1933 they rented a house together in Palm Springs while Dearholt was in the Caribbean and Central America, apparently on business. The date was four months before Burroughs left Emma.

Dearholt stayed away for three months. Perhaps nothing especially intimate occurred between Burroughs and Florence during that time; but when Dearholt arrived home, there was no question that the domestic landscape had changed radically. On March 2, eight days after Burroughs's Palm Springs trip with Florence, he was invited to dinner at the Dearholts, which suggests one of three possibilities: that he and Florence were still just "best friends"; that their friendship had progressed to something more, and Dearholt didn't yet know; or that he *did* know and just didn't mind. Adding to the intrigue was the presence of a woman whom Burroughs identifies in his diary as "Enca" Holt. Her real name was actually Ula Holt, not Enca; for Burroughs to have gotten it wrong implies that he had not paid much attention to her, which in turn implies that he, and perhaps Florence, too, did not know at the time that Dearholt and Ula were already having an affair. Regardless of what was spoken or unspoken that evening, everyone was apparently on their best behavior. They got along so well that five days later, Dearholt, Florence, and Burroughs all had dinner again, this time as Burroughs's guests at the Garden of Allah.

The next few weeks were a zany blend of decorum and decadence. Dearholt, Florence, Ula, and Burroughs were inseparable. They went to parties together, had dinner together, visited Gay's Lion Farm together, though which lady was on which gentleman's arm can only be conjectured. The picture finally came clear on March 29, when Burroughs's diary reported perfunctorily, "The Dearholts were divorced today." Apparently it was no surprise to anyone, and it scarcely disrupted social calendars. During the first two weeks of April, Burroughs and Florence continued to see a great deal of each other. (He later insisted their urge to be together was purely a case of misery loving company.) And to show that he had nothing to be ashamed of—and as testimony to his friendship with Dearholt—he had him and Ula over to dinner two weeks after the divorce, though on this occasion Florence was absent.

In trying to understand the curious chronology and choreography of separation, courtship, and realignment, one more piece of the puzzle deserves consideration: *The Swords of Mars,* written between November 6 and December 15, 1933, before Burroughs had left Emma and well before the supposed start of his affair with Florence. *Swords* opens with the narrator on a camping trip in the White Mountains of Arizona, the same locale Burroughs had visited the previous July. The narrator is sitting up late in his cabin, reading a murder mystery in a detective magazine, when he is interrupted by a noise at the door: it is John Carter, direct from Mars. Carter proceeds to recount a novel-length adventure in which he leaves home, incognito, on a mission to wipe out a guild of assassins in the distant and hostile city of Zodanga. The action and exposition have a lean, hard-boiled tone that sustains a clever plot involving Martian mind control and industrial espionage between rival spaceship manufacturers. Especially given the turmoil in Burroughs's life at the time he was working on *Swords of Mars,* it stands out as a particularly remarkable piece of writing, and in fact is one of his very best novels.

The question, though, is, did Burroughs write it in spite of his personal life or, to at least some extent, as a *result* of it? Certain scenes in *Swords* are suggestive of events much closer to home. One example: John Carter rescues the pretty young slave Zanda from her master, a mad scientist who wants to destroy her brain. Zanda pledges herself to Carter, who chuckles modestly that she has merely chosen the lesser of two evils. "You see," he quips, "the young lady does not know me very well; when she does, she will very probably change her mind." Was Burroughs pondering his own worthiness as a mate for Florence?

Another example: later, on the Martian moon of Thuria, John Carter meets Ozara, a queen imprisoned in her husband's castle. She asks Carter to help her escape, explaining that her husband has begun looking for her replacement. "He changes his jeddaras [queens] often," she says. "I think that he has found one to his liking already, and that my days are numbered." Knowing that Florence was not Dearholt's first wife, that Dearholt fancied himself a lady killer, and that Ula Holt was younger and perhaps already in the picture, these lines read like an inside joke and a wicked one at that.

One other aspect of *Swords of Mars* that relates to Burroughs and

Florence cannot be dismissed as coincidence. In the manuscript he submitted to *Blue Book*, dated January 8, 1934—a full month before he left Emma—the first letter of the first word of each chapter, when strung together, spell out "TO FLORENCE WITH ALL MY LOVE ED."

FLORENCE and Dearholt continued to behave cordially toward each other after their divorce, just as they had in the days leading up to it. The two children, Caryl Lee and Lee, stayed with their mother, and when Dearholt came to visit, sometimes with Ula, they acted as if nothing untoward had happened. Nor did Dearholt seem to mind that Burroughs and Florence were now quite obviously an item. If anything, he seemed pleased to have finally struck a deal with his good friend, however odd that arrangement might seem to the outside world. Stranger still, Dearholt and Burroughs—cuckold and cuckolder—were again discussing going into business together.

Meanwhile, Burroughs's relationship with his own family was at best strained. Emma kept hoping that he would come to his senses and return home, but as the weeks stretched to months, she became despondent and even more besotted. "I break down every morning," she confessed to Jack in May. "I am so depressed. I do not think I will ever be any other way again." Burroughs saw Emma only two more times that year—once at Jack's graduation from Pomona and at a funeral later in the summer. After that, they were never together again.

Of the three children, Joan was the most bitter. She resented the fact that her father had taken up with Florence, her girlfriend. She avoided him and quit speaking to Florence. Hully and Jack were far more understanding and tried to be peacemakers, though they were never entirely comfortable around Florence or with Burroughs when he was around her. Of the three Burroughs children, Hully saw their father the most; that winter he had joined ERB, Inc., and was given the title of vice president. Predictably, Burroughs had grown impatient with using a middleman on the radio show and in April had severed ties with American Radio Features and put Hully in charge of producing and syndicating the series.

Jack, who had graduated magna cum laude, had decided to pursue a career as an artist. Burroughs had used a variety of illustrators for his book jackets over the years, most notably J. Allen St. John of Chicago.

When ERB, Inc., began publishing its own books in 1931, he had replaced St. John with his nephew Studley Burroughs, a struggling commercial artist in Chicago. But one year and three jackets later, he had to let Studley go and rehire St. John, who likely would have done covers forever if Jack Burroughs had not come along soon after. Jack took his art very seriously and threw himself into everything from traditional studio painting to the newest animation technology. By the time he was twenty-four, he was illustrating all of his father's book jackets. Later he would create a comic strip and even ghostwrite a Burroughs story, "John Carter and the Giant of Mars."

Burroughs needed all the support he could get, for despite the beneficial effect the recent Tarzan movies had had on business, the Depression had not left ERB, Inc., entirely unscathed. The latest Burroughs book, *Pirates of Venus,* had sold only three thousand copies in the first edition. The Tarzan novels were doing better, but even their popularity had begun to slide. Magazine editors were now calling for shorter stories and offering lower word rates for them. *Liberty,* which had raised Burroughs's hopes of permanent promotion to the slicks, rejected *The Swords of Mars;* so did *Argosy,* and the story finally went to *Blue Book* for fifty-five hundred dollars, half of what *Liberty* had paid for *Tarzan and the Lion Man* the year before. In a fit of sarcasm and frustration, Burroughs published *Lion Man* in the fall of 1934 with the jacket blurb, "Mr. Burroughs believes this to be the poorest Tarzan novel he has ever written." He did it to get the reviewers buzzing, but those who knew him heard a not-so-subliminal cry of self-doubt.

An even more startling gambit was Burroughs's decision to proceed with his partnership with Dearholt. One of the things that he had always liked about Dearholt was his spirit of adventure. Like Burroughs, Dearholt loved "auto-gypsying" and had converted a trailer into a "land yacht"—a proto-mobile home—that he and Florence had towed around the West, just as Burroughs had done with his family. When Dearholt suggested filming Tarzan in "a series of adventures throughout interesting and unusual parts of the world," Burroughs was intrigued by both the daring and originality of the idea. On September 12, he signed an agreement forming Burroughs–Tarzan Enterprises (BTE); Burroughs received a 40 percent interest and Dearholt and his two partners, George Stout and Ben Cohen, 60 percent. "I would not sell you any dreams," Dearholt promised Burroughs, predicting that the motion picture project would make a million.

Fueling Dearholt's bravado was the recent success of MGM's *Tarzan and His Mate*, the second feature starring Johnny Weissmuller and Maureen O'Sullivan. After *Tarzan the Ape Man*, MGM had given Burroughs forty-five thousand dollars for the right to make a sequel and had secured an option to make two additional features. To top the first Weissmuller Tarzan and to ensure that there would be no comparison to the mediocre Buster Crabbe Tarzan, MGM went all out, spending more than a million dollars.

The story picks up where *Ape Man* leaves off. After the death of her father, Jane stays behind in Africa with Tarzan. Her old suitor Harry Holt (played again by Neil Hamilton) also reappears in Africa; he still has designs on Jane and the ivory secreted in the fabled elephant's graveyard. Holt and lecherous sidekick Martin Arlington (Paul Cavanagh) try to woo Jane with jazz records and stylish gowns so that she will reveal the secret of the graveyard's location. Jane is as intoxicated by the worldly trinkets as Holt and Arlington are by the prospect of a bounty of tusks, but Tarzan sees through it all, and in due course the sanctity of the jungle is preserved.

Tarzan and His Mate is easily the best of all the Tarzan pictures, though the story line is not necessarily what makes it shine. Credit must again go to Weissmuller, O'Sullivan, and their wonderful chemistry; to MGM for escalating the action; and most especially to director Cedric Gibbons for appreciating the essence of *Ape Man* and making it even more provocative. Today, Gibbons is best remembered as a production designer—and as the designer of the Oscar, the Academy Award statuette, eleven of which he won during his career. He left his flourishes on everything from *Ben-Hur* to *Grand Hotel*, *The Merry Wives*, and *The Thin Man*, though the only movie he was ever given credit for directing is *Tarzan and His Mate*. (He in fact did not stick with *Mate* through the entire production; regardless, it would not have been the same picture without him.)

In at least one very obvious way, *Tarzan and His Mate* was a direct response to *King Kong*, RKO's box office buster of the previous year, starring an overgrown and plainly man-made ape. In *Mate*, Gibbons and MGM consciously expanded the role of Cheetah, a real and extremely endearing ape, who had been such a scene stealer in the previous Tarzan. They also added a series of animal stunts that set new standards for realism. Their version of King Kong was an enormous, twenty-foot-long mechanical crocodile made of steel and rubber and immersed in a large tank on the MGM lot. The underwater footage of Weissmuller being thrown about by the leviathan makes Buster Crabbe's croc tussle in *Fearless* seem like a day at the beach. This time the critics did not chortle at the "trickery." Quick camera cuts, the violent articulation of the crocodile, and the obvious danger to Weissmuller as he dodges the flailing tail and finally sinks his knife in the reptile's throat all make for a stupendously riveting scene.

In another stunt, Tarzan is called on to ride a rhinoceros, a trick never attempted on film before. MGM imported Mary, a rhino from the Hagenbeck Zoo in Hamburg, Germany, especially for the scene. Unlike lion wrestling—central to any Tarzan repertoire and always handled by a professional lion man—a rhino rodeo was something Weissmuller was game to try himself. Much to everyone's relief, he managed to gallop around the MGM lot safely, sacrificing only a few strips of skin to the coarse hide of an otherwise well-mannered Mary.

The best scene in *Tarzan and His Mate*, however, is one that few audiences ever saw. The morning after Holt and Arlington entice Jane into a French gown—one of the few cinematic interludes in which the goal of the lothario is actually to *dress* a woman ("These are clothes," she later explains to Tarzan. "Women wear them because they hope men will like them."), Tarzan and Jane wake up and decide to take a swim. Jane, who has slept in her silk, is poised to dive into the jungle pool. Tarzan gives her a playful shove, keeping hold of the dress, and Jane plunges into the water in her birthday suit. Tarzan dives in after her.

The underwater ballet that follows is sensational. Weissmuller wears his usual skimpy loincloth (though this one seems even skimpier than the one he wore in *Tarzan the Ape Man*), but Olympic swimmer Josephine McKim, doubling for O'Sullivan, slides through the scene entirely nude. Together they are a pair of lissome otters executing a series of joyous underwater loops and slaloms, their gorgeous limbs rippling like synchronized ribbons. "It is a very beautiful and artistic shot," Burroughs wrote to Hully in August 1933, after seeing the daily rushes at MGM. "Their movements under water are naturally slow and extremely graceful. I saw nothing objectionable in it." Still, he added, "it may get by the censors and it may not."

MGM had chosen the worst possible time to test the industry's code of propriety. In the wake of the Fatty Arbuckle, William Desmond Taylor, and other scandals of the early 1920s, the Motion Picture Producers and Distributors of America (MPPDA), the industry's trade association, had tried to impose a higher standard of morality through self-censorship. But over the years, the Hays Office, named for MPPDA's appointed czar of taste, Will Hays, had grown lax, at least in the view of American conservatives, particularly American Catholics. At their annual conference in November 1933, the nation's Catholic bishops called for the formation of a "Legion of Decency" to pressure Hollywood to clean up its act. By winter, millions of Catholics had signed pledges promising to boycott any movie judged by the Legion to be immoral.

Perpetually sensitive to charges that a largely Jewish-owned industry was out of step with Christian America, the MPPDA named Legion member Joseph Breen as the Hays Office's chief censor; for all intents and purposes, the new set of standards Breen brought to bear on American cinema bore the imprimatur of the Vatican. The Legion code not only frowned on the usual sins of profanity, nudity, and promiscuity, but also proscribed such acts as miscegenation, disrespect for the flag, and ridicule of clergy. A movie could be censored not just for specific imagery or dialogue, but for its overall message—for instance, a story in which crime went unpunished or in which philandering led to a happy ending. Not surprisingly, Breen cracked down promptly on Mae West, whose bawdy movies had made her Hollywood's most conspicuous sinner; but he also threatened to withhold the "seal of purity" from the movie adaptations of seemingly virtuous novels such as Somerset Maugham's *Of Human Bondage* and Leo Tolstoy's *Anna Karenina*.

In such a climate, it was a wonder that *Tarzan and His Mate* was released at all. MGM could not have done a more effective job of baiting the censors (who were in especially high dudgeon after Hedy Lamarr had appeared nude in the Czech-made *Ecstasy* the year before). Tarzan's paucity of cover was the least of the film's problems; after all, Weissmuller hadn't worn much more as a competitive swimmer. But what about Jane? In *Tarzan the Ape Man*, she is amply dressed; come *Mate*, she is a full-fledged denizen of the jungle and clad in a brief bustier and her own revealing loincloth—two flaps of leather that leave her thighs and hip bones exposed.

Also problematic was her matrimonial status, or lack thereof, which is flaunted in the movie's title, *Tarzan and His Mate*. While it is plain from the start that she and Tarzan are truly in love, there is never any suggestion that they are married. "From a Park Avenue penthouse to a tree-top love nest in the jungle!" proclaimed one of the MGM's lobby posters. "But what girl would not make the change for Tarzan?" And what man would not be tempted by such an apparent libertine? When Holt and Arlington try to seduce Jane with worldly trinkets, their forwardness is fanned by the unspoken understanding that, despite her avowed faithfulness to Tarzan, she is legally still an *available* woman and doubtless not a virgin. (When pestered about the marriage issue in the Tarzan books, Burroughs reminded his puritanical critics that Tarzan and Jane had been married by Professor Porter at the end of *The Return of Tarzan*.) Adding a nude swimming scene to all this was like slipping pepper into the Legion of Decency's communion goblet.

Amazingly, the censors insisted that only the swim scene be cut. (A few unexpurgated prints made it into circulation in several states, but most of the world was unaware of the excised morsel until 1986, when Turner Entertainment discovered it in the MGM archives and returned it to its rightful place in the video version of the film.) Even without it, *Tarzan and His Mate* stands out as one of the last uninhibited movies Hollywood made before the Legion of Decency lowered the boom. Nearly two decades would pass before another studio would take the chances MGM did in 1934. And despite all the claims that Hollywood had lost touch with American values, the public and the critics absolutely adored *Tarzan and His Mate*, marveling at the extraordinary photography and especially at the aerial and animal stunts. "If you try to keep the children away from this," teased one columnist, "you'll have juvenile riots on your hands. If you let them go, you'll have to deal with juvenile nightmares. Take your pick." Legion pledges or no, most Americans chose the latter, and MGM had its second Tarzan hit in a row, the first time a studio had been able to sustain any momentum with the character.

BURROUGHS did not take the good news impassively. True to form, he grasped that if someone else could make money off of his property, then he could make just as much or more by doing it himself. BTE had no intention of interfering with MGM, but the law of the commercial jungle held that there was always room for one more Tarzan, especially the one Burroughs and Dearholt had in mind.

He had never abandoned his desire to see the complete Tarzan brought to the screen, a lord of the jungle who was both savage and sophisticated. Dearholt concurred, envisioning a character who was a cross between Weissmuller and Douglas Fairbanks. "Then there will be light and shadow," he told Burroughs. And so the call went out for Tarzan No. 8.

After a succession of auditions—one source claimed an even hundred—BTE finally settled on Herman Brix, the former University of Washington football star and shot-putter who had narrowly missed winning Weissmuller's job at MGM three years earlier. Brix agreed to take the part at seventy-five dollars a week, an astoundingly low salary compared to the two thousand dollars that BTE had agreed to pay Jiggs, the chimpanzee who had played Cheetah in *Tarzan and His Mate* and also appeared in Buster Crabbe's *King of the Jungle*. BTE cast Jiggs as Nkima, the real Cheetah of the Tarzan novels.

Finding a leading lady was less difficult. The part went to Ula Holt, though she had virtually no acting experience save for brief appearances in Grantland Rice's *Sportslights* one-reelers.

Money was a factor from the start and much more difficult to come by than actors. For all their vaunted experience in the business, neither Dearholt nor his partners, Stout and Cohen, could secure financing for the project, which now bore the working title *Tarzan in Guatemala*. At the last minute, as production was about to commence, Burroughs had to guarantee a loan from Citizens National Bank of Los Angeles himself. Negotiations over financing were further complicated by the fact that in October he had established residence in Las Vegas, Nevada, in anticipation of filing for divorce from Emma.

If Burroughs had stopped to think, he might have noted the extent to which *Tarzan in Guatemala* was starting to imitate *Tarzan and the Lion Man*. The novel had made fun of *Trader Horn*, as well as *Tarzan the Ape Man*, for mounting an expedition to film a movie in a faraway jungle. In both *Trader Horn* and *Lion Man*, the leading man is an athlete with little or no acting experience and the leading lady a sweet young thing who enjoys special favor with the leader of the safari. *Lion Man* laughs at *Trader Horn* for traipsing all over Africa at great risk and expense in order to collect "authentic" footage—and now BTE was preparing to do the same thing.

Shooting began at the Selig Zoo on November 28, three days after Burroughs had secured the bank note. Then on December 1, Dearholt, a crew of twenty-eight, and a four-ton sound truck sailed for Guatemala.

According to the press releases, the trip was shaping up very much like *Trader Horn* revisited. A photo distributed to screen magazines shows Dearholt in bandanna and goatee, his pith helmet shading a Nimrod stare. Others had braved the world's remote regions "to bring realism to the screen," one clip exclaims, but "it has remained for Dearholt . . . to transport what was literally a fully equipped studio to Central America, and to drag, by means of motor trucks, tons of freight through parts of the jungle and over high mountain passes hitherto deemed inaccessible— even to men afoot or on muleback."

All told, the "Dearholt Expedition" spent four months in Guatemala, filming in and around Guatemala City, Chichicastenango, Antigua, and the Mayan ruins of Tikal. Initially everything seemed to go well. "We have enjoyed the rushes tremendously," Burroughs wrote to Dearholt after reviewing the first footage sent from Guatemala. "You have some wonderful shots, and with the sets, crowds and backgrounds, it looks like a million dollar picture. It would certainly have cost MGM that much if they had made it on their lot." In fact, BTE would have loved to have had one-tenth of the money MGM had spent on its last Tarzan movie. As it was, when the Citizens National Bank note came due on February 25, BTE was not immediately able to meet its obligation. Finally, more financing was secured thanks to guarantees from distributors, but for the entire time that the crew was in Guatemala, cash was in short supply.

Tarzan in Guatemala, eventually renamed *The New Adventures of Tarzan,* is essentially one long chase presented in serial, rather than feature, format. Venerable archeologist Major Markling and an entourage travel to Guatemala in search of the Green Goddess, an ancient Mayan statue said to be packed with priceless jewels as well as the formula to "the most powerful explosive the world has ever known." Also on the goddess's trail is Raglan, described in the BTE promotional text as a "rascally explorer" in the employ of an "unscrupulous munitions manufacturer." On the heels of both parties is the determined and enigmatic Ula Vale (Ula Holt), who seems to know more about the goddess than anyone. Then, of course, comes Tarzan, who has traveled from Africa to Guatemala in search of his old friend Lieutenant D'Arnot, whose plane has crashed somewhere in the interior.

In the course of twelve chapters—e.g., "River Perils," "Fatal Fangs," "Angry Gods," "the Devil's Fireworks"—the goddess is found, lost, and stolen, with and without the code book that tells how to open it. Every episode has its battle royal, gator pit, panther attack, cave-in, blowup, hurricane, donnybrook, and cliffhanger ending. At one point, Burroughs had worried that so much local scenery had been eliminated from the episodes that the whole thing might just as well have been shot in Hollywood. But in the final edit, enough Mayan ruins, colonial cities, and Guatemalan Indians survive to create a richly exotic and authentic backdrop. And for once, Tarzan is able to swing through trees other than the sycamore and eucalyptus so predominant in earlier films shot in or near Los Angeles.

To his credit, Herman Brix looks like an honest-to-goodness Tarzan. At six foot one, 190 pounds, he was as lithe and sinuous as Weissmuller and perhaps even more catlike. Like Weissmuller, Brix did not know how to act, and therein lay a distinction. Weissmuller's charm was that he knew *not* to act, or at least his performances appeared that way. By contrast, Brix *acts* as if he is acting, a blunder made worse by a script even stiffer than his on-camera persona.

True to Burroughs's wishes, Brix is both Greystoke and Tarzan—though on balance he is neither. In the opening episode, he appears in tweeds and ascot, speaks proper English, and is addressed as Lord Greystoke. When he is in his loincloth, which is most of the time, he is called Tarzan and performs impressive feats of strength, agility, and bravery. Yet never does he evince either true aristocracy or true wildness. For instance, he talks to Nkima like a schoolteacher, not with the intimate indulgence of a man who once lived among apes and believed he was one himself. His jungle yell—"*Mmmm-an-gann-eee,*" which is authentic Burroughs ape-speak for "I am ape"—is also unconvincing, especially compared to the theatrical paradigm set by Weissmuller.

And unlike every previous Tarzan movie and story, all of which have romance at their core, *New Adventures* has none whatsoever. In the final scene of the final chapter, Tarzan simply lays his hand on Ula Vale's and thanks her for helping to track down the Green Goddess (it turns out she is a British secret agent), and that's all. No kisses. No chivalrous guarding of the lady's lair. No water ballet. No "Tarzan . . . Ula . . . Tarzan . . . Ula."

Shortcomings aside, however, BTE had much to be proud of. Dearholt had pulled off a Herculean feat just to complete the film in the face of such great financial, technical, and physical hardship. His crew was too small and grew smaller as various members succumbed to fever. One of Jiggs's trainers was called upon to play the wicked Mayan queen. When Don Castello, the actor cast as Raglan, fell by the wayside early on, Dearholt gamely took his place. Herman Brix had the roughest road of all and was in fact lucky to get out of Guatemala alive. Except for the jaguar- and lion-fighting scenes, he performed his own stunts, for which he paid a high price. In nearly every episode, he was pummeled and thrown about by Guatemalan Indians, and he had to do a decathlete's share of running, climbing, swinging, diving, and falling. He came down with a tropical fever—not surprising, considering his chronic exhaustion and the amount of time he spent in the less-than-pure Guatemalan rivers and lakes—and had to be hospitalized several days for a leg injury.

When the crew finally returned to Los Angeles, it faced a new set of trials. BTE had come home with enough footage to make not only a twelve-chapter serial, but a seventy-five minute feature as well. The plan was to let distributors take their pick. The feature was completed first and previewed in April—only to be greeted with disheartening reviews. "The reaction was most unfavorable.... [I]t was a body blow," Dearholt reported to Burroughs. Distributors felt there was "not enough Tarzan," disparaged the sound, and scoffed at the story line.

But unbeknownst to anyone at BTE, the fix had been in against *New Adventures* well before the lights had been dimmed at the first screening.

While BTE was completing its Guatemala production, MGM was preparing to shoot its third Weissmuller–O'Sullivan feature, *Tarzan Escapes.* To protect its turf, MGM quietly but emphatically put the word out to bookers that they did not want another Tarzan crowding the marketplace. Thanks to MGM's back-channel threats, BTE cold not secure block booking for *New Adventures* in first-tier theaters and had to distribute to independent theaters, catch-as-catch-can. As a result, neither the feature nor the serial sold well in the United States—though they did somewhat better in Britain and France, where fans craved Tarzan in any form and distributors could not be so easily strong-armed by the major studios. Eventually *New Adventures* did make money, but apparently not much. Reviews never softened—"pretty tedious stuff," shrugged the *New York Times*—and Burroughs, Dearholt, and company were angry, embarrassed, wounded, and in no hurry to launch another Tarzan expedition. (Postscript: Despite his stiff performance as Tarzan and near-death experience, Herman Brix survived as an actor; he changed his name to Bruce Bennett and acquitted himself admirably in films such as *Dark Passage* and *The Treasure of the Sierra Madre.* As for Ula Holt, she never acted again, though she did become the new Mrs. Ashton Dearholt shortly after returning from Guatemala.)

WHILE *New Adventures* was struggling to be born, Burroughs, in self-exile in Nevada, was immersed in his own melodrama. In its first half century, Las Vegas had been nothing more than a tank town in the eastern Mojave Desert. Then in 1931, two seismic events occurred. The United States Bureau of Reclamation began construction of Hoover Dam on the Colorado River, thirty miles away; it was the largest civil engineering project since the Panama Canal, employing at its peak more than five thousand workers. Almost simultaneously, Las Vegas legalized gambling and quickie divorces in hopes of stimulating an economy recently weakened by a regional decline in mining. Overnight, the former Mormon outpost became Sin City, packed with off-duty dam builders, hustlers, prostitutes, and spouses killing time till they could establish legal residence in order to finesse their divorces. Speakeasies didn't even pretend to hide their identities. "If I had wanted a drink," Burroughs wrote to Jack from the "New Air Cooled" Apache Hotel, the only nice hostelry in town, "I couldn't have gotten near enough a bar to have gotten one—they were all jammed."

Burroughs would have preferred to keep a low profile during the six weeks it took to qualify for Nevada residency. When anyone asked, he said he was "gathering material for a new novel" or writing a story on Hoover Dam. But by mid-November, his cover was blown by gossip columnist Walter Winchell, who reported that, "a man named Edgar Rice Burroughs is at the Apache Hotel . . . for the usual reason—after 34 years of marriage. His next bride will be Florence Dearholt of Queens Road, Hollywood."

Burroughs's lawyer had not been idle during his client's weeks away. For months Emma had been vowing to contest the divorce, partly because she believed Burroughs would eventually come to his senses and take her back. Separation of property under any conditions is messy, and in Burroughs and Emma's case, it was made even stickier due to the fact that they were both stockholders in ERB, Inc. Finally, on December 3, the day before Burroughs's six weeks were up, the ERB, Inc., board of directors (Burroughs, Hully, Rothmund making a quorum) came up with the idea of putting Emma on salary as "editor-in-chief" of the company. Two days later, Burroughs filed for divorce in Las Vegas, and Emma's attorney announced that she would abstain from filing a countersuit. The public was informed that "a satisfactory property settlement had been effected."

On Christmas Day, Burroughs and Florence announced their engagement at Florence's mother's house. That afternoon, Joan, Hully, and Jack received the news when they came to Burroughs's apartment to exchange gifts. Someone, presumably one of the other partners in BTE, must have shared the news with Dearholt, who was by then deep in the heart of Guatemala with the *New Adventures* crew. (Burroughs had never mentioned the engagement in any of his communiqués to Dearholt at the time.) A week later, Dearholt sent a cheerful postcard to Burroughs, assuring him that filming was proceeding on schedule. He then closes with "Everything Great. Write about kiddies [Dearholt's, soon to be Burroughs's stepchildren, Caryl Lee and Lee]. Regards Ash." In short, no hard feelings, old boy.

On and off for the previous eight months, Burroughs had been at work on a Tarzan story, which he finally completed on January 19, 1935. At first glance, it is simply one more saga of jungle peril; seen in another light, it provides a commentary on Burroughs's relationship with Florence. Specifically, it marks the return of Jane, who had not figured in a Tarzan story since *Tarzan and the Golden Lion*, thirteen years earlier.

Returning from a trip to London, the airplane carrying Jane Clayton crashes in the jungle, stranding her with a hopelessly timorous and dubiously credentialed prince, his title-hungry American wife, and their two servants. Until Tarzan can come to the rescue, it falls to Jane to keep the group alive. She takes charge firmly but fairly, delegates camp duties, stalks and kills antelope to feed her hapless cohorts, and when need arises, swings through the trees in a manner befitting the wife of the lord of the apes. The pilot, Neal Brown, a street-smart Chicagoan and the ablest of the lot, is immensely impressed by her overall poise: "She was not at all the sort of person that he had imagined a titled English woman would be. He had always thought of women of her class as pampered, helpless creatures. It seemed strange to him now that he should look up to one as a trusted, dependable leader. . . . He had never followed a man in whom he had greater confidence, or for whom he had more respect, than this slender, beautiful lady of quality." Coincidentally or not, these were traits that Burroughs saw in Florence; she was slim, beautiful, and above all, game. Once upon a time, he had admired Emma for her pluck. Now he had a new wife to worship.

Burroughs wanted to call the story "Tarzan and Jane," but *Blue Book* changed the title to "Tarzan and the Immortal Men," preferring to stress the plot's most sensational aspect. (As a book, it became *Tarzan's Quest.*) Eternal youth was by now a well-established theme in Burroughs's fiction: John Carter is essentially ageless; the Vapajans of Venus have discovered a "serum of longevity"; Ras Thavas, the mad scientist of *The Master Mind of Mars,* ghoulishly swaps old bodies for young; and "God" of *Tarzan and the Lion Man* has his own diabolical formula for the fountain of youth. But "Tarzan and the Immortal Men," written just after Burroughs had replaced an old and relatively torpid wife with a vigorous one precisely half his age, takes Burroughs's obsession to an unprecedented extreme. "[It] seems to be a bully good yarn," chided *Blue Book* editor Donald Kennicott, "except for one element—the sacrifice of young girls to produce an elixir of youth."

Despite her best efforts to avoid danger, Jane is inevitably captured by the Kavuru, an all-male tribe whose chief has discovered an antidote to age. The potion's ingredients include the spinal fluid of leopards and the glands and the blood of young women. Jane steadfastly refuses the chief's sexual advances and his offer of "deathless youth"; she will not break her vow of fidelity to Tarzan for any price. "Not for anything," she says.

Miraculously, Tarzan arrives just as Jane's time seems to have run out, and they flee the evil Kavuru temple—but not before pilot Brown snatches a box of eternal youth pills. The story ends with Tarzan, Jane, and Brown (the prince and princess have perished) sitting around the fireplace of the Greystoke's African bungalow, dividing up the pills.

On April 4, Burroughs and Florence flew to Las Vegas and were married in a civil ceremony at the county courthouse. They were back in Los Angeles by sundown, greeted at the airport by five newspaper cameras. The following day, they embarked on a honeymoon to Hawaii aboard the liner S.S. *Lurline* and sat at the captain's table all the way to Honolulu.

They stayed at the Royal Hawaiian, one of Honolulu's best hotels, where they kicked off their shoes and relaxed for the first time in ages. Florence, a natural athlete, took her first swimming lessons. Burroughs, feeling spry and wanting to prove he still had a few tricks left, one-upped her by taking a surfing lesson. By the end of their month-long stay, they were tan and thoroughly enamored of the islands. Ten days after their return to Los Angeles, they had Dearholt and Ula to dinner at the house they had rented at 806 Rodeo Drive, in Beverly Hills.

The first months of marriage were a whirlwind of gaiety and games. Life in Tarzana had been comparatively sedate, with early bedtimes greatly outnumbering the forays into town. Now, married to a young partner and seduced by bright city lights, Burroughs allowed his schedule to turn upside down. His diary itemizes a relentless parade of parties, dinners, and theater. Whereas he had come to frown on alcohol at Tarzana, an evening in the city would often begin—and sometimes end—with cocktails at Rodeo Drive or someone else's house. Burroughs, who had always been an early riser, found it hard to keep the candle lit at both ends. And it didn't help that he had to commute over the mountain to Tarzana each morning. He kept shorter work hours, and on some days he didn't go to the office at all.

The year's distractions and adjustments had a direct and deleterious affect on his work. After *Tarzan's Quest,* he completed only one more story in 1935: *Back to the Stone Age,* a plodding Pellucidar tale, which elicited little enthusiasm from a variety of editors but was finally accepted a year after completion by *Argosy.*

Many of the pulps were having a hard time paying the bills during the Depression; movies were siphoning off what little disposable income people still had, and radio was the favorite form of home entertainment. Magazine editors came and went with no warning, making it even harder for Burroughs to maintain his publishing momentum. Two years earlier, he could count on ten cents a word, seven or eight thousand dollars for a story. But lately rates had plummeted. In April, while he was on his honeymoon, *Blue Book* offered only three thousand dollars for *Tarzan's Quest,* which he accepted reluctantly. "Now that we are satisfied that your offer . . . was not based on the merits of the story and that you think it is really a good story, we have decided to let you have it for that price," he wrote to Donald Kennicott, who was still holding on at a very shaky *Blue Book.* "[B]ut please understand that this is not to be construed as a precedent for future Burroughs stories." In fact, it was worse than a precedent.

The following year, Kennicott offered five hundred dollars for a Tarzan story, and even after Burroughs groused, Kennicott would go no higher than seven hundred and fifty dollars.

It was diversity that kept him going. The comic strip now appeared in more than 250 papers, and there was even some discussion of starting a John Carter strip to compete with the popular *Buck Rogers* and *Flash Gordon* comics. At the same time, MGM was expecting big things from *Tarzan Escapes,* although for reasons that had nothing to do with the perceived encroachment of *New Adventures,* the release date had been pushed back to 1936.

Also comforting was the knowledge that ERB, Inc., was in good hands, even on the occasions that Burroughs was absent from the office. Whether by decision or default, shortly after his marriage to Florence, he had relinquished the majority of day-to-day decisions of the company to Rothmund and Hully.

Since the divorce, Hully and Jack had moved with their mother to a house in Bel-Air, a stylish suburb west of Beverly Hills. Burroughs, meanwhile, had become more of a stepfather than he had anticipated. Dearholt never stopped seeing Florence and Burroughs, and his marriage to Ula in July only seemed to cement the foursome's pact of friendship further. Even so, as time passed, he saw less and less of his daughter and son, and Burroughs, like it or not, became their effective father. Of the two children, four-year-old Caryl Lee adjusted the best and in no time at all grew to worship her new stepfather, and the affection was mutual. Burroughs recycled all the old bedtime stories he had told his own children and showered her with little favors. Young Lee, six, was far more withdrawn and Burroughs far less indulgent with him. As with his own sons, he sent mixed signals of discipline and leniency and pushed Lee to ride horses (though he was allergic to them) and to be generally more athletic. Eventually he persuaded Florence to send the boy to military school. "We just kind of put up with each other," Lee recalled sixty years later.

In mid-October, Burroughs and Florence moved out of the Beverly Hills house (which was then rented to Fred Astaire) and moved to Palm Springs. Located in the high desert one hundred and ten miles east of Los Angeles, Palm Springs had grown gradually from a retreat for tuberculars to a resort for California's smart set. The lifestyle was quieter and less expensive than in the big city, but not by much. In 1934, actors Ralph Bellamy and Charles Farrell, both tennis fanatics, had opened the Palm

Springs Racquet Club, which, though first and foremost a serious tennis venue, instantly became the hub for all manner of recreation. Bellamy and Farrell had little difficulty recruiting a raft of Hollywood friends to join, and by the time Burroughs and Florence became members in October 1935, the Racquet Club was already one of *the* places to winter. Florence became an avid player, and her place on the tennis ladder improved her position on the social ladder. Burroughs took up tennis with characteristic enthusiasm, although, having begun at sixty, he never became much more than an affable doubles partner. Regardless of the discrepancy in ages and ability, all was bright and cheerful in the new cottage Burroughs and Florence rented on club grounds.

For three weeks, anyway. On November 9, Burroughs was admitted to the Good Samaritan Hospital in Los Angeles for yet another operation on his bladder—this one much more serious than anyone had expected.

12

VANISHING POINT

urroughs hated the idea that his body was beginning to fall apart, and he preferred to view his operation as a trip to the garage for mechanical repairs. Clearly, though, his ailment was more serious than that. His previous surgery, five years earlier, had not been entirely successful and had caused bouts of discomfort ever since. He never spelled out the specifics; bladder troubles are patently embarrassing and hardly a topic of polite conversation, especially for a man of Burroughs's vanity. But not talking about his condition had not made it go away. By the time he entered Good Samaritan Hospital in November 1935, his doctors were quite alarmed. In a letter to Hully and Jack afterward, Burroughs confessed that the surgeon had given him no better than a fifty-fifty chance of recovery. On the eve of the operation, Florence was so distraught that Ashton Dearholt, her ex-husband and Burroughs's current business partner, escorted her back to her hotel to wait.

The surgery went better than expected, though convalescence called for another long hospital stay. By the first of December, Burroughs was still weak, but spunky enough to scribble a tongue-in-cheek dirge, "Dear Old Eight-two-three," which was his room number at Good Samaritan:

The doctors come and see me;
They shake their heads and say,
"You for dear old eight-two-three
Until the judgement day."

He surprised everyone with how quickly he bounced back. Initially, he had been advised that it would be at least six months before he could resume exercise and a normal lifestyle. But he was in Palm Springs by Christmas and by late January he was cleared to play tennis. "I am greatly encouraged," he wrote his sons. And in his diary, he saluted his wife for her devotion throughout the ordeal: "Florence has been with me every minute that she could. . . . She has been very faithful."

Dearholt, too, had proven his loyalty to Burroughs, though in quite a different way. He had kept Burroughs–Tarzan Enterprises alive through the fall and winter, with the help of overseas returns from *The New Adventures of Tarzan,* and he had big plans for the company in the near future. At the end of December, BTE had changed its name to Burroughs–Tarzan Pictures (BTP). The principals remained the same—Burroughs, Dearholt, Stout, and Cohen—but the company's portfolio broadened. The aim was still to make movies of Burroughs stories; *The Mad King* and *Tarzan, Lord of the Jungle* were the two titles mentioned most often, and Herman Brix was still the Tarzan of choice. But because BTP needed to increase its cash flow as quickly as possible, Dearholt bought the rights to several non-Burroughs stories that could be rushed into production.

The first was *The Drag Net,* an underworld drama based on a recent stage play. The lead went to Rod LaRocque, who had been dropped from the cast of *Tarzan and His Mate* two years earlier, and the entire film was written, shot, edited, and shipped in less than two months. BTP's next production was *The Phantom of Santa Fe,* a Zorro-esque western starring Norman Kerry, filmed in color. It was ready for release by July, though the sound and color were of disappointing quality.

As quickly as Dearholt had completed these two pictures, he could not get them into theaters fast enough to keep BTP ahead of its creditors. On July 16, George Stout was obliged to report to Burroughs that the company's situation was "most acute." *The Drag Net* was bringing in a paltry three hundred dollars a week, none of BTP's employees had been paid in three weeks, and Stout could not find a soul willing to loan the money needed to complete a third picture, *Tundra,* a thrilling but low-budget Jack

London/*Nanook of the North*–type survival story set in Alaska. BTP was convinced that the film would create a huge sensation, if only the snarling lienholders could be kept at bay. On August 3, 1936, Dearholt confessed to Burroughs, "[O]ur noses are flat into a wall of disheartening facts." The only solution was "money P.D.Q." Fifty thousand would be nice, though five thousand would at least keep the doors open. Burroughs caved in and loaned the lesser amount.

It was the best he could do at the time, for he was now strapped for money himself. The remaining acreage he still owned in Tarzana was costing him ten thousand dollars a year in mortgage and maintenance. The move to Palm Springs had helped trim expenses, but then in May he and Florence moved back to Los Angeles, where they rented a succession of comfortable apartments. Meanwhile, his income from book sales, which had enjoyed a brief spurt in the early 1930s, was now "nearing the vanishing point," or so he claimed to former publisher Joe Bray. In 1935, ERB, Inc., had sold fewer than 100,000 books, at least a third of which were giveaways sponsored by the makers of Tarzan ice-cream cups. His latest book, *Tarzan's Quest,* was not selling at all, New York agent Michael Mill reported.

In the fall of 1936, the situation brightened somewhat. During a quick trip to New York with Florence, Burroughs signed an agreement with the William Morris Agency to market the radio show, which he hoped would give it a new lease on life. Then in October, he sold Sol Lesser the movie rights to all of his published stories for a period of seven years, with the understanding that Lesser, in conjunction with Twentieth Century-Fox, would produce at least one Tarzan feature a year.

After the success of *Tarzan and His Mate,* Burroughs had fully intended staying with MGM, but the studio had run into unforeseen difficulty completing its third Tarzan, *Tarzan Escapes,* and had lost its enthusiasm for the series—a circumstance that Lesser turned to his advantage. Throughout the delicate negotiations surrounding Lesser's own Tarzan, *Tarzan the Fearless,* he and Burroughs had remained friends, and despite the limited success of *Fearless* compared with that of the first two MGM Tarzans, he was eager for another chance. The exact price he offered Burroughs for the rights to his stories is not known, but in order to match MGM's most recent fee, he would have had to pay at least forty thousand dollars per picture.

MGM finally succeeded in releasing *Tarzan Escapes* in November

1936. In stark contrast to *Tarzan the Ape Man* and *Tarzan and His Mate*, *Escapes* plays down the physical intimacy between Tarzan and Jane and instead stresses a Swiss Family Robinson wholesomeness that not even the Legion of Decency could find fault with. Jane trades her floor show fig leaves for a shift that covers shoulders, midriff, and thighs. And when she performs her underwater ballet, this time she doesn't leave her wardrobe high and dry. Tarzan is still the monosyllabic, immodestly clad lord of the jungle, but he is so much tamer; now when he slays wild game, he is simply a jungle shopper providing a roast for his lady's table. The centerpiece of MGM's million-dollar production is an elaborate tree house, a replacement for Tarzan and Jane's crude and vaguely prurient love nests of yore. It is furnished with turtle shell sinks, running water (a procession of bamboo scoops delivered by a vine-and-pulley system), an ape-powered fan, and an open-air elevator attended by an obsequious elephant. (MGM bragged that the feasibility of these primitive appliances had been checked by anthropologists from the University of California. Even so, Burroughs was privately embarrassed by the "penthouse" treatment.)

Again the story is one of paradise disturbed by outsiders. Two of Jane's relatives, Eric and Rita Parker, arrive from England and convince Jane that she must return to London to claim an inheritance. They are guided by a shifty-eyed white hunter whose clandestine ambition is to capture Tarzan. Other familiar elements include the juju-shrouded Mutia Escarpment, the fearsome Giboni (who are eventually upstaged by the Hymandi, named after MGM producer Bernard Hyman), and outtakes from *Trader Horn, Tarzan the Ape Man,* and *Tarzan and His Mate.* Cheetah, whom one reviewer described as "the Martha Raye of chimpanzees," once again provides charismatic comic relief.

Though *Tarzan Escapes* was ready for release by the end of 1935, it was not distributed to theaters until almost a full year later. Adults who previewed it complained of a weak central story, while children, who were MGM's target audience this time around, were overly frightened by the final escape scene in which Tarzan leads Jane and her relatives' safari through an underground swamp filled with lizards and vampire bats. (An early working title for the movie was *Tarzan and the Vampires.*) The studio quickly pulled the film, and replaced director James McKay with a more conservative Richard Thorpe, who reduced the gruesome parts and beefed up the melodrama between Tarzan, Jane, and the interloping safari. The result is a slower-paced film, essentially a rehash of previous Tarzans. Regretting the time and money it had spent producing what it perceived to be a humdrum product, MGM made the additional mistake of relinquishing the Tarzan franchise to Sol Lesser.

In November, just as *Tarzan Escapes* was (re)opening, Sol Lesser began a very public search for his own Tarzan. One of the first candidates mentioned was baseball player Lou Gehrig. Not that Lesser was serious about casting Gehrig, but by merely auditioning the famous Yankee slugger, he created a flutter of publicity for his upcoming movie. Burroughs admired Lesser's stunt, if not his nominee for leading man: "Having seen several pictures of you as Tarzan and paid $50 for newspaper clippings," he ribbed Gehrig in a telegram, "I want to congratulate you on being a swell first baseman."

Gehrig's chunky physique notwithstanding, he was precisely the sort of celebrity Lesser needed. The past three Tarzans had been Olympic medalists whose fame and figures had given a terrific lift to their respective movies. The biggest star of the recent 1936 Olympics in Berlin had been sprinter Jesse Owens; but despite his world-record dash, which had embarrassed Adolf Hitler and made Owens's name a household word, his black skin disqualified him as the next Tarzan. That left Glenn Morris, the gold medalist in the decathlon. Like Weissmuller, Crabbe, and Brix before him, Morris had no acting experience, but he was six foot two, 190 pounds, and looked terrific in a loincloth. And down deep, he was a bit of a wild man, though perhaps Sol Lesser didn't realize as much.

Morris was born in rural Colorado and went on to star in both football and track at Colorado A&M (now Colorado State) University. Though Jesse Owens had hoarded most of the headlines at the Berlin Olympics, Morris, as the master of ten different events, had won bragging rights as the world's greatest athlete. Among the legion of spectators who had observed Morris's record-breaking performance, one who remembered the clean-limbed Coloradan above all others was Leni Riefenstahl, the Third Reich's anointed documentary filmmaker. Her film of the 1936 games, *Olympia*, would eventually be appreciated as a quintessential portrait of Nazi ideals and one of the finest documentaries ever made.

In her memoir, published fifty years after the Berlin Olympics, Riefenstahl describes meeting Morris between decathlon events. In order to film the games, she had permission to roam the stadium, where one afternoon she was introduced to Morris, who was relaxing on the grass. "It was an incredible moment and I had never expected anything like it," she wrote. "I tried to choke down the feelings surging up inside me and to forget what had happened. From then on I avoided Morris, with whom I exchanged barely a dozen words, and yet this meeting had had a profound impact on me."

Later in the games, Riefenstahl was on hand to watch Morris receive his gold medal. "The dim light prevented any filming of the ceremony," she recalled, "and when Glenn Morris came down the steps, he headed straight toward me. I held out my hand and congratulated him, but he grabbed me in his arms, tore off my blouse, and kissed my breasts, right in the middle of the stadium, in front of a hundred thousand spectators. A lunatic, I thought. I wrenched myself out of his grasp and dashed away. But I could not forget the wild look in his eyes."

If Sol Lesser recognized the same look, he did not succeed in capturing it on film. It hardly seems possible, but *Tarzan's Revenge,* released in 1938, is even worse than *Tarzan the Fearless.* Burroughs had urged Lesser to reread *Tarzan of the Apes* and *The Return of Tarzan* before beginning the picture, hoping that Lesser would give his hero a Greystoke shading, but the Morris Tarzan was the most simplistic to date. In the entire film, he speaks only four words, gives three Tarzan yells (his *"Ah-AHH-ah"* is better than Brix's and Crabbe's, but a far cry from Weissmuller's), and tussles with one lion, which he allows to escape.

In every important scene, Morris is outacted by a spunky Eleanor Holm, who plays Eleanor Reed (no Jane this time), a wholesome lass who has come to Africa with her parents and fiancé to gather animals for an American zoo. Holm was an Olympian, too, though she was hardly a paragon of athletic dedication. She had won a gold medal in the backstroke in the 1932 games in Los Angeles. Afterward, she had acted in a few movies and done some nightclub singing. She kept up her swimming, admitting, however, that she trained on champagne and cigarettes. Her reputation as an unretiring vamp caught up with her in the summer of 1936, when she was observed drinking and shooting craps aboard the ocean liner carrying the American Olympians to Germany and was promptly kicked off the team. She was not allowed to compete in Berlin, though she boasted that she could have beaten the summer's competition "with a champagne bottle in either hand."

In *Tarzan's Revenge,* Holm not only gets all the lines, but it is she, not Morris, who is called on to outswim the crocodile—which she does easily, wearing a stylish two-piece swimsuit. Morris, meanwhile, succeeds in communicating neither Johnny Weissmuller's naive sensuality nor Herman Brix's martial endurance. He throws a spear with authority, but his mute demeanor and enigmatic grin suggest Harpo Marx more than any Burroughs hero. While physically strong, he is sexually so bland, so unavailable—nothing like the bodice-ripper of Berlin. (Hollywood gossips reported that Holm, who was far from a prude, couldn't stand Morris and refused to kiss him.) Reviews justly branded *Tarzan's Revenge* "inferior entertainment" and the choice of Morris "unfortunate." When Lupe Velez, the tempestuous latina actress married to Johnny Weissmuller, encountered Morris at a Hollywood party sometime later, she reportedly kicked him in the shins and dressed him down: "You are not *heem!* There is *onlee* one Tarzan. And that's my Johnny!"

Velez was absolutely correct. Weissmuller was still the world's Tarzan—a verity that MGM came to appreciate with some chagrin. Whatever doubts the studio had once had about Tarzan's durability vanished when its own *Tarzan Escapes,* written off prematurely as a star-crossed dud and released ahead of Lesser's *Revenge,* wound up grossing two million dollars. With fresh resolve, MGM came back to Burroughs in July 1937, tendering a proposal to make three Tarzan pictures for seventy-five thousand dollars. The one stumbling block was Sol Lesser, who still had six years left on his contract with ERB, Inc. The deal took a year to consummate, but once Lesser realized that his second Tarzan was not likely to do any better than his first, he sold his rights back to MGM for a handsome sum. Upon completing the deal, Burroughs had to laugh at fortune's fickleness: he had nearly lost his shirt making his own lousy Tarzan, but because Sol Lesser had made one that was equally lousy, he wound up back in the money.

IN JUNE, he and Florence felt flush enough to move to the Sunset Grove, a stylish art deco apartment building above the Sunset Strip; fellow residents included Ralph and Catherine Bellamy, as well as high-profile mobster Johnny Roselli and his wife. On the rare evenings that the Burroughses did not make the rounds of restaurants, clubs, and theaters, they stayed up late playing bridge, backgammon, or mah-jongg with the

Bellamys and other neighbors. Burroughs's diary entry for February 10, a Wednesday, describes a virtual decathlon of gaiety: "To the Turf Club for steaks. Then to Coconut Grove—dancing. Then to gambling house on Sunset near Doheny. Played roulette—won a little—about $12.00. Bed about 2 a.m." And for September 9: "Worked at apt. Swam. Watched Florence & [Mrs. Johnny] Roselli play tennis in p.m.; then played a little myself. To Clara Bow's 'It' restaurant for dinner. To [Grauman's] Chinese [Theater] to see 'Wife, Doctor, & Nurse' with Loretta Young. Also 'Charlie Chan on Broadway.' Stopped at Beachcomber to try a Zombie." Finally he had to confess to his diary, "Don't know how much more I can stand."

Vacation left him even more exhausted. On a summer trip to Northern California, he took Caryl Lee and Lee fishing, as he used to do with his own children. But at sixty-one, he was not as hardy as he once had been. "I rowed for about two hours," he noted. "2 sets of tennis after lunch. Nearly dead. Old angina pains after I got to my room. They come and go, some day I'll go with them."

The grueling social schedule made it harder than ever to focus on his fiction, and the Tarzan novel of 1937, a pairing of two stories, "Tarzan and the Magic Men" and "Tarzan and the Elephant Men" (published as *Tarzan the Magnificent*), was a struggle. Tarzan is pitted against two witch doctors who derive their power from two priceless gems, one an emerald, the other a diamond. Each "magic man" surrounds himself with an army of fierce women warriors and male slaves. As a subplot, Burroughs fusses with the perennially prickly subjects of racial purity and miscegenation. But his larger intent, to the extent that he has one, is to warn against the deleterious side effects of material wealth and the insidious power women can hold over men. He himself was supporting two women at the time, and though his financial picture had improved markedly of late, he dared not let his guard down.

Now more than ever, he saw the business of selling stories as a crapshoot. Since placing *Tarzan and the Lion Man* in *Liberty*, he had continued to submit stories to the slicks, but none had taken him seriously. The pulps were scarcely more hospitable. It was humiliating enough that they kept reducing the fee they paid to one of their most popular authors; worse, they had lately begun treating him as if he was no longer good enough for their impoverished pages. "[E]nthusiasm fails me," wrote *Blue Book*'s Donald Kennicott to explain his offer of a token five hundred dollars for the forty-thousand-word "Tarzan and the Magic Men." Burroughs eventually succeeded in selling it to *Argosy*, but for only fifteen hundred dollars, and nine months later *Argosy*'s rejection of the sequel, "Tarzan and the Elephant Men," was accompanied by one of the most withering critiques he had ever received. There were "too many characters, with too many objectives," iterated editor Jack Byrne. The suspense was "so diffuse that it does not catch hold." The escapes were "haphazardly achieved," and Tarzan suffered from "a complete lack of verve."

To be sure, "Tarzan and the Elephant Men" is not a masterpiece; nor, on the other hand, is it leagues worse than most of Burroughs's previous adventures. But with Tarzan now having to compete with a growing roster of pulp heroes—the Shadow, the Phantom, Doc Savage—and with a new generation of editors calling the shots, Burroughs's ape-man was viewed increasingly as faded goods. "Frankly," wrote Byrne of *Argosy* in ravaging "Elephant Men," "I think you are making a mistake in your latter day tendency to make Tarzan into a deus ex machina who blunders into minor situations that concern rather uninteresting characters and proceeds to solve these difficulties after passing through a certain amount of danger himself. Tarzan needs to have some really personal interest to motivate him."

What had Byrne expected—*Gone With the Wind*? Unlike the characters in Margaret Mitchell's best-seller of 1936, Tarzan was not a glib gallant with a troubled inner soul. For better or worse, he had been an aloof wayfarer for at least fifteen years. Stolid independence, formerly a strength, was now viewed as a weakness—in Tarzan and Burroughs both. "Haven't you been playing the lone wolf too long," Byrne wondered in a subsequent letter, "and failing to throw your plot ideas against the sounding boards of other minds?"

Older and wiser, and with Ralph Rothmund doubtless staying his boss's temper, Burroughs played the obedient servant. "I should not be at all surprised to find that you are right," he wrote back stiffly, "and I appreciate the friendly interest you have shown and shall try to profit by your criticisms."

Carson of Venus, his next book-length story, was hardly a new beginning. Once again, Carson Napier and Princess Duare set out for a safe Venusian haven only to land in harm's way. Their first encounter is with the Samary, a race whose men are frail, gossiping homebodies and whose women are cruel, callous warriors: "They were strapping specimens, broad shouldered, deep chested, with the sturdy limbs of gladiators. . . .They were not unhandsome, with their short hair and bronzed skins; but even though their figures were, in a modified way, those of women, there seemed to be no trace of femininity among them."

Once they fight their way clear of the Samary, Carson and Duare face the Zanis, who in both letter and spirit bear a strong resemblance to Nazis. Less than five years earlier, many of Burroughs's views had not differed greatly from those of Hitler (and on the topic of eugenics, they were still in accord). But by the summer of 1937, he and nearly every other American had ceased to regard the Third Reich as a beacon of conservative order and stern common sense; now the Nazis were profoundly sinister. Another war was already on the horizon, and Burroughs, as ever, had climbed on the bandwagon of public concern.

In *Carson of Venus*, a "strange cult" has arisen, "conceived and led by a common man named Mephis." Mephis has taken control of the capital and most of the country of Amlot. In order to build a "super race," Mephis has ordered that the large-eared "Atorians"—mostly scholars and scientists, and plainly the Venusian equivalent of Jews—be segregated or, worse, tortured and killed. Citizens must greet one another by shouting, "Maltu, Mephis," an obvious play on "Heil, Hitler"; Mephis's army, the Zani Guard, marches with a funny hop step, a parody of the Nazi goose step; and when Mephis passes through the streets, men stand on their heads, literally, or risk losing them. At every Amtorian theater, the same play is performed endlessly: a 101-act tribute to the life of the maniacal leader.

Perhaps because of the satiric currency of *Carson of Venus*, Burroughs had hopes of selling it to the slicks; but for the umpteenth time, he received rejection letters from *The Saturday Evening Post, Collier's, The Ladies' Home Journal,* and *Liberty. Blue Book* bid a trifling two thousand dollars, which was only five hundred more than it had paid for "Elephant Men," a story half its length. The previous Tarzan hadn't given newsstand sales "any special kick," *Blue Book*'s Kennicott explained. He liked the Carson story, but he couldn't justify a handsome fee. *Argosy*'s offer of three thousand dollars wasn't much better, but Burroughs had to accept it.

*   *   *

By January 1938, as *Carson of Venus* was running humbly in *Argosy*, several of Burroughs's other endeavors were struggling, as well. The radio show was coming to a halt after six years on the air, and though the comic strip was still one of the five or six most popular nationally, Joe Neebe's Famous Books and Plays, the agency in charge of producing and syndicating the strip, was on the verge of running out of material.

From the start, the Tarzan comics had fed off the novels; but even with liberal padding by writers and illustrators, the strip had consumed the Burroughs library faster than he could replenish it. Neebe had already been obliged to adapt movie scripts and even radio scripts, and by 1938, he had begun turning Tarzan manuscripts into comics months before they appeared in magazines or as books. That shelf was about to be bare, and United Features, in charge of syndicating the strip, wondered if the time was not ripe to begin mining some of Burroughs's characters besides Tarzan. The most likely candidate was John Carter, whom Jack Burroughs had recently begun adapting for a comic book called *The Funnies*. As proud as Burroughs was of his son's talent, he did not want to retire his star attraction so hastily. Instead, he directed Famous Books and Plays to begin coming up with its own material for the Tarzan strip.

While the comic strip was sputtering, Burroughs–Tarzan Pictures was collapsing altogether. In March 1938, BTP released its fifth and final picture, a re-edited version of the *New Adventures* serial, trimmed very clumsily to seventy-two minutes and retitled *Tarzan and the Green Goddess*. It was a pathetic attempt to keep the company alive and a case of too little, too late. BTP folded within the month, with losses to all involved, especially Burroughs. In business as in personal matters, he and Ashton Dearholt remained civil through the hard times, but after BTP ceased to exist, they saw very little of each other.

Burroughs's disappointment over the demise of BTP was offset somewhat by the recent re-signing with MGM. Nor did he seem to mourn the loss of the radio show. Jim and Joan Pierce had left the show several years earlier; besides, he had already come up with an idea to replace it. The new show would be called *I See by the Paper*. The setting, as outlined in letters to several syndicators and in two sample scripts, was to be the office of the *Tarzana Tribune*, a fictional newspaper published in Tarzana, California. The main characters would be the grumpy editor, a dense blonde stenographer, a ne'er-do-well office boy, and columnist

Edgar Rice Burroughs, who perpetually arrives late to the office and receives more "pan" letters than fan letters. ("Dear Sir: I like your column; it's full of meat—balony.") The possibilities for humor and human interest were "illimitable," Burroughs promised, though the lame gags and Blondie–Dagwood–Dithers repartee he submitted were hardly side-splitting. "[T]he whole market is over-columned," apologized George Carlin of United Features in turning down *I See by the Paper*.

Undeterred, Burroughs proposed yet another radio show in 1939, this one simply a string of quips relating to current events—war had just broken out in Europe—and the quirks of everyday life. His new title was *Quiet, Please!* Sample scripts are full of scorn for Franklin Roosevelt's pacifism and the President's decision to run for a third term. Between acidic flicks at Hitler, Stalin, and Churchill, Burroughs grouses about the man who would not return Florence's lost watch until a reward had been posted and denounces the innovation of wrapping cigarette packages in cellophane. He was clearly not the next Walter Winchell, and his efforts to sell *Quiet, Please!* were met with stony silence.

Nonetheless, he kept cooking up new ideas. He wrote an outline for a story in which a group of German officers secretly assassinate Hitler and replace him with a "perfect double"—a 1938 version of *The Mad King*. He never did get around to writing the actual story; perhaps experience had finally taught him that editors cared only for his "fantastic" fare. Still suspicious that he was being rejected as much for his byline as his stories, he again tried out the nom de plume John Tyler McCulloch. One pseudonymous effort was "'Two Gun' Doak Flies South," a hackneyed tale of muddled identity. Having resisted a marriage arranged by their fathers, the hero and heroine fall in love anonymously while escaping from the gangsters who have hijacked their transcontinental flight. Mostly, though, "'Two Gun' Doak" is just an excuse to lampoon the other passengers: Mrs. J. Witherington Snite, "the lady hippopotamus" married to a wealthy restaurant owner; Gladys Klump, the young wife of an aging candy manufacturer (her "sugar daddy"); and E. Allan Smith, stuffy, hypocritical book reviewer for the *New York Times,* whose own fiction has been spurned by every editor in the country. Secret identities, though they might work in romances, did not work for their author. Neither the slicks nor the pulps were interested in "'Two Gun' Doak" or John Tyler McCulloch, and the story was never published.

Relief from the social and professional turmoil of the past year and a half finally came in August 1938, when Burroughs and Florence took a second trip to Hawaii, this one for six weeks. But shortly after their return, Burroughs was back in the hospital. In November, he was operated on for a double hernia. "I wasn't going to mention it," he wrote to his three children, "but I feared you might be hurt if I didn't let you know. . . . It is not a serious operation. . . . Evidently I am slowly coming apart, just like an old car. The Pierce is doing the same thing. . . . A couple of wrecks going hand in hand to the junk heap."

Several weeks later, he wrote a more sober letter to his former book publisher Joe Bray, who at age seventy-seven had long since retired and was within months of dying. "It has been a long time since I have heard from you, although I often think of you," Burroughs began warmly. "We are plodding along here in the same old rut with Tarzan, although the rut seems to be thinning out. . . . I shall never forget asking you many years ago what my life as an author would be, and you replied that if I were lucky I might go for ten years; so I must have been unusually fortunate to wiggle through for a quarter of a century. I have no kick coming. . . ."

There was a shred of truth to his hangdog claim that his best years as a writer were behind him. The stories he wrote between October 1937 (*Tarzan and the Forbidden City*) and February 1940 (*Tarzan and the Madman*) are uniformly disappointing, with the exception of the imaginative *Synthetic Men of Mars*, in which John Carter tracks down "Master Mind" Ras Thavas, who has become imprisoned by his own fiendish surgical creations. The mad scientist's experiments in biological engineering ultimately fill his entire laboratory with "a billowy mass of slimy, human tissue. . . . Protruding from it were unrelated fragments of human anatomy—a hand, an entire leg, a foot, a lung, a heart, and here and there a horribly mouthing head. . . . Theoretically, it would never cease to grow. . . . Eventually it would cover the entire surface of the planet." If Burroughs was attempting a totalitarian metaphor, warning against the dangers of communism or fascism, *Liberty* didn't see it that way; instead, it saw only the grotesqueness of *Synthetic Men* and turned it down. *Blue Book*, on the other hand, passed on the story because "it didn't hit us quite hard enough." Jack Byrne of *Argosy* played Goldilocks this once: to him, *Synthetic Men* was just right, and he offered twelve hundred dollars.

*　　*　　*

HAVING BEEN whipsawed so cruelly by *Argosy* and *Blue Book* in recent years and having no residual loyalty to either magazine, Burroughs continued to look for another outlet. For a brief period in 1939, he thought he had found one in the Standard Magazines, publisher of *Thrilling Adventures* and a score of other pulps, several of which used the word *Thrilling* in their titles. Editorial Director Leo Margulies had once been an assistant to Bob Davis at the Munsey Company and was a longtime devotee of Burroughs's work. In August, Burroughs wrote Margulies, wondering if he might be interested in "That Damn Dude" or *Pirate Blood,* neither of which had been published. Margulies passed on *Pirate Blood,* explaining that the "overtone of sex" and glorification of "wanton murderers and thieves" were inappropriate for a Standard readership. The western, however, was "the kind of yarn we like." He offered five hundred dollars, which Burroughs accepted with gratitude and relief. It was published in *Thrilling Adventures* as "The Terrible Tenderfoot," and the following year as an ERB, Inc., book, *The Deputy Sheriff of Comanche County.*

Two months later, Margulies rescued another of Burroughs's orphans, a series of Tarzan murder mysteries that had recently been cast aside by *Argosy.* "I have in mind combining the Northwest Mounted Police and super-sleuth ideas, and making Tarzan something of a jungle Sherlock Holmes," Burroughs had pitched to *Argosy*'s Jack Byrne earlier in the year. In each story he would solve a mystery, "such as the murder of a Colonial official; or a search for a royal big-game hunter, who has become lost; or a diamond shipment that has been stolen; or perhaps the apprehension of a white-slaver who had stolen a girl." To Burroughs, the series seemed a sure thing. Detective stories were a burgeoning subgenre that he had yet to exploit beyond his brief foray into "Murder Mystery Puzzles" in 1932. Byrne showed interest, but given the poor national economy, he could offer no better than two cents a word upon acceptance.

Burroughs wrote the sixteen-thousand-word "Tarzan and the Jungle Murders" in less than two weeks, but by the time the manuscript arrived at *Argosy,* Byrne had quit. His successor, G. Worthington Post, who was even stiffer than his patrician name suggested, didn't care for "Jungle Murders" at all. The one remaining hope was Margulies.

But even Margulies, a diehard fan, was ambivalent toward the Tarzan mystery. "Frankly," he wrote Burroughs, "I was a bit disappointed in it, especially since it would be the first Tarzan story for our *Thrilling*

Adventures magazine. . . . In its present shape, I cannot use it. However, there is a good story in the yarn, and I took the liberty of turning it over to one of our editors for a revision job. It was revised according to what we think a Tarzan story . . . should be like."

How far Burroughs had fallen. In more robust years, he had insisted that nothing be changed in his manuscripts, except for typographical errors, and he had commanded eight and even ten cents a word. Now he raised no objection whatsoever to Margulies's rewrite and accepted two cents a word "in the hope that it will create a demand for my stories in your magazines and thus warrant a higher rate in the future." Later, when Margulies asked Burroughs for a brief autobiography to run in the magazine, he suggested, somewhat sarcastically, that Margulies assign "a member of your staff to write [it] for me, as he could undoubtedly do a better job than I."

The thrill of *Thrilling* was over almost as quickly as it had begun. Three weeks after accepting "Jungle Murders," Margulies rejected *Land of Terror*, the sixth Pellucidar novel (and it was never published in a magazine). "There's really no plot," he stated frankly, just a "series of incidents and adventures" lacking in continuity and suspense. Whatever professional adoration Margulies may once have had for Burroughs was gone. Over the next few years, Burroughs submitted several more stories to Margulies, but never again succeeded in selling one to the *Thrilling* stable of magazines.

By far the most positive occurrence of 1939 was the release of MGM's new movie, *Tarzan Finds a Son.* Over the years, Burroughs had come to accept that Hollywood's Tarzan—Johnny Weissmuller specifically (and not Herman Brix or Glenn Morris)—was the engine that powered the Burroughs omnibus. "Of course, it is a real thrill to see real persons enact one's pet characters," he wrote in a bylined story circulated on the eve of the release of the new movie. "I am no longer a critic of my own stories on the screen. Johnny Weissmuller is just Tarzan to me . . . [and] Weissmuller is what the public accepts as Tarzan."

Weissmuller had not appeared in a movie since *Tarzan Escapes*, three years earlier. MGM had kept him under contract in the interim but had not cast him in any other roles or loaned him to other studios for fear that his image as *the* Tarzan might become fuzzy. Weissmuller had spent the time golfing, sailing, nightclubbing, and trying to keep up with his free-spirited and spendthrift wife, Lupe Velez. He had kept in shape by performing in aquacades and giving swimming exhibitions, and when filming began in Silver Springs, Florida (famous for the "world's clearest water"), he was still Tarzan in body and persona.

Maureen O'Sullivan was a different story. Since *Tarzan Escapes,* she had appeared in at least ten movies, playing a variety of roles and had come to be regarded as one of Hollywood's leading actresses. Only reluctantly did she agree to act in the next Tarzan film, and citing impending motherhood, she vowed that it would be her last. She had married John Farrow, the screenwriter who had revamped *Tarzan Escapes,* in 1937, and by the time shooting began on *Son,* she was several months pregnant with their first child. The Hays Office did not need to concern itself with suggestive costumes in this picture. O'Sullivan's Jane dresses conservatively—maternally, that is—and in a number of scenes, she was filmed strictly from the waist up or behind various props to conceal her swelling tummy.

With O'Sullivan not long for the jungle, MGM was again faced with the problem of how to preserve and perpetuate its Tarzan interests. Ultimately, someone came up with the solution of having Jane die, though not before giving Tarzan a son. The public might weep—a calculated plus for the box office—but the series would live on as family entertainment.

Killing off Jane was easy enough, or so it seemed to screenwriter Cyril Hume. Delivering a baby, however, was a thornier task. In print, Tarzan and Jane were legally married, and in *Tarzan and His Mate* they had referred to each other as husband and wife. But from the standpoint of the censors, their relationship was ratified by neither license nor sacrament. To permit Tarzan and Jane to conceive their own offspring from their own loins was, perish the thought, to condone out-of-wedlock sexual intercourse.

Under the circumstances, Cyril Hume took the one course available: virgin birth, or the closest thing to it. The plane carrying Lord Greystoke's "favorite nephew" Richard Lancing, Lancing's wife, and infant son crashes on the Mutia Escarpment. The parents are killed and Tarzan and Jane adopt the baby. Tarzan wants to name him Elephant, for his precocious strength, but finally they settle on Boy. "The king has a son," Jane announces, beaming at the bundle in its treetop cradle.

Five years later a search party of Lancing relatives arrives in the jungle; the senior Lancing, Sir Thomas, hopes to find the family alive, but Austin Lancing and his wife hope to uncover proof that all are dead so they can inherit the Greystoke fortune. When they encounter Tarzan and family, Jane tells a lie, informing them that all three Lancings have perished in the crash and that Boy—played by Johnny Sheffield and, in the dangerous scenes, doubled by thirty-two-year-old "Midget Strong Man" Harry Monty—is her biological son. Before long, the Lancings discover Boy's true identity and convince Jane that he would be better off growing up in civilized England (where they can steal the inheritance). When Tarzan protests, Jane plays a cruel trick in order to get him out of the way, and she and Boy sneak off with the London-bound safari. Inevitably the party is captured by the Zambelis (named for MGM producer Sam Zimbalist) and faces unspeakable torture and certain death. In helping Boy escape—he knows his way home to Tarzan—Jane is felled by a Zambeli spear.

This, at least, was how the movie was supposed to end. But when the demise of Jane leaked out in prerelease newspaper articles, fans protested so vociferously that MGM shot a new ending in which Jane pulls through and is forgiven her double-cross by a wet-eyed Tarzan. In the final scene, Tarzan and Jane ride over the hill on the back of a loyal elephant, trailed by Boy aboard the pachyderm's capering offspring.

Audiences found much to like in *Tarzan Finds a Son* besides the happy ending. They got another chance to see Tarzan ride Mary the rhinoceros and glimpsed the final bits of *Trader Horn* wildlife footage. They revisited Tarzan and Jane's fantastic treehouse with its elephant elevator and learned Jane's recipe for ostrich egg omelets.

The best element of all, however, is Boy. Weissmuller is said to have selected Johnny Sheffield himself from a pool of three hopeful "Boys," and Big John and Little John, as they were known on the set, got along famously. (One reviewer called Sheffield "a chimp off the old block.") Underwater swimming scenes, like lion-wrestling scenes and Cheetah-runs-amok scenes, had become a staple of the MGM Tarzans, and in terms of aesthetics and athleticism, Tarzan and Boy's swimming interlude in *Son* is second only to the Johnny Weissmuller–Josephine McKim footage, which of course had been cut from *Tarzan and His Mate*. They play hide-and-seek among sunken logs in gin-clear Silver Springs—sheer father-son delight evidently an adequate substitute for oxygen. At one point, Tarzan grabs the tail of a passing sea turtle, Boy grabs Tarzan's ankle, and they glide across the screen like two mermen taking their finned pet for a stroll.

The retooled, untragic *Tarzan Finds a Son* accomplished precisely what MGM had hoped for: Boy upstages Jane, and Jane is tidily relegated to the role of Mom, keeper of home and hearth. Maureen O'Sullivan's future in the series was still uncertain, but after *Tarzan Finds a Son,* if she happened to disappear, violently or contractually, the studio had confidence that its franchise would survive.

Burroughs and ERB, Inc., also hoped to benefit from the Boy bonanza. By 1939, there was hardly a male in America, or the world for that matter, who had not read a Tarzan story, seen a Tarzan movie, or imagined himself as lord of the jungle. Over the years, Burroughs had received thousands of letters from fans expressing their delight, nitpicking narrative flaws, or soliciting his blessing before running away to Africa. In his consummate diligence, he saved and answered every fan letter he ever received. "When you play Tarzan in the trees, be careful that you don't fall out," he gently advised. He was particularly taken with Jackie Strong, the seven-year-old who had survived three days and nights alone in the Oregon wilderness by practicing woodcraft he had picked up from Tarzan stories. With the introduction of Boy—a virtual *every* boy—the bond between Tarzan and his millions of protégés was that much stronger. In the early 1930s, Signal Oil had enlisted 125,000 children in its Tribes of Tarzan, but membership had evaporated as soon as Signal stopped sponsoring the radio show. Perhaps the time was once again ripe to revive the notion of a nationwide Tarzan fan club.

In early May, several weeks before the official release of *Tarzan Finds a Son,* Burroughs and Ralph Rothmund printed up a thirty-two page *Official Guide of the Tarzan Clans of America,* containing details on: "How to form a Tarzan Clan. Duties of Chief and other officers. Tarzan Pledge. Secret Initiation Ritual. How to make Tarzan weapons and shield. Tribal dances. Tarzan Games. Tarzan Songs. How to hold Clan and Tribal Field meets. A Dictionary of the Ape Language." The fee for joining was one dollar, for which a "warrior" would receive a membership card, an *Official Guide,* and last but not least, a copy of the latest Burroughs novel. With clans in "every hamlet, village, and city in The Union," Burroughs reasoned, enrollment could easily reach two million.

His hope was that MGM would follow Signal Oil's example and throw its considerable promotional resources behind the clan idea. But while the studio readily granted ERB, Inc., permission to name Johnny Weissmuller "Chief of Chiefs," it chose not to circulate a large number of clan booklets or otherwise solicit memberships in the lobbies of movie theaters showing *Tarzan Finds a Son*. As a result, enrollment was a fraction of what Burroughs had envisioned; certainly book sales did not jump appreciably in 1939 or 1940.

In the end, the most noteworthy secondary lift he received from *Tarzan Finds a Son* came from a more mature fan. Fifty-year-old Alva Johnston was one of the most highly respected journalists in the country, having won a Pulitzer Prize for science reporting in the 1920s and more recently having completed a splendid biography of Samuel Goldwyn. In mid-May, *The Saturday Evening Post* dispatched him to Tarzana to interview Edgar Rice Burroughs. His profile, entitled "How to Become a Great Writer," appeared in the July 29 issue, just as *Tarzan Finds a Son* was filling the movie houses. Johnston's assignment, or so he asserted, had been to search out America's greatest living writer, using the following criteria: "1. The size of the writer's public. 2. His success in establishing a character in the consciousness of the world. 3. The possibility of being read by posterity." Without question, Johnston averred, "Edgar Rice Burroughs is first and the rest nowhere. No other literary creation of this century has a following like Tarzan. Another character with a world-wide public is Mickey Mouse, but he belongs to a different art. The only other recent works of imagination in this class are Charlie McCarthy and The Lone Ranger, but their vogue is confined to the English-speaking peoples and they are still novelties rather than assured immortals."

In making his case, Johnston exercised considerable rhetorical license and was guilty of the occasional inaccuracy. He stated that 25 million copies of the Tarzan books had been sold, an unverifiable figure that Burroughs had probably supplied him. And he sketched a Horatio Alger version of Burroughs's past, stressing the "dullness, wretchedness and futility" of his years as a cowboy, miner, policeman, office manager, and peddler—information Johnston must have picked up from reading Burroughs's uncompleted autobiography. Judging from Burroughs's background, in order to become a great writer, one should: "1. Be a disappointed man. 2. Achieve no success at anything you touch. 3. Lead an unbearably drab and uninteresting life. 4. Hate civilization. 5. Learn no grammar. 6. Read little. 7. Write nothing. 8. Have an ordinary mind and commonplace tastes, approximating those of the great reading public. 9. Avoid subjects that you know about."

Kidding aside, Johnston's observations on Burroughs's craft are quite astute. Of *Tarzan and the Apes* he wrote, "[T]he reader can put his finger on the passages where Burroughs is the dream-disciplined artist and on the passages where he is the self-conscious amateur. . . . [Yet] he did not win his world public solely through mediocrity. There are pages of his books which have the authentic flash of storytelling genius."

As for Burroughs the man, Johnston, if not exactly charmed, was appreciative of his interviewee's pragmatism and lack of pretense: "There is probably less literary foppery about Burroughs than about any other living writer. He has enough fame for a thousand ordinary lions of the literary teas, but it has never meant anything to him except as it has boosted royalties. He has known few writers personally and does not like them as a class; he thinks they spend their leisure sitting around and trying pathetically to say smart things. . . . If anybody compliments him to his face, Burroughs bristles, supposing that he is being heckled. But he is not mortified to learn that over in Japan little boys have been named Edgar after the author of Tarzan."

Burroughs was delighted by the article for reasons he claimed were strictly economic. Johnston did a "swell job," he told George Carlin of the United Features Syndicate. "I am wondering what effect it will have, not on me personally, but what the reaction will be insofar as my books and the [comic] strips are concerned." Carlin declined to make a firm prediction, "but the fact remains," he told his client, "that Tarzan will be getting about twenty-five thousand dollars' worth of promotion that ought to mean something."

The irony, of course, was that *The Saturday Evening Post* had turned down every story Burroughs had ever submitted, and in a final twist of the knife, the *Post* summarily rejected "Tarzan and the Champion," his latest submission, two months *after* Johnston had declared him the world's "greatest living writer." "Champion," in which Tarzan tangles with a prize-fighter, contained no "flash of storytelling genius," advised a *Post* fiction editor, who evidently was not a close reader of his own magazine. *Collier's* declined the ten-thousand-word story as well, and it was finally bought by *Blue Book* the following spring for two hundred and fifty dollars.

Notwithstanding the fact that one of the nation's leading magazines had declared Tarzan "the best-known literary character of the twentieth century," by decade's end it was clear that the ape-man and his creator had grown stale. After reading and rejecting Burroughs's next story,

"Tarzan and the Madman," another Post—*Argosy*'s G. W. Worthington Post—griped that "Tarzan doesn't seem to be Tarzan any more." As a matter of fact, Post charged, Tarzan was barely visible: "[He] takes, I should guess, something under fifty per-cent of the wordage. And when he does appear, he is simply a safety net in the rescue of the other characters. His own immediate problem is slight, his own perils are few, and the jams he gets into himself are the sort Tarzan, as we very well know, could get out of with both hands tied behind him."

Burroughs blamed his jangled lifestyle. In the four years that he and Florence had been married, their social life had never slowed down. They still ran back and forth to Palm Springs and stayed out late several nights a week. His diary for May 24, 1939 mentions they went to the "Olympic Auditorium to see 'Tarzan' White [one of a score of athletes who had taken the nickname] wrestle the Masked Marvel. [Burroughs was a big fan of professional wrestling and boxing, too.] Tarzan won and unmasked the Marvel all the way to his waist. Then to Wilshire Bowl, but did not stay—too crowded. Then to Marvel's [a nightclub] where we heard Gertrude Mess sing." Alva Johnston, who had interviewed Burroughs a week before, had described him as "powerfully built" and "fairly rugged," but behind the "poker face" and "iron-gray" bristles Johnston had detected a vague edginess. Burroughs was not getting any younger, no matter how deep his tan or how much tennis he played.

In passing, Johnston had also mentioned that MGM intended to shoot its next Tarzan film in Africa. More important, he stated that "Burroughs has been asked to accompany the expedition for publicity purposes and is inclined to accept. . . . He would like to see some of the country about which he has written hundreds of thousands of words."

In fact, the plan to go to Africa was a pipe dream. War ensured that the next Tarzan would be filmed in Hollywood and Florida again. In early 1940, as his sixty-fifth birthday neared, Burroughs conceived an entirely different itinerary. If there was war in Africa and Europe, then he and Florence would go in the other direction. He had enjoyed the previous two visits to Hawaii. Perhaps he could be content there for the rest of his days.

13

MAROONED

henever anyone asked, Burroughs said he had moved to Hawaii because he had "reached the end of my rope financially on the mainland." Claims of penury to the contrary, he in fact was not on the verge of bankruptcy. It is true that the magazine market was moribund and that, despite a variety of schemes to increase his book sales—Ralph Rothmund even proposed selling books in vending machines—they, too, were at an all-time low. But on the positive side, his contract with the movies guaranteed ERB, Inc., at least twenty-five thousand dollars annually, assuming that a new Tarzan came out every other year. With some modest budgeting, he should have been set for a good long while.

The trouble was, he had never been any good at managing money. Beginning with his purchase of Tarzana Ranch in 1919, and onward through his acquisition of cars, Thoroughbreds, and an airplane, he had fallen into a pattern of living beyond his means. Without a doubt, he was adept at squeezing the most out of his literary property. When he tried to put his earnings to work, though, he wound up losing his entire investment in Apache Motors and in his own film company, and he never made a dime in real estate—a performance that, if nothing else, must be regarded as one of the great anomalies of Southern California at the time. His was not so much a case of fortunes won and lost, but considering his gross earnings over the previous twenty-nine years as a writer, he very easily could have been a wealthy retiree. Instead he was an aging upper-middle-class businessman who, through his company or by his own salary, supported his grown children, his ex-wife, his new wife, and two young stepchildren, not to mention an executive secretary, a stenographer, and a maid. Alva Johnston had been kind to him in *The Saturday Evening Post*, but six months shy of Burroughs's sixty-fifth birthday, he had to wonder just what all his hard work and struggle really amounted to. He had never aspired to be Gatsby, but he would be damned if he would muddle along forever as Babbitt, either. He calculated that in Hawaii he could cut his expenses to a third of what they were in California and still enjoy the good life.

On April 18, 1940, Florence, her two children, and a maid, with a Packard sedan stowed in the hold, embarked for Honolulu aboard the S.S. *Matsonia*. Burroughs stayed another week to tie up loose ends, including assigning certain signatory authority to Ralph Rothmund and securing a tenant for the house he had purchased in Beverly Hills the previous summer. Hully, with help from Jack and Joan, would keep his eye on the business, though Burroughs had complete faith in Rothmund's ability—a confidence that was reaffirmed when Rothmund succeeded in selling the movie rights to *The Jungle Girl* on the eve of Burroughs's departure aboard the S.S. *Monterey*.

On the trip over, he felt lonesome and "terribly blue." He would be reunited with Florence in a week, but he had no idea when, or if, he would see California or his own children again. Another sobering image was the American flag painted on the side of the ship to make its registry more visible to anyone gazing through the periscope of a submarine. Fighting had begun in Europe the previous September; shortly thereafter, Congress had repealed the embargo forbidding sale of arms to belligerent powers, making the Stars and Stripes more a target than a shield. "This is the closest I have been to war," Burroughs noted in his diary on April 25, three days before arriving in Hawaii.

Florence had rented a house on Kailua Bay, in Lanikai, on the opposite side of the island from Honolulu, "smack on the ocean, with a nice, white sandy beach," Burroughs recorded. Despite frequent rain the first several weeks they were there, he was still taken with the casual island atmosphere. He readily adopted the local dress of shorts, untucked shirt, and sandals. A devout sunbather, he tanned to a deep bronze. The children, Caryl Lee and Lee, loved the water and the adventure of a new place. For the first few months, they did not have to go to school.

Though off the beaten path, Burroughs and his family were scarcely isolated. Living nearby were good friends Hal Thompson, a film editor, and his wife, Rochelle Hudson. Hudson had been a teenage starlet and a childhood friend of Hully and Jack. In 1940, she appeared in three pictures, *Girls Under Twenty-one*, *Men Without Souls*, and *Island of Doomed Men*, though her meteoric career was already dimming. Another acquaintance was actor John Halliday and his wife, Eleanor. Halliday's career was waning as well, though he would distinguish himself in one of the biggest films of 1940, *Philadelphia Story*.

During the day, the couples and children would get together for swim outings, picnics, and tennis. Evenings were crowded with cocktails, bridge, and luaus—which Burroughs characterized as "one of those damned things where you are supposed to eat dried octopus, raw fish, disinterred pig, and library paste which they try to disguise under the alias of poi." He may not have liked the diet, but he never turned down an invitation.

To Burroughs, whom Alva Johnston had described as still looking "a little military," the bustle of the navy at nearby Pearl Harbor and the army at Fort Ruger, Fort Shafter, Schofield Barracks, and Hickam Field was much more fetching than any picnic or party. On May 7, he took the family to Pearl Harbor for a closer look. "[T]hey wouldn't let us in," he wrote in his diary. "Finally, after I identified myself, a Marine Sergeant got authority from the Capt of the Yard to detail a corporal to accompany us and show us around." As soon as the *Honolulu Advertiser* published a profile of the island's newest author in residence ("Hawaii Not Rugged Enough for Tarzan, Says His Creator at Lanikai Hideway"), all doors and docks were open. The captain of the *California* invited Burroughs on a personal tour of his ship, moored on Pearl Harbor's famous Battleship Row. Soon he and Florence were thick with most of the top brass on Oahu. In 1940, Hawaii was still considered easy duty, and officers had plenty of time and inclination to mix with civilians, especially someone of Burroughs's renown. He, needless to say, enjoyed the company of military men more than he did that of authors or Hollywood notables.

Despite Hawaii's inherent tranquillity, the topic of safety had begun to creep into daily conversation. The surf of Honolulu was a long way from the beaches of Dunkirk, where in May and June, more than 300,000 British and French troops made the narrowest of escapes; nevertheless, if America and Japan were to enter the war, which seemed increasingly likely, though not yet inevitable, "[a]n enemy from the West would probably try to mess up this island," Burroughs wrote to Bert Weston. Like most Hawaiians, he still considered an attack a long shot, "an extremely remote contingency" that could occur only in the unlikely event that "the British fleet is scuttled . . . or captured by Hitler." Even then, he couldn't imagine being overrun. "The entire island of Oahu is an immense fortress," he wrote to his brother George (his only surviving sibling since the death of Harry Burroughs in January). "Every point and headland is heavily fortified. In addition to the navy and the army and the navy air corps, there are twenty-five thousand troops here—the largest force stationed anywhere in U.S. territory." Though the rest of the world was "going to pot," he concluded, "I still refuse to worry."

On the evening of May 23, he and Florence drove to the top of Mount Tantalus, overlooking Honolulu, to observe a blackout rehearsal. "There were several couples there, including the usual quota of Admirals and Colonels," he wrote to his children. "These admirals are so numerous over here that they are always getting between your feet and in your hair. I have to comb them out every time I come home from any place." The blackout was very entertaining, he reported, "although there were a few Fifth Columnists who left their lights on. The [mock] enemy planes dropped flares, and our side filled the heavens with flood lights." To hear Burroughs tell it, the defense of Hawaii was all just a marvelous game.

A much more palpable concern to Burroughs and a large number of Hawaii's white inhabitants was the presence of so many Japanese and Japanese-Americans on the islands. The first Japanese had come to Hawaii in the late 1800s to labor on the sugar plantations—invited by the "Big Five" growers as a preferable alternative to Chinese workers, who were viewed as racially inferior. By 1940, one out of three Hawaiians was of Japanese heritage, either issei (first generation and ineligible for U.S. citizenship) or nisei (their descendants, born in Hawaii and thus American citizens). From a white (haole) perspective, the Japanese were an integral but worrisome underclass. Despite the fact that the vast majority of Japanese on Hawaii were conservative, hard-working souls whose roots in the Hawaiian soil ran as deep as those of most whites, a number of events over the years, including labor strikes, epidemics, and several sensational cases of interracial violence, had perpetuated an atmosphere of suspicion and latent disdain between the two populations.

For years, white reactionaries had warned against a conspiracy by issei and nisei to "Japanize" Hawaii. Now, with the heightening of tensions between the United States and Japanese governments, the jingoist perspective was gaining more and more adherents. It was noted that many Japanese in Hawaii had relatives still living in Japan, and indeed many Japanese Hawaiians were still Japanese citizens. If war broke out, the alarmists asked, to which flag would the issei and nisei pledge allegiance? A large percentage of whites, including the Burroughses, employed Japanese servants. Were they spies? How many were waiting, inscrutably, for a signal from the homeland to slit haole throats and bring Hawaii to its knees?

Burroughs may not have believed that the islands could be successfully attacked from without, but his tendency toward racial stereotyping made him a ready subscriber to the anti-Japanese movement. His stepson Lee remembers him calling the Hawaiian Japanese "black ants." Several weeks after their arrival on Oahu, Burroughs took Lee and his sister to a movie. "The place was crowded with orientals," he noted in his diary, "and stank to high heaven." And when he discovered a Yoshiko Burroughs in the Honolulu telephone directory, he asked the local police if they wouldn't mind conducting a brief background check. "I had almost thought that I had almost a clear lineage of English blood, with the exception of one Pennsylvania Dutchman [his mother's father] who sneaked in about a hundred years ago," he explained in his letter to the police. "[B]ut now up pops a Japanese Burroughs, and I don't know what the hell I am." If it wasn't too much trouble, would the police department mind "diplomatically ascertaining how Yoshiko annexed that surname"? He insisted that he was motivated by idle curiosity only; yet it rankled that he and a Japanese might be related somehow. "I am sure that Yoshiko is an upstanding citizen and a credit to our common ancestor," he joked testily in his letter, but he obviously considered something as minor as a Japanese Burroughs in the phone book a blot on his family genealogy.

*   *   *

THE LANIKAI house had no spare room for an office, so Burroughs set up his Underwood typewriter on a workbench in the garage, with a crate for a chair. Casting about for story ideas, he inevitably looked seaward. In the first tale he wrote in Hawaii, "Slaves of the Fishmen," Carson Napier and his mate Duare are captured by the Myposans, a race of amphibious humans with bulging eyes, protruding lips, and gills, who raise their young in swimming pools. The moral of the story seems to be that if man was intended to spend so much time in and under water, he should have been born there. In a letter to daughter Joan, written while he was in the middle of "Fishmen," Burroughs confessed his own inadequacy as a swimmer: "I have been sixty-four years trying to learn, and up to now arrived nowhere. I go in the ocean with the children and jump up and down as the rollers come in. I'm too damned scared to swim out."

"Slaves of the Fishmen" is only twenty-four thousand words, a length that suited Raymond Palmer, editor of *Amazing Stories* and *Fantastic Adventures.* The previous year, Palmer had bought "Beware!," which had languished in Burroughs's drawer since 1922. Palmer paid only a penny a word, or two hundred and forty dollars, but Burroughs was thrilled to have unloaded the musty manuscript and to have discovered a hospitable editor, a rarity in recent years. Subsequently, Palmer rejected the book-length *Land of Terror,* but indicated that he would be much more receptive to shorter stories, roughly the length of "Beware!"

The prospect of not having to sustain an entire novel was liberating. Burroughs adopted a schedule that would allow him to turn out a succession of "novelettes" that could be strung together to make a book, and in the first six months he was in Hawaii, he wrote eleven stories—four Venus, four Mars, and three Pellucidar—each approximately twenty thousand words. All were accepted by Palmer and appeared either in *Amazing Stories* or *Fantastic Adventures.* (Eventually they were published in book form as *Escape on Venus, Llana of Gathol,* and *Savage Pellucidar.*) It was one of the most productive periods of Burroughs's career. It was also the last big burst of writing he would do in his life.

In the *Escape on Venus* stories, Carson Napier and Duare traverse Venus in an airplane (on Venus, an anotar), endeavoring to reach their island home in the southern hemisphere. After fleeing the fishmen, they must reckon with the Goddess of Fire, who turns out to be the long-lost Betty Callwell, a Brooklyn girl transported to the land of the green-skinned Brokols, whose offspring grow on trees, like fruit. "Here was a race of people," Napier reflects, "who not only had family trees but family orchards." Next the aeronauts descend to Voo-ad, which at first blush appears to be a sort of Venusian Shangri-la, not unlike Hawaii. As Carson and Duare step from their airship, they are showered with flowers and songs of welcome. At a banquet in their honor, however, they are doped—paralyzed from the neck down—and soon find themselves hung like exotic taxidermy in the Museum of Natural History. The final story in the set, "War on Venus," divulges just how familiar Burroughs had become with Hawaii's military materiel. Carson and Duare inadvertently find themselves caught up in a war between the Pangans and Falsans. The dispute has an Old West flavor—it begins over grazing rights—though the actual fighting is a Burroughs hybrid: naval-type warfare fought on land. On the plain of Anlap, Carson's anator comes upon the Falsan fleet, comprised of superdreadnaughts and the equivalent of cruisers and destroyers, which in many ways resemble the ships docked at Pearl Harbor, with their decks and armor, pennants and big guns. Though Carson acknowledges that he is originally from California, "a little country that's not at war with anybody," he eventually becomes commander of a Falsan athgan, the land version of a PT boat, and wins the day for his adopted flag.

Hawaii figures much more explicitly in the opening Martian story of *Llana of Gathol*. John Carter finds his earthling nephew, narrator of previous Martian tales, on the beach of Lanikai, gazing idly at the moonlit sea. "Lanikai is a district, a beach, a Post Office, and a grocery story," the nephew begins. "It lies on the windward shore of the Island of Oahu. It is a long way from Mars. Its waters are blue and beautiful and calm inside the coral reef, and the trade winds sighing through the fronds of the coconut palms at night might be the murmuring voices of the ghosts of the kings and chieftains who fished in its still waters long before the sea captains brought strange diseases or the missionaries brought mother-hubbards."

John Carter interrupts the reverie: "Well, well . . . asleep on a beautiful night like this!" Carter explains that he has missed his nephew, "the last of my Earthly kin whom I know personally. . . . After you are dead, and it will not be long now, I shall have no Earthly ties—no reason to return to the scene of my former life."

The nephew, thrilled to see Carter again, assures him that even after he is gone, his children will welcome the Martian warlord. After all, they are blood kin. "Yes . . . I know," Carter replies, "but they might be afraid of me."

"Not my children," the nephew assures him. "They know you quite as well as I. After I am gone, see them occasionally."

"Perhaps I shall," answers Carter, himself quite ageless.

Burroughs was wondering when he would see his own children again, though he did not allow any further mawkishness to soften the Martian escapades that followed. In "The City of Mummies," John Carter rescues his granddaughter, Llana of Gathol, from the pits beneath the dead city of Horz, inhabited by the remnants of a race of white-skinned, blond-haired Barsoomians that once dominated the planet but then declined as the Martian oceans dried up. Fleeing Horz, Carter and Llana are then captured by the Black Pirates of Barsoom, who though not the dominant race of Mars, are indisputably its oldest. "They are an exceptionally handsome race," Carter notes, "clean-limbed and power-ful, with intelligent faces and features of such exquisite chiseling that Adonis himself might have envied them. I am a Virginian; and it may seem strange for me to say so, but their black skins, resembling polished ebony, add greatly to their beauty." The attractiveness of the First Born does not forgive their manifest cruelty, nor the fact that they, as blacks, have enslaved John Carter, a white man, and have even worse plans for Llana. To escape, Carter cleverly dons blackface and slips through his enemy's guard.

In the third episode, John Carter must rescue Llana from "the hot-house city of the frozen North," where the megalomaniacal tyrant Hin Abtol has been stockpiling thousands of warriors in his deep freeze toward the day that he can thaw them out and conquer all of Mars. And in the final leg of the perilous journey back to Gathol, Carter and Llana are imprisoned within the Forest of Lost Men, possessors of a pill that renders them invisible. The highlight is a duel between Carter and Motus for the bragging rights of best swordsman on Barsoom. Carter makes mincemeat of his opponent—"from the waist up he looked like a plate of raw hamburger"—biding his time till his own pill of invisibility activates and allows him to vanish with Llana. Not wishing to reveal his true iden-tity to the Lost Men, he fights under the pseudonym "the Sultan of Swat," which was also the nickname of baseball slugger Babe Ruth.

Burroughs's humor was in good form throughout the Pellucidar sto-ries of 1940. At one point, Hodon the Fleet and comely O-aa, the central characters in "The Return to Pellucidar," are thrown together with an ancient Cape Cod mariner, whose whaling ship strayed through the opening at the North Pole a century earlier. The Cape Codder is an incorrigible cannibal, forever sizing up his next human snack. "Ol' Bill wa a mite tough and rank," he says of a former shipmate, "but there was a Swede I et who was just about the nicest eatin' you ever see."

In the next novelette, David Innes arrives in Tanga-tanga, where he allows himself to be worshipped as Pu, the one true God, if for no other reason than to avoid being taken prisoner. When it comes time to plot escape, he invents the sacrament of confession in order to learn the secrets of the priests. "What are you going to do?" O-aa asks as he prepares to debrief the ranking clerics of the land. "I am going to scare the pants off him," Innes replies. "What are pants?" wonders the innocent O-aa, whose shapely figure has never known even a suit of underclothes, much less a Mother Hubbard.

Raymond Palmer loved this stream of Pellucidarian, Martian, and Venusian adventures and was impressed by Burroughs's ability to fire them off in such rapid succession. There was only one problem: having accepted more than 200,000 words of Burroughs prose in a six-month period, both *Fantastic Adventures* and *Thrilling Stories* were booked up till at least the end of 1941. "Mr. Burroughs now understands that you wish no more Mars, Venus, or Inner World stories from him," Ralph Rothmund wrote to Palmer on December 6, "and therefore the enclosed 'Invisible Men of Mars' is the last we will send you." Burroughs never got around to writing the fourth story in the Inner World series, "Savage Pellucidar," until October 1944.

FACED with a hefty backlog, he turned his attention elsewhere. In late October, he decided to explore an entirely new planet, this one located in a distant solar system. As he had done with Mars, Pellucidar, and Venus, he began by drawing a map, inventing an alphabet, and figuring a calendar and clock for his brave new world. The twenty-thousand-word "Beyond the Farthest Star" was intended to be the first installment of at least a four-novelette series.

Farflung locale aside, the story hit close to home, offering an unmistakable commentary on World War II. It also represented a radical shift in Burroughs's views on war in general. In nearly thirty years of writing, he had never been squeamish in his descriptions of human combat. The fighting in his stories is invariably bloody, sometimes with tens of thousands of warriors killed in a single battle. Indeed, more people die violently in Burroughs's stories than in all pulp westerns or detective stories combined. Skulls are cloven, hearts pierced, limbs severed, and the ground is often slick with the viscera of the fallen. Yet as gory as these scenes may be, Burroughs always washed them with a noble light: Tarzan obeys the law of the jungle; John Carter is a chivalrous Civil War veteran. Guns, whether they fire rays or bullets, kill and wound in many stories, particularly the ones written after Burroughs became a pistol owner himself. But for manly combat, the blade (in Tarzan's case, a knife; in John Carter's, a sword) is still the weapon of choice. Not even World War I—in which wholesale, mechanical butchery replaced the time-honored notion of war as romantic gauntlet—seemed to have much of an effect on his literary arsenal. By the end of 1940, however, he finally acknowledged that the style of swashbuckling combat practiced by John Carter so recently in *Llana of Gathol* belonged to a bygone sensibility.

He had first alluded to the modern horror of World War II in "The Return to Pellucidar," written earlier that fall. David Innes's inventor sidekick, Abner Perry, has succeeded in making the first Pellucidarian plane. "Just what do you propose using an aeroplane for?" Innes inquires. "To drop bombs, of course," Perry answers academically. "Just think of the havoc it will raise! Think of those poor people who have never seen an aeroplane before running out from their caves as it circles overhead. Think of the vast stride it will be in civilizing these people!" Burroughs offers his own opinion of aerial bombardment by having the plane burn up on the runway before it can do Perry's bidding.

In "Beyond the Farthest Star," his revulsion is even more pronounced. The hero of the tale, a pilot who chooses not to reveal his name, is shot down during a dogfight with three German Messerschmidts in September 1939. With a machine gun bullet to the heart, he plummets to what he presumes, in his waning seconds of consciousness, will be his death. But like John Carter in *A Princess of Mars* and Ulysses Paxton in *The Master Mind of Mars*, he awakens unhurt—and in a faraway land. The setting this time is the city of Orvis, in the country of Unis, on the planet Poloda, which orbits the star Omos, 450,000 light years from Earth. (By Polodan calculation, the distance is 547,500 light years, though, the narrator notes, "What's one hundred thousand light years among friends, anyway"?) The Polodans are a lot like earthlings—except of course for the women, who are more beautiful and customarily dress themselves in red boots and gold sequins that appear to have been pasted on their bare skin.

The pilot, who is given the name Tangor (literally, "from nothing"), discovers that the Polodans are in the one hundred and first year of an air war with the country of Kapara. Houses and most buildings are constructed in elevator shafts so they can be lowered out of harm's way during bombardments. The cost of war has curtailed luxury. All the motorcars are identical, "each one seating four people comfortably, or six uncomfortably," and clothing, including the sequins worn by women, is standardized. "I could not but wonder what American women would do if the Nazis succeeded in bringing total war to the world," Tangor ruminates. "I think that they would arise to the emergency just as courageously as have the women of Unis, but it might be a little galling to them at first to wear the same indestructible costume from the time they got their growth until they were married. . . . It was rather a strain on my imagination to visualize Elizabeth Arden hoeing potatoes."

In short order, Tangor is piloting his own plane and dogfighting with his Kapar counterparts, and though he acquits himself with signature Burroughsian flair, personal valor is overshadowed by the absurdity of a conflict fought for so long, so destructively. "There is no chivalry in complete war, I can assure you," Tangor confesses after killing two more Kapars. And even if he can accept the premise that war is "the natural state of man," as his friend Balzo Jan avers, it pains him to think of the toll it has taken on Polodan women. "Yes, it is hard on them," Balzo Jan admits. "The men only have to die once, but the women have to suffer always. Yes, it is too bad, but I can't imagine what we would do without war."

Burroughs completed "Beyond the Farthest Star" in two weeks and then dashed off the short, uninspired "Quest of Tarzan" (*Tarzan and the Castaways*), in which a ship carrying Tarzan, an Arab slave trader, a mutinous German, several prim Englishmen, a French ingenue, and an ark's worth of African beasts is wrecked on a Pacific island inhabited by a lost tribe of bloodthirsty Mayans. Quickly, though, he returned to Poloda, completing the twenty-thousand word "Tangor Returns" in five days. This time Tangor is sent to Kapara as a secret agent with the assignment to steal the drawings to an "amplifier" that will enable planes to fly to Tonos, the nearest planet in the solar system. The Polodans are finally tiring of war and contemplating emigration to a new home; they don't want the Kapars to follow them.

There is no mistaking the subtext of "Tangor Returns." Burroughs had regretted alienating German readers with *Tarzan the Untamed* twenty years earlier; by December 1940, however, he had no qualms about taking Nazism to task. When Tangor finally meets Pom Da, a Kapar version of Adolf Hitler, he discovers that he is "not a large man . . . and appears even smaller than he is because of his very evident nervousness, fear, and suspicion." Nor does Pom Da surround himself with good lieutenants: "[T]he Kapars are not highly intelligent, their first Pom Da having killed off a majority of the intelligent people of his time and his successor destroying the remainder, leaving only scum to breed." Burroughs saves some of his sharpest invective for the Zabo, the Kapar equivalent of the Gestapo: "The army fears the Zabo, the Zabo hates the army." And everyone fears Pom Da.

At least one magazine editor did not think that Burroughs's trip beyond the farthest star was worth the effort. G. Worthington Post of *Argosy* ignored the topical subtext of the first Polodan story, dismissing it as "merely a long travelogue about a fictitious and not extremely interesting planet." Donald Kennicott of *Blue Book*, who had recently turned down a story on the grounds that "there is [already] so much actual horror in the world just now," was willing to make an allowance for "Beyond the Farthest Star." However, he offered only four hundred dollars, which Burroughs begrudgingly accepted. "Tangor Returns," the sequel, was never accepted anywhere, for any price.

BY JANUARY 1941, Burroughs was at a loss for what to write next, having extruded nearly three hundred thousand words in the previous eight months. "I think plots are like eggs," he wrote to his son Jack. "A hen is born with the potentialities of just so many eggs, and after she has layed [*sic*] the last one she can sit on her nest and strain and grunt and never squeeze out another. Perhaps a writer is born with just so many plots. I have been straining and grunting and rearranging my feathers for a long time, but I can't squeeze out a single new plot, and the old ones have commenced to smell."

Finally, though, he managed to complete the four-thousand-word

"Misogynists Preferred," which, though never published, is an important story in light of the events that were about to occur in his personal life. It features John Alexander, a wealthy globetrotter whose hatred for all women can be traced to the abrupt departure of his wife, "who stuck nobly by him until he lost his money." After making a second fortune, he recruits four like-minded men, including a black servant, through a classified advertisement ("Misogynists preferred") to live with him on a remote Pacific island, whose only distinguishing characteristic is its historic dearth of women. Their new home, Nui Papaya, is "an Eveless Garden of Eden . . . a place of peace, *sans* gabble, lipstick, red toenails, permanents, and perfume at forty dollars a drop. "This is Heaven," one of the men declares. "[N]ot a skirt; not even a grass skirt."

The stag party is short-lived, for soon a yacht carrying Minerva Johnson, her secretary, black maid, and two "super-pulchritudinous" girlfriends—all of whom have been done wrong by men at some time or another—is tossed onto the beach of Nui Papaya. Predictably, familiarity erodes contempt, and after eighteen months, the sexes have mixed (though not the races) and the population of the island has jumped to fifteen—"five men, five women, and five babies, one of them black."

Comparable contentment was hard to find in Hawaii, especially amid proliferating rumors of war. The house of Lanikai, which at first had seemed like such a sanctuary, turned out to be a poor fit. The view and proximity to the beach were nice, but Florence complained that the bungalow was overrun with bugs and rats. Burroughs did not have a proper place to work, and most of their friends lived over a twisty mountain road in or near Honolulu. Finally in August, the family left the beach and took a house in Honolulu, in time for Caryl Lee and Lee to begin school in the city. Burroughs rented office space downtown. Then, two days after Christmas, the family moved again, to the Niumalu Hotel on Kapiolani Boulevard, a compound of residential cottages with a central dining room and lounge. "The grounds are a jungle of coconut trees and other tropical vegetation," Burroughs reported to Jack, though apparently the hotel had the misfortune of being located near a canal that discharged the city's wastewater into the sea. "I call it 'Hovel-on-Sewer,'" he said of their three-bedroom accommodations. "When the wind is from the south, the children do not swim—no one does."

The atmosphere within the Burroughs bungalow was not much healthier. Difference in age had always been an issue with Burroughs and

Florence, but, ironically, he was the one who acted immaturely more frequently. According to Florence, he wanted to go out every night. She never drank very much; he kept the flat well stocked with liquor. (Florence claimed he kept a case of bottles under his bed.) He took to calling her "Mama," and she remembers him constantly urging, "C'mon, Mama, have one more," or, "C'mon, Mama, let's have some fun."

Burroughs had been a terrific father to his own children. Likewise, he got along marvelously with Florence's younger child, Caryl Lee, who was nine in 1941. Eleven-year-old Lee was more of a problem. Unlike Hully and Jack, Lee was not particularly athletic, and Burroughs was always pushing him to take up one sport or another. Nor was he a particularly zealous student. Years after she and Burroughs had parted, Florence hinted that he had been too strict with Lee and on occasions may have been verbally abusive.

While Lee was an easy target, he was by no means the only one. On January 24, Burroughs wrote an unusual letter to his daughter, Joan. Until then, his letters to her had been nothing but sweet. This time, though, he exploded with bitter frustration:

> If anyone says a kind word about my work nowadays, as you did, I nearly break down and cry. I have had so many refusals lately and had my classics so gratuitously insulted . . . that I have lost confidence in myself. I am getting damned sick of hearing people apologize to me for reading my stories, or pretend[ing] to grouse because they have had to read them to their children, or say[ing] that they used to read them while they were in kinder-gar[t]en but have not read any for years and years. It used to amuse me, but I guess I must be losing my sense of humor. I think I shall come right back at the next one with a retort such as: "Well, you homely looking abortion, if you had the brains of a cross-eyed titmouse you'd keep your fool mouth shut instead of knocking inspired literature that has entertained . . . a hundred million people for over a quarter of a century!"

Three weeks later, though, Burroughs was not so outspoken when he and Florence spied Ernest Hemingway in a Honolulu restaurant. In a way, he and Hemingway had a great deal in common. They were two of the best-known authors of their day. Both were men's men, hard drinkers, and lovers of the outdoors. (And by coincidence, both had lived for a time in the Chicago suburb of Oak Park.) In 1941, Hemingway had a new wife, too, the journalist Martha Gellhorn, and the newlyweds were stopping over in Hawaii on their way to China, where Gellhorn was to cover the Sino-Japanese War. It was Florence who spotted them first.

She pretended to swoon. At first Burroughs didn't think it was Hemingway seated across the restaurant. When he finally conceded that their fellow diner *was* Hemingway, Florence prodded him to go over and say hello. But he wouldn't. Instead he grew furious at her for being so starstruck. She did her best to unruffle his feathers and again urged him to introduce himself. "Obviously you need to meet this man," she recalled saying. "Maybe you and Ernest should get together on some island sometime." Burroughs sat rooted to his chair, and the evening ended without Hemingway knowing that Burroughs was in the room.

As near as he had been to Hemingway, he understood that they were in fact oceans apart. Just before the trip to Hawaii, Hemingway had finished *For Whom the Bell Tolls,* a romance set in the Spanish Civil War. Reviewers would praise the novel for its skill at balancing "delicacy" and "brutality," qualities Burroughs instilled in all of his heroes, though none of his novels had ever received the serious attention paid to Hemingway's. If Florence didn't realize the critical gulf separating the two authors, Burroughs surely did, and his glowering silence was as good as an admission.

Perhaps at another time, in another place, he might have sauntered over and introduced himself to Hemingway, but lately he had been in too sour a mood to make his usual social overtures. "[W]e do practically nothing," he told Joan in his next letter, overlooking the fateful nonencounter with Hemingway. It was as if he and Florence were both waiting for the next shoe to drop. Surely they would not have moved to the Niumalu Hotel if they were planning to make Hawaii their permanent home.

Finally on March 14, the break came, though neither Burroughs nor Florence was willing to acknowledge its finality. "Florence and the children returned to the mainland," Burroughs wrote to Bert Weston. "It is so difficult to get reservations and the possibility of war with Japan so definite that we thought it best to get them off while we could. I shall finish up my business here and follow in about a month." The war made a convenient smoke screen, covering up the more private war that he and Florence had apparently been waging over the previous several months. Nothing in his correspondence or diary indicates that he took any definite steps to book a return passage in the weeks following Florence's departure. Instead he fell into a deep despondency that quite nearly killed him.

On March 27, he scribbled in his diary: "Had a very bad night last night from worry about Florence and finances. Early this morning when I woke I thought I had had a slight stroke in my sleep. (I think of the cutest things.) My arm still feels funny—the left one—sort of numb." More likely he had suffered an attack of angina pectoris—not his first and definitely not his last. He didn't tell anyone at first, save for his diary. In letters to his children he continued to present a cheerful face, but in reality he had retreated into a shell of self-pity. He quit seeing friends and attending parties, preferring to go to bed immediately after dinner. On April 11, Good Friday, he wrote in his diary, "What's good about it? . . . Bed 7:30." The following day's entry was more verbose, but no less glum: "I just realized that I go for days without speaking except to say 'morning' a few times and to order my meals—which are scarcely worth ordering. To my surprise, I do not mind being a sort of recluse."

Somehow he managed to complete two new stories: *I Am a Barbarian*, an account of a Briton slave to the Roman Emperor Caligula, and *The Wizard of Venus*, a Carson Napier yarn about a Merlin-esque tyrant who hypnotizes his rivals into believing he can turn them into the Venusian equivalent of swine. Neither found a publisher. All the while, he tried to ignore the rehearsals for war that were underway all around him. "Every morning," he wrote Joan, "I hear, faintly, the sound of reveille from nearby Fort Ruger at 6:15, whereupon I thumb my nose and turn over for two more hours of sleep. Later in the morning, I hear big guns and little guns booming in the distance and the roar of the motors of fighters and bombers overhead; then I turn over on the other side and contemplate the horrors of war, but not fearfully, as I realize that some two hundred thousand armed men, the United States fleet, and a swell air corps are gathered all about to protect me."

He conveyed no such sense of well-being to Ralph Rothmund two days later. Quite the opposite, his letter bore the imprint of a man contemplating departure from the living. "I don't need to tell you how much I have appreciated your friendship or what pleasure it has been to work with you all these years," he wrote to his loyal assistant. "As you have had to share many of the burdens of my later life, you will probably have no objection to arranging for the disposal of my remains. My personal desire is that there be no funeral and no services, but in that matter I shall bow to the wishes of the members of my family. Please see, however, that it is done with the least expense and fuss." Perhaps he was simply tying up loose ends—he had written a will much earlier—but if death was an appointment, even an imminent one, he was prepared to keep it.

Still, he wasn't exactly giving up. He made a concerted effort to regain his health: he began going to bed early, quit drinking entirely, took vitamins, and lost a dozen pounds. "I'm something of an optimist," Carson Napier says in *The Wizard of Venus*. "How much of an optimist I am, you may readily judge when I admit that I have been hopefully waiting for years for seven spades, vulnerable, doubled, and redoubled," a reference to Burroughs's own obsession for contract bridge.

But then on June 1, he took an abrupt turn for the worse. "Had a bad night last night and am scared," he confessed. "[My] old trouble seems to be returning," meaning of course his bladder condition; he could urinate only with great difficulty and discomfort. His doctor suggested that he resume drinking, but after two highballs, his first in two months, he was awake most of the night. "[A]m back on the water wagon, Dr. or no Dr.," he wrote in his diary. "I know when I feel well and I feel like hell this morning."

On June 12, he was admitted to the hospital, where a wire was inserted into his urethra via his penis in order to widen the opening of the bladder, which had become partially occluded with scar tissue after his earlier operations. He was sent home the next day but was out of commission for ten days. On the twenty-second, he phoned his doctor, who advised him to return to the hospital. Instead he drank five highballs, went to a baseball game, and took three more drinks when he came home. "I'm either going to kill or cure myself," he declared. Three days later, however, he relented, and returned to the hospital, where he remained for thirteen days. Back at the Niumalu Hotel, he tried to get back to writing and a semblance of normal living. His convalescence was interrupted on July 23 by a phone call from a reporter from the *Honolulu Star-Bulletin*, wanting a reaction to an item that had just come across the wire: "Actress Florence Gilbert announced through her attorney . . . today that she is filing a suit for divorce against Edgar Rice Burroughs, the author, charging him with mental cruelty." Burroughs's comment, which ran in the next morning's paper, was, "News to me."

August was a month of torture. He had little energy to worry about the divorce and left the details to Rothmund and his attorney in Los Angeles. Meantime, his doctor ordered a repetition of the invasive wire procedure, accompanied by a dosage of sulfa, a promising new antibiotic, to stave off infection. "I went to Dr. Brown's office this afternoon," he wrote on the eighth. "Everything was fine and I felt like a million dollars until about 7:30 P.M. Then . . . my temp went up; during the night it reached 103; I was delirious, vomited, had muscular convulsions. People pounded on the walls to make me shut up. I was unable to get out of bed to call a doctor until morning." He wasn't dying, but on the days he visited Dr. Brown's office, living wasn't much fun.

At first his children took his casual mentions of health troubles at face value, and when he drafted a new will on August 13, they understood that it was a necessary part of his divorce strategy. Yet eventually the thought of their father expiring all alone on a Pacific island was too much to contemplate. They met and decided that, of the three, Hully, the only unmarried sibling, should sail to Hawaii and rescue dear "O.B."— Old Burroughs, his children's pet name for their father. Upon hearing that Hully was on his way, Burroughs's spirits soared. "Gosh! you can't imagine what that means to me," he told Joan.

HE WAS SO excited that he rode out on the tugboat that greeted Hully's ship, the *Mariposa,* bearing the traditional gift of a fragrant lei. A photo taken on deck shows father and son shoulder to shoulder. They are not looking at the camera, but squarely into each other's eyes, broad grins lighting their faces.

Much to Hully's surprise and relief, his father looked quite fit, especially considering the setbacks of the past six months. Except for the strong reaction to his bladder treatments, which took a day or two to get over, he said he felt as fine as could feel a man who had just passed his sixty-sixth birthday. He and Hully did their best to ignore the pall that hung over each month's visit to the doctor. Neither did anything to expose the myth that Hully had come over strictly for "vacation." Burroughs was too stoical to admit he needed Hully, and Hully was too gracious to patronize his father. They moved into new quarters at the

Niumalu Hotel: a bedroom, sitting room, and bath, with Hully bunking on a pullout in the sitting room. Burroughs made little pretense of working. They ate late breakfasts, lingered over lunch, and spent afternoons driving around the island, sunbathing, fishing, or playing Burroughs's new favorite sport, paddle tennis. Evenings often began with cocktails. "I am leading your little brother astray," Burroughs wrote Jack. "He now drinks a rum collins. . . . And he mixes them himself. He is now afraid that he will become the town drunkard. It is getting to the point where I feel that I shall have to hide the rum bottle—or there won't be any rum left for me."

It was a poor attempt at humor, especially in light of his children's deep concern for their mother, whose alcoholism was no laughing matter. He was also aware that Joan's marriage was in trouble due in large part to Jim Pierce's drinking problem. Nor did Burroughs's joke fairly explain what was really going on in Hawaii. Hully was privately concerned that his father was becoming an alcoholic as well, and despite his apparent endorsement of the drinking life, he was in fact endeavoring to curb his father's behavior. Instead of tippling into the night, as had been Burroughs's habit previously, Hully made sure that the cocktails ended with dinner, after which he took his father to movies, or they attended professional wrestling matches, which Burroughs found "hilariously exciting" in their sweaty theatricality and hokey sadism. On other nights, they turned in right after supper and slept for twelve hours.

In his letters to Jack and Rothmund, Hully talked of bringing his father home, possibly as soon as mid-November 1941. Burroughs, who had once regarded his move to Hawaii as permanent, was now quite amenable to returning to the mainland. He had not lived in his own house among his own things for a year and a half; he hardly knew his grandchildren. The only hitch was the divorce. His lawyers still had not ironed out an agreement; until then, they advised he stay put in Hawaii.

Had Burroughs and Hully been more anxious about the war, they might have found a way to leave the islands sooner. But even though the rest of the world worried about Hawaii's vulnerability, they still did not. "I don't see how any foreign power could possibly make a successful attack on [Pearl Harbor]—least of all the Oriental pip-squeak," Hully commented several days after his arrival. Burroughs seconded the sentiment in a letter to a California friend: "There is no war fear here except for an occasional individual who must always find something to be pessimistic about. I think this is one of the safest places under the Flag."

As Hully's stay stretched to three, then four, months, father and son tried to make the most of their time together. In a charming reprise of Tarzana days, they fell into a regimen of friendly rivalry. Every afternoon's paddle tennis match was a test of experience versus youth. "Papa plays a damned good game for a man of his age," Hully wrote to Jack. "He beat me yesterday a set at 9–8. Day before he beat me 5–3." Weight reduction was another forum of competition: Burroughs got down to 182, a loss of sixteen pounds since the summer; Hully boasted that he got as low as 177. Together they quit drinking, and Burroughs quit smoking.

Hully was frankly amazed by his father's new lease on life. One afternoon they were walking back to the hotel along a fence line. "Papa didn't like the idea of walking all the way around the fence," Hully reported, "so damned if he didn't lightly jump up, swing a leg over and drop neatly down the other side. I stood there flabbergasted because the fence was chest high. I knew *I* couldn't get over it." In a letter to Joan, Burroughs summed up his dramatic turnaround with the bluff assurance: "Don't worry about my health. I am too damned mean to die."

Death, however, was closer than anyone knew. On Sunday, December 7, he and Hully rose early to take advantage of the cool morning, as they had lately become accustomed to doing. Burroughs's diary entry for the day notes dispassionately, "Watched Japan bomb Pearl Harbor and Hickam Field while we played tennis. . . ."

14

CAME THE WAR

The precision and temerity of the Japanese attack on Pearl Harbor were beyond immediate comprehension. That the raid occurred on a Sunday, at a peaceful hour on a peaceful island, only contributed to the incongruity. "When we awoke Sunday morning, December 7th, we heard a great deal of firing, some of it very loud," Burroughs wrote to his children two days later. "[B]ut we . . . had been informed by the newspapers the day before that heavy guns would be fired from various parts of the island during the ensuing several days; so we thought nothing of it and went to breakfast."

After eating, he and Hully changed clothes and proceeded to the tennis court on the Niumalu grounds, where they began their usual game. "There is an area of sand for sun bathers beyond . . . the court," he explained, "and soon a great many of the hotel guests were congregated there watching the show. Bombs were falling on Pearl Harbor. We could hear the detonations and see the bursts quite plainly [although an intervening hill prevented them from seeing the actual naval base, three miles away]. . . . Bombs were falling in the ocean not far from us. Black smoke was billowing up. . . . One among us, brighter than the others, said it was a practice smoke screen.

Through it all, Burroughs and Hully alternated tennis with "watching the show." And even after they learned that the attack was "the real McCoy," they continued to play. "There was nothing that we could do, as orders were constantly being broadcast to civilians to keep off the streets, to stay home, and not to use the telephone," he explained. In both his December ninth letter and an unpublished article, "Came the War," which he drafted from it, he interrupts his eyewitness account to digress on the virtues of paddle tennis, leaving the unfortunate impression that he was just as excited about the hotel's tricky court as he was about the tactics of Japanese dive bombers. His point, apparently, was to stress how unflappable he and his fellow Americans were in the face of wicked assault. "I should like to say right here that all the people were calm and unafraid," he asserted. If he himself was scared, he didn't let on.

For most of the day and night following the early morning raid, the island of Oahu had no assurance that more strikes would not follow. There were constant rumors of Japanese paratroopers landing in the mountains, of troops pouring onto remote beaches. Every nisei and issei was suspected of being a fifth columnist or at least a Japanese sympathizer for whom the attack on Pearl Harbor was a signal to rise up and seize the island.

Shortly after noon on Sunday, a call went out over the radio for all able-bodied men to report to the waterfront. At sixty-six, Burroughs could easily have stayed home. Instead, he, Hully, and a fellow hotel guest, Anton Rost—whom Burroughs described as a corpulent "dog fancier and kennel show judge"—drove to the docks in Burroughs's Buick. After several false starts, they were issued Springfield rifles and assigned to guard a tuna-packing plant, where military police had arrested twenty-two Japanese fishermen whose heritage and radio-equipped sampans were viewed as threats to island security. Burroughs dubbed Hully, Rost, and himself "the Three Musketeers."

Later, while Rost continued to guard the tuna plant, Burroughs and Hully were ordered to patrol a mile-long stretch of Ward Avenue. Rain fell most of the night. Accustomed to going to bed at seven o'clock, Burroughs was kept awake only by the pain in his feet. Sometime after midnight, he and Hully were detailed to help escort another group of Japanese to an immigration station. "By this time," he announced with humility, "both my collar bones had caved in beneath the weight of my Springfield, and my feet had practically ceased to exist as such. . . . Before we got there, the seat of my pants [was] dragging on the ground; and I knew just how Napoleon felt on the retreat from Moscow." Returning to the tuna plant, they and Rost spent the rest of the night trying to sleep on a cement floor. "I lay down for a while," Burroughs recorded, "but I had so much difficulty getting up again that I decided to ossify in a sitting position." At first light, they emerged from the tuna plant, "where people commenced ordering us around once more. Presently there was another alarm, and we were ordered to take cover. Everyone lay or squatted behind sandbags, lumber, or what-have-you, with guns pointing in all directions, for no one knew from what direction the enemy would pop up on us. I say everyone, but there was one exception. I did no squatting nor lying down. . . . I was not animated by any excess of courage, but by a definite conviction that if I once got down, I should never be able to get up again. Portions of my anatomy that ordinarily bend fairly well seemed on the verge of bending no more. About eight o'clock, having gotten the war off to a good start, we went home."

His wit, it turned out, was his most effective weapon. On December 12, he was summoned to the office of Col. Kendall Fielder, whom he knew well from cocktail parties. Fielder had sized Burroughs up as a quipster, if not a soldier, and asked him to consider writing a newspaper column that would "reflect the lighter side of what we are passing through." Burroughs jumped at the chance, and the first "Laugh It Off" appeared in the *Honolulu Advertiser* the following day. "Whatever else the civilian population of the island of Oahu may lack, it is long on cooperation, guts, and a sense of humor," he wrote. "Since the Japanese attack . . . I have seen more grins and heard more laughter and jokes than ever before in all the time I have spent in the Paradise of the Pacific." Most of the column repeated the anecdotes of his December 9 letter. His one attempt at comedy was to tweak an unnamed colonel and a captain for falling into a trench during a blackout.

Blackouts proved to be a major source of levity in many of the columns that followed. He told of the spy whose code signals turned out to be merely a lantern in the hand of an old man milking a cow. He made fun of a woman who, attending to her toilette in the dark, inadvertently shampooed her hair with cough syrup and brushed her teeth with white shoe polish. Other jokes related to the perceived threat of local Japanese. When the rumor circulated that fifth columnists had poisoned the drinking water, Burroughs hooted at pet owners who sampled the water themselves before allowing their dogs to drink. Much to his delight, when Japanese aliens were ordered to turn in all firearms, one fellow relinquished a bow and arrow.

He relished his role as pundit and propagandist and had no desire to return to fiction anytime soon. Even after he quit writing the column in the end of January—once Hawaii had regained a modicum of composure—he continued to wear a green armband with a red C on it and carried the credentials of an official correspondent.

Hully likewise wanted to cover the war in an official capacity. In January, while his father was still writing "Laugh It Off," he enlisted in the Army Air Corps at nearby Hickam Field, with the idea of putting his photography skills to good use. Like any parent, Burroughs worried about his son's safety, but was nonetheless supportive. "I'm very proud of you," he wrote Hully two days after his enlistment. "My heart swelled and the tears started to my eyes when I saw you in the uniform of the land we both so love. I know you will make a great soldier. A man who has been such a fine son, friend, and companion could not do otherwise. You epitomize all that is fine and clean in young American manhood." Contrarily, Burroughs was loath to see Jack follow in his brother's footsteps. "Under present circumstances he should not serve," he confided to Joan. "With Hulbert it was different: he has no wife and isn't going to have a baby." Jack's first child was born in June, and he never did serve in the military.

It never occurred to Burroughs that he should sit out the war himself. Shortly after quitting "Laugh It Off," he enlisted in the Businessmen's Military Training Corps, a civilian guard intended to deter any thoughts of a local uprising and to aid police in the event of air raids. He quickly advanced from the rank of corporal to second lieutenant and then to major. The BMTC's nickname was the Opus Guard, *opu* meaning potbelly in Hawaiian, though Burroughs was a noteworthy exception. Tennis and regular "setting-up" exercises had helped him lose nearly thirty pounds since arriving in Hawaii, and as he proudly admitted, he looked "sylphlike" in his khaki uniform, a Colt .45 revolver on his hip. He relished the weekly drills, a throwback to his youth in military school, the cavalry, and the Illinois militia. His primary duty with the BMTC was not as military policeman or even instructor, but as publicist, a job he performed with flair and excellent results.

By May, he was pleased to report to Hully that the sulfa drugs had finally cleared up his bladder infection and that he no longer needed wire treatments. For the first time in twelve years, his doctor gave him a clean bill of health. Almost simultaneously, he received word from the mainland that his divorce from Florence had been finalized. Suddenly all the old reasons for staying in Hawaii had evaporated. But now that he was free to go home, he didn't want to. "In comparison [to Hawaii], life in California would be pretty dull," Hully wrote Jack, explaining why their father had chosen to remain in Honolulu. "After all, he is in the thick of history being made, and why not let him share in momentous times?"

One of the topics that continued to preoccupy Burroughs was the Japanese presence in Hawaii, which he described in a letter to United States Senator Hiram Johnson as "a Damoclean sword hanging constantly over our heads." He elaborated on his concerns in an article entitled "What Are We Going to Do About It?" He accused America's haole establishment of being naive or in some cases soft in respect to the threat posed by the presence of 159,000 "potential fifth columnists" in Hawaii. He referred to Hawaii's congressional delegate, Samuel Wilder King, as "Sampan" King. And he claimed, on good authority, that 80 percent of Hawaii's nisei secretly hoped that Japan would win the war. All nisei, he asserted, have been under "the influence of the enemy aliens all their lives. After American school hours, they were required to attend Japanese language schools where they were taught many things beside the Japanese language, literature, and culture. And it is doubtful that loyalty to America was any part of the curriculum." He did not explicitly call for the deportment of all Japanese from Hawaii, as he had done in his letter to Senator Johnson, but his message was clear just the same: "My considered judgment is that something should be done. . . . I leave the deductions to you."

Fortunately for the thousands of loyal Japanese-Americans living on Hawaii or serving in the armed forces, his agent George Carlin had no success in placing "What Are We Going to Do About It?" Burroughs's disappointment was short-lived, for he already had his eye on a much bigger prize.

That summer, Hully had received a commission (thanks in part to his father's influence with higher-ups) and had been sent off to the Pacific as an aerial photographer. His accounts of bombing raids in the Solomon Islands and close calls on Guadalcanal only heightened Burroughs's appetite to see the war for himself. He resigned from the BMTC in September and, against all odds, applied for and received credentials as a combat correspondent for United Press. "I really never thought I would get a break like this," he wrote Hully when his papers finally came through. "I'm a lucky guy."

After more than a month of "sitting on the edges of chairs with pants full of ants," he finally received an assignment. On December 5, he boarded a B-24, bound for New Caledonia, via Canton Island and Fiji. "Everybody on the transport plane was a fan," he noted with pleasure. "And so it was throughout. I shone in the reflected glory, as the name [of Tarzan] aroused nostalgic memories of boyhood in the minds of the hundreds I met—from privates to generals."

On Canton Island, water rationing reminded him of his rough-and-tumble youth: "[M]y experience in the 7th Cavalry in Arizona and as a cowpuncher in Idaho had long since impressed me with the fact that washing may be reduced to a minimum or done away with entirely." Yet the hardships he encountered in the South Seas were nothing like those he had endured in the wild West. Airplane seats may have been uncomfortable. Mosquitoes were often pernicious. It could rain for days, and his clothes were often soaked. On several occasions he was obliged to board ships by climbing cargo nets, a challenge for any sixty-seven-year-old, no matter how fit. But more often than not, he was given preferential treatment because of his celebrity, his age, and his credentials as a correspondent. He complained about the jeeps assigned him—"Bouncing Babies"—but had to admit that they were better than hitching rides or walking, which most correspondents had to do. The bunks were not always the best, the toilets and latrines less than four star, but he was always given the best available. And each time he shifted quarters, he never had to carry his own luggage. "I have forgotten who helped me with my gear," he noted in his diary after one decampment, "but somebody did. Somebody always did."

In three months, Burroughs filed twenty-five stories, though, strangely, none was ever published. He doubted that they even reached United Press and presumed that they wound up "mouldering in the War Department in Washington." As a result, the only extant record of his journey is "The Diary of a Confused Old Man," a fifty-nine-page, single-spaced travelogue that he extrapolated from his diary for the edification of "my children, my children's children, and anyone else dumb enough to read it." Far from a methodical war report, it more closely resembled the "Auto-Gypsying" journal he had compiled in 1916.

After a brief stop in New Caledonia, he arrived in Sydney, Australia, where he spent a great deal of his three weeks towning around with various uniformed cronies. Everyone wanted to have a drink with him, and even when liquor was hard to come by, someone always knew how to find a bottle for the occasion. Scotch was the libation of choice, cold beer was a welcome luxury, and Canadian whiskey or rum was also potable in a pinch. The higher the rank, the greater the access to good spirits, and Burroughs made friends with dozens of officers throughout his trip. "I seem to be drinking my way through this war," he acknowledged, "and I don't know of any better way of getting through a war."

Amid the barhopping, he somehow found time to tend to a bit of unfinished business. The war had wounded ERB, Inc., on several fronts. Due to paper rationing, the company had been obliged to cease publishing books, and a number of newspapers had eliminated *Tarzan* from their trimmed-down comic sections. Jack Burroughs's comic, *John Carter of Mars*, had finally debuted in the Sunday funny pages on, of all days, December 7, 1941, a guarantee of its almost immediate demise. Another problem created by the war had to do with collection of overseas royalties. More than three thousand dollars in Tarzan radio-show royalties had been frozen in a Sydney account since Australia's entrance into the war in 1939. There was little Burroughs could do to loosen the other constraints on ERB, Inc.'s, affairs, but he vowed not to leave the country without his money. On January 9, he finally succeeded in converting the overdue and sorely needed income into U.S. war bonds.

In Australia, he was also able to further the cause of MGM's newly released *Tarzan's New York Adventure*—the first time since leaving California that he had had any direct involvement with Hollywood. Over the previous two years, Republic Pictures had produced a fifteen-chapter serial of *Jungle Girl*, which Burroughs may not even have seen, and MGM had released *Tarzan's Secret Treasure*, which he had watched, incognito, in a Honolulu theater. By contrast, MGM's Australian executives gave him a special screening of *Tarzan's New York Adventure* and set up a number of print, radio, and newsreel interviews, which he handled with the aplomb of a visiting statesman.

The movie needed all the help it could get. By 1942, Maureen O'Sullivan was sick of playing Jane yet again, and Johnny Weissmuller's swinging Hollywood lifestyle had finally softened his Olympian physique. MGM had decided that this would be its last Tarzan. Rather than set the story in Africa, the studio opted for the Big City—sure proof of its disenchantment with the jungle genre. In *New York Adventure*, Boy is shanghaied and put to work in an American circus. Tarzan and Jane track him to Manhattan, where civilization-as-wilderness is the not-so-subtle conceit. Tarzan takes a shower in his suit, vaults from one skyscraper to another, and dives off the Brooklyn Bridge. He rescues Boy after a perilous car chase, and as the curtain closes, Tarzan, Jane, and Boy are headed back to the relative peace of Africa. Barely seventy minutes long, *New York Adventure* was MGM's shortest Tarzan and arguably its weakest, though still a moneymaker. (The movie must have made an especially strong impression on the Australians, for it seems to have served as inspiration for *Crocodile Dundee*, the 1986 Australian film about an unsophisticated but savvy son of the outback who is tossed into the midst of an even more savage New York.)

On January 10, Burroughs flew from Australia back to New Caledonia, and finally his coverage of army activities began in earnest. In Nouméa, the capital, he registered at the comfortable Grand Hotel du Pacifique, where he was glad to see several familiar faces, including that of navy Lt. Hal Thompson, husband of Rochelle Hudson. For one of his first assignments, he joined a field artillery training exercise deep in the jungle. Due to the overgrown, mountainous terrain, the only way to get to the battalion's camp in the Dumbea Valley was by horse and mule, a hardship he found thrilling. "There is no USO, no movie stars, no glamor girls for [these troops]," he reported.

There was no enemy to fight, either. Perhaps the closest encounter with real combat came during a visit to a military hospital, where he was thronged by bandaged enlisted men, who told him vivid, bloody stories "of courage, of loyalty, of miracles." That night he toasted these plucky heroes at a meeting of the Nouméa Chowder & Marching Club, a loose fraternity of officers who convened regularly for drinking and cards.

After three weeks in New Caledonia, he boarded the USS *Shaw*, a destroyer hobbling home after running aground on a coral reef in the Solomons. "[H]er keel was badly wrinkled, some of her plates were sprung, and she had holes in her bottom that had been patched up with concrete," he observed none too happily. The captain confided in him that a heavy storm, or even the concussion of its own depth charges, could sink her. As wartime crossings went, however, the *Shaw*'s homeward voyage was fairly uneventful. Burroughs spent a good deal of time on the bridge looking for whales, sharks, and, perversely, corpses. "My interest in floating corpses has been almost lifelong," he admitted. "It derives from a story I read many years ago of a voyage on a windjammer way down in the Antarctic in an area practically never traveled by ships, where the narrator saw the body of a man floating. How did it get there? Where had it floated from? The intensely cold water must have preserved it. It may be floating around down there yet."

He wrote his final three United Press dispatches onboard ship and one evening, to pass the time, began writing a murder mystery of his own. "None of the [murder mysteries] I had read had enough corpses to wholly satisfy me," he joked. By the time he had finished it (back in Hawaii), his story had fourteen. But neither his gallows humor nor the title, "More Fun! More People Killed!," appealed to magazine editors, and the story, like his war correspondence, was never published.

The final run across the Pacific was disturbed by a number of submarine alarms, though most proved false. On one such occasion, Burroughs recounted, the captain ordered, "'Stand by to drop depth charges!' The great moment had come! The moment for which I had been hoping. I also hoped that the Shaw wouldn't break in two and sink. A moment later, the lookout beside whom I was standing announced: 'School of porpoises off port bow!'"

Three months after leaving Hickam Field, he arrived safely in Honolulu, having seen a lot of the world but very little of the war. Still, at his age, he was proud to have come through in such fine shape, and he overflowed with patriotism and appreciation for his fellowman. "[Y]ou just can't imagine how wonderfully everyone has treated me," he wrote to Joan shortly after his return. "As you know, I have always been just a little bit cynical about homo sapiens. But now I guess that I shall have to admit that God made a pretty good job when he whittled him out. And for me, the best of them are our own people. . . . I am so damned proud of being an American that I am on the verge of bursting."

The news from California, which had not caught up with him for three months, was less heartening. Joan and Jim Pierce had separated. Jim had gone off to Nogales, Mexico, purportedly to build an airport, though Ralph Rothmund was convinced that the deal was a shell game and that Jim was doing little more than hiding out from his creditors. Pierce had fallen so deeply into debt that he had hocked some of the family furniture and sold some of Joan's rings. "Jim has taken the Burroughs clan for as big a ride as one can possibly imagine," Rothmund remarked bluntly. "[He] is the worst and biggest bum in the world." By the time Burroughs returned from the South Pacific, Joan had "no place to go and nobody to support her," according to a letter from Jack, and she had taken her children to live with Emma in Bel-Air, which was scarcely a sanctuary.

Emma's condition was pathetic, as Hully made clear to family attorney Michael Shannon:

> [M]y mother is the victim of chronic alcoholism. . . . I know because I have seen my mother's affliction ever since the days of my childhood when I was too young to know what the trouble was. Since my mother and father separated and later divorced, the condition has become intolerably worse. At the time I came to Hawaii before the war, the periods of sobriety were very short— about two or three weeks—followed by ten days to two weeks of continuous drinking usually in a state bordering on delirium tremens and the resultant need of physician's attention. . . . It went on at this killing pace for over six years following the divorce with seldom more than a month or two abstinence. . . . I am convinced that the tragedy of her affliction will follow—or lead—her to her grave.

Assuming a grim and foregone conclusion, Hully suggested that the only thing the family could do was "try to make her life as happy and as free of worry as conditions will permit, and to control as far as possible the means whereby she can injure herself." Through conferences and correspondence, a new plan emerged: Emma's maid and her driver, who were apparently enabling her bingeing and taking advantage of her financially, were abruptly fired, and Rothmund was put in charge of all of Emma's day-to-day finances.

Once Burroughs was brought up to date on Emma's situation, he was profusely grateful to Jack and Rothmund for handling the matter so deftly. Emma had not seen him in at least five years but had kept tabs on him through the children. At certain times, she had figured to punish him by urging Joan, Hully, and Jack to stay away from their father, but she had not succeeded. For his part, Burroughs never stopped worrying about Emma, though he carried not the dimmest torch for her romantically. Rather, he saw her as a chronic liability and, as the mother of his children, a constant source of pain. One of the few direct communications he had with Emma after the divorce was a letter he wrote on June 9, 1943. It had to do with some Christmas presents Emma apparently had sent to him, which he received after getting back from Australia and New Caledonia. His response was clearly a ratification of Ralph's and Jack's efforts to curb her financial profligacy, but it also revealed his fundamental disdain for his ex-wife. "[B]elatedly, I thank you," he told her. "The gifts were lovely, but you should not have spent the money on me. Please do not do so again."

Meanwhile, he was hardly a model of self-control himself. "Would that I had the wings of a B17 . . . that I might cruise to far islands—and Australia, where there are beef, lamb, and Scotch," he commented in a newsletter circulated among his fellow United Press correspondents. "All that is left here is bathtub gin and I don't like gin." He was kidding about the limited choices of liquor, though. Friends—most of whom, he admitted, were "two-fisted drinkers"—were constantly showing up at his cottage at the Niumalu, sometimes before lunch, sometimes after he had gone to bed, with a bottle and offers that he rarely refused. "Life here has ceased to be very interesting," he said half-facetiously to Joan. "I am ashamed to say that outside of a little bridge, a little poker, and an occasional cocktail party I do nothing."

He did very little writing after returning from his trip, except to complete "More Fun! More People Killed!" and several perfunctory commentaries for United Press. Instead he did a lot of reading, plowing through the *Encyclopedia Britannica*, volume by volume. Another diversion was professional wrestling, which he considered "one of the most remarkable phenomena of the Twentieth Century." The broad, hammy theatricality of men throwing one another about in the ring was the athletic equivalent of his own pulp fiction, though he preferred to stress the sport's classical origin: "Hundreds of years before Christ, the Greek wrestling impresarios were putting on even better shows than Al Karasick [a Hawaiian promoter and a friend of Burroughs]. No holds were barred, not even strangling, butting, kicking, or finger crushing." The big difference was that modern-day wrestling, rather than mirroring the human suffering that was going on around the world, offered escape from it. "[R]ight now we can laugh at Al Karasick's comedies," he pointed out, "because we know that they are mostly play acting and that it is seldom that any of the actors get hurt."

          ✻   ✻   ✻

IT WAS nearly impossible to ignore the war for even an hour or two. Everyone was expected to do their bit, if not in uniform, then through rationing, war bonds, and labors that increased preparedness and pro-ductivity. The universal criterion for almost every decision was, will it help win the war? No lifestyle or profession was exempt, least of all the entertainment industry. Tin Pan Alley obligingly (and opportunistically) cranked out a series of patriotic songs, ranging from the pugnacious "Praise the Lord and Pass the Ammunition" and "The Sun Will Soon Be Setting on the Land of the Rising Sun" to more romantic ditties such as the memorable plea for home-front chastity, "Don't Sit Under the Apple Tree (With Anyone Else but Me)" and the less wholesome but no less inspirational "He Loved Me Till the All-Clear Came." Hollywood played an even larger role, turning its dream factories to the manufacture of propaganda and dispatching its screen heroes to entertain the troops or, in a number of instances, to join the actual fight. Jimmy Stewart, Henry Fonda, Clark Gable, and Robert Montgomery were among the most conspicuous enlistees. Women did their share, too. Besides building the morale of the army and navy through generous public appearances, Dorothy Lamour, Bette Davis, Hedy Lamarr, and Rita Hayworth helped sell millions of dollars in war bonds. No woman gave more to the cause than Gable's wife, Carole Lombard, who died in a plane crash on a 1942 bond tour.

The propaganda potential of movies was deemed too important to be left to the discretion of the studios alone. Shortly after Pearl Harbor, the Office of War Information established the Bureau of Motion Pictures (BMP), which very closely resembled the Hays Office in its authority to censor and shape movie content and tone. The BMP urged that films "show people making small sacrifices for victory"—everything from scrimping on sugar to giving up train seats for servicemen. Moreover, movies were expected to demonstrate admiration for American allies and to "stress national unity." For instance, the BMP's *Manual for the Motion Picture* suggested, "Show colored soldiers in crowd scenes." By mid-1942, one out of three movies was a war picture, and a public that had retreated behind blackout curtains in the months following Pearl Harbor returned to theaters to watch films ranging from the foxhole tragedy *Bataan* to the more uplifting *We've Never Been Licked.* Even cartoonists pitched in: Chuck Jones, the creator of Daffy Duck, doused Hitler and Mussolini with satiric ink in *The Ducktators,* and able-bodied sailor Popeye stormed the Pacific in *Scrap the Japs.*

It was only a matter of time before Tarzan entered the fray. After the release of *Tarzan's New York Adventure,* MGM had rid itself of the series, and in 1943 the film rights that MGM had bought from Sol Lesser five years earlier reverted to Lesser once again. A congenital grand-stander in war as in peace, Lesser was all too happy to sic his ape-man on the Axis. In the spirit of the day, he titled his picture *Tarzan Triumphs.*

The two Johnnies, Weissmuller and Sheffield, had agreed to follow Lesser, but Maureen O'Sullivan had finally bid adieu to treehouses, vine trapezes, and spiteful chimps. In *Triumphs,* Lesser finessed her departure by placing Jane off-camera in London, where she is said to be visiting her sick mother. From there, she gets word to Tarzan of the outbreak of world war; shortly thereafter, a Nazi safari arrives in the jungle and enslaves Tarzan's peaceful neighbors, the Palandrians. Tarzan initially hews to a policy of nonintervention—until news reaches him that Boy has been kid-napped by the Nazis. "Now Tarzan make war!" he exclaims, a line that drew cheers from wartime audiences. His hackles up at last, Tarzan saves Boy and the Palandrians (including the lovely Zandra, played by Frances Gifford, who had starred in *Jungle Girl* two years earlier) and lures the jackbooted German commanding officer into a pit containing a very annoyed lion (shades of the World War I-era *Tarzan the Untamed* and "The Little Door"). The seventy-eight-minute movie was nothing extraor-dinary, not even by Lesser's standards, but given the country's gung-ho appetite, it proved to be a solid hit. By September, after the movie had been out six months, Lesser was able to inform Burroughs that on top of his twenty-five thousand dollar advance, his royalty on *Tarzan Triumphs* had surpassed one hundred thousand dollars, "and the end is not yet in sight."

Lesser was so confident in Tarzan's resurgent appeal that he rushed another picture, *Tarzan's Desert Mystery,* into production. It, too, had a wartime message—Tarzan is asked to deliver a secret fever medicine to Allies in Burma—but with Jane still "away" in London, it offered negli-gible romance and only the broadest of plots. To reach the vines that contain the fever serum, Tarzan and Boy must cross a formidable desert (in fact, the dunes of California's Mojave); along the way, they tangle with a German spy and rescue a beautiful wild stallion and a gorgeous American girl (Nancy Kelly, a starlet from the RKO stable). All ends as it should when Tarzan delivers the German into the web of a man-eating spider.

Burroughs did not see either of Lesser's new *Tarzans,* at least not right away. "I haven't seen a Tarzan picture since I was in Sydney," he wrote the producer. "When they show here, there is a line from the box office to kingdom-come, and I won't stand in line for anything but hootch." Now that Lesser seemed finally to have found the golden touch, Burroughs was even more adamant about keeping his distance. When Lesser solicited feedback on the script of a third picture, *Tarzan and the Amazons,* he politely declined. "I am in no position to offer suggestions. But I appreciate the beau geste," he advised, ribbing his old friend for having patterned *Tarzan's Desert Mystery* on the much more artful film *Beau Geste* (1939).

BURROUGHS had been pessimistic about his chances of getting another war assignment—because of his age, because of the number of other reporters already in the field, and because he had had so little success on his previous trip. "As a war correspondent I have probably set a world record as All-American flop," he confessed to his boss at United Press. It came as a great surprise, then, to be given a second chance in March 1944.

His destination this time was Tarawa, in the Gilbert Islands, eighty miles from the equator. The previous November, a thousand Marines had lost their lives in driving the Japanese from Tarawa's coral bunkers, enabling Tarawa's airstrip to serve as a critical staging area for the invasion of the Marshall Islands to the north. By February, the navy, marines, and army had captured the three most fortified of the Marshalls: Kwajalein, Eniwetok, and Parry—and with that, the noose around the Marianas, Iwo Jima, Okinawa, and the Japanese mainland tightened dramatically. Even so, by late March, when Burroughs arrived in the Western Pacific, not all of the Marshalls had been secured, the smaller ones having been leapfrogged in the race to take the big three.

On Tarawa, two delightful coincidences occurred—though perhaps they had been orchestrated before leaving Honolulu. First, Burroughs was reunited with Hully, who was stationed there briefly as an aerial photographer. Second, he renewed his acquaintance with Brig. Gen. Truman H. (Ted) Landon, commanding general of the Seventh Army Air

Force Bomber Command. Burroughs had known Landon socially in Honolulu and was immediately invited to share the general's Tarawa living quarters and all the amenities that rank afforded. "I was treated like a rich uncle," he bragged to Bert Weston. "At different times two generals carried my gear, and one of them washed a uniform for me after seeing the God-awful mess I had made of it."

Privilege aside, living conditions on Tarawa and neighboring islands were nowhere near as cushy as those he had encountered on his tour of Fiji, New Caledonia, and Australia. He and General Landon had to dig their own foxhole; drinking water was brackish, booze scarce, and the defoliated atoll scorching. On one occasion, they even had to step around a few Japanese corpses. "They smell like ripe camembert," he wrote a friend in Hawaii.

On the nearby island of Jaluit, the enemy was very much alive, and well armed. At last Burroughs had found the war. He had spent the past half century imagining himself in the line of fire, and when the moment finally came, he behaved admirably. "Was on two bombing missions (daylight), with ack ack and other trimmings," he noted nonchalantly, though another account, filed years later, suggests that his experiences had been anything but routine. The first time Burroughs flew in Landon's B-24 Liberator bomber, according to Oliver Franklin, a member of the crew, the general

had the Marine ordnance boys load six 500-pound bombs in the rear bomb bays. As we neared the target, Ed stationed himself at the right waist window, equipped with headset and throat microphone. Coming in at 7000 feet the enemy guns opened up, so the general decided to do a precision job on the gun position at the east edge of Jabor town [on the island of Jaluit]. We made short, timed runs over the target, dropping one bomb each run, while clearly and calmly over the interphone came Ed's voice calling off: "Ack-ack burst at 3 o'clock high." Or, "Burst low, straight underneath." After each "bomb away," he would put his head so far out the open waist window that the 200-m.p.h. slip stream almost blew away his scanty gray hair, but he simply held onto his headset with one hand until he could see the bomb burst and then he would call out: "Bomb slightly over and a bit left of gun position." After using up our bombs without success,

I was cheered to hear Ed grumble: "Too bad we didn't have one more bomb. We were getting closer every time."

On the next trip, General Landon decided to fly to Eniwetok to inspect a landing strip that had been rebuilt after the American invasion a month earlier. "Almost the entire Marine garrison was watching the first four-engine bomber landing on their island," crewman Franklin recounted.

As the general eased the plane forward to touch the nose wheel to the ground, it folded up, and the bomber slid to an inglorious stop with the nose scooping up coral gravel. It was a mechanical failure, and even the best pilot in the world could not prevent it. . . . All hands, climbed out, Ed and the general crawling out of the bomb bay together. Then and there Ed proved his high caliber as a diplomat and a gentleman. Instead of looking at the plane with its nose rooting into the ground, he ignored it completely and began exclaiming about the desolate appearance of the island. . . . Taking our cue from Ed, the rest of us did the same. The general has a quick sense of humor, so in a moment his expression changed from red-faced embarrassment to quiet amusement. As the first Marine jeeps rolled up, I thought I heard him say: "Thanks a million, Ed. You're the perfect guest."

Carson Napier could not have displayed more cool, and while thousands of other men had chalked up closer calls in the Pacific, at least Burroughs could quit complaining that he had arrived too late for the thrill.

THOUGH he had not by any stretch been bloodied in battle or fired a single shot in anger, he was a changed man. Most notably, his exposure to the Japanese in the Western Pacific had a surprising effect on his attitude toward Japanese-Americans. Soon after his return from the Marshall Islands, he submitted an article to *Hawaii* magazine entitled "Our Japanese Problem," in which he accepted the inappropriateness of wholesale deportation of nisei from Hawaii. Where once he had been blinded by "bitter prejudice," now he allowed that, with only a few exceptions,

Japanese-Americans were decent and law-abiding and had never posed any threat to whites. Clearly, he realized, the Hawaiians of Japanese ancestry whom he saw every day in Honolulu were worlds apart from the Japanese corpses and prisoners he had seen on his recent trip. Not the least of their differences was that Japanese-Americans were "larger and better looking."

By the summer of 1944, the capitulation of Japan was considered not so much a matter of if but of when, and many pundits were volunteering suggestions on what to do with Japan and the Japanese after the war. In the final paragraphs of his *Hawaii* article, Burroughs proposed sending loyal, capable Japanese-Americans to Japan to set up a new, Western-minded government and economy. "As strongly as I [once felt that] both we and the Japanese would be better off if there were none of them on our soil," he concluded, sending volunteers to Japan was a far better solution than the mass deportation and disenfranchisement that many extremists were advocating.

It was a strange, patronizing, and squarely racist proposal, but given the intense anti-Japanese sentiment of the day, particularly in Hawaii, California, and Washington, D.C., it was received by many readers as progressive. One Hawaiian nisei wrote to congratulate him on his "real courage," and a group of prominent Japanese-American professionals invited him to discuss the issue in person. Like John Carter venturing into an unexplored region of Mars, Burroughs went expecting alien creatures, only to be pleasantly surprised by how much he and his hosts had in common. "What will interest you most about my experience," he wrote to Don Jackson, a marine friend, "is that both Bourbon and Scotch flowed freely; and our hostess, a very lovely woman, served delicious hors d'oeuvres. These were the first high class Japanese I had ever met. They were just as American as you or I." Class and alcohol were two languages that Burroughs spoke fluently, and thereafter he stuck up for Japanese-Americans both publicly and privately.

On the other hand, he showed Japan and the Japanese no quarter in his next book. He had not written a Tarzan story since *Tarzan and the Castaways* in 1940, partly because he did not see a lucrative outlet and partly because he had been so distracted by the war. Any number of people had urged him to send Tarzan into battle, as Sol Lesser had done with his two Tarzan movies, but Burroughs was hesitant. "In regard to your suggestion about sending Tarzan out to fight the Japs, it is something to think over," he wrote to agent George Carlin, "but for my own part I didn't like very much [Tarzan's] previous experience in fighting the Germans in North Africa." (He chose not to mention his anti-Nazi allegories in *Carson of Venus* and "Tangor Returns.") In June, he finally caved in, and over the next three months, he wrote *Tarzan and the Foreign Legion.*

The new novel was, above all, a reassertion of ideals. The bombing of Pearl Harbor had shot holes in one of the fundamental tenets of Burroughs's fiction—namely that a white man of courage and conviction would always prevail against a vastly greater force of savages. On the printed page, at least, it was time to retake the high ground.

Tarzan and the Foreign Legion begins where Burroughs's Pacific trip had left off: aboard a B-24 Liberator. Col. John Clayton, aka Lord Greystoke, of the Royal Air Force has joined the plane's American crew on a reconnaissance mission over Japanese-held Sumatra in the Netherland East Indies. The Americans, particularly Sgt. Tony "Shrimp" Rosetti of Chicago, dismiss Clayton as a stuffed English shirt. But after the bomber is shot down, the three survivors come to appreciate his physical prowess and junglecraft. When Colonel Clayton kills a tiger with his knife and gives the victory cry of the bull ape, pilot Jerry Lucas exclaims, "Lord Greystoke—Tarzan of the Apes!" At which point Shrimp Rosetti blurts in his best Chicagoese, "Is dat Johnny Weis[s]muller?" Later he speculates that if Clayton were to perform his remarkable tree swinging back in the States, he just might win a job "wit Sol Lesser out in Hollywood."

The Tarzan who fights the Japanese in the East Indies is every bit the warrior who had fought the Germans twenty-five years earlier. One of the Dutchmen, remembering that his father had read of Tarzan when he was a boy, asks how he has managed to stay so young. Tarzan explains to his comrades that he is the beneficiary of an eternal youth potion—the pills passed around at the end of *Tarzan's Quest.* In fiction or in fact, Burroughs implies, Tarzan could last forever.

From the standpoint of propaganda, Burroughs outdoes even Sol Lesser's flag-waving in the most recent Tarzan movies. He salutes the Foreign Legion, as the ragtag group of Dutch guerrillas and downed airmen dub themselves, for their fortitude and denounces the "Japs" occupying the island as craven "vermin" who communicate by "monkey jabber." They are rapists, torturers, cold-blooded murderers, deserving of a "just hate—a grand hate." When Corrie, a pretty Dutch freedom fighter, stabs a Japanese soldier to death, avenging the murder of her parents, she announces, "I have not killed a man. I have killed a Jap." Even Tarzan, who generally never takes a life except for food or self-preservation, makes a point of single-handedly stalking and killing an entire squad of Japanese for the sheer pleasure. In another skirmish, Tarzan slays a tiger, a species that had eluded him ever since the zoological faux pas in *Tarzan of the Apes* four decades earlier.

Burroughs finished *Tarzan and the Foreign Legion* in September 1944 and over the next several months tried to sell it to the slicks and the pulps. Despite its frothy topicality, no one was interested, and it never appeared in a magazine. (When it finally became a book three years later, he dedicated it to Brig. Gen. Truman H. Landon.)

On November 6, while Burroughs was still waiting to learn the fate of *Foreign Legion,* he received word that Emma had died of a stroke the day before in Bel-Air. During the previous year and a half, she had been in and out of sanatoriums but had always reverted to drunkenness after being sent home. The family, while stricken with grief, acknowledged that her decline had been inevitable and her death merciful. "I cannot help feeling that our real mother died many years ago," Hully wrote to Joan and Jack after receiving the news. "It was a relief, as her condition was hopeless," Burroughs confided to Ted Landon and Bert Weston. He and Hully were granted leave by the army—Burroughs's for forty-five days, Hully's for thirty—and they flew to California together on November 17.

Even though the instigation for the trip was an unhappy one, he was nonetheless excited to be back. It was the first time he had been home since April 1940, and the Thanksgiving and Christmas he spent with his family were the first since leaving Emma eleven years earlier. One of the biggest treats was meeting Jack's boys, Johnny and Danton, ages two years and five months respectively, both of whom had been born while their grandfather was in Hawaii.

He took charge of family business as if he had never been away, drafting a list of repairs needed at Emma's Bel-Air house and catching up on corporate matters with Ralph Rothmund, whom he had missed as much as his own kin. In a different sort of reunion, he had lunch with Florence at a Los Angeles restaurant, their first meeting since their separation. She had remarried; her new husband was Dr. Alfred Chase, a physician they both had known and consulted in California. Burroughs also made a point of seeing Caryl Lee, with whom he had exchanged letters off and on over the past four years. Caryl Lee still worshipped her former stepfather, even if her mother did not, and for a while begged to be allowed to use the surname Burroughs, rather than Chase, the name thrice-married Florence had taken.

In the end, though, his stay in California was dispiriting—first, because the army expected him back in Hawaii soon, and second, because in late December he was obliged to undergo hernia surgery for the second time in his life, a setback that delayed his departure but left him uncomfortable and somewhat unsociable during the latter part of his stay. When he finally arrived in Honolulu on February 1, the palm trees and familiar faces could not mitigate his melancholy. "My life here runs in pretty much of a rut," he wrote at the end of March. "I haven't done a lick of work since I returned. I sun bathe, read, and go to cocktail parties."

Finally, in April, for lack of anything better to do, he resumed writing his "Laugh It Off" column, submitting it to *Hawaii.* It contained mostly off-the-cuff reactions to the headlines of the day. On May 8, V-E Day, he listened to the radio in the morning, but like most residents of Hawaii, he saw it as cause for only moderate celebration. "The Nips say they will fight for a hundred years," he wrote upon hearing the news of Germany's surrender.

The war was indeed a long way from over. Two weeks after the collapse of the Third Reich, Burroughs boarded the USS *Cahaba,* an oiler bound for the Carolines and other islands in the Western Pacific. Once again, he was given preferential treatment. "Am living and eating much better than I do at the Niumalu," he wrote Joan while at sea. "The Captain [Julian Burnbaum] installed me in his quarters—two big rooms, a swell bath, a steward and a mess attendant." Though the *Cahaba*'s role as a refueler of the fleet was a supportive one, the crew nonetheless felt part of "a great historical event," he remarked in one of his few dispatches to be published. "Perhaps this is the Navy's last great strike at the enemy's shattered fleet and homeland."

The *Cahaba* sailed as far as Kerama Retto, an atoll to the west of Okinawa. Though the marines had liberated it at the end of March, a smattering of Japanese were still at large. While accompanying a shore party, he came under sniper fire. No one was hit, he reported jauntily, but on the way back to the ship, the aim of the Japanese was much truer: "[J]ust after we passed an admiral's flagship we heard firing. Sticking our heads out on each side of the gig we saw a Jap plane close over us, saw him bomb the admiral's ship and then suicide dive into another big ship." Several more ships were hit by bombs or kamikazes in the days the *Cahaba* was anchored at Kerama Retto.

There was nothing dangerous about Burroughs's next visit ashore, but it made a deep impression just the same. On one of the islands in the Ulithi atoll, in the Western Carolines, he was permitted to land with a small party of officers, doctors, and nurses. He reported that the island was largely off limits to military personnel, and the natives were said to live much as they had before the war. In contrast to the drunken Apache scouts he had met in Arizona, the island men were uncorrupted and wore "nothing but a sketchy G-string," he wrote in his United Press dispatch. "Up to the age of five, no one wears anything, then the girls wear grass skirts until they marry and graduate to lava lavas. The little boys wear lava lavas until they reach the G-string age." Forty-three years earlier, under the influence of various myths and travelogues, Burroughs had concocted Tarzan. Now, at last, he believed he was seeing the noble savage in the flesh.

Much later it would become embarrassingly clear that he had not been the only writer to admire the Ulithians. In 1956, eleven years after his trip to the Caroline Islands, a former naval officer by the name of William Brinkley wrote a satiric novel, *Don't Go Near the Water* (which became a best-seller and then an even more popular movie). Brinkley, who had served in the Western Pacific in 1945, begins his send-up of naval snafus with a story of a group of self-conscious and semi-inept naval public relations officers whose biggest wartime challenge on the fictitious island of Tulura is the arrival of a "really large name." "Tarzan is on his way here!" announces the executive officer noisily but nervously. "That is to say, Edgar Rice Burroughs, the creator and author of Tarzan—and therefore the same as Tarzan for our purposes. . . . He's coming as a correspondent." After a great deal of hand-wringing and head-scratching, the navy decides that the way to squeeze the greatest amount of publicity out of the event is to "take Burroughs down to some atoll-like island and photograph him with a bunch of these natives like they have in Tarzan." It's "picturable," declares the head photographer—"babes, children, dogs, natives" and Burroughs. "Sound-wise," adds the radio man, it will be perfect to have Burroughs surrounded by natives "jabbering away." As good as *Trader Horn,* someone else suggests.

There is only one problem: the natives won't behave like natives. "Why, they wear pants and shirts . . . just like anybody else!" one of the military PR men reports at a later meeting, after the plan has already been approved and set in motion. "And this old goat who's sort of their chief or mayor seemed to actually resent it when I suggested they put on breechcloths for the filming." Finally, an ensign considered simpatico with the natives is sent on a mission of persuasion, and after a night of drinking and joke swapping with the Tulurans, he is able to report besottedly to his superiors, "They'll wear the jockstraps."

And so the novelized Tarzan tour comes off without a hitch. The newsreel footage shows Burroughs disembarking from the landing craft like MacArthur. Whereupon he is surrounded by natives, all of them wearing brand-new breechclouts. "Tremendous!" exclaims the executive officer when he first sees the newsreel. "What a natural! What a plug for the Navy! Probably cost you a million dollars to buy that kind of publicity. . . . The looks of those natives! Why, they almost seem to giggle, I'll swear! They just loved it, didn't they? How innocent and childlike they are! And that talk of theirs! How authentic!"

To the Tulurans, of course, the performance was a magnificently ribald spoof. History has yet to divulge if the actual event that Burroughs witnessed in 1945—and which Brinkley obviously had shared or at least read about—was a charade, but it seems likely that Burroughs's impressions of that day were his and his alone. True or not, he had seen what he had always wanted to see, and that was what mattered.

Burroughs left the *Cahaba* in mid-July and flew to Guam in a plane piloted by one of Hollywood's men in uniform, Lt. Tyrone Power, and then caught another hop to Hawaii, arriving home on the fifteenth. In two months, he had sailed more than ten thousand miles and flown another five thousand. But unlike his previous two trips, this time the experience did not rejuvenate him. "I am suffering from acute antiquity," he confessed shortly after unpacking at the Niumalu.

In fact, he was suffering from something much more specific than old age. Aboard the *Cahaba,* his angina had returned. After a navy doctor had prescribed codeine, the symptoms had gone away, and shortly after arriving in Honolulu, he had a general checkup and was apparently fine. Three days later, however, he noted in his diary, "Angina Pectoris, or whatever it is, hurts like hell today."

The discomfort nagged him throughout the remainder of the summer, the only respite occurring on August 14, when word reached Hawaii that Japan had accepted the Allied terms of surrender. Burroughs was in the middle of typing a letter to Jack when the all-clear sirens sounded and thousands of automobile horns chimed in. "Thank God," he wrote. "I could cry for happiness. I'll finish this after I sober up." He and his fellow Niumalu residents started in on scotch, then a punch of brandy and champagne. "We drank and drank and drank," he reported when he finally returned to the typewriter. "The town is a mad-house. . . . We have been very close to the war for nearly four years, and the relief is uninhibiting—if there is such a word. We are on the loose." Later that night, he, Hully, and Hully's girlfriend, Marion (whom he would soon marry) celebrated together at the home of a good friend. "All in all," Burroughs wrote in his diary, "it was a large day."

Hully left for California a week later. With his correspondent's job over, Burroughs was eager to follow but did not want to pack up until he had a definite place to settle in California. He marked his seventieth birthday on September 1 without any family members to help him celebrate, and shortly thereafter his angina flared up. "I am having these attacks too frequently," he wrote in his diary. "Wish I were home." On the sixteenth, his doctor prescribed more codeine and sent him to bed. In explaining his condition to friends and family, he no longer soft-pedaled its seriousness. "I don't know whether you knew it at the time or not," he wrote to Captain Burnbaum of the *Cahaba*, "but I had a heart attack . . . in the Philippine Sea; and then I had another attack in Honolulu. . . . I guess I ran up and down too many ship's ladders for an old man."

Throughout his correspondence, he mistakenly uses the terms *heart attack* and *angina pectoris* interchangeably, but whichever had occurred (perhaps both), his doctor considered his case grave enough to keep him in bed for six weeks. Plenty of friends dropped by to cheer him up and drop off everything from cigarettes to steaks, but he was desperate to be home. "Soon I shall be in your midst, and that is all that I can think of," he wrote to the children on October 20, addressing them as "Beloved idiots" and signing his customary "O.B."

Finally, on October 28, he boarded a plane at Hickam Field and the next morning arrived at Hamilton Field, outside San Francisco. Jack was there to meet him, and they celebrated in several bars in and around Chinatown. They took two days driving south along the coast, and on November 1 arrived in Los Angeles in time for dinner with Joan and Hully. In his diary, Burroughs declares simply, "It was wonderful to see them all again." He had no idea what he would do next, and he could not have cared less. For now, just being back was heaven.

15

DAMN OLD AGE

The robust man who had moved to Hawaii five-and-a-half years earlier returned home a virtual invalid. His heart had been damaged in the Pacific, and he doubted he would ever get his strength back. "I cannot imagine anything as weak as I feel," he confided to his flying comrade, Ted Landon, in January, several weeks after arriving in California. With the help of his children, Joan particularly, he bought a small, two-bedroom bungalow on a half-acre lot. The address was 5465 Zelzah Avenue, just a few blocks from the ERB, Inc., office. Because the house was located on the north side of Ventura Boulevard, Burroughs was officially a resident of Encino, not Tarzana. He didn't mind, though. Owning his own home more than compensated for the address and modest size of his new quarters, and he apparently harbored no nostalgia for the old Otis mansion on the hill, which had been occupied by the Coastal Defense Command during the war (the empty swimming pool making an ideal position for an antiaircraft gun). Being so near his children and grandchildren was more important. Joan, Hully, and Jack all lived within a fifteen-minute drive.

In February, Burroughs's life was made easier by the arrival of two live-in Japanese-American servants, Frank and Mitzi—"my Nisei," he called them. Mitzi proved to be an able cook and housekeeper and Frank a superb gardener and handyman. Burroughs was openly devoted to them, marveling at their various domestic skills and worrying how he would manage if they ever left him.

He was grateful for such good care, but as the weeks grew into months, he had to accept that his health was not improving. For years he had defied time, if not as well as Tarzan, then as admirably as any normal man could. Now he was resigned to its passage. "I never thought anyone could age so damned fast in a few months," he told an old Niumalu neighbor. "You ask what I do with my days," he replied to another friend. "I spring lightly out of bed at nine or ten o'clock and stagger to my office anywhere from eleven to one. I annoy Ralph and Mildred [Jensen, the secretary] for a short time and then come home and read until first drink time. . . . I try to stay awake after dinner a few hours, but I usually fall asleep in my chair, senility creeping up on me."

The regimen of the first few months became the pattern of the next five years. Even when he endeavored to break out of his listlessness, he was not often successful. "I tried to do something more strenuous the other day and had another heart attack," he told Bert Weston, "so I have taken up sitting again."

He did make a couple of stabs at writing, turning out eighty-three pages of a Tarzan story in 1946 before setting it aside. The following year, he tried again on another Tarzan, but it never saw the light of day, either.

His business carried on both with and without him, as it had while he was in Hawaii and the South Pacific. Now that the paper shortage was finally over, ERB, Inc., resumed publishing books, first *Escape on Venus,* then *Tarzan and the Foreign Legion* and *Llana of Gathol.*

The comic strips, both daily and Sunday, never regained the popularity they had achieved in the mid-1930s, but the movies seemed unstoppable. Sol Lesser continued to produce one a year. With the departure of Maureen O'Sullivan, wholesome, blonde Brenda Joyce became the new Jane, beginning with *Tarzan and the Amazons* in 1945, though the public would not acknowledge her as anything but a Jane-come-lately. Johnny Sheffield was the next cast member to leave. By 1947, he had grown too old for the part of Boy, though he was not too grown-up to take the part of Bomba the Jungle Boy in a series of movies that began in 1949.

As early as 1944, Burroughs had written to Sol Lesser, suggesting that it might be time to ease Johnny Weissmuller out of the role of Tarzan. "How many more pictures do you think this poor old soul will last?" he wondered, facetiously imagining the day when Weissmuller would have to be "pushed on to the set in a wheelchair." Weissmuller was only forty at the time, but his chin had doubled, his waist had thickened, and his chest (though still powerful) had begun to sag. He hung on for four more movies (making a total of twelve); his final appearance as Tarzan—the role that he had defined, and had defined him—came in *Tarzan and the Mermaids,* a good deal of which was filmed in Acapulco, Mexico, in 1947. He was still far too young to retire, and so from 1948 till 1956, he played Jungle Jim, a courageous (but clothed) African adventurer, in movies and then in a television series. Weissmuller lived to the ripe old age of seventy-nine, dying in Acapulco in 1984. A tape of his Tarzan yell was played at his burial.

One cannot imagine a tougher act to follow than Weissmuller's Tarzan, and in 1948 Burroughs urged Sol Lesser to conduct a well-publicized national search, as had been done in the 1920s. Finally, Lesser, who had bombed with his previous two Tarzan choices—Glenn Morris and Buster Crabbe—settled on Lex Barker, a thirty-year-old Princeton dropout, to take the lead in *Tarzan's Magic Fountain.* Fifty-nine-year-old Elmo Lincoln was hired as an extra. Barker was trim, handsome, and quite athletic, but for fans to accept him as the new lord of the jungle meant betraying the Weissmuller archetype. In the end, Barker was probably better known for his marriages to actresses Arlene Dahl and Lana Turner than for his five Tarzan features.

Regardless of whose name appeared on the marquee, the Tarzan movies reaped handsome royalties throughout the remainder of Burroughs's life. In August 1949, *Writer's Digest* reported that Lesser and RKO were paying ERB, Inc., two hundred thousand dollars a picture; all told, the movies were said to have paid ERB, Inc., nearly three million over the years. These figures were likely high, as were some of the other numbers cited in the article; for instance, *Writer's Digest* also stated that ERB, Inc., received well over fifty thousand dollars a year in royalties on the comic strip, although, according to Burroughs's own correspondence, the company never made more than thirty thousand dollars a year from comics, and by 1946 was making only half that. Whatever the truth, Burroughs's income was more than sufficient to support the modest lifestyle he had adopted in California, with plenty left over to pay his employees and to spread among his children, all of whom were stockholders in ERB, Inc.

In Tarzana (Encino, actually), he made no attempt to reestablish a social life. He had kept up with his old friend from military school, Bert Weston, of Beatrice, Nebraska, and they had several reunions in the late 1940s. His only other steadfast friend was Sol Lesser, their mutual respect extending far beyond the context of business.

Most of the time, though, he seemed content to be by himself. Sometimes, when he got lonesome or grew a little stir-crazy, he would get in his Buick Roadmaster, purchased upon his return from Hawaii, and drive down Ventura Boulevard to observe the goings-on. Much had changed since the summer of 1893 when he had driven a battery-powered car around the grounds of the Chicago World's Fair, and the Tarzana he had first visited in 1919 seemed a world away, as well. The growth of the San Fernando Valley, in which Burroughs had played such a seminal role, had accelerated after the war and now defined the new American ideal of strip, drive-in, and sprawl. He was not thrilled by what he saw, and the irony that a town bearing the name Tarzana had become a whizzing suburb was not lost on him. Nor did he approve of the sort of people who had become his neighbors. In a letter to his nephew Studley, he lamented that Joan's teenaged daughter Joanne "has few opportunities to meet very nice people, as the high school . . . seems to be overrun by hot rod drivers and other morons with dirty finger nails and no Emily Post training." Class, as ever, was a sticking point.

Eventually, he became a virtual shut-in, seeing few people beyond his children and grandchildren. "I have almost completely folded up . . . like a mollusk," he confessed in January 1948. On Frank and Mitzi's day off, Joan would drop by to cook his dinner. Most nights, he watched baseball, boxing, and wrestling on his ten-inch television set. Occasionally Hully and Jack would drop by and watch with him, while their kids pumped nickels into Burroughs's other favorite appliance, a slot machine. At one point, he tried to give up drinking again, but determined that he felt better off the wagon than on. "My bar is at my elbow," he wrote an old Honolulu neighbor. "You know we angina pectorials have to keep our arteries dilated." When bourbon didn't work, he took nitro-glycerine tablets.

Ever since he had been diagnosed with a heart murmur at Fort Grant, Arizona, in 1896, he had joked about having one foot in the grave.

"Fifty-two years ago an Army doctor gave me six months to live," he wrote to another wartime acquaintance, "and I'll bet the goddam old drunk has been dead twenty years." But by mid-1948, he sensed that the end was near. "[T]here is something else the matter with me, as I have difficulty in walking," he admitted to the doctor who had treated his bladder. The diagnosis this time was paralysis agitans, better known as Parkinson's disease. Within six months, he was so shaky he got about the house mostly by wheelchair.

Burroughs did not profess to be a religious man; certainly he never went to church. Yet he was not exactly an atheist, either. Throughout his fiction he had ridiculed false prophets and people simple or foolish enough to follow them, but mostly he was railing against the dogmatism of organized religion. The trouble with the world, an African witch doctor informs Jane in *Tarzan's Quest,* is that men have *imagined* God instead of seeking God among themselves. "God should be a leader," the shaman says, "and a leader should be a tangible entity—something men can see and feel and touch." Similarly, in *Tarzan at the Earth's Core,* Tarzan acknowledges that, to the extent that he thinks about God at all, "he liked to think of Him privately, as a personal God. And while he realized that he knew nothing of such matters, he liked to believe that after death he would live again."

Even in the last year of his life, Burroughs did not reflect much on spiritual matters, and, if anything, contemplation of the hereafter struck him as a waste of time. "I'm afraid I don't know how to grow old gracefully," he told *Writer's Digest* in what proved to be his last published interview. "I hate old age! Damn old age! I hate dull, old people and I hate death!" He had given life a fair run, he figured, and that was good enough. Not only had he beaten the army doctor's prognosis, but he had also done better and lasted longer as a writer than any of his editors or publishers had predicted. With Hully and Rothmund in control of ERB, Inc., he could rest assured that his affairs were in good order. He wouldn't live forever, but Tarzan, John Carter, David Innes, and Carson Napier had a fighting chance.

In December 1949, Burroughs suffered a serious heart attack which imprisoned him in an oxygen tent for several weeks. He improved sufficiently to escape the tent, but he never got far from his bed—which was where his housekeeper discovered him on Sunday, March 19, 1950, slumped over the morning paper. Apparently he had been reading Tarzan in the funny papers when his heart stopped beating. At least it is pleasant to think so. He was five months shy of his seventy-fifth birthday.

After his funeral and cremation, his ashes were buried under the walnut tree that grew in front of the stucco, Spanish-style office of ERB, Inc.—the same spot where, twenty years earlier, he had interred his mother's remains. Today the walnut tree has been replaced by a mulberry that not only shades ERB, Inc., but provides a buffer from the constant roar of traffic on Ventura Boulevard.

ERB, Inc., has carried on in the half-century since the death of its founder. The neighborhood has given way to hair salons, fast-food joints, and copy shops, but ERB, Inc., remains virtually unchanged. Burroughs's handcarved mahogany desk still commands his office. On a nearby shelf rests one of the pencil sharpeners he was attempting to sell at the time he wrote *A Princess of Mars,* along with samples of various paperback and foreign editions of his books. In the outer office, facing the reception desk, hangs the original oil painting of Tarzan that N. C. Wyeth had painted for *New Story*'s serialization of *The Return of Tarzan.* Indeed, so little has changed at ERB, Inc., since its construction in 1927 that a visitor half expects to find Burroughs himself seated behind the big desk. Instead, the chair is occupied by his grandson Danton, director and secretary-treasurer of ERB, Inc., who, in the dim light of the deep-eaved building, bears a striking resemblance to the long-deceased patriarch.

Nearly all of Burroughs's books are still in print, and most of the manuscripts unpublished during his lifetime—including *Minidoka, Marcia of the Doorstep, Pirate Blood,* and *I Am a Barbarian*—are now under cover, as well, or will be soon. ERB, Inc., still holds the copyright to the Tarzan name and to most of the Burroughs titles, from which the company and Burroughs heirs continue to receive significant income. The company warehouse is jammed to the ceiling with everything from Tarzan pajamas to plastic action figures, which on cue emit a mechanical Weissmuller-esque ululation.

Every few years, Hollywood takes another crack at Tarzan. Succeeding Lex Barker were Gordon Scott, Denny Miller, Jock Mahoney, and Mike Henry. Ron Ely played Tarzan in sixty-four television episodes in the late 1960s. Other highlights of the genre include *Greystoke: The Legend of Tarzan* (1984), the first Tarzan movie since Burroughs–Tarzan Pictures' *New Adventures of Tarzan* to portray the blue-blooded side of the character. Less admirable but still memorable is *Tarzan, the Ape Man* (1981), in which Bo Derek plays a pulchritudinous Jane and Miles O'Keeffe, as Tarzan, utters nary a word. And now comes Disney's animated, musical version of Tarzan, surely the most colorful departure from the original Tarzan to date. Doubtless many more Tarzans will follow, a fertile vine entwined in the history of movies, television, and video. Yet just as Sean Connery will always be *the* James Bond, Johnny Weissmuller will always be *the* quintessential Tarzan.

Parody is said to be a form of flattery, and one the best measures of Tarzan's success and saturation has been the degree to which he has been mocked. As early as 1934, the same year *Tarzan and His Mate* was released, Jimmy Durante played "Schnarzan" in MGM's *Hollywood Party*. In the 1960s, Andy Warhol titled one of his avant-garde films *Tarzan and Jane Regained . . . Sort of,* and not long after that, pop singer Ray Stevens had a hit with his novelty song, "Gitarzan (and His Jungle Band)." The Kinks followed with "Apeman." Disney's 1997 comedy, *George of the Jungle* (whose intermediate inspiration was the television cartoon of the same name), turns MGM's Tarzan on his politically incorrect head. The most bizarre permutation of the Tarzan character, however, has to be *Jungle Heat,* an X-rated, interactive CD-ROM, in which, according to those who viewed it before ERB, Inc.'s, lawyer had it quashed, Tarzan plays "the wrong kind of swinger."

A few unauthorized developments have been welcomed by ERB, Inc. Beginning in the mid-1940s, for instance, *Webster's* included "Tarzan" in its dictionaries, defining it generically as "a well-built, agile, and very strong man." In 1972, science fiction writer Philip José Farmer published *Tarzan Alive,* a faux biography of Lord Greystoke/Tarzan, which fills in details, however speculatively, that Burroughs had left out of his Tarzan stories. Farmer's wry contention is that Tarzan was a real person, and the author even vouches that he once met Lord Greystoke in the flesh. The book is all in good fun and certainly has not been taken to heart by Burroughs buffs, except to the extent that it places Tarzan against a credible historical, cultural, and geographic backdrop. If nothing else, *Tarzan Alive* serves as proof that Tarzan has a life of his own, a life beyond Burroughs.

Today, vintage Tarzan books (and comics and bread wrappers and lobby cards) are bought and sold for thousands of dollars, another reflection of the American hunger for artifacts from a past seemingly only minutes old. Meanwhile, academics, clustered beneath the rubric of "popular culture" have stirred up their own feeding frenzy. Recent additions to their weighty canon bear titles such as "The Tarzan Myth and Jung's Genesis of Self," "*Tarzan of the Apes:* Foreign Policy in the Twentieth Century," and *You Tarzan: Masculinity, Movies, and Men.*

Burroughs would have chuckled over the brouhaha generated by a character he thought up one chilly winter in order to "entertain" pulp audiences and feed his wife and young children. He did not live long enough to witness monkeys rocketed into orbit (much less a robot land on Mars), but in August 1996, an unusual incident occurred at a Chicago area zoo that certainly must have caused the leaves of a certain mulberry tree in Tarzana to rustle without the influence of wind or temblor. According to print and television accounts, a young boy visiting the zoo fell over a protective parapet into the gorilla exhibit. Witnesses looked on in horror, expecting the worst, as a notoriously fierce female gorilla approached the unconscious child. Then, much to the amazement of all, except perhaps for the ghost of O.B., the great anthropoid ape tenderly picked the youngster up in her arms and carried him to safety—in this case, the zookeeper's door.

A hundred or so members of the Burroughs Bibliophiles, who, quite by coincidence, had that very day gathered for their annual convention in Southern California, just down Ventura Boulevard from Tarzana, received the news with knowing nods. After all, this was a story as old as the hills, and nobody, they pointed out in a hastily called press conference, had ever told it better than Edgar Rice Burroughs.

ACKNOWLEDGMENTS
AND
BIBLIOGRAPHICAL NOTES

In 1962, Irwin Porges, author and professor of English at Valley College in Van Nuys, California, took a notion to write a biography of Edgar Rice Burroughs. It was not until 1967 that Porges received the approval and cooperation of Edgar Rice Burroughs, Inc. The fruit of his perseverance, *Edgar Rice Burroughs: The Man Who Created Tarzan*, was finally published in 1975 by Brigham Young University Press. For nearly twenty-five years, Porges's biography has stood as the most comprehensive treatment of the subject—because of its length (820 pages) and because of the toil that went into it.

Gaining access to the Burroughs storerooms and file cabinets, Porges and his wife, Cele, sifted through tens, perhaps hundreds, of thousands of pages of manuscripts, letters, diaries, and notes, photocopying thousands they considered germane and transcribing hundreds more. Burroughs, they quickly came to appreciate, had made a science out of paper movement and management—a discipline he had acquired during his brief tenure as head of the stenography department at Sears, Roebuck. Burroughs kept virtually every letter he ever received and made a carbon of every one he wrote. His files contain all of his correspondence with editors, publishers, agents, and movie producers; they also include letters to and from his parents, brothers, and children, and a lifelong exchange with his school chum Bert Weston. Likewise, Burroughs kept scrapbooks, photos, and a series of journals; some entries, such as his chronicles of cross-country trips, are longwinded, while others are shorthand records of the day's weather, mood, and appointments. Besides drafting an autobiography (never completed, never published), he preserved his childhood poems and mementos from military school, the army, and his western adventures. As a staunch believer in the importance of bloodlines, his genealogical records of family are thorough and orderly. Like most writers, he kept manuscripts of his stories and novels in a safe place; but like no other, he also made work notes on every story he wrote, recording the day and sometimes even the minute he commenced and completed a story, along with its precise word length and brief notes on the plot and characters. Ever attuned to publicity, he collected scores of articles written about him and, through a clipping service, accumulated reviews of all of his books and the movies based on them. That he was able to manage so much material, albeit with the help of a secretary, and still write several hundred thousand words of fiction a year is mindboggling. That Irwin and Cele Porges were able to sort through it all in a mere eight years is an astounding achievement in its own right.

I had wished to express my gratitude to Mr. Porges in person on a visit to Southern California in August 1998. Sadly—and rather spookily—Porges died from a long-standing illness the morning I arrived to make his acquaintance. Now I can say thanks only posthumously, in writing.

Truly the Porges book has been a great help to my own project. But even more valuable, exponentially so, have been the many thousand Burroughs papers which the Porges pulled from the warehouse—hereafter referred to as the "Porges Papers" and officially titled the Porges Archives of Edgar Rice Burroughs; they are now part of the Burroughs Memorial Collection at the University of Louisville in Kentucky. Because so much of the information used herein is from the Porges Papers, I have chosen not to flag every reference.

Just as Irwin Porges will not have the last word on Burroughs, neither are the Porges Papers, however substantial, the *only* source for my own work. For there is another benevolent giant who inhabits Burroughsiana: George McWhorter, curator of the Burroughs Memorial Collection. A passionate bibliophile and esteemed rare books librarian, McWhorter has devoted his life to collecting and archiving everything related to Edgar Rice Burroughs. While the Porges Papers are an important part of the Burroughs Collection—from a biographer's standpoint, they are the crown jewels—in terms of sheer shelf space, they are dwarfed by the abundance of other delights amassed over the years by McWhorter, often with his own money. The collection contains a complete set of Burroughs first editions, in every language. Here, too, are all the Tarzan comic strips, tapes of the Tarzan movies and radio shows, movie stills, Tarzan figurines, promotional ephemera, and even Burroughs's uniform from military school. In the Burroughs atlas, Tarzana, California, will always be the Greenwich meridian, but thanks to George McWhorter, Louisville is now Mecca. No, make that Opar. It is with gratitude and respect that I dedicate this book to my friend and mentor. I will forever cherish the days and dinners George and I shared during my time in Louisville. No researcher could hope for more cordial, considered attention. His many musings on Burroughs, particularly those in the pages of *The Burroughs Bulletin,* of which he is editor, are informed and enlightening. And his books, *Burroughs Dictionary: An Alphabetical List of Proper Names, Words, Phrases and Concepts Contained in the Published Works of Edgar Rice Burroughs* (1987) and *Edgar Rice Burroughs Memorial Collection: A Catalog* (1991), are indispensable to anyone wishing to reach the upper terraces of Burroughs understanding.

If George McWhorter is Burroughs's honorary godfather, then Burroughs's grandson Danton is the official keeper of the Burroughs flame. Only with his permission was I able to begin this book and only with his adroit assistance have I managed to complete it. Like his grandfather, whom he knew briefly as a very small boy, Danton has applied the right balance of protectiveness and munificence in serving the interests of ERB, Inc. He welcomed me into the ERB, Inc., offices in Tarzana and dazzled me with his own personal collection of Burroughs material, especially letters and photos once in the possession of his father Jack and Uncle Hully and heretofore unavailable to Burroughs buffs and scholars. "O.B." can rest easily knowing that Dan Burroughs sits behind the carved mahogany desk at 18345 Ventura Boulevard. We should all have such conscientious heirs.

There are others who deserve thanks: Eddie Gilbert, brother of Florence Gilbert; Cindy (Caryl Lee) James and Lee Chase, Florence's children; Sandra Galfas, president of ERB, Inc.; Ralph Herman, owner of what remains of the Tarzana ranch and a painstaking Tarzana historian in his own right; Phillip Burger, nimble Burroughs scholar and essayist; Robert Barrett, Joan Bledig, and Roy and Dela White, equally dedicated to giving Burroughs his due; Kathie Tovo, Richard Lester, Rachel Feit, diligent researchers of the zeitgeist; Marianne Lesher, superb innkeeper; George McWhorter's hospitable colleagues in the rare book collection at the Ekstrom Library, University of Louisville; all of the Burroughs Bibliophiles; and my father, Jack Taliaferro, for his observations and research on World War II and Burroughs's movements in the South Pacific.

Finally, in addition to the Porges biography, I would like to acknowledge the influence of several other Burroughs-related books: Richard A. Lupoff, *Edgar Rice Burroughs: Master of Adventure* (1965); Robert W. Fenton, *The Big Swingers* (1967); Erling B. Holtsmark, *Edgar Rice Burroughs* (1986); Henry Hardy Heins, *A Golden Anniversary Bibliography of Edgar Rice Burroughs* (1964); Robert B. Zeuschner, *Edgar Rice Burroughs: The Exhaustive Scholar's and Collector's Descriptive Bibliography of American Periodical, Hardcover, Paperback, and Reprint Editions* (1996); and Sarkis Atamian, *The Origin of Tarzan: The Mystery of Tarzan's Creation Solved* (1997).

CHAPTER ONE: THE SUM OF THE PARTS

H. G. Wells coins the term *practical incredibleness* in *The Time Machine* (1895, Bantam Books reprint, 1991).

CHAPTER TWO: A JUNGLE OF SORTS

My reading on Chicago and its West Side included Donald L. Miller's tour de force, *City of the Century: The Epic of Chicago and the Making of America* (1996); Richard Sennett, *Families Against the City: Middle Class Homes of Industrial Chicago* (1970); John Drury, "Old Chicago Neighborhoods," *Landlords Guide: The Trade Paper of Chicago's Apartment Owners* 38:7 (July 1947); and "Tarzan Was Born in Chicago," *Chicago History,* New Series 1:1 (Spring 1970).

For my knowledge of Burroughs's activities and whereabouts in Idaho and Arizona, I am greatly indebted to Phillip Burger for his master's thesis, "Glimpses of a World Past: Edgar Rice Burroughs, the West, and the Birth of an American Writer" (Utah State University, 1987). Burger was extraordinarily kind to share his as-yet unpublished research on Burroughs's cavalry service. I also recommend Burger's "Sweetser and the Burroughs Boys," *The Burroughs Bulletin* 19, New Series (July 1994). Additional descriptions of Fort Grant and army life in southeastern Arizona can be found in John G. Bourke, *On the Border with Crook* (1891, reprint 1971). For a crisp summation of the Apache Wars, see David Roberts, *Once They Moved Like the Wind: Cochise, Geronimo, and the Apache Wars* (1993). The single best source on Charles King is Don Russell, *Campaigning with King: Charles King, Chronicler of the Old Army* (1991).

Upton Sinclair's "hog-squeal" of the Chicago stockyards emanates from *The Jungle* (1906); Rudyard Kipling's denunciation of Chicago appears in *American Notes* (1891); Carl Sandburg describes Chicago's feline climate in his poem "Fog" (1913); and Hamlin Garland's "vicious boars" take to the streets in *Rose of Dutcher's Coolly* (1895).

My glimpses of the World's Columbian Exposition include Robert W. Rydell, *All The World's a Fair* (1984); Ralph W. Dexter, "Putnam's Problems Popularizing Anthropology," *American Scientist* 54:3 (1966), 315–331; Frederick Starr, "Anthropology at the World's Fair," *The Popular Science Monthly* 43 (September 1893), 610–621; Edward B. McDowell, "The World's Fair Cosmopolis," *Frank Leslie's Popular Magazine* 36:4 (October 1893), 407–416; John C. Eastman, "Village Life at the World's Fair," *The Chautauquan* 17 (1893), 602–4; William H. Dall, "Anthropology," *The Nation* 57 (September 28, 1893), 224–6; Harlan Ingersoll Smith, "Man and His Works: The Anthropological Building at the World's Columbian Exposition," *The American Antiquarian* 15 (March 1893), 115–7; Quandam (Charles M. Stevens), *The Adventures of Uncle Jeremiah at the Great Fair* (1893); "Through the Looking Glass," *Chicago Tribune*, November 1, 1893, 9; and John McGovern, ed., *A Portfolio of Photographic Views of the World's Columbian Exposition* (1894).

The role of the Seventh Cavalry in settling labor disputes is deftly explained in Richard Slotkin, *Gunfighter Nation: The Myth of the Frontier in Twentieth-Century America* (1992). Slotkin also has quite a bit to say about Burroughs.

CHAPTER 3: THE EFFICIENCY EXPERT

The throne-room genre exemplified by the Graustark novels et al. is plumbed in Raymond P. Wallace, "Cardboard Kingdoms," *San José Studies* 13:2 (Spring 1987), 23–34.

Burroughs's approach to science fiction in general, and Mars specifically, is discussed ably in Richard A. Lupoff, *Edgar Rice Burroughs: Master of Adventure* (1965); Lupoff, *Barsoom: Edgar Rice Burroughs and the Martian Vision* (1976); John Flint Roy, *A Guide to Barsoom: The Mars of Edgar Rice Burroughs* (1976); Erling B. Holtsmark, *Edgar Rice Burroughs* (1986); Sam Moskowitz, *Explorers of the Infinite: Shapers of Science Fiction* (1963); Moskowitz, "A History of 'The Scientific Romance' in the Munsey Magazines, 1912–1920," in Moskowitz, ed., *Under the Moon of Mars: A History and Anthology of "The Scientific Romance" in the Munsey Magazines, 1912–1920* (1970), 291–433; Paul A. Carter, *The Creation of Tomorrow: Fifty Years of Magazine Science Fiction* (1977); Brian W. Aldiss, *Billion Year Spree: The True History of Science Fiction* (1973); Richard Kyle, "Out of Time's Abyss: The Martian Stories of Edgar Rice Burroughs, A Speculation," *Riverside Quarterly* 4:2, 110–122; Benjamin S. Lawson, "The Time and Place of Edgar Rice Burroughs's Early Martian Trilogy," *Extrapolation* 27:3 (Fall 1986), 208–219; and John T. Flautz, "An American Demagogue in Barsoom," *Journal of Popular Culture* 1:3 (Winter 1967), 226–275.

Regarding Percival Lowell and the history of Mars-gazing, see William Graves Hoyt, *Lowell and Mars* (1976); John Noble Wilford, *Mars Beckons: The Mysteries, The Challenges, The Expectations of Our Next Great Adventure in Space* (1990); James Trefil, "Ah, but there may have *been* life on Mars," *Smithsonian* 26:5, 71–77; Mark R. Hillegas, "Martians and Mythmakers: 1877–1938," in Ray B. Browne et al., eds., *Challenges in American Culture* (1970); and Richard D. Mullen, "The Undisciplined Imagination: Edgar Rice Burroughs and Lowellian Mars," in Thomas D. Clareson, ed., *SF: The Other Side of Realism; Essays on Modern Fantasy and Science Fiction* (1971).

Other excellent sources on the origin and nature of science fiction include Kingsley Amis, *New Maps of Hell: A Survey of Science Fiction* (1960); Moskowitz, *Science Fiction by Gaslight: A History and Anthology of Science Fiction in the Popular Magazines, 1891–1911* (1986); and L. Sprague de Camp and Catherine Crook de Camp, *Science Fiction Handbook, Revised* (1975).

The rise of the ten-cent and pulp magazines is chronicled in Lee Server, *Danger Is My Business: An Illustrated History of the Fabulous Pulp Magazines* (1993); Ron Goulart, *Cheap Thrills: An Informal History of the Pulp Magazines* (1972); Tony Goodstone, *The Pulps: Fifty Years of American Pop Culture* (1970); Frank Gruber, *The Pulp Jungle* (1967); John Tebbel, *The American Magazine: A Compact History* (1969); Frank Luther Mott, *A History of American Magazines, 1885–1905* (1957); and George Britt, *Forty Years—Forty Millions: The Career of Frank A. Munsey* (1935).

For a wholesome discussion of Burroughs's preoccupation with rape, see Richard D. Mullen, "Edgar Rice Burroughs and the Fate Worse Than Death," *Riverside Quarterly* 4:2, 186–191.

CHAPTER FOUR: WHITE APE

The high and low points of African history are described concisely in Thomas Pakenham, *The Scramble for Africa: White Man's Conquest of the Dark Continent from 1876 to 1912* (1991).

Rudolph Altrocchi's essay, "Ancestors of Tarzan," appears in his book *Sleuthing the Stacks* (1944).

The literature on the wild-child phenomenon is broad and fascinating. My reading included Philip José Farmer, ed., *Mother Was a Lovely Beast: A Feral Man Anthology; Fiction and Fact About Humans Raised by Animals* (1974); Douglas Keith Candland, *Feral Children and Clever Animals* (1993); J. A. L. Singh and Robert M. Zingg, *Wolf-Children and Feral Man* (1939); Charles Maclean, *The Wolf Children* (1977); Roger Shattuck, *The Forbidden Experiment: The Story of the Wild Boy of Aveyron* (1980); François Truffaut and Jean Grualt, *The Wild Child* (1973); Mary Charles McNeil, Edward A. Polloway, and J. David Smith, "Feral and Isolated Children: Historical Review and Analysis," *Education and Training of the Mentally Retarded* 19:1 (February 1984), 70–79; Armando R. Favazza, "Feral and Isolated Children," *British Journal of Medical Psychology* 50: 1 (March 1977); and Jennifer Wicke, "Koko's Necklace: The Wild Child as Subject," *Critical Quarterly* 30:1 (Spring 1988), 113–27.

For insight into Tarzan's classical roots, the arcadian ideal, and primitivism, see Holtsmark, *Tarzan and Tradition: Classical Myth in Popular Literature* (1981); Gary Topping, "The Pastoral Ideal in Popular American Literature: Zane Grey and Edgar Rice Burroughs," *Rendezvous* 12:2 (1977), 11–25; Tom Henighan, "Tarzan and Rima," *Riverside Quarterly* 3:4 (March 1969), 256–265; Brian V. Street, *The Savage in Literature: Representations of "Primitive" Society in English Fiction 1858–1920* (1975); Peter J. Schmitt, *Back to Nature: The Arcadian Myth in Urban America* (1969); Hoxie Neale Fairchild, *The Noble Savage: A Study in Romantic Naturalism* (1961); Roderick Nash, *Wilderness and the American Mind* (1967); Leo Marx, *The Machine in the Garden: Technology and the Pastoral Ideal in America* (1967); and Richard Hofstadter, *The Age of Reform; From Bryan to F.D.R.* (1955).

Bernarr Macfadden and the Physical Culture Movement come to life in William R. Hunt, *Body Love: The Amazing Career of Bernarr Macfadden* (1989); Harvey Green, *Fit for America: Health, Fitness, Sport, and American Society* (1986); David Armstrong and Elizabeth Metzger Armstrong, *The Great American Medicine Show* (1991); Ben Yagoda, "The True Story of Bernarr Macfadden," *American Heritage* 33:1 (December 1981), 22–29; William H. Taft, "Bernarr Macfadden," *Missouri Historical Review* 63:1 (October 1968), 71–89. Special thanks also to Terry Todd, professor of kinesiology, University of Texas at Austin, for pointing out Tarzan's departure from the Physical Culture stereotype.

On the subject of apes, the Dum-Dum, and missing links, my sources (in addition to those cited in the text itself) include Vernon Reynolds, *The Apes: The Gorilla, Chimpanzee, Orangutan, and Gibbon—Their History and Their World* (1967); Ramona and Desmond Morris, *Men and Apes* (1966); Herbert Wendt, *From Ape to Adam: The Search for the Ancestry of Man* (1971); Matthew A.

Edey, *The Missing Link: The Emergence of Man* (1972); John E. Pfeiffer, *The Emergence of Humankind* (fourth edition, 1985); Richard E. Leakey, *The Making of Mankind* (1981); Donald C. Johanson and Maitland A. Edey, *Lucy: The Beginnings of Humankind* (1981); Charles Blinderman, *The Piltdown Inquest* (1986); Jane van Lawick-Goodall, *In the Shadow of Man* (1971); George B. Schaller, *The Year of the Gorilla* (1964); Wolfgang Kohler, *The Mentality of Apes* (1925); and Robert M. Yerkes, *Almost Human* (1925).

CHAPTER 5: FAST AND FURIOUS

Albert Payson Terhune tells his life story (without mentioning Burroughs) in *To the Best of My Memory* (1930).

San Diego's and Southern California's appeal to tourists is explained in Carey McWilliams, *Southern California Country: An Island on the Land* (1946, reprint 1973); Ann Farrar Hyde, *An American Vision: Far Western Landscape and National Culture, 1820–1920* (1990); and Earl Pomeroy, *In Search of the Golden West: The Tourist in America* (1957).

Jack London's career is assessed in Robert Barltrop, *Jack London: The Man, the Writer, the Rebel* (1976); James Lundquist, *Jack London: Adventures, Ideas, and Fiction* (1987); Irving Stone, *Jack London, Sailor on Horseback* (1937); Charles N. Watson Jr., *The Novels of Jack London: A Reappraisal* (1983); and Dale L. Walker, *The Fiction of Jack London: A Chronological Bibliography* (1972).

My favorite account of the early days of motion pictures remains Neal Gabler, *A World of Their Own: How the Jews Invented Hollywood* (1989).

CHAPTER 6: MOTION PICTURES

In addition to the sources cited in chapter 5, Kevin Starr's *Material Dreams: Southern California Through the 1920s* (1990) is required reading for anyone intent on understanding the region and its boom. Irvin S. Cobb's "Corn Belt" remark is quoted in McWilliams, *Southern California Country*, 181.

The life and works of L. Frank Baum are properly appreciated in Martin Gardner and Russell B. Nye, *The Wizard of Oz and Who He Was* (1957); Frank Joslyn Baum and Russell P. MacFall, *To Please a Child: A Biography of L. Frank Baum, Royal Historian of Oz* (1961); Raylyn Moore, *Wonderful Wizard, Marvelous Land* (1974); L. Frank Baum, *The Wonderful Wizard of Oz; An Exhibition of His Published Writings in Commemoration of His Birth, May 15, 1856* (catalogue, Columbia University Libraries, 1956); and Daniel P. Mannix, "The Father of the Wizard of Oz," *American Heritage* 16:1 (December 1964), 36–47, 108–9.

Instances in which racist language was edited in later paperback editions are itemized in Jerry L. Schneider, "Tarzan the Censored," *The Burroughs Bulletin,* New Series 28 (Fall 1996), 30–36.

My information on World War I propaganda and the activities of the Four-Minute Men comes from David M. Kennedy, *Over Here: The First World War and American Society* (1980).

Regarding Elmo Lincoln's Tarzan and all the subsequent Tarzan movies, I am greatly indebted to Gabe Essoe, *Tarzan of the Movies: A Pictorial History of More Than Fifty Years of Edgar Rice Burroughs' Legendary Hero* (1968); and David Fury, *Kings of the Jungle: An Illustrated Reference to "Tarzan" on Screen and Television* (1994).

CHAPTER 7: TARZANA

The saga of Harrison Gray Otis, the Owens River aqueduct, and the development of the San Fernando Valley is fleshed out, then dissected, in Starr, *Material Dreams* (1990); McWilliams, *Southern California Country* (1946, reprinted 1973); Robert Gottlieb and Irene Holt, *Thinking Big: The Story of the Los Angeles Times, Its Publishers and Their Influence on Southern California* (1977); Marshall Berges, *The Life and Times of Los Angeles: A Newspaper, a Family, and a City* (1984); Jack R. Hart, *The Information Empire: The Rise of the Los Angeles Times and the Times Mirrors Corporation* (1981); Abraham Hoffman, *Vision or Villainy: Origins of the Owens Valley–Los Angeles Water Controversy* (1981); William L. Kahrl, *Water and Power: The Conflict Over Los Angeles' Water Supply in Owens Valley* (1982); Margaret Leslie Davis, *Rivers in the Desert: William Mulholland and the Inventing of Los Angeles* (1993); Catherine Mulholland, *The Owensmouth Baby: The Making of a San Fernando Valley Town* (1987); W. W. Robinson, *The Story of San Fernando Valley* (1961); Lawrence C. Jorgenson, "Subdivisions and Subdividers," in Lawrence C. Jorgenson, ed., *The San Fernando Valley: Past and Present* (1982); and Remi Nadeau, "The Men Who Opened the Valley," *Westways* 55:5 (May 1963), 24–27.

The formation of United Artists is examined in Tino Balio, *United Artists: The Company Built by the Stars* (1976).

The Red Scare of 1919 and 1920 commands chapters in William E. Leuchtenburg, *The Perils of Prosperity, 1914–1932* (1958); and Starr, *Endangered Dreams: The Great Depression in California* (1966).

CHAPTER 8: IMAGINATION WITHOUT TRUTH

For an unapologetically sensational glimpse of Hollywood in the 1920s, see Kenneth Anger, *Hollywood Babylon* (1975). The subgenre of the Hollywood novel is inventoried in Nancy Brooker-Bowers, *The Hollywood Novel and Other Novels About Film, 1912–1982: An Annotated Bibliography* (1985); and

Anthony Slide, *The Hollywood Novel: A Critical Guide to Over 1200 Works with Film-Related Themes or Characters, 1912 Through 1994* (1995).

Romance magazines are nicely reviewed in Thomas H. Uzzell, "The Love Pulps," *Scribner's Magazine* 103:4 (April 1938), 36–41. For an intellectual appreciation of western fiction, all trails lead to John G. Cawelti, *Adventure, Mystery, and Romance: Formula Stories as Art and Popular Culture* (1976); Christine Bold, *Selling the Wild West: Popular Western Fiction, 1860 to 1960* (1987); and Slotkin, *Gunfighter Nation* (1992). Owen Wister's and Clarence Mulford's careers are recapped in John Tuska and Vicki Piekarski, eds., *Encyclopedia of Frontier and Western Fiction* (1983); and Geoff Sadler, ed., *Twentieth-Century Western Writers* (second edition, 1991). Frank Gruber offers a kind but frustratingly thin account of Zane Grey's life in *Zane Grey* (1970). Robert Easton does a much better job with Max Brand in *Max Brand: The Big "Westerner"* (1970).

Burroughs's career is most often compared to that of Zane Grey, but in terms of literary substance, he has much more in common with Max Brand. Brand's first story for *All-Story Weekly,* "The Untamed" (1918), features a sort of Tarzan-in-boots, Whistlin' Dan Barry. Found wandering alone in the desert, whistling to himself, Dan grows into a strong, agile, mercurial man who is most at home in the naked western landscape and in the companionship of his black stallion and wolf dog. "I see in Dan a man who's different from the common run of us," says the rancher who found and raised him. "He knows animals because he has all the powers that they have. An' I know from the way his eyes go yellow that he has the fightin' instinct of the ancestors of man." Whistlin' Dan's Jane is Kate, who falls for his Aryan good looks and quiet dignity and draws him to the civilizing glow of her fire. (Brand's title, "The Untamed," appeared a year before Burroughs published *Tarzan the Untamed.*)

Ernst Haeckel's hypothetical *Pithecanthropus alalus* comes to life in Wendt, *From Ape to Adam.*

My knowledge of the anti-Semitic draft of "Marcia of the Doorstep" comes by way of a synopsis prepared by longtime Burroughs authority Henry Hardy Heins, who reviewed the manuscript at the request of Hulbert Burroughs in July 1966; a copy of Heins's exegesis is included in the Porges Papers.

Raymond Dart's missing link is described in Edey, *The Missing Link,* and Pfeiffer, *The Emergence of Mankind.*

Among the many thorough and enthralling treatments of the Scopes trial are Ray Ginger, *Six Days of Forever* (1974); Tom McGowen, *The Great Monkey Trial: Science Versus Fundamentalism in America* (1990); and L. Sprague de Camp, *The Great Monkey Trial* (1968).

Joseph Kennedy's affair with Hollywood is exposed in Doris Kearns Goodwin, *The Fitzgeralds and the Kennedys* (1987).

James Pierce published an autobiography, *The Battle of Hollywood* (1978), an exercise in selective memory if there ever was one.

The sad and mysterious case of Charley McComas is investigated in Marc Simmons, *Massacre on the Lordsburg Road* (1997). Also see John G. Bourke, *An Apache Campaign in the Sierra Madre* (1886, reprint 1987); Jason Betzinez with Wilbur Sturtevant Nye, *I Fought with Geronimo* (1959, reprint 1987); Anton Mazzanovich, *Trailing Geronimo* (third edition, 1931); Dan L. Thrapp, *Al Sieber, Chief of Scouts* (1964); and Thrapp, *General Crook and the Sierra Madre Adventure* (1972).

The library on comics includes Reinhold Reitberger and Wolfgang Fuchs, *Comics: Anatomy of a Mass Media* (1970); Robert C. Harvey, *The Art of the Funnies: An Aesthetic History* (1994); Jerry Robinson, *The Comics: An Illustrated History of Comic Book Art* (1974); George Perry and Alan Aldridge, *The Penguin Book of Comics* (1967); and David Manning White, *The Funnies: An American Idiom* (1963).

Hickman's defense attorney Richard A. Cantillon gives the bloody details of the murder, trial, and execution in *In Defense of the Fox: The Trial of William Edward Hickman* (1972).

The evolution of evolutionary thought and the eugenics movement are chronicled and critiqued in a wide range of texts, the most cogent of which is Daniel J. Kelves, *In the Name of Eugenics: Genetics and the Uses of Human Heredity* (1985). Other compelling sources include Mark Haller, *Eugenics: Hereditarian Attitudes in American Thought* (1963); Annemarie de Waal Malefijt, *Images of Man: A History of Anthropological Thought* (1974); George W. Stocking Jr., *Race, Culture, and Evolution: Essays in the History of Evolution* (reprint, 1982); John S. Haller Jr., *Outcasts from Evolution: Scientific Attitudes of Racial Inferiority, 1859–1900* (reprint, 1995); Derek Freeman, *Margaret Mead in Samoa: The Making and Unmaking of an Anthropological Myth* (1983); Franz Boaz, *The Mind of Primitive Man* (1911); Stephen Jay Gould, *Ever Since Darwin: Reflections in Natural History* (1977); Gould, *The Mismeasure of Man* (1981); Gould, *The Flamingo's Smile: Reflections in Natural History* (1985); and Richard Hofstadter, *Social Darwinism in American Thought* (1944).

Richard Dugdale's Juke research is deflated in Samuel Hopkins Adams, "The Juke Myth," *The Saturday Review* 38:14 (April 2, 1955), 13, 48–9. Franz Boaz takes Madison Grant's *The Passing of the Great Race* to task in "Inventing a Great Race," *The New Republic* 9:115 (January 13, 1917), 305–7, and gives Lothrop Stoddard's *The Rising Tide of Color* similarly stern review in "The Rising Tide of Color," *The Nation* 3:2892 (December 8, 1920), 656.

The Symmes Hole and related hollow-Earth speculation are explored in Martin Gardner (no apparent relation to Marshall Gardner), *In the Name of Science* (1952, reprinted as *Fads and Fallacies in the Name of Science,* 1957); and Harold Beaver's introduction to Edgar Allan Poe, *The Narrative of Arthur Gordon Pym of Nantucket* (1838, Penguin Classics reprint, 1975).

CHAPTER 10: "JANE . . . TARZAN"

In addition to Essoe, *Tarzan of the Movies,* and Fury, *Kings of the Jungle,* the fortunes of Johnny Weissmuller, Maureen O'Sullivan, *Trader Horn* and *Tarzan the Ape Man* are told in Narda Onyx, *Water, World & Weissmuller* (1964); Connie J. Billips, *Maureen O'Sullivan: A Bio-Bibliography* (1990); Bosley Crowther, *The Lion's Share: The Story of an Entertainment Empire* (1957); James Robert Parish and Gregory W. Mank, *The Best of MGM: The Golden Years (1928–59)* (1981); John Douglas Eames, *The MGM Story: The Complete History of Fifty Roaring Years* (1975); Bob Thomas, *Thalberg: Life and Legend* (1969); Robert C. Cannom, *Van Dyke and the Mythical City, Hollywood* (1948); Rudy Behlmer, ed., *W. S. Van Dyke's Journal: White Shadows in the South Seas (1927–1928)* and *Other Van Dyke on Van Dyke* (1996); Behlmer, "Tarzan, Hollywood's Greatest Jungle Hero," *American Cinematographer* 68:11 (January 1987), 38–48; Behlmer, "Tarzan and MGM: The Rest of the Story," *American Cinematographer* 68:2 (February 1987), 34–44; Behlmer, "Johnny Weissmuller: Olympics to Tarzan," *Films in Review* 47:7/8 (July–August 1996), 20–33; and Byron Riggan, "Damn the Crocodiles—Keep the Cameras Rolling!," *American Heritage* 19:4 (June 1968), 38–44, 100–3.

The rise of radio and the appeal of particular radio characters are recounted in Erik Barnouw, *A Tower in Babel: A History of Broadcasting in the United States, Volume I—to 1933* (1966); Barnouw, *The Golden Web: A History of Broadcasting in the United States, Volume II—1933 to 1953* (1968); J. Fred MacDonald, *Don't Touch That Dial! Radio Programming in American Life, 1920–1960* (1979); and Charles Panati, *Panati's Parade of Fads, Follies, and Manias: The Origin of Our Most Cherished Obsessions* (1991).

The inhabitability of Venus is weighed in James Jeans, *The Universe Around Us* (1929).

CHAPTER 11: THE NEW GIRL FROM HOLLYWOOD

The most illuminating writing on *Tarzan and His Mate* is Behlmer, *Behind the Scenes* (1982); and Behlmer, "Tarzan: Hollywood's Greatest Jungle Hero."

The liveliest books on Hollywood censorship, the Hays Office, and the Legion of Decency are Gregory D. Black, *Hollywood Censored: Morality Codes, Catholics, and the Movies* (1994); Leonard J. Leff and Jerold L. Simmons, *The Dame in the Kimono: Hollywood, Censorship, and the Production Code from the 1920s to the 1960s* (1990); and Murray Schumach, *The Face on the Cutting Room Floor: The Story of Movie and Television Censorship* (1964). Other pertinent sources include Martin Quigley, *Decency in Motion Pictures* (1937); Raymond Moley, *The Hays Office* (1945); Paul W. Facey, *The Legion of*

Decency: A Sociological Analysis of the Emergence and Development of a Social Pressure Group (1974); William E. Berchtold, "The Hollywood Purge," *The North American Review* 238:6 (December 1934), 503–12; Ben Ray Redman, "Pictures and Censorship," *The Saturday Review of Literature* 19 (December 31, 1938), 3–4, 13–14; Richard Corliss, "The Legion of Decency," *Film Comment* 4:4 (Summer 1968), 24–61; and Francis G. Couvares, "Hollywood, Main Street, and the Church: Trying to Censor the Movies Before the Production Code," *American Quarterly* 44:4 (December 1992), 584–616.

Las Vegas rises from the desert in Stanley W. Paher, *Las Vegas: As It Began—As It Grew* (1971); Ralph J. Roske, *Las Vegas: A Desert Paradise* (1986); Eugene P. Moehring, *Resort City in the Sunbelt: Las Vegas, 1930–1970* (1989); and Robert D. McCracken, *Las Vegas: The Great American Playground* (1996).

Ralph Bellamy reflects on his role in the development of Palm Springs in his autobiography, *When the Smoke Hit the Fan* (1979).

CHAPTER 12: VANISHING POINT

Leni Riefenstahl's autobiography, *Memoiren* (1987), was published in English as *The Sieve of Time* (1992). Eleanor Holm expresses few regrets for her outré insouciance in Sally Guard, "Still Very Much in the Swim," *Sports Illustrated* 76:23 (June 15, 1992), 12–16. Lupe Velez's tempestuous movies and marriages are savored in Floyd Conner, *Lupe Velez and Her Lovers* (1993).

CHAPTER 13: MAROONED

Views of Hawaii before the war are provided in Stanley D. Porteus, *And Blow Not the Trumpet: A Prelude to Peril* (1947); Lawrence H. Fuchs, *Hawaii Pono: A Social History* (1961); Gavan Daws, *Shoal of Time: A History of the Hawaiian Islands* (1968); and Eleanor C. Nordyke and Y. Scott Matsumoto, "The Japanese in Hawaii: A Historical and Demographic Perspective," *The Hawaiian Journal of History* 11 (1977), 162–174.

Ernest Hemingway's and Martha Gellhorn's visit to Honolulu and the positive reception of *For Whom the Bell Tolls* are noted in Carlos Baker, *Ernest Hemingway: A Life* (1969), and Michael Reynolds, *Hemingway: An Annotated Chronology* (1991).

CHAPTER 14: CAME THE WAR

For the blow-by-blow of December 7, 1941, Walter Lord, *Day of Infamy* (1957), and Gordon W. Prange, *At Dawn We Slept: The Untold Story of Pearl Harbor* (1981), are as riveting as any newsreel.

The entertainment industry's part in the war is saluted in Richard R. Linge-man, *Don't You Know There's A War On? The American Home Front, 1941–1945* (1970); Colin Shindler, *Hollywood Goes to War: Films and American Society, 1939–1952* (1979); Otto Friedrich, *City of Nets: A Portrait of Hollywood in the 1940s* (1986); and Stefan Kanfer, *Serious Business: The Art and Commerce of Animation in America from Betty Boop to Toy Story* (1997).

The war in the Pacific is chronicled vividly and rigorously in Samuel Eliot Morison, *History of United States Naval Operations in World War II,* particularly volumes VII (1951) and XIV (1960). Also useful is P. E. Culetta, ed., *United States Navy and Marine Corps Bases Overseas* (1985).

CHAPTER 15: DAMN OLD AGE

Once again, thanks to Essoe, *Tarzan of the Movies,* and Fury, *Kings of the Jungle,* for their guidance in tracking Tarzan on film.

A fuller but by no means complete list of articles and books dealing specifically or incidentally, lightly or soberly, with Tarzan and Burroughs includes, in no particular order: Michael Orth, "Utopia in the Pulps: The Apocalyptic Pastoralism of Edgar Rice Burroughs," *Extrapolation* 27:3 (Fall 1986), 221–233; Allen Carey-Webb, *"Heart of Darkness,* Tarzan, and the 'Third World': Canons and Encounters in World Literature, English 109," *College Literature* (October 1992/February 1993), 121–141; Eric Cheyfitz, *"Tarzan of the Apes:* U.S. Foreign Policy in the Twentieth Century," *American Literary History* 2 (Summer 1989), 339–359; David Cowart, "The Tarzan Myth and Jung's Genesis of the Self," *Journal of American Culture* 2:2 (Summer 1979), 220–230; David Leverenz, "The Last Real Man in America: From Natty Bumppo to Batman," *American Literary History* 3:4 (Winter 1991), 753–781; Derral Cheatwood, "The Tarzan Films: An Analysis of Determinants of Maintenance and Change in Conventions," *Journal of Popular Culture* 16:2 (Fall 1982), 127–142; James R. Nesterby, "The Tenuous Vine of Tarzan of the Apes," *Journal of Popular Culture* 13: 13:3 (Spring 1980), 483–487; Nesterby, "Tarzan of Arabia: American Popular Culture Permeates Yemen," *Journal of Popular Culture* 15:1 (Summer 1981), 39–45; John Hollow, "Rereading Tarzan; Or, 'What Is It,' Lady Alice Whispered, 'A Man?'" *Dalhousie Review* 56:1 (Spring 1976), 83–92; Paul Mandel, "Tarzan of the Paperbacks," *Life* 55:22 (November 29, 1963), 11–12; Leslie A. Fiedler, "Lord of Absolute Elsewhere," *New York Times Book Review,* June 9, 1974; Margo Jefferson, "Empire, Nature and a Good Look at the Male Body," *New York Times,* May 3, 1998; Marianna Torgovnick, *Gone Primitive: Savage Intellects, Modern Lives* (1990); Pat Kirkham and Janet Thumim, eds., *You Tarzan: Masculinity, Movies and Men* (1993); Bram Dijkstra, *Evil Sisters: The Threat of Female Sexuality and the Cult of Manhood* (1996); Anthony Haden-Guest, "A Trip to

Tarzana," in *The Paradigm Program: Travels through Muzak, Hilton, Coca-Cola, Texaco, Walt Disney and Other World Empires* (1973); S. J. Perelman, "Cloudland Revisited: Rock-A-Bye, Viscount, in the Treetop," in *The Most of S. J. Perelman* (1958); and Gore Vidal, "Tarzan Revisited," *Esquire* 60:6 (December 1963), 192–3, 262, 264. It would be folly for me to pick favorites from the hundreds of articles published in *The Burroughs Bulletin, ERB-dom, ERB-APA, ERBania, ERBivore, Tarzine,* and the other Burroughs-devoted journals that have existed over the past half century. Cheers to all of them.

INDEX